The Near Northwest Side Story

The Near Northwest Side Story

Migration, Displacement,
and Puerto Rican Families

Gina M. Pérez

UNIVERSITY OF CALIFORNIA PRESS

Berkeley / Los Angeles / London

University of California Press
Berkeley and Los Angeles, California

University of California Press, Ltd.
London, England

Library of Congress Cataloging-in-Publication Data

Pérez, Gina M., 1968–.
    The near northwest side story : migration, displacement, and Puerto
Rican families / Gina M. Pérez.
        p.   cm.
    Includes bibliographical references and index.
    ISBN 978-0-520-23368-3 (pbk. : alk. paper)
    1. Puerto Ricans — Illinois — Chicago — Migrations.   2. Chicago (Ill.) —
Emigration and immigration — History.   3. San Sebastián (P.R.) —
Emigration and immigration — History.   I. Title.

F548.9.P85P47   2004
305.868'7295077311 — dc22   2004048010

Manufactured in the United States of America
13   12   11   10
10   9   8   7   6   5   4

Printed on Ecobook 50 containing a minimum 50% post-consumer waste,
processed chlorine free. The balance contains virgin pulp, including 25%
Forest Stewardship Council Certified for no old-growth tree cutting,
processed either TCF or ECF. The sheet is acid-free and meets the minimum
requirements of ANSI/NISO Z39.48–1992 (R 1997) (Permanence of Paper).♾

In memory of Félix Antonio Pérez, 1945–1997
Lover of ideas, laughter, justice, and family

Contents

Figures

Maps

Tables

Preface

Chicago's Near Northwest Side has been an important site for the North American cultural imaginary. Nelson Algren's classic thriller *The Man with the Golden Arm* takes place along Division Street and in the neighborhoods of Humboldt Park and Wicker Park. Saul Bellow's *Humboldt's Gift* is a nostalgic memoir of European immigrant life in Humboldt Park before Puerto Rican migrants arrived in the 1960s, transforming the ethnic composition and character of the neighborhood into what one character described as a "smelly West Indian slum." And most famously, journalist Mike Royko often used Humboldt Park, Logan Square, and West Town — the community areas composing the Near Northwest Side — as a backdrop for the "average white ethnic" wisdom and social critique that characterized his political commentary and satire. This area was also, for a short time, home to French feminist Simone de Beauvoir, and it is one of the neighborhoods depicted so vividly in Sara Paretsky's mystery novels featuring the adventures of detective V. I. Warshawski.

Located in the northwestern region of Puerto Rico, San Sebastián de las Vegas del Pepino has played an equally important role in Puerto Rico's cultural and political imaginary. Its cultural festivals — La Novilla in January and La Hamaca in July — are popularly regarded as "typical" of official island folklore. Many *pepinianos*[1] consider their town, along with the neighboring municipality of Lares, to be the cradle of Puerto Rican independence and nationalism. While San Sebastián is home to many generations of *pepinianos,* it is also home to thousands of *puertorriqueños* from other parts of the island who, according to town lore, succumbed to the town's magical charms after drinking the water from its river: *El que bebe agua del río Culebrinas se queda en el Pepino* (Those who drink water from the Culebrinas River remain in Pepino).

This ethnography of different places connected by a long transnational history of circulating people, ideas, relationships, and goods details the history and present of these communities in order to challenge enduring myths about Puerto Rican migration, poverty, and identity. The book's title plays on the 1961 film *West Side Story*, which recounts the love story of a Puerto Rican girl and a white American boy, a love destined for destruction because of ethnic/racial fear fueling violent battles to control urban space. Perhaps unlike any other film, *West Side Story* penetrated the American cultural imagination in ways that continue to shape many Americans' popular perceptions of Puerto Ricans — and Latinos more broadly — and to inform racialized stereotypes of U.S. Latinas and Latinos as hypersexualized, violent people. Although this *Near Northwest Side Story* shares important themes with the movie — namely how the politics of belonging, identity, structure, and agency, as well as a racialized struggle for urban space, continue to shape the lives of many poor and working-class Puerto Ricans both on the island and on the mainland — it challenges pernicious myths used to explain Puerto Ricans' poverty, and describes how many Puerto Ricans struggle to make ends meet and to build meaningful communities in marginal economic and social circumstances.

This book would not have been possible without the support and love of many people. Acknowledging all of them is one of the most gratifying parts of this long project. I am extremely grateful and indebted to the women and men in Chicago and San Sebastián, Puerto Rico, who opened their lives and homes to me throughout my research and who must remain anonymous. I especially want to thank my G.E.D. students from the Ruiz Belvis Cultural Center in Chicago (known as the Centro), as well as the Centro's staff and board members, all of whom inspired me to write about their struggles and encouraged me over the years. I am indebted to the kindness of my father's extended family in San Sebastián, who received me warmly into their homes and regaled me with stories about family, migration, struggle, and community. I especially want to thank Justina Pérez, Liono Ramos, Fidencia Vélez, Gin Morales, and all other *pepinianos y pepinianas* who shared their stories with me.

This book began as a dissertation in the Department of Anthropology at Northwestern University. My advisor, Micaela di Leonardo, provided incredible support and guidance throughout the process and continues to be an important source of strength both personally and professionally.

Josef Barton, Mary Wiesmantel, and Karen Tranberg Hansen contributed to my thinking about this project in invaluable ways. Beyond Northwestern University, Patricia Zavella, Jorge Duany, Brett Williams, Arlene Dávila, and Juan Flores commented on various drafts of my dissertation and this book manuscript, and provided critical insight for improving my analysis.

Field research and writing of this ethnography were supported by the Social Science Research Council (Minority Dissertation Workshop on International Migration 1996), the Graduate School at Northwestern University (1998–99), the Ford Foundation Dissertation Fellowship (1999–2000), and the Professional Staff Congress of the City University of New York (2001–2002).

I am particularly indebted to my colleagues at the Center for Puerto Rican Studies at Hunter College, City University of New York, where I was provided with space, time, and intellectual sustenance for more than three years. Caridad Souza, Carlos Vargas Ramos, Félix Matos-Rodríguez, and Ismael García read and commented on various chapters of this book, and I benefited enormously from ongoing conversations and intellectual engagement with them, as well as from discussions with Pedro Pedraza and Ramón Bosque-Pérez, who consistently provided me with critical computer assistance in moments of crisis. The Centro's administrative unit, especially José de Jesus, Catrize Ortiz, Mayra Torres, and Eudenis Castillo provided inexhaustible technical and moral support, and I enjoyed as well the collegiality and friendship of Ivelisse Rosario-Natal, Yamila Sterling, Carol Chacón, Rossy Matos, and Yasmín Ramírez. Carolynn Julien, Tara Smith, Anne Marie Rivera, and others in the Research Administration Office at Hunter College were consistently helpful in sharing information about funding for research projects and shepherding me through lengthy protocols and application processes. I also want to thank the staff of the Centro's library and archives: Pedro Juan Hernández, Nélida Pérez, and Jorge Matos have been extremely generous, both at the dissertation and postdissertation stages, in locating documents from the Migration Division Office. My gratitude goes to José Camacho and Félix Rivera in the library, as well to Idilio Gracia-Peña, Nitza Medina, and Carmen Fontán, who consistently engaged me with their thoughts about the wealth of information contained in the Migration Division Archives. My thanks to Gamaliel Ramos and Marisol Berrios for technical assistance with the maps in this book. Carlos Vargas Ramos helped me organize the book's tables, and with Xavier Totti provided editorial advice and help with countless translations. *Gracias*.

Over the years I have been extremely blessed with the personal and professional support of many colleagues and friends. I want to thank especially Michelle Boyd, who not only read and commented on countless versions of this manuscript but, together with Regina Deil-Amen, Heather McClure, and Deborah Parédez, sustained me with friendship, love, critical insight, and encouragement throughout graduate school and beyond. I am also grateful to friends and colleagues Isar Godreau, Yarimar Bonilla, Ivelisse Rivera-Bonilla, Rima Brusi, Frank Guridy, Adrián Burgos Jr., Wilson Valentín, Elizabeth García, Ana Yolanda Ramos-Zayas, Nicholas De Genova, Mérida Rúa, and Jacalyn Harden, who organized panels, presented papers, and collaborated with me in so many ways. An incredibly inspiring group of women colleagues/mentors — Marixsa Alicea, Maura Toro-Morn, Nilda Flores-González, Arlene Torres, Irma Olmedo, and Luz del Alba Acevedo — provided moral and intellectual support over the years in both Chicago and Puerto Rico; thanks as well to long-time friends and colleagues Tedra Osell and Liesl Haas and to my colleagues at Oberlin College, where I was warmly received and generously supported as I completed this book.

I owe a great deal to Naomi Schneider at University of California Press for encouraging me through the end of this intellectual project. My sincere thanks as well to the Press's anonymous reviewers and its Editorial Committee reader, who provided challenging, insightful comments as I finished this book.

My mother, Leeann Pérez, and my brothers and sisters, Peter, Lorna, Teresa, and Eric, have provided much-needed emotional and spiritual grounding over the years. And warm thanks to my *suegros,* Roland and Sofia Pineda, as well as my brother-in-law André Pineda, for their encouragement throughout this process.

I would not have been able to finish this book without the love and intellectual strength provided by my husband and *compañero,* Baron Leon Pineda. Over the years, he has provided critical insight into this project, supported me during summer fieldwork in Chicago, and been a constant source of love, intelligence, humor, and peace. He and Antonio and Pablo Amado, our sons, have brought a tremendous amount of joy to my life, and I am a better person because of them. My father, Félix Antonio Pérez, has been the most important and influential person in my life, offering me moral, spiritual, and intellectual guidance. I dedicate this book to his memory.

CHAPTER I

Introduction

A Gendered Tale of Two Barrios

On a cold, rainy Chicago morning in late October 1997, I left my Humboldt Park apartment and drove my red pickup truck south on California Avenue. From Armitage Street, I went past the Western Union billboards, Moos Elementary School, and the Wright College Extension Campus directly across the street from the single-room occupancy hotel on the northwest corner of North and California Avenues. I continued south along the eastern entrance of Humboldt Park, which faces a row of impressive greystones, each housing multiple families, many of them proudly displaying large Puerto Rican flags from their windows. On a typical morning, this area of the park bustles with the quiet activities of people sleeping in the park, younger folks jogging or walking along the park's pathways, and older Latino and African American men — occasionally accompanied by young boys — fishing in the lagoon.

Turning east onto Division Street, I passed a Kentucky Fried Chicken on my left and then, across the street, Lily's Record Shop, which sells a wide range of music in Spanish — *salsa, merengue, música jíbara* — and hundreds of T-shirts, with everything emblazoned on them from the Puerto Rican flag to a *pava*-wearing *coquí* dancing with an animated creature draped in the Mexican flag. Plastic and ceramic *recuerdos de Puerto Rico,* including a plate of *arroz con habichuelas* in shiny plastic miniature, dolls, and musical instruments, crowd the small, cramped store, which pipes loud music to the street on most afternoons. This section of Paseo Boricua, the popular name of the six-block area between the two fifty-ton Puerto Rican flags on the eastern and western ends of Division Street, is filled with dollar stores, small family-run grocery stores, barber shops, restaurants, and the Boriken Bakery, providing the best *pan de agua, quesitos,* and *pastelitos de guayaba* in Puerto Rican Chicago. I continued east under the Puerto Rican flag, past Roberto Clemente High School and the St. Elizabeth's Hospital complex, beyond the new, hip restaurants and bars frequented by young white professionals, students, and artists, all newcomers to the area. Finally, I passed the old Polish bakery — a reminder of the neighborhood's earlier ethnic composition — before turning south onto Paulina Street, where I drove three blocks to pick up Aida Rodríguez and her teenage daughter, Milly Vargas, at their second-floor apartment in the quickly gentrifying West Town neighborhood.[1]

Aida has lived in this two-story wooden house almost all her life. Her father bought the building in 1977, after renting various apartments within West Town and the adjacent neighborhood, Wicker Park. In fact, except for the three years in the mid 1980s when she lived in Brooklyn with her husband, Eli, and their children, and the short time she was sent to live with her paternal relatives in Vega Baja, Puerto Rico, Aida has lived all her life within a four-block radius of this home. In 1990, no longer able to pay taxes on the building, her father sold the family house and moved Aida's mother and their youngest children to a rented apartment nearby. The following year, Aida rented a second-floor apartment from the new owner. I visited her there, where she would remain until December 1999, when she and her five children would move to the Belmont Cragin neighborhood, northwest of West Town.

Music filled the narrow stairwell as I climbed the stairs to Aida's small apartment, where she and her three daughters were watching hip-hop videos in the living room. As we waited for Eli and their two sons to return from repairing a flat tire, Aida and I played Pacman on her son's Gameboy, and Milly and her sisters chatted about the music videos and their favorite performers, including the rap artist Tupac and *salsero* Jerry Rivera. Shortly after Eli arrived, Aida, Milly, and I left the apartment, squeezed into the cab of my truck, and drove to Aida's parents' house on Shubert Avenue in Logan Square, just as her father and younger brothers finished their breakfast of fried eggs, deli ham, and white bread, and prepared to move more boxes to a newly rented home down the block. Aida's mother, Magda Quiñones, was excited about the move, saying that it would be the third house they'd lived in on that same block — perhaps even on the same side of the street. She was confident that as long as the owner didn't sell the house, she and her husband and youngest daughters would live there quite comfortably for a long time, since the new house had not been subdivided into smaller apartments for multiple renters and thus provided ample room. Aida had invited me to spend the day with her and her family, something we have done together on countless occasions, and she was particularly excited about introducing me to her cousin Mayra, who lived directly across the street. Mayra, Aida, and I spent most of the day together, talking about the usual topics — problems with children, health, housing, and jobs, and their hopes and dreams for a better life for themselves and their children — before returning to her parents' home later in the evening, where Magda and her husband, Carmelo, were watching Spanish-language television in their living room. Milly had spent the day trying on clothes with one of her *tías* — Aida's youngest sister, who was slightly older than Milly.

As soon as we walked in the door, Magda offered us *café con leche*. Carmelo asked Aida if she would take a look at some papers he had just received from public aid, and Magda invited me into the kitchen while she made the coffee. I have known Aida and her extended family for more than two years and have celebrated holidays, birthdays, weddings, and other special events with them. On several occasions, I asked Magda if I might interview her, since Aida frequently directs me to her mother when I have questions about her family's history in Chicago and Puerto Rico. Each time I approach Magda, however, she refuses, insisting she has nothing interesting to say and instructing me to speak with her husband, who, she assures me, will provide information that would be of greater interest to me. But today Magda ushers me into the kitchen, quickly closing the door behind me. She says to me suddenly and quite seriously, "*Ahora* te voy a dar mi historia" (*Now* I will tell you my story).

"Aida is raising Milly too strict," she begins in English, suggesting that Aida is likely to push Milly into making bad decisions. When I suggest that Aida simply wants the best for Milly and is trying to prevent her from making the same mistakes Aida made as a teenager — getting pregnant and not finishing high school — Magda shakes her head and insists that Aida is making the same mistakes she herself did with Aida and her sisters: being too strict, unreasonable, and, in the end, pushing them to do things behind her back. "Se van a meter las patas igual" (They'll get pregnant anyway), she says sadly. "Yo apretaba demasiado con mis muchachos, y mira como salieron" (I was too strict with my children, and look how they turned out), referring to the fact that, despite her best efforts, her three oldest daughters were teenage mothers. This, she explains, is part of her own sad story of *sufrimiento*, which began with her migration from Utuado, Puerto Rico, to Chicago at the age of ten to live with an aunt who needed help raising her family in the absence of extended kin. "Fue un infierno. Y yo era una esclava" (It was hell. And I was a slave), she says mournfully. Not only did Magda have to do all the work in her aunt's home, but she was also forbidden to leave the house alone, since her aunt felt responsible for protecting her. Magda eventually fled her aunt's home in the middle of the night. She stayed with a neighbor until she was able to contact a woman from her home town who was also living in Chicago and who had given Magda her phone number, saying to call if she ever needed help. The woman allowed Magda to stay with her, but it proved to be more of the same. She paid Magda ten dollars weekly for doing the same work she had been required to do at her aunt's house, but she still had no freedom. It was at this time that she met Carmelo, who was ten years older. They were permitted only short visits, and eventually she married him in order to leave the house and have more autonomy.

As Magda told me her story, she connected it to her own decisions on how to raise her children. "Yo apretaba demasiado con mis muchachos," she repeated sadly. When Aida was thirteen, Magda was so worried about her daughters getting pregnant that she sent Aida to Puerto Rico to live with family for a short time, *para que no se dañara* — so she wouldn't be ruined. Despite Magda's best efforts, Aida returned from Puerto Rico after only a month — she describes her stay in Puerto Rico as horribly traumatic — and got pregnant with Milly the following year. Life in Puerto Rico, Magda explained, is *más sana* — healthier, safer, and purer — than in Chicago. On the other hand, Chicago provides employment and broader economic and educational opportunities, and for these reasons, Magda insisted on remaining in Chicago, while preserving good relations with her own and her husband's kin in Puerto Rico through letters, phone calls, and hosting family and friends. As for many Puerto Rican families, this connection to the island has become an important resource that Magda — and even Aida — can draw upon when necessary. These ties, however, are episodic, intensifying and fading according to the changing needs of families. While remaining firmly rooted in Chicago, Magda and Aida imagine themselves as belonging to something beyond the city's borders that provides meaning and important possibilities in their lives.

The implications of Magda's actions became clearer to me after I moved to Puerto Rico the following year and met people like Willy Arroyo, who had equally complicated experiences of place and belonging. Born and raised in San Sebastián, a small town in the northwestern region of Puerto Rico, Willy moved with his mother and sisters to Chicago when he was fifteen and lived on Chicago's Near Northwest Side for six years. In 1993,

Willy returned with his girlfriend, Raquel Ramos, and their one-year-old son to live with his maternal aunt, Antonia, in the brightly painted, modest cement home she owns near the center of town. Unlike his mother, Mercedes Rubio, Willy has lived a relatively settled life in San Sebastián, having been raised primarily by Antonia, who has never lived outside of Puerto Rico but whose home is filled with glossy photographs, posters, and ceramic figurines with the names of U.S. cities — Chicago, New York, and Orlando — emblazoned on them. Despite having lived primarily in San Sebastián, Willy's connections to Chicago are strong: He follows Chicago sports teams religiously, his walls are filled with Chicago Bulls championship pennants, he and his son, Tito, stroll around town in matching Bulls jerseys, and he often talks nostalgically about the places he visited, the friends he made, and the jobs he had while living in Chicago. His main reason for returning to Puerto Rico was his problems with gangs. He was never involved in a gang, he assured me repeatedly, but young men hassled him as he walked the streets, accused him of belonging to opposition gangs, and once fired into his apartment when he, Raquel, and Tito were sleeping. Shortly after the shooting, they returned to San Sebastián, eventually renting a small wooden house from his uncle, who moved in temporarily with Antonia. In the six years since Willy returned to San Sebastián, the composition of his household has fluctuated dramatically as he took in his sisters and their children and his mother and her youngest children, and as they moved around San Sebastián and between San Sebastián and Chicago. He has held a number of poorly paid jobs and is now steadily employed as a messenger for a local doctor, making some three hundred dollars a month, far less than he would like to earn.

That is probably the main reason why, one sticky afternoon in April, Willy announced, to everyone's surprise, that he was thinking of returning to Chicago. Willy's brother-in-law, Ralphy, had mentioned earlier that Willy was spending time with Richie, an old friend from Chicago who was visiting his family and friends in Lares, a town just east of San Sebastián. According to Ralphy, Richie had been boasting about how much money he was making in Chicago. He encouraged Willy to go to Chicago with him, promising to help Willy find a job where he could make much more money than he currently did — "Maybe even a thousand dollars a week," Ralphy explained to me. He elaborated, "Willy was thinking, 'If I can make a thousand a week there and only $120 here, why should I stay?'" Willy later explained to me that all that prevented him from leaving was the gangs and the fear of raising his son in a dangerous place like Chicago. But now, with Raquel working three part-time jobs just to make five hundred dollars a month and him making even less, the allure of going to Chicago for a better-paid job was strong and had become a source of tension between him and Raquel.

The stories told by Magda, Aida, and Willy of urban fear, migrant aspirations, and interminable strategizing are familiar to many poor and working-class Puerto Rican families both on the island and on the mainland. It is not uncommon to hear older Puerto Ricans — the first generation of migrants, who left the island in the late 1940s and 1950s, at the height of Puerto Rican emigration — tell stories of their journeys to cold northern cities, such as New York and Chicago, the sacrifices they made leaving kin and friends in Puerto Rico in order to find jobs and *mejor ambiente,* a better life abroad, and their struggle to raise families in those new places. Their adult children, whether in Puerto Rico or the United States, have decidedly different migration tales, frequently involving forced relocation to live with grandparents, aunts, and uncles on the island because of real or perceived danger. Or living with the constant *possibility* of being sent away in moments of crisis. At other times, they speak of perhaps migrating themselves — for better jobs, improved housing, reliable healthcare. Many second- and third-generation Puerto Ricans have never migrated, but they still think about these other places in their lives, which are often animated by the stories of older kin, and they understand their lives and themselves in relation to these places because of their emotional connection to them. It is impossible to understand life in either community without taking the other into account. Over time, migrants and their children have been actively involved both in creating a transnational community and in building meaningful place in marginal economic circumstances.

Puerto Ricans' enduring connections with multiple communities typify the behavior of late-twentieth-century immigrants, who sustain long-term transnational ties with sending and host communities. Emotional, cultural, social, and economic connections between island and mainland communities have persisted over several generations and, in some cases, have been strengthened by the participation of second- and third-generation Puerto Ricans. These connections are certainly facilitated because of the ease with which Puerto Ricans, who are U.S. citizens, can travel between the island and the United States, but they are not exclusive to them. Advances in telecommunication technology and transportation, as well as government recognition of the rights of migrants abroad, have transformed the ways migrants remain connected to sending communities around the world. Moreover, because these ties and ways of understanding often involve being firmly rooted in one place and they are used by people who may have never even visited the island or left Puerto Rico, it is clear that mobility is not necessary for one to feel part of a transnational community. Transnational practices and imaginings have gradually become interwoven with the fabric of a community, binding it up with other places and people, who fasten and loosen ties as necessary.

This book is about these ties between places and people, connected by a long transnational history of circulating people, capital, information, and ideologies. In subsequent chapters, I explore the impact of migration on two communities — Chicago, Illinois, and San Sebastián, Puerto Rico — and their residents, and the ways in which transnational practices and imaginings have shaped the cultural, economic, social, and political landscapes in both places. I focus specifically on how people create rich, meaningful lives in marginal circumstances, and how several generations of Puerto Rican families fashion ideas of place, culture, and migration critical to sustaining their families, households, and communities. Because my primary concern is to present a portrait of daily life in one kind of transnational community, I emphasize the role of power in shaping the terrain of human activity, past and present, and explore how people respond to, accommodate, and resist its various manifestations. Migration, whether voluntary or involuntary, is fundamentally about power relations — between countries, economies, and individuals — and it raises important questions about the nature and scope of power hierarchies, including those of race, class, gender, sexuality, and nation. Why do people move, and who benefits from this movement? Under what circumstances do people forge transnational connections, and how do they change over time? Do these ties affect all people equally? In what follows, I foreground one of these power hierarchies, that of gender, in order to advance our understanding of how gendered power relations shape transnational practices, including men's and women's distinctive experiences in local labor markets, their often divergent opinions regarding migration and return, and their differential access to resources, such as education, housing, and kin networks, that are critical for their survival. In doing so, I reveal that the history of Puerto Rican migration and displacement is simultaneously a narrative of gender, and show its embeddedness in development ideologies, labor history, place-making, and ethnic identity construction in a transnational context.

A Gendered Reading of Puerto Rican Migration

Magda Quiñones and Mercedes Rubio come from a long line of women who, until recently, have been all but invisible in migration studies.

Their stories of displacement are sobering, a reminder of how women's productive and reproductive work is absolutely critical for economic and social policy on both local and global levels. Magda Quiñones, for example, is just one of many Puerto Rican girls who migrated to Chicago in the 1950s in order to assist female kin with the reproductive tasks of a newly migrant household reliant on men and women's wage labor outside the home. Two decades later, Mercedes Rubio would follow a similar path, following an older sister to Chicago and sharing a residence with her as they both struggled to find jobs and raise children in a new environment. In Chicago, both women changed residences frequently, moving into different households, sometimes establishing their own, but almost always doing so in marginal economic conditions, in response to rising rents, inadequate housing, and the consequences of uneven urban development, including urban renewal projects and gentrification. These experiences of displacement in Chicago stem from a series of public policy decisions and economic shifts in Chicago and Puerto Rico that made women's postwar migration to Chicago both possible and necessary.

In Puerto Rico, the decades-long concern with the island's perceived overpopulation problem prompted the Puerto Rican government to promote migration as a strategy for ameliorating the demographic pressures allegedly hampering Puerto Rico's economic development. Overpopulation, Laura Briggs persuasively argues, was a key economic narrative in the postwar era, not only in Puerto Rico but throughout the developing world, as U.S. policymakers worried that "excessive, uncontrolled reproduction was an obstacle to capital formation," or, in other words, "development."[2] U.S. philanthropists, social scientists, and policymakers regarded international family planning — more specifically, modifying and regulating Third World women's sexual behavior — as one way of advancing economic development. In the case of Puerto Rico, these powerful interests also encouraged emigration to the mainland, the unofficial policy that, along with family planning, became the cornerstone of the island's economic development policy.

In 1947, for example, the Puerto Rican government established the Bureau of Employment and Migration, which later became the Migration Division of the Department of Labor, a new government office charged with encouraging Puerto Rican migration to the United States by providing information about employment opportunities abroad and job training, even helping to secure employment through contract labor programs. This planned migration strategy was accompanied by the implementation of Puerto Rico's export-oriented industrialization program, later named Operation Bootstrap, which based the island's economic development on foreign and domestic private investment, encouraged by tax holidays, loan assistance programs, and wage and rent subsidies. Puerto Rico's industrialization project served as a template for the later capital importation — or *maquiladora* — model familiar throughout the developing world, an economic arrangement that feminist scholars have shown is contingent on women's labor and their "emancipation" from "traditional" constraints, such as family, land, and community.[3] The developmentalist ideology guiding Puerto Rico's industrial policy, as well as its migration program, was deeply gendered, as poor women of child-bearing age were both encouraged to migrate to U.S. cities like Chicago and recruited to work in new factories throughout the island.[4]

In Chicago, equally powerful policy and economic concerns encouraged the arrival of Puerto Rican migrants. In 1946, single young Puerto Rican women were recruited by a Chicago-based employment agency to remedy the city's "maid shortage." The abundance of industrial work for both men and women further encouraged Puerto Ricans' arrival. As I demonstrate in subsequent chapters, a feminist reading of Puerto Rican economic and migration history, as well as an analysis of postwar U.S. economics, politics, and family ideologies, throws in sharp relief how gendered power relations support, rationalize, and advance economic development programs, public policy, and migration on the island and the mainland.[5]

The social conditions enabling Puerto Rican women and men to be mobile subjects — or at least imagine themselves as flexible actors — are the result of historically specific processes conditioned by Puerto Rico's persistent colonial status, as well as a longer history of exploration, conquest, and empire characterizing the entire Caribbean region. A distinctive feature of the Caribbean, for example, is that it is a region in which countries simultaneously experience emigration and immigration.[6] Puerto Rico is no exception to this regional trend. Since the 1940s, the island has witnessed the displacement of more than 1.5 million people to the United States, where, according to the 2000 census, nearly half of all Puerto Ricans now reside. This massive displacement from the island is accompanied by substantive immigration to Puerto Rico, with more than 9 percent of the island's current population classified as foreign born, a statistic that includes children born to Puerto Rican parents abroad as well as Dominicans, Cubans, and others.[7] Scholars have employed a variety of metaphors to capture this tremendous mobility, referring to Puerto Rico as "a nation on the move" or the "commuter nation," and to Puerto Rican migrants as "passengers on an airbus." Such metaphors are useful in high-lighting tremendous mobility, but more importantly, they point to how the geographic displacement of Puerto Ricans, whether forced or volun-tary, has come to define Puerto Ricans' social and political identity. Like Mexican Americans who either crossed international boundaries or had borders "cross them," the consequences of Puerto Ricans' displacement, past and present, loom large in historical memory and contemporary local and national politics.[8] The internationally visible struggle around the Puerto Rican island of Vieques, for example, is not only about demand-ing an end to military operations off the island; more profoundly, it con-cerns historical and contemporary Puerto Rican displacement as a result of land concentration and subsequent land expropriation in the service of American capital and military power.[9]

The U.S. occupation of Puerto Rico in 1898 and the subsequent con-solidation of U.S. agrarian capitalism and shrinking small-scale subsistence cultivation helped set in motion population movements to places like Hawaii, Arizona, California, and, most notably, New York City. Between 1900 and 1940, more than ninety thousand Puerto Ricans left the island, although many returned after working in New York, Pennsylvania, and New Jersey.[10] As a result of the Migration Division's efforts and the struc-tural changes in the rapidly industrializing Puerto Rican economy, the exo-dus from the island increased sharply in the early postwar years, peaking in the 1950s, as Puerto Ricans went to cities like New York, Chicago, and Philadelphia, where there was great demand for low-wage workers in manufacturing industries. Approximately one-third of the island's popu-lation circulated or emigrated to the United States between 1955 and 1970, as Puerto Ricans continued to leave the island in large numbers. By the early 1970s, however, deindustrialization in Northeastern and Midwestern cities resulted in a decline in manufacturing jobs, making emigration a less attractive option for working-class migrants until the mid 1980s and 1990s, when migration from the island increased once again. And while cities like New York, Chicago, and Philadelphia continue to serve as home to large Puerto Rican populations, 2000 census data confirm a geo-graphic dispersal of Puerto Rican migrants and communities to such des-tinations as Florida beginning in the 1980s.[11]

Puerto Rican migration, however, has not been unidirectional. Return migration beginning in the mid 1960s increased dramatically by the early 1970s and in some years even surpassed emigration from the island, a trend that continued through the early 1980s.[12] A number of studies have doc-umented this flow of return migrants and have analyzed its impact on the island, focusing largely on economic and cultural effects of return migra-

TABLE 1. Puerto Rican Population in the United States by State, 2000

State	Puerto Rican Population	State	Puerto Rican Population
New York	1,050,293	Oklahoma	8,153
Florida	482,027	Louisiana	7,670
New Jersey	366,788	Missouri	6,677
Pennsylvania	228,557	Minnesota	6,616
Massachusetts	199,207	Kentucky	6,469
Connecticut	194,443	Alabama	6,322
Illinois	157,851	New Hampshire	6,215
California	140,570	Kansas	5,237
Texas	69,504	Oregon	5,092
Ohio	66,269	New Mexico	4,488
Virginia	41,131	Utah	3,977
Georgia	35,532	Mississippi	2,881
North Carolina	31,117	Iowa	2,690
Wisconsin	30,267	Alaska	2,649
Hawaii	30,005	Arkansas	2,473
Michigan	26,941	District of Columbia	2,328
Maryland	25,570	Maine	2,275
Rhode Island	25,422	Nebraska	1,993
Indiana	19,678	West Virginia	1,609
Arizona	17,587	Idaho	1,509
Washington	16,140	Vermont	1,374
Delaware	14,005	Montana	931
Colorado	12,993	South Dakota	637
South Carolina	12,211	Wyoming	575
Nevada	10,420	North Dakota	507
Tennessee	10,303		

SOURCE: U.S. Census Bureau, Census 2000, Summary File 1

tion and, to a lesser extent, on its political consequences.[13] Still others emphasize the circular nature of Puerto Rican migration, one in which the flow of goods, people, ideas, and capital connect island and mainland communities.[14] Like many late-twentieth-century migrations, Puerto Rican migration has evolved to include a variety of new destinations, multiple movements, and sustained connections among different places, a phenomenon popularly regarded as a "va y ven" (or *vaivén*) movement, an experience of coming and going familiar to many Puerto Ricans, and one that has provoked serious debate both inside and outside the academy.

For some scholars, the *vaivén* tradition is a result of economic changes both on the island and on the mainland and has become a culturally conditioned way for migrants to improve their economic and social position; as sociologist Marixsa Alicea has noted, it is a way for migrants and their families to create and make use of "dual home bases."[15] Other writers, however, argue that the continual circulation of Puerto Rican migrants is a key contributor to increased economic immiseration and poverty among Puerto Ricans on the mainland, since such movement disrupts families and people's participation in the labor market.[16] More recently, scholars like anthropologist Jorge Duany have re-engaged with this debate, arguing that circular migration — or "mobile livelihood practices" — is, in fact, a flexible survival strategy enhancing migrants' socioeconomic status. In response to poor economic conditions on both the island and the mainland, Puerto Rican migrants have created and make use of extensive networks, including multiple home bases in several labor markets. These transnational practices, he argues, not only compensate for the fact that economic opportunities are unequally distributed in space, but they also undermine "the highly localized images of space, culture, and identity that have dominated nationalist discourse and practice in Puerto Rico and elsewhere."[17] The complicated patterns of migration, return, and subsequent movement present theoretical and methodological challenges to traditional ways of analyzing migration and migrant practices. For this reason, new debates proposing a transnational approach to migration are useful in capturing Puerto Ricans' lives both on the island and abroad.

Migration Studies and a Transnational Perspective

For the past decade, writers both inside and outside of the academy have invoked the term *transnationalism* to refer to everything from the unfettered circulation of North American companies and capital to the movement of people, commodities, information, and ideas. Within the social sciences, the term has been particularly visible, appearing in the titles of countless conferences, working papers, articles, and presentations, where it has been linked to a variety of traditional areas of academic inquiry, such as transnational labor, transnational capital, transnational feminisms, and transnational migration. Frequently, *transnationalism* and *globalization* (perhaps an equally ubiquitous term) are used interchangeably, an unfortunate tendency that often mystifies rather than explains important social phenomena that are certainly related but analytically distinct processes.

Transnationalism refers to those processes that are "anchored in and transcend one or more nation-states," while *globalization* involves processes that are "largely decentered from specific national territories and take place in a global space." The conflation of these terms says a lot about late-twentieth-century sensibility, in which transnational corporations push us to think of ourselves as part of a "global village."[18] In short, *transnationalism* is "in the air," and its proliferation within the social sciences matches the term's increasing ambiguity.[19]

This is particularly true in migration studies, where, since the late 1980s, some scholars have advanced the idea of "transnational migration" to capture the different ways in which immigrants integrate themselves into their new environment while creating and sustaining ties with the communities from which they come. This transnational perspective keeps in focus immigrants' border-spanning activities, including political activities, various income-generating practices, and the reconfiguration of families and households involving migrants and nonmigrants alike. And although migration scholars still struggle with the proliferation of terms used to capture these complicated migration processes (transnational circuits, transnational communities, trans-localities, transnational villages, and transnational social fields and contexts, to name a few), it is clear that the transnational model is an important corrective to earlier migration theories, which have traditionally treated migration as a unidirectional flow of people who eventually settle permanently into host societies.

Borrowing from economic theory, for example, the neoclassical equilibrium approach to international migration — the "push-pull" model — emphasizes the individual motivations of migrants as they are "pushed" from poor industrializing economies characterized by labor surplus, and "pulled" to developed, labor-scarce countries. Historical-structural models, on the other hand, focus on the structural consequences of a global capitalist system organized by an international division of labor and a global political hierarchy that in turn creates mobile populations moving from poor nations on the "periphery" to developed "core" countries. The direction of these migration flows — from Jamaica to Great Britain, Algeria to France, and the Dominican Republic to the United States, for example — is not arbitrary. Instead, they reflect the political and economic expansion of countries whose colonial, imperialist, and/or military interventions have had the unintended consequence of stimulating international migration. Migrants' networks increase the likelihood that movement will continue, as nonmigrants draw on the social ties of kinship and friendship connecting them to migrants and former migrants and providing them with the knowledge and resources necessary for their own movement. Taken together, neoclassical and historical-structural migration theories, as well as migrant network analysis, help to explain both the structural and individual forces shaping migration processes and patterns. But, as sociologist Douglas Massey aptly notes, such models were developed during the industrial era and do not adequately explain "a more complex migration regime" involving more people, more destinations, faster communication and travel, and "rising government intervention and greater circularity of movements."[20]

A transnational approach to migration has proven a useful frame for understanding the complicated ways in which individuals, communities, organizations, and even countries simultaneously shape (and are affected by) migration, and for explaining the persistence of ties across generations. In their seminal 1992 edited volume on transnationalism and migration, anthropologist Nina Glick Schiller and her colleagues defined transnationalism as "the process by which immigrants forge and sustain multi-stranded social relations that link together their societies of origin and settlement."[21] This perspective no longer regards immigrants as "uprooted" people who are eventually "transplanted" in a new environment.[22] Instead, the transnational frame provides a far more complicated portrait of migrant life, including migrants' simultaneous participation in the economic, social, and political life of both the society from which they came and their new community of residence. Rather than sever ties with sending communities, "transmigrants" are understood to live their lives "across international borders," establishing "transnational social fields" consisting of dense migrant networks and connections that become institutionalized over time.[23] Invariably, migrants and nonmigrants alike are enmeshed in these transnational social fields, and over time migration becomes part of the fabric of places, as people begin to imagine themselves as part of a larger community that extends beyond their place of residence. This happens in concrete, historically specific ways, through, for example, cultural festivals in which migrants are honored, the proliferation of institutions like travel agencies and money-wiring businesses that help facilitate movement and communication, and political parties, community organizations, and sports clubs that bring together, physically and/or psychologically, people from different places. Thus, while transnational migration draws our attention to the border-spanning activities that shape people's lives and the communities in which they live, we cannot forget that these practices are "embodied in specific social relations established between specific people, situated in unequivocal localities, at historically determined times."[24] In other words, the transnational cannot eclipse the local, and we need to reflect on the different power hierarchies in which transnational practices are embedded. We need to conceptualize place-making within transnational migration.

It is in this regard that attention to Puerto Rican migration is extremely relevant and revealing. To date, much of the literature focusing on U.S. transnational migration has drawn on examples from the Caribbean, Mexico, and Central America — an understandable trend given the proliferation of immigrants from Latin America, the long-standing relationship between the United States and the Caribbean, and the region's proximity to the United States.[25] According to the U.S. Census Bureau, slightly more than 50 percent of the county's foreign-born population hails from the Caribbean, Mexico, and Central and South America, a demographic trend that has prompted media, policy experts, and social critics to speculate on the consequences of this new latinization of the United States.[26] Moreover, many immigrants, particularly *mejicanos,* have lived "transnationally" for more than a century, starting long before the term was popularized, and long before, as anthropologist Carlos Vélez-Ibañez notes, "that imaginary political division called the U.S.-Mexican border" came into existence.[27] Despite recent theorizing of Latin American and Caribbean transnational practices, however, critical attention to Puerto Rican migration is noticeably absent. This is surprising, since it is arguably one of the longest sustained migrations to the United States, and therefore offers a unique opportunity to examine the construction, maintenance, and reconfiguration of transnational social fields over several generations. Some scholars may be reluctant to consider Puerto Rican migration as a transnational phenomenon, since Puerto Ricans are U.S. citizens and do not cross the geopolitical — or international — boundaries that define one's legal status. The absence of international boundaries, the logic goes, allows Puerto Ricans to move easily (and, more importantly, legally) between the island and the mainland, and therefore renders their experience qualitatively different from undocumented immigrants residing in the United States.

These concerns are certainly valid. As U.S. citizens, Puerto Ricans do not cross political boundaries in quite the same way as other immigrants, nor are they enmeshed in the discourse of illegality that stigmatizes undocumented immigrants and increases their exploitability. In fact, Puerto Ricans often use the stigma of illegality to distance themselves from Spanish-speaking immigrants and make claims to economic, political, and civil rights based on their citizenship status.[28] Puerto Ricans do, however, cross colonial, ethnic, and cultural *borders* — the geographic, cultural, and linguistic contact zones that often differ from formal boundaries of nations, yet still have the power to determine inclusion and exclusion in the imagined American nation.[29] As racialized colonial subjects hailing from a dependent U.S. territory, Puerto Ricans have always had an uneasy relationship with borders and boundaries as they define the limits of citizenship for Puerto Ricans. In the United States, for example, Puerto Ricans are free to exercise all rights of citizens, although on the island they do not have Congressional representatives and cannot vote in federal elections, including U.S. presidential races. When Puerto Ricans travel to the United States mainland, Jorge Duany notes, their luggage not only must pass through the U.S. Department of Agriculture inspections, but Immigration and Naturalization Service (INS) officers may ask passengers for proof of U.S. citizenship. Moreover, "some airline, train, and courier companies, as well as banks and retail businesses, classify Puerto Rico as an international or overseas destination."[30]

By underscoring the similarities between Puerto Ricans and other migrants, I do not wish to downplay or ignore the tremendous power states yield with regard to undocumented migrants. Recent events, including the indefinite detention of hundreds of foreign nationals in the wake of the World Trade Center and Pentagon attacks in September 2001, attest to the importance of geopolitical borders and show that the federal government can use its power to detain and deport noncitizens as it deems necessary. Instead, I wish to highlight how state power regimes beyond U.S. immigration law structure migrants' lives. It is a belief shared by many — including some academics — that as American citizens, Puerto Ricans should be doing far better than other Latin Americans, who frequently live and work in the United States as undocumented immigrants.[31] Indeed, on several occasions, Puerto Rican and non–Puerto Rican Latinos — especially those of the middle and upper-middle classes — have asked me to explain to them why Puerto Ricans fare so poorly compared to Mexicans and "even African Americans" in Chicago. Scholars who have conducted fieldwork among mixed Latino groups, especially in the New York metropolitan area, where most Puerto Ricans on the mainland still reside, have documented similar queries.[32]

While the INS certainly contributes to immigrant exploitability and limits undocumented workers' economic possibilities, most Latin American immigrants — including Puerto Rican migrants and other legal immigrants — also face other, equally powerful forms of state power that circumscribe their economic, social, and political lives. The lack of universal healthcare, federal neglect of urban schools, increased privatization of the housing market — concomitant with federal cutbacks in subsidized housing construction and municipal failure to maintain low-cost housing — and an emerging carceral society based on questionable policing in poor minority neighborhoods all contribute to migrants' economic and social marginalization.[33] For second- and third-generation migrants who do not face the problem of illegality, there are other barriers to full participation in the social, economic, and political life in the United States, including how they are racialized in different contexts. Filipinos and other Asian Americans, for example, are popularly regarded as "non-Americans," or "the 'foreigner-within,' even when born in the United States."[34] The same is true for many Mexican Americans, who continue to be defined as foreigners or newcomers despite several generations of U.S. residency and citizenship. This study of Puerto Rican migrants and their families keeps in focus these racialized power asymmetries and reveals the limits of citizenship with regard to poor and working-class racialized minorities.

A Gendered Ethnography of Place

Like most human experiences, the consequences of displacement are extremely gendered. Men and women may experience displacement quite differently, not because of inherent or "natural" differences between them, but rather because so many areas of life, "including sexuality, family, education, economy, and the state . . . are organized according to gender principles and shot through with conflicting interests and hierarchies of power and privilege."[35] The stories of Magda Quiñones and Willy Arroyo, for example, are suggestive of how gender shapes people's lives, making some things possible and others not. Both Magda and Willy arrived in Chicago as a result of women's social networks based on kinship; once in Chicago, their divergent experiences continued to be shaped by gender, as well as class, race, sexuality, and generation. Magda's unhappy residence with her maternal aunt was characterized by generational conflicts concerning reproductive work, sexuality, and gendered norms of respectability and behavior, conflicts that culminated in her flight from her aunt's home. And Willy's experiences with gangs compelled him to leave Chicago for San Sebastián, where he and his family lived with his maternal aunt, resulting in a reconfiguration of households and a series of intergenerational and gendered conflicts. Feminist scholars, by focusing their attention on gendered power relations in migration, have been critical in uncovering the many ways in which gender circumscribes migrants' lives and in identifying other areas of rich inquiry regarding migration, displacement, and the construction of place.

Feminist scholars have long noted the absence of women's experiences in migration research.[36] As in the social sciences more generally, feminist migration research beginning in the 1970s sought to correct this bias. Since that time, it has passed through a number of different stages in order to do so. Some of the earliest works to consider women in migration treated sex as one of many variables to assess — for example, changes in the labor force participation rates of immigrant women.[37] Other accounts, such as Hasia Diner's work on Irish immigrant women or Evelyn Nakano Glenn's research on Japanese immigrant women and their children, are more descriptive, providing rich details of immigrant women's experiences and the social and economic conditions shaping their movement.[38] Building on these writings, scholars have focused on the role of household and social networks in facilitating and sustaining migration. Such studies are important because they make visible women's reproductive work. They also challenge prevailing assumptions of the household as a unified entity and reveal that migration is often the source of tremendous gendered and intergenerational conflict, as migrants balance the demands and expectations of those who remain behind with the obligations and duties ensuing from new interpersonal and institutional relationships in their "host" communities.[39]

Most recently, scholars have treated gender and sexuality as central organizing principles of migration, an approach that emphasizes how sexuality and gender ideologies, relations, and identities create, sustain, and transform migration experiences, as well as the social spaces in which migration occurs.[40] In so doing, writers have explored how sexuality shapes migrant networks, as well as the critical role women's reproductive work plays in sustaining transnational connections. Notions of stratified reproduction, transnational motherhood, and international kinship highlight the relationship between women's productive and reproductive labor, as these women live and work abroad while remaining deeply connected to people in their sending communities.[41] Women's migration can also be understood as important "kin work," what anthropologist Micaela di Leonardo describes as "the conception, maintenance, and ritual celebration of cross-household kin ties." In the case of transnational migration, kin work frequently includes caring for sick or elderly kin, and for adolescents who may be sent to live with family members in order to protect them from actual or perceived dangers.[42] This work is done by women in the aggregate and is unremunerated labor. In this way, family members affirm ethnic and cultural identities through women's labor and networks connecting their households across different communities.

Many Puerto Rican women migrants have engaged in these transnational practices since the late 1940s, and they have continued to cultivate similar ties into the present, although these networks, while providing critical support to women and their kin, may also be fraught with conflict, friction, and even resentment, as Cecilia Menjívar has shown in her research among Salvadoran immigrant women.[43] In treating gender and sexuality as central organizing principles of migration, scholars like Menjívar have not only helped to correct a bias in migration research, which often romanticizes immigrant women's networks, treating them as static entities based on bonds of mutual sharing and reciprocity; perhaps more importantly, these writers have directed attention to the dynamic processes that shape the political, economic, social, and cultural contexts in which many impoverished migrants live and to the "potential deleterious effects of poverty on their informal sources of assistance, and to their remarkable capacity to survive, even when they have very little, if anything, going for them."[44]

The following chapters employ this gendered perspective to highlight the experiences of Puerto Rican migrants in Chicago and San Sebastián and their various attempts to resist and accommodate the political-economic forces that shape their lives. My ethnographic and historical approach allows me to provide an account of transnational living that neither exaggerates the uprootedness of migrants and their kin nor ignores the fact that many poor *puertorriqueños* are unable to take advantage of the mobility and innovations late capitalism offers.[45] While Chicago Puerto Ricans and *pepinianos* do indeed lead deeply transnational lives, they do so while remaining firmly rooted in particular places, even if many continue to be oriented to places that are not their current residences.[46]

The Study and Its Settings

In February 1995, I began working as a volunteer at the Ruiz Belvis Cultural Center in the city's Near Northwest Side. Since my arrival in Chicago in 1993, I had hoped to become involved in the city's Puerto Rican community, a desire fueled in part by my previous experience as a volunteer in several U.S. cities and as a community organizer in Latin

America in the early 1990s. This time, however, I was primarily motivated by the unique opportunity to work among "my own people." As a Brooklyn-born, California-raised Puerto Rican, I never really knew any other Puerto Rican families — except for the wonderful Aliceas, the only other non-Mexican Latinos my family knew in Stockton, who, thankfully, attended the same Catholic Church and school we did. Living and studying in Chicago was my chance to finally inhabit a world that both fascinated me and evoked deep feelings of insecurity and loss. My father's stories about growing up in Brooklyn among a large extended family and the ethnic networks and neighborhoods in which they were enmeshed and my frequent trips to New York City as an undergraduate to visit my aunts and grandmother had whetted my desire to live and work among other Puerto Ricans.[47]

At the Centro, I was immediately placed on a planning committee for its annual *jornada abolicionista,* a series of programs, workshops, and cultural events celebrating the abolition of slavery in Puerto Rico in 1873. A few months later, I was appointed the Centro's G.E.D. instructor, a position that allowed me to work with men and women ranging in age from sixteen to sixty. This experience unexpectedly transformed me. I initially wanted to teach G.E.D. classes because it was a way for me to use my talents and skills to help others. I enjoyed the challenge of a mixed-age group of students, and I was sobered by students' stories about their daily lives and the reasons why they were spending their summer studying for a high school equivalency exam. Their daily essays, journal entries, and discussion of current events revealed a public school system that had failed them — or pushed them out, as the Centro's staff explained to me — and how troubles with gangs, drugs, and daily violence, struggles with public aid, and a dominant perception of them as lazy, dangerous, and undeserving shaped their daily lives. By summer's end, I had decided to construct a dual-site research project that would examine the lives of first- and second-generation Puerto Rican migrants in Chicago and Puerto Rico.

Later that summer, I made my first trip alone to Puerto Rico to begin my research on migration. I spent most of my time in Río Piedras reading island newspapers, struggling to identify where I might conduct fieldwork on the island, and discussing my project with willing and supportive faculty members at the University of Puerto Rico. I also made several trips to San Sebastián to visit my father's relatives, whom we had not seen in more than fifteen years. Initially, these trips were strictly personal, a time to reconnect with my extended kin and to enjoy the beauty and peacefulness of *el campo.* But I quickly realized through conversations with

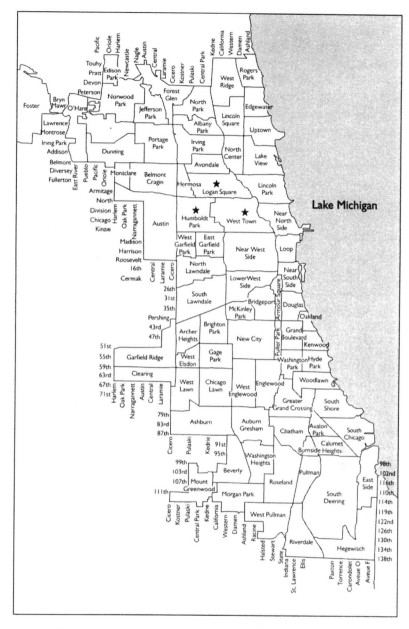

MAP 1. Chicago Community Area Map. Starred neighborhoods make up Near Northwest Side. Source: City of Chicago Department of Planning.

MAP 2. Puerto Rico Political Map. Source: U.S. Central Intelligence Agency 1976 (University of Texas Library Online).

return migrants in my great aunt Cristina's store and with other *pepinianos* traveling to Pepino for the weekend that the town was filled with people who had lived *afuera* — literally, "outside" in the United States — in places like New York, Newark, and Chicago, and who still maintained important connections with family and friends in these places. Learning more about San Sebastián's migration history cemented my decision to choose it as my field site. In January 1998, I returned to the town and lived with my *tía* Cristina and her family for six months as I conducted interviews, made use of my tenure working in *la tienda* to be a participant observer, and gathered historical data about the town's migration history.

San Sebastián is located in the western central highlands of Puerto Rico and is bordered by a cluster of smaller agricultural communities that depend on the town for its vibrant commercial life.[48] And while the town's main productive base continues to be agriculture, its current population of over 44,000 and its increasingly diverse economy — including small factories, a bustling service economy, and until recently, one of the island's largest sugar refineries — attest to its economic and political importance. San Sebastián's extensive migration history, which dates back to the nineteenth century, has created a context in which population shifts are part of the social fabric of the town. In the 1940s, men and women were recruited to work in mainland homes and factories. Many of these migrants went to Chicago. Beginning in the 1960s, many *pepinianos* returned to San Sebastián in response to changes in the island and mainland economies, a trend that, as Carlos Vargas Ramos notes, characterizes Puerto Rico's northwestern and southeastern regions more broadly, making the Aguadilla Statistical Metropolitan Area (which includes San Sebastián) one that indexes above-average rates of return migrants.[49] The facts that some *pepinianos* left San Sebastián again in the 1980s and 1990s for cities like Chicago, and that many have never left the town but are profoundly affected by the changes occasioned by these different migration patterns, point to the need to examine how circular migration and transnational practices shape people's lives and communities in northwestern towns like San Sebastián.

This book is based on two years of ethnographic and historical research in San Sebastián and Chicago. Using local newspapers, government documents, in-depth interviews, and kinship and household analysis, it details the migration histories and imaginings of members of twenty-two different households, as they migrate, return, and settle in both communities. In both settings, I relied on multiple and overlapping networks — as a teacher, neighbor, community worker, family member, and eventually a friend — to meet people, most of whom I formally interviewed. In Chicago, my work at Ruiz Belvis was an important entrée into people's lives and the larger Puerto Rican community. A number of students from my first G.E.D. class, during the summer of 1995, were particularly helpful, and they are some of the most important people featured in these pages: Aida Rodríguez, Yvette Jiménez, and Lorena Santiago were all part of this first group of students.

Shortly after I began teaching that summer, I learned that these women and other students were just as fascinated by my life as I was by theirs. They were particularly intrigued by the fact that at the age of twenty-five, I was "still in school," single, and childless. The fact that I lived far from my family and shared an apartment with another single Puerto Rican woman — also a graduate student — was equally foreign. The older women in the class very sweetly tried to compensate for my lack of family in the area by occasionally bringing to class carefully prepared meals they insisted I take home *por si acaso* — just in case I didn't have time, or wasn't able, to cook for myself. The older men concerned themselves with my physical safety, insisting on walking me to the train after class and giving me advice about which parts of the neighborhood I should avoid. And the women who were my contemporaries would initiate long conversations about what it was like "living single" in the city and having my own apartment. Most of these women either still lived with their own parents — usually together with their husbands or boyfriends and children — or with extended kin (their own or their partners'), and they expressed a deep longing for a place of their own.

When I returned from Puerto Rico later that fall, I contacted some of my students and tried to make plans to see them and conduct interviews. Most of the women agreed to meet me only at the Centro. After a number of unsuccessful attempts to meet at their homes, I finally realized why they had not invited me to visit them; like other poor and working-class families in the Near Northwest Side, they usually lived doubled-up with extended family and friends or in extremely cramped conditions, and people like Yvette and Lorena were reluctant to bring me home because they were not sure how I would react to their living arrangements. They were ashamed of their apartments, which were usually very old, drafty, and cluttered with clothes drying on lines in their living rooms and kitchens. Their homes were also painfully loud, with multiple conversations competing with blaring television and radio, which were almost always turned on. One woman was horribly embarrassed and almost cried when a large cockroach scurried across the table as she served me a delicious cup of *café con leche*. And others worried that I wouldn't feel "cómoda" (comfortable) in their homes. Painfully aware of how their class background differed from my own, these women did everything they could to hide the "injuries of class."[50]

The first time Aida invited me to her home, I climbed the steps to her second-floor apartment, eager to spend the evening with her large family. But she quickly led me outside to a nearby coffee shop, where I interviewed her for the first time over hamburgers and fries. When the check arrived, she surprised me by grabbing it and insisting on paying for our meal. When I objected, telling her there was no way I would allow her to pay for our meal — she was supporting herself and her five children on her husband's sporadic wages and the little she received from welfare — she cocked her head, lowered her eyes, and pointed at me angrily. "Aren't we friends? Huh? If we're friends, then you have to let me pay every once in a while, you know. I got my money too, you know." I explained that I didn't have the kind of expenses she had with all of her children, and that it was the least I could do. She responded by saying that just because she didn't live in a nice apartment, it didn't mean she couldn't pay for a couple of cheap burgers. I quickly realized that for Aida, and many of my students, bringing me home was risky since it revealed their sometimes unsuccessful struggle to create decent and respectable living spaces in their marginal economic circumstances. For that reason — and surely others of which I am unaware — many of my initial interviews, formal and informal, occurred either at the Centro or in other public spaces.

As a volunteer at the Centro and as the G.E.D. teacher the following year, I continued to meet people willing to share their stories about migration and life in Chicago. In the fall of 1996 I moved to Humboldt Park and lived on the third floor of a neat, relatively quiet apartment building near the corner of Armitage and California Avenues. I chose the apartment because it was affordable, relatively quiet, and conveniently located near Puerto Rican grocery stores, Mexican *panaderías,* and the park. Most of my neighbors in the building were also young students, but the rest of the neighborhood was filled with working-class Puerto Rican and Mexican families living in apartment buildings and single family homes. Because I was initially unsuccessful in meeting people on the street, I began to wash my clothes at Paradise Wash, the local laundromat, which offered free drying and hours of conversation with men and women representative of the neighborhood. Many of the women I met were African American, but most who spoke with me at length were Mexican or Puerto Rican. From my hours at Paradise Wash, I learned more about the increasing tensions between Puerto Ricans and Mexicans; the sexual division of labor at home (women always arrived with multiple bags filled with their family's clothes, and when I saw men, they were usually washing only their own); and Humboldt Park's thriving informal economy (vendors always stopped inside to sell *tamales, pasteles,* clothing, music, and bootlegged videos). I spoke with people at length about their perceptions of the neighborhood and how it was changing. When I could, I shopped in nearby grocery stores. These experiences in the neighborhood and at the Centro make up the bulk of my Chicago ethnography.

In San Sebastián, working in Tía Cristina's store allowed me to meet neighbors and friends who had lived for varying lengths of time *afuera.* This was my main entrée into people's lives. I would serve beers, *palitos de ron* — shots of rum — and sodas to the *viejitos* who frequented the store. And along with Tía and my father's cousin Lydia, who also lived with Tía Cristi and her husband, I played countless games of dominoes and pool with men, young and old. Women did not usually play dominoes, Lydia informed me. And respectable women would never be found at *la tienda.* But since we were Tía Cristina's help and family, we would have no problems, she assured me. Because *la tienda* was directly across the street from the local basketball courts and baseball fields, I also met people, mostly men, from other areas around San Sebastián who introduced me to families who had lived in Chicago.

In town, I would strike up conversations with people, usually women, in *la plaza,* the *cafeterías,* and the local library. Because San Sebastián is small enough for old-timers to recognize family names, being from a family with a long history in Pepino was very helpful. One librarian introduced me to a local community activist and *independentista,* who in turn introduced me to local artisan Jorge Colosio, who shared with me his story of *huyendo de la caña* — fleeing the cane — to Florida and then Chicago in 1951. He also introduced me to Congressman Luis Gutierrez's parents, who had returned to San Sebastián in the 1970s after many years in Chicago. Finally, *pepinianas* I knew in Chicago, like Mercedes Rubio, put me in contact with extended family in San Sebastián. My conversations and interviews with these people — usually conducted in their homes, their *marquesina* (carport), or at the store — provided the rich data for this ethnography.

My ethnographic study was complemented by historical research in Chicago, Puerto Rico, and New York. In Chicago, I made extensive use of the Chicago Historical Society's archive of municipal documents and newspapers detailing the arrival and popular perceptions of Puerto Rican migrants from the late 1940s to the present. In Puerto Rico, I had access to private newspaper collections in San Sebastián, and I read other island dailies, government documents, and magazines in the Colección Puertorriqueña at the University of Puerto Rico in Río Piedras. And in New York, I used the Historical Archive of the Puerto Rican Migration to the United States at the Center for Puerto Rican Studies at Hunter College. I focused exclusively on documents from the Migration Division Office of the Department of Labor, paying particular attention to monthly and annual reports from the Midwest and Chicago offices detailing the housing, employment, and social needs of new Puerto Rican migrants in the city. I also analyzed all annual reports from 1948 to 1968 from the division's New York office, since they frequently contained information about the growing "Puerto Rican problem" in New York and made reference to Chicago's Puerto Rican population. Like the migration experience of many Puerto Ricans, my research led me to many locations on the mainland and the island. I also found myself involved in the painful, but tremendously instructive, politics of research.

A Puerto Rican Yuppie and the Politics of Research

After my first summer teaching G.E.D. classes, I continued my work with the Centro by volunteering as a tutor, collaborating with cultural and educational programs, and serving on its board of directors. When I for-

mally began my Chicago field research in the fall of 1996, I moved to
Humboldt Park and was reappointed as the Centro's G.E.D. instructor.
By this time, my students from the summer before had moved on. Some
had passed the exam, while others were simply unable to continue their
studies at that time. To my dismay, the new group of students didn't meet
my expectations from previous experience. There were more young men
and fewer women and mothers my age, and it was very clear that we were
equally concerned about how we would get along. A few weeks into the
course, however, we relaxed around each other and began telling stories
and sharing experiences beyond the classroom. One October morning,
my students excitedly talked about Fox's television program *Faces of
Death,* which had aired the night before. Those who had seen the program provided gruesome details about the show's death scenes and
argued over which was the most disgusting. When they asked me if I had
seen the program, I told them that I hadn't and that I really didn't enjoy
scary movies or horror films. Surprised, José, a twenty-four-year-old
Puerto Rican student, turned to me and said, "You know, you're different.
You're like, um, a Puerto Rican yuppie." I was absolutely shocked. I
couldn't believe that my students thought I was a yuppie. For me, yuppies represented consumerism, materialism, and an inability to see that
one's life and actions are deeply political — all values I find problematic.
In my field notes that night, I recorded the morning's painful events:

For me, that is possibly the worst thing someone could say to me. I must have
looked shocked — and completely caught off-guard — because José just looked at
me and said, "Ooooo," as if he thought he had really made me mad. I responded,
"I can't be a yuppie. I don't have enough money to be a yuppie." "You don't have
to," he responded. Leo Chacón agreed, "Yeah, just look at all these people around
here," meaning Wicker Park/West Town. "All you need is enough money to
travel." At this point, I am getting even more defensive. Not only was I compared
to the gentrifiers about whom my students constantly complain, I was told that
being a yuppie is somehow equated not with money or the display of money or
looking rich. It has to do with travel — which I do a lot — which, in turn, has to
do with an attitude about life. My students could not have touched on a more vulnerable subject with me.

   Leo continued, "Nah, you're not a yuppie." "You're alternative," José interrupted. "Nah, she's not alternative. She's earffy." "Earffy?" I asked. "What's that?"
"You know," he explained. "You don't wear any makeup, you're laid back, care-
free, and well, you're always *happy.* Man! You're *always* smiling." "Yeah, you're
always so *happy,*" Jose added. [I later figured out that "earffy" was "earthy."]

   I was so taken aback by all of this. I guess I knew that I was different and that
both my students and my friends in Humboldt Park saw me as being very

different. But I really never knew how. And now I know. And I don't know if I like it, or if I really know what they mean by all of this. As I have said before, this neighborhood is experiencing quite a bit of gentrification, and I really don't want to be seen as part of that process. And I am not sure if that is what they mean by their comments. Clearly, I am not just a yuppie — I'm a *Puerto Rican* yuppie, as José pointed out. They see me as similar, yet different.

My students' comments that day reminded me of my insider/outsider status, and of the ways in which my class position, education, and cultural capital marked me in very specific ways. Once I overcame the shock and embarrassment of being labeled a Puerto Rican yuppie, I started thinking about the different ways in which the Centro and other Puerto Rican institutions tried to emphasize my similarities — a shared ethnic identity — with these students and other youth frequenting the Centro. Like other professional Puerto Ricans and college students in Chicago, I was presented as a "role model" to the students. And that, I was told, was one of the reasons why I, and others like me, were encouraged to serve in leadership positions and collaborate in the Centro's activities. Initially, I was extremely willing to be this role model, believing that it was an important way to "give something back." But I soon realized that such thinking is actually dangerous and quite regressive: It smoothes over extremely important differences of class and education within ethnic groups. It also ignores individual agency, suggesting that poor young people will unreflectively imitate those who are presented to them. This idea of ethnic role models also elides the important issue of political-economic power that structures people's lives quite distinctively, offering instead the promise of class mobility based on the conservative rhetoric of hard work, personal sacrifice, and self-reliance.[51]

My status as an insider/outsider in Puerto Rico was equally complicated and mapped onto the perennial debate surrounding Puerto Rican identity. Because I was Cristina's great niece, neighbors who frequented her store were willing to speak with me and answer my informal queries about their migration experiences. I was, in fact, like many of their own daughters and granddaughters who were born and raised *afuera* and now lived in Puerto Rico. And because these people knew my extended family quite well, I was also understood within the "patriarchal connectivity" constructing and defining all people in the neighborhood.[52] People would introduce me as "la hija de Tony" or "la nieta de Pedro y Juanita" and would use similar terms to present newcomers to me.

Once friends and neighbors knew who I was, many would spend hours debating the issue of Puerto Rican identity with me. On several occasions, I was asked if I considered myself Puerto Rican. This, of course, was almost always a trick question. Rubén, one of the regulars at the store, asked me this on a regular basis. When I answered that I did consider myself to be Puerto Rican, he would respond, "You're not Puerto Rican. You are of *Puerto Rican parents*. But because you weren't born in Puerto Rico, you're of Puerto Rican *descent*." Those nearby would sometimes agree; others — usually those born in the United States — would take issue and debate for hours who was actually Puerto Rican. Still others would defend me, saying that I was "una muchacha decente," and pointing to the markers in dress, language, class, and education that demonstrated that I was indeed Puerto Rican and remarkably different from *los jóvenes de afuera* — the youth born in American cities.

In this context, agreeing with my defenders meant affirming these negative portraits of mainland Puerto Ricans. Yet allowing others to define me as *not* Puerto Rican only reproduced essentialized and very narrow definitions of gendered ethnic identity. My shifting and contested identity influenced how people interacted with me. Young men and women who had resided in places like Chicago and New York were particularly eager to talk with me, but they often did so when the old-timers were not around. And the opposite was also true. As in Chicago, I navigated these relationships, tensions, and expectations with as much grace and respect as possible, paying close attention to the way in which my positionality elicited particular reactions.

In the pages that follow, I present an account of people's lives in San Sebastián and Chicago. For reasons of *confianza y respeto,* the names of the people who shared their lives with me have been changed. The narrative structure is organized in the circular pattern that has characterized many *puertorriqueños'* experiences: migration, return, subsequent movements, and enduring transnational connections. My hope is to present their stories with all the complexity and richness they shared with me, while preserving their anonymity and their trust.

CHAPTER 2

"Fleeing the Cane"
and the Origins of Displacement

Today the journey from San Juan to San Sebastián is neither long nor complicated, thanks to Puerto Rico's expressway, *la 22.* Until the early 1990s, when the expressway from San Juan to Arecibo was completed, the trip easily lasted four hours, and travelers in private cars or *carros públicos* (taxis) would make the trip more enjoyable by stopping along the way at one of the many roadside restaurants, kiosks, and bakeries for sandwiches, *frituras,* and *café* or soda. One can now complete the trip in just under two hours, although this does not change older people's perceptions of the distance or their need to stop mid-journey for a drink or to stretch their legs. Nor does it dissuade my tía Cristina from loading up my car with *guineos* (bananas) and sodas *por si acaso,* just in case I get hungry or thirsty on my occasional research trips to San Juan.

After exiting the freeway in Arecibo, the picturesque highway 119 leads south, descending into a verdant valley bordered by the Camuy Caverns on the east, and eventually to Lares, the cradle of the Revolution. Lares and San Sebastián are connected by a windy road thick with vegetation, *la 111,* which continues west past brightly painted wood and cement houses hugging the mountain road and past *el Salto de Collaso,* a cascading waterfall, and into the town of San Sebastián. A deep green knoll topped with colorfully arranged flowers spelling out the words "San Sebastián de las Vegas del Pepino" assures newcomers they have finally arrived in El Pepino.

Even though getting to San Sebastián is much easier than before, on my last visit there, in May 2001, I got lost. With one of my sisters and my toddler son in tow, I was excitedly telling them stories of San Sebastián, the people they would meet, and the town's quaint, warm appeal, as we descended along *la 111,* when I realized that I had missed the usual detour through town, past the Puerto Rican Telephone Company offices and the bustling *cafeterias,* and was instead on an unfamiliar road lined with strip malls packed with new chain stores like Pep Boys, Western Auto, and Pitusa. I eventually found the road leading to the neighborhood of Saltos, where Tía Cristina and my father's cousin anxiously awaited us. When I told them and others in Tía Cristina's store that I lost my way into town, they laughed, saying that was the price of *progreso,* or progress, in Pepino. Pepino was growing, changing, "finally progressing into the twenty-first century," they assured me, a familiar refrain I had noted in my fieldwork three years earlier.

The idea of *progreso* in San Sebastián is a familiar one, whose roots reach back to the early stages of Puerto Rico's industrialization program in the 1940s, sustaining local understandings of the town's history and present. *Pepinianos'* postwar migration to the United States, shifts in the town's productive base, and changes in local cultural practices as a result of industrialization, return migration, and intensified transnational connections between San Sebastián and U.S. cities are largely understood within this ideology of progress. And although many *pepinianos* lament and even resist what they regard as the negative consequences of *progreso* — the proliferation of strip malls filled with megastores and transnational fast food chains, as well as bigger roads and parking lots to accommodate the rising number of cars in the town — others encourage these changes, which symbolize the town's modernity, processes I analyze in greater detail in subsequent chapters. Here I focus on San Sebastián's economic and migration histories to explore how notions of "progress" and "modernity" became inextricably linked to mobility, both actual and imagined, and displacement. San Sebastián is not unique in this regard. In fact, the transformations characterizing the town in the postwar era reflect important islandwide economic, political, and cultural changes and reveal quite dramatically the ideological underpinnings of Puerto Rico's industrialization program, including the ways in which the island's rural population and women have been implicated in these processes. For the architects of Puerto Rico's industrialization program, the project's success rested largely on mobilizing residents of places like San Sebastián as industrial laborers, migrants, and ultimately transnational actors.

San Sebastián's Changing Economy

San Sebastián is approximately 71 square miles in size, and while the town of slightly more than 44,000 residents is by no means a large city, it ranks as one of the most important agricultural centers in Puerto Rico and is an important commercial hub for the surrounding municipalities of Lares, Moca, Las Marías, and Isabela.[1] Located in the western central region, San Sebastián lies at the crossroads of the island's sugar- and coffee-producing regions and, because of the town's diverse topography, produces both commodities, as well as other agricultural products, including plantains, dairy products, and livestock. San Sebastián's Plaza del Mercado — an all-night marketplace — draws vendors and buyers from all over the island interested in its offering of fruits, vegetables, livestock, plants, and even small appliances, clothes, and other goods typical of flea markets. The town's cultural festivals, Festival de la Novilla in January and Festival de la Hamaca in July, also draw thousands of islanders and international visitors interested in participating in "typical" cultural activities.

Pepinianos are extremely proud of their town and readily boast of its important historical events and people, although who is included in this list varies according to one's political philosophy and reflects the island's political history. Many residents would remind me, for example, of San Sebastián's role in *El Grito de Lares*[2] and would also point out that the first Puerto Rican soldier drafted into the U.S. military during World War I, shortly after the passage of the Jones Act conferring U.S. citizenship on Puerto Ricans, was from San Sebastián. Puerto Rico's beloved singer Sophy also hails from Pepino, as do musician, director, and composer Angel Mislán, Congressman Luis Gutierrez (whose parents still reside there), and Puerto Rican political prisoner Oscar López. These names, as well as other facts about San Sebastián, are readily shared with newcomers, who are also warned of the town's seductive powers, of how visitors to San Sebastián become so enchanted that they never leave, a feeling captured in a popular expression, "El que bebe agua del Rio Culebrinas, se queda en el Pepino" (Those who drink water from the Culebrinas River remain in Pepino).

While San Sebastián continues to be an important agricultural center on the island, its residents are largely concentrated in the public sector as government employees (29 percent) and in manufacturing industries (20 percent), as well as in the service sector. According to the 1990 census, unemployment and poverty rates in San Sebastián, at 25 percent and 70.1 percent respectively, are significantly higher than islandwide rates (20 percent and 59 percent), a problem attesting to the deep regional inequalities characterizing Puerto Rico.[3] The decline in manufacturing employment has exacerbated a precarious economic base in San Sebastián, as factories like Avon, Hanes, and P.J. have moved much of their production elsewhere. Workers' economic security is even more endangered because the companies remaining in San Sebastián increasingly rely on temporary workers subcontracted from businesses like Kelly Temporary Services, which place workers in desirable jobs but without the same wages, protections, and benefits previously provided by employers. The 1996 closing of Central La Plata, San Sebastián's sugar refinery, which had generated close to $17 million annually for the local economy and provided income, either directly or indirectly, for more than half of the town's residents, was the final blow to the town's struggling economy.[4] Its closure was a bittersweet ending to an important chapter of San Sebastián's economic history, in which sugar played a complex and defining role. Bernardino Robles, a seventy-year-old *colono* (small landowner) and return migrant, reflected on *pepinianos'* relationship to sugar: "[Working in the cane] was a good, decent job. You could make good money . . . . Parents would send their children to study with the money they made working the cane. 'Study, my son. Study. [Working in] the cane is hard.' Parents sent their children to study; to study with money [they made working] the cane."

Bernardino's comments speak to important tensions and contradictions characterizing many *pepinianos'* — and by extension Puerto Ricans' — relationship to sugar. On the one hand, the iconic images of the sugar industry — *el machete,* the (male) worker in the cane, ox-drawn carts, and hills green with unharvested sugarcane — are ubiquitous, adorning wooden plaques, posters, and T-shirts marketed for tourist, and even local, consumption. They have also become powerful symbols of resistance and ethnic pride that are deployed in cultural nationalist struggles on the island and throughout Puerto Rican communities on the mainland. On the other hand, agricultural work in Puerto Rico is devalued and rests largely on the shoulders of older *colonos,* who grow crops for household consumption, informal exchange, and local sale, and on the shoulders of Dominican immigrants, who are often socially, culturally, and economically marginalized in Puerto Rican society. Although sugar production now plays a very minor role in the Puerto Rican economy, these contradictory images reveal the enduring cultural importance of a commodity that transformed the island's economic, cultural, and social history after the U.S. invasion in 1898.

Already in the first decades of U.S. political and economic control, sugar dominated the island economy. Prior to 1898, under Spanish colonial rule, coffee had been Puerto Rico's primary export, and hacienda-based coffee production had dominated the regional economies of the island's mountainous interior.[5] Although San Sebastián never produced as much coffee as the neighboring municipalities of Lares and Las Marías, which are located at higher altitudes, the town's economic welfare still relied heavily on coffee production, especially from 1877 to 1898. Historians of San Sebastián have noted that the town's coffee industry benefited from significant population growth early in the nineteenth century, as *colonos* and *agregados* (landless agricultural workers), displaced from the coasts as a result of increased cane cultivation and land concentration, migrated to the interior in search of land. Internal migrants from Aguada, Añasco, and Mayaguez settled in San Sebastián, as did Spanish immigrants from Venezuela and Santo Domingo, who were encouraged to settle in the region by the Spanish government, which provided inexpensive landholdings and, most importantly, credit to support their commercial and agricultural endeavors. With this kind of support, Spanish immigrants quickly became the town's principal landowners and most profitable commercial actors. "Whether it was in agriculture or commercial areas," Helen Santiago Méndez notes, "being an immigrant was, with few exceptions, a passport to success in the nineteenth century."[6]

Throughout the nineteenth century, *criollo* and immigrant agriculturalists grew coffee, cotton, rice, and even small amounts of sugarcane for household consumption and local sale, although coffee quickly became the region's most lucrative agricultural commodity. In response to a global demand for coffee in the nineteenth century, Spain invested heavily in Puerto Rico's coffee industry by providing extensive credit to Spanish *cafetaleros* (coffee producers) and imposing tariffs to protect Puerto Rican coffee on the world market. Both *peninsular* (Spanish-born residents) and *criollo* (island-born residents) coffee growers — who dominated coffee production in San Sebastián and Lares — benefited from Spain's economic policies, and the region's coffee production flourished after 1877, reaching peaks in 1892 and 1897. Coffee's economic importance in the region was, however, short-lived. With the American occupation of Puerto Rico in 1898, the coffee industry lost its primary market, as well as access to Spanish and European credit, upon which the coffee industry depended. Moreover, the United States failed to protect Puerto Rican coffee with tariffs, and in fact raised import taxes on the commodity, making it unable to compete with less expensive coffee imports from Brazil and other South American countries.[7] These political-economic changes, as well as the devastating 1899 hurricane San Ciriaco, all contributed to the eventual replacement of coffee with sugarcane as San Sebastián's most important agricultural commodity.[8]

By establishing political control in Puerto Rico, the United States laid the foundation for unfettered economic expansion throughout the island, particularly in the sugar industry, which was dominated by powerful U.S. corporations within the first two decades of occupation. As Sidney Mintz notes, capitalist penetration of Puerto Rico's sugar industry "continued unabated for fully twenty-five years, within which time every feature of sugar production in Puerto Rico, and the very scale of the industry underwent revolutionary change." Land concentration occurred at unprecedented rates, especially on the coasts, where U.S. corporations were most powerful. Here irrigation was introduced, and sugar processing was increasingly centralized as a result of the "corporate land-and-factory" model. By 1910, U.S. industries controlled more than 62 percent of the land dedicated to sugar production in the island, and by 1940, two-thirds of Puerto Rico's exports consisted of sugar.[9]

The rapid expansion of commercial sugar production in Puerto Rico had severe consequences for other sectors of the island economy and set in motion renewed internal migration, this time to coastal sugar regions. Coffee planters, who had survived crises in 1898 and 1899, could no longer obtain sufficient credit to maintain their agricultural production. As a result, many coffee farmers were forced to reduce production levels and, in more extreme cases, to abandon their farms and move to the burgeoning urban centers on the island. San Sebastián was no exception to these trends, albeit with important exceptions. Although coffee dominated San Sebastián's economic base in the late nineteenth century, its diversified topography also allowed agriculturalists to grow cane on a much smaller scale — less then 1 percent of cultivated land in 1896 — and provided the basis for greater agricultural investment in cane cultivation after 1898.[10] As sugar began to dominate the island economy, *pepinianos* increasingly invested in cane cultivation. Newcomers to the town also invested in sugar production, contributing to the town's significant population growth of nearly 60 percent from 1899 to 1930, particularly in rural barrios like Hato Arriba, Pozas, and Saltos, which would eventually dominate the town's cane cultivation.

In the first decade of the twentieth century, San Sebastián's sugar industry developed slowly, with *colonos* growing and grinding cane on small and medium-sized haciendas that were also used to cultivate minor crops and raise animals for household consumption, although coffee production still predominated in the region. By the 1920s, however, a number of factors secured the primary importance of sugar production in the town, including a continuing drop in coffee prices, the destruction wrought by hurricane San Felipe, which wiped out the remaining small coffee producers in the region, U.S. promotion of sugar production through easy access to credit and other tax incentives, and finally the establishment of a sugar refinery in the town. In July 1910, private investors established La Plata Agricultural Company, an industrial and agricultural society dedicated to sugarcane cultivation in San Sebastián, Moca, and Aguadilla. Later that year, they founded Central La Plata, one of the area's most important sugar mills, under the auspices of La Plata Sugar Company.[11]

San Sebastián's land ownership structure avoided the "corporate land-and-factory combine" characterizing much of the island's sugar production. Unlike many *centrales,* which integrated agricultural production and processing on large tracts of land, La Plata was solely a sugar refinery, purchasing sugarcane from local *colonos,* 99 percent of whom owned small or medium-sized farms of five hundred acres or less that supported both cane cultivation and subsistence farming. In contrast, historian Carmen Whalen notes that in five south coast *municipios,* 60 percent of farms comprised five hundred acres or more. This land structure had a dramatic impact on San Sebastián, protecting it from the consequences of the sugar economy's sharp decline in the 1930s as a result of the Jones-Costigan Act of 1934 and the Sugar Act of 1937, which "limited the production and marketing of sugar for all areas supplying sugar to the United States, including Puerto Rico."[12]

While the island's sugar industry contracted and many of the *centrales* closed beginning in the late 1930s — including La Central Carmen in Toa Alta, Central el Caribe in Salinas, and Boca Chica in Ponce — La Plata continued to thrive and expand because its *colonos* remained financially solvent with their cane production and their diversified productive base. Women's wage labor in the needle trades and in manufacturing also provided critical economic support for *pepinianos'* household economies during that time. *Pepinianas'* employment in the needle trades was part of an island-wide increase in the home needlework industry during World War I, when, as Carmen Whalen notes, the United States suspended European imports, such as hand-sewn gloves and embroidered handkerchiefs, which were subsequently produced in Puerto Rico through a system in which "contractors and subcontractors handled the distribution and collection of materials, and rural women added the hand details at home, earning piecework wages."[13] The needle industry was concentrated in rural areas, especially in Mayaguez and the surrounding region, to such an extent that by 1935, more than half of all island women in the labor force were involved in home-based needlework, factory-based needle trades, and other factory employment, such as cigar and tobacco production, contributing necessary income to cash-strapped households.[14] According to the 1940 census, more than 2,200 *pepinianas* were employed in the home needlework trade, 2,600 in apparel and other textile production, and 2,600 as "operatives and kindred workers." Women's subsistence and informal economic activities also helped to sustain households, as did their reproductive work, which was largely unremunerated.[15]

As was true throughout the island, rural households in San Sebastián survived based on a combination of commercial agriculture, subsistence farming, and the needlework industry. But for many agricultural households in Pepino, La Plata was key to their survival. By 1939, La Plata was grinding nearly 130,000 tons of sugar annually, soon becoming the eighth most important of Puerto Rico's thirty-two sugar refineries.[16] Despite the varied subsistence strategies that sustained them, many rural households were also dangerously dependent on seasonal and sporadic income-generating activities in order to buy basic foodstuffs. By the mid 1930s, Puerto Rico's cost of living had surged to such a degree that the price of basic foodstuffs sold on the island — 80 percent of which were imported from the United States — was almost 15 percent more than in New York City, where workers earned tenfold wages.[17] The inflation, in conjunction with a worsening economic context caused by the faltering sugar economy, devastated Puerto Rico's economy to such an alarming degree that President Roosevelt and his New Deal strategists directed their attention first to Puerto Rico, not only to provide emergency relief but also to use it as "a political testing ground for the exportability of New Deal recovery strategies." In 1934, President Roosevelt commissioned Dr. Carlos Chardón, chancellor of the University of Puerto Rico, to preside over the Puerto Rican Policy Commission, designated to investigate the socioeconomic conditions of Puerto Ricans and formulate a development plan to address the island's economic crisis.[18]

The Chardón Plan and the Resurrection of the Overpopulation Debate

The Chardón Plan, as it was later labeled, was important for a number of reasons. First, it approached Puerto Rico's economic and social problems not as "a depression emergency" but instead as "the chronic maladjustment of a land-hungry and sugar-dominated economy that it was in reality," and proposed radical structural changes that would address the root of Puerto Rico's economic crisis.[19] To that end, the Chardón Plan urged the Roosevelt administration to enact an agrarian reform program that included the enforcement of the Five Hundred Acre Law provided under the Foraker Act of 1900, the diversification of agriculture, the rehabilitation of coffee and tobacco areas through the establishment of subsistence farms, and a rural electrification project. It also recommended the creation of an industrialization program, beginning with state sponsorship of local development projects, such as the construction of a cement factory and the development and expansion of social service programs in education, healthcare, and public housing. Finally, the plan called for a comprehensive program that would address overpopulation and unemployment in Puerto Rico through planned migration.[20]

The Chardón Plan was never fully implemented. In fact, it seemed doomed to failure by its emphasis on an agrarian reform program that challenged powerful sugar growers and industrialists. Instead, a more modest reconstruction program was implemented by a new government bureaucracy, which also served as a vehicle for the political ascent of local Puerto Rican technocrats, bureaucrats, and professionals who would later became the primary political force in island politics, the Partido Popular Democrático (PPD).[21] Throughout the next decade, three key elements of the Chardón Plan — the call for a planned industrial development strategy, a deep concern regarding rural communities and rural-based economic strategies, and a resurgence of the overpopulation discourse — symbolically defined the reformist political-economic agenda of the PPD and its populist slogan, *Pan, tierra y libertad* (Bread, land and freedom). For my purposes, the plan's concern with overpopulation — and specifically, the ideological construction of rural peoples as a surplus population — is significant in that it resurrected the island's long-standing overpopulation debates, which can be traced back to the U.S. invasion of Puerto Rico, when American officials forecasted social disaster due to widespread poverty, overpopulation, and ill health of island residents. The Chardón Plan echoed these earlier sentiments, noting that even if industrial development were to improve "progressive landlessness" and "chronic unemployment," the achievements would "be unavailing . . . if population growth cannot be checked, or at least reduced."[22]

At the time of the plan's release, urban growth had increased substantially while the island's rural populations had slowly declined. Contrary

TABLE 2. Population and Population Change by Decade, San Sebastián, 1899–2000

Year	Population	Percent Change from Previous Census
1899	16,412	
1910	18,904	15.2
1920	22,524	19.1
1930	25,691	14.1
1940	30,216	17.6
1950	35,376	17.1
1960	33,451	-5.4
1970	30,157	-9.8
1980	35,690	18.3
1990	38,799	8.7
2000	44,204	13.9

SOURCES: Junta de Planificación, Urbanización, y Zonificación, Population Statistics, 1899–1940; U.S. Census Bureau, Characteristics of the Population 1950–1990; U.S. Census Bureau, 2000 Census, Redistricting Data Summary File

TABLE 3. Population and Population Change by Decade, Puerto Rico, 1899–2000

Year	Population	Percent Change from Previous Census
1899	953,243	19.4
1910	1,118,012	17.3
1920	1,299,809	16.3
1930	1,543,913	18.8
1940	1,869,255	21.1
1950	2,210,703	18.3
1960	2,349,544	6.3
1970	2,712,033	15.4
1980	3,196,520	17.9
1990	3,522,037	10.2
2000	3,808,037	8.1

SOURCES: Junta de Planificación, Urbanización, y Zonificación, Population Statistics, 1899–1940; U.S. Census Bureau, Characteristics of the Population 1950–1990; U.S. Census Bureau, 2000 Census, Redistricting Data Summary File

to islandwide trends, however, San Sebastián's population had increased by nearly 20 percent in the 1930s and 1940s, with much of that growth occurring in rural barrios. San Sebastián's growth can be attributed, in large part, to a brief period of agrarian reform and populist policies under the PPD, which improved rural infrastructure with new roads, sanitation, and electricity and enhanced the quality of life with better education and public health services. In the 1930s, the number of *colonos* in San Sebastián increased, as did the amount of cane ground in the La Plata sugar mill, reaching close to 130,000 tons by 1939, a trend that continued through the 1940s.[23] Thus San Sebastián's rural population was increasing precisely at the same time as the Chardón Plan proposed a social policy of population control based on planned emigration and a "scientific scheme of birth control":

It is estimated by [the Federal Emergency Relief Administration (FERA)] that there are in Puerto Rico not less than 150,000 heads of families permanently unemployed. This covers roughly about half the population. A study of the possibilities should determine what proportion of these may be absorbed over a period of years by the maximum industrial development as determined by present knowledge and conditions. Unemployment remaining beyond such possibilities of industrialization must obviously be taken care of by the return of the land in small farms to agricultural workers and by emigration that will provide employment in other regions. *Although a scientific scheme of birth control should be part of any far-sighted policy for Puerto Rico,* it cannot be hoped that it will be socially effective until the standard of living, and therefore the sense of responsibility of the mass of the population, has been substantially improved. It will probably be effective in keeping the rate of growth down in the future, after the improvement brought about by economic reconstruction has begun to be felt by the population as a whole [emphasis added].[24]

While the Chardón Plan clearly advocated a birth control policy in concert with emigration and improved economic conditions, its explicit reference to such a policy at the beginning of the two-hundred-page report is particularly noteworthy. Soon after the plan's release, the Puerto Rican Emergency Relief Administration authorized a portion of its funds to be used for the creation of the Maternal Health Clinic, an experimental birth control clinic and a division of Puerto Rico's School of Tropical Medicine. Between October 1935 and June 1936, FERA expanded the birth control effort by opening sixty-seven maternal clinics, which provided services to more than ten thousand island women.[25]

Government involvement in the creation and funding of birth control clinics in the 1930s was preceded by private efforts to promote birth control leagues and associations in Puerto Rico in the 1920s. In 1925, La Liga para el Control de Natalidad de Puerto Rico (the Birth Control League of Puerto Rico), the island's first birth control association, started providing educational information and materials to women interested in contraception. The league also worked with American organizations to repeal the Comstock Laws, which prohibited the teaching and distribution of birth control methods in the United States. Ideologically, the league was attuned to the prevailing ethos, which Laura Briggs describes as a "modernizing nationalism of birth control rhetoric," deeply informed by socialist thought and the desire to "produce happy families, a healthier working class, and a wealthier nation through birth control."[26] In 1922, for example, Luis Muñoz Marín succinctly argued that the problem of poverty in Puerto Rico could be approached

[by] reducing the population or increasing the wealth. . . . I believe that reducing the population is the most important, the most practical, and the cheapest. . . . I favor Malthusianism, the voluntary limitation of childbearing, supported by the government. Scientific methods of avoiding conception should be taught to all *poor* families who wish to learn them. And an active campaign should be carried out so that the largest possible number of *poor* families will want to learn them [emphasis added].[27]

Muñoz Marín, league members, and other island elites advocating expanded birth control programs in Puerto Rico were heavily influenced by Margaret Sanger and her American Birth Control League.[28] Puerto Rican reformers were also aware of eugenic social movements in Europe, the United States, and Latin America that targeted "socially unfit" groups based on race and class, and readily subscribed to such eugenicist views (as seen in Muñoz Marín's emphasis on a birth control program for *poor* families), as did the island press.[29] In the days following the founding of the Birth Control League of Puerto Rico, the island's most prominent newspaper, *El Mundo,* celebrated the event by focusing on the island's rural population, the *jíbaros* (the popular and folkloric label for rural people who worked the land), as the appropriate objects of eugenic measures: "[The *jíbaros* are] a generation undermined since childhood, destined, even before its birth, to pass uselessly through life, a victim of itself, of the fatal legacy left by its parents."[30]

Despite popular support, the league's existence was short-lived, dissolving as a result of strong opposition from the Catholic Church in Puerto Rico and the United States. This group laid the foundation, however, for the work of nurses and social workers with a broad political agenda that included "the consolidation of social work and nursing as autonomous professions, the creation of maternal and child health programs, the ending of illegitimacy, obtaining suffrage for literate women (exclusively), and the extension of mainland minimum-wage legislation to the working classes of Puerto Rico." From 1932 to 1936, nurses and social workers played a key role in the creation of the island's birth control clinic movement, with the 1932 opening in San Juan of the first clinic to provide contraceptive services for women, and the subsequent establishment of birth control clinics in Lares and Mayaguez, although these institutions quickly folded as a result of religious opposition and lack of funds.[31]

For its part, the Chardón Plan provided the ideological rationale for government funding of the island's birth control movement — albeit for a short period of time — and for American economic support.[32] In 1936, island elites, with the help of American philanthropists and private capital, organized the Association of Maternal and Child Care, opened twenty-three clinics, and successfully fought in 1937 to introduce and pass birth control legislation. In that year, the Puerto Rican legislature passed Acts 116 and 136, creating a Eugenics Board to oversee the sterilization of women "unfit" for reproduction. These measures opened the floodgates to the most extreme approaches to family planning.[33] By the mid 1940s, the Health Department's district hospitals, serving primarily poor, rural women, had curtailed contraceptive programs and begun to promote, in their place, sterilization as an appropriate birth control method. Between 1944 and 1946, over one thousand sterilizations were performed in district hospitals — a number that does not include the unrecorded sterilizations performed in municipal hospitals. Sterilization was promoted by hospital policies that admitted only those women having three or more children who agreed to postpartum sterilization.[34]

The Chardón Plan helped to set in motion public and private efforts to control poor women's reproductive practices in the name of progress and enlightened social policy.[35] It also tapped into — borrowing from Raymond Williams — dominant "structures of feeling" that continue to operate today.[36] During my fieldwork in San Sebastián, for example, casual conversation often turned to one of the most popular and volatile topics of discussion: Puerto Rican politics. And almost universally people would tell me that Puerto Rico's biggest problem is "que somos un pais sumamente sobrepoblado" — we are an extremely overpopulated country. Puerto Ricans on the mainland shared this sentiment, offering it as a reason why they would not want to live in Puerto Rico. This notion has been an official tenet of geographic education in Puerto Rico for a very long time,[37] and its persistence speaks to the seductiveness of Malthusian approaches to poverty, which emphasize impoverished women's reproductive practices rather than limited economic and social development as an explanation for high fertility rates and population problems. Interestingly, even some of the most ardent supporters of aggressive family planning strategies in Puerto Rico in the 1950s, such as demographer Paul Hatt, insisted that the Malthusian analysis of over-population was inadequate in that Puerto Rico was actually less densely populated than Rhode Island and New Jersey and closely mirrored density rates in New York. These states, of course, have thrived economically and, in the case of New Jersey and New York, were popular destinations for Puerto Rican migrants.[38] As James Dietz and other scholars demonstrate, overpopulation — or labor surplus — does not necessarily undermine capitalist development. Indeed, it is a demographic law of capitalism.[39]

As a dominant structure of feeling, "overpopulation" was an important piece of what Emilio Pantojas-García refers to as the "developmentalist ideology" that guided Puerto Rico's industrial policies. Women figured prominently in this development discourse, although they were rarely, if at all, mentioned explicitly until Puerto Rico's industrialization program and planned migration strategy were fully implemented in the 1950s. The overpopulation debates of the 1930s and 1940s, however, fixed poor women squarely within national discussions about the relationship between population control and modernization. Government officials heeded policy experts' calls to reform poor women's reproductive practices, but they also maintained that they did not encourage sterilization programs. Anthropologist Iris López counters these claims, arguing that despite the government's denial, "the role that they played was actually one of acceptance and tolerance of continued sterilization. . . . [I]t was the withdrawal of government funds that led to the rise in numbers of private sterilization clinics. Once private clinics began to proliferate, the government made no attempt to restrict or regulate them."[40]

It is clear that for government officials, poor women were a "problem," reproducing too many offspring and thereby contributing to rural surplus labor. But as wage earners in the needlework trade, for example, women were actually an important solution to the problems of unemployment and poverty, a crucial point overlooked by the Chardón Plan as well as concerned policymakers.[41] The discourse of industrialization beginning in the late 1940s elided women's crucial material and ideological role in economic development, although by the 1950s, Operation Bootstrap's architects focused their policy gaze squarely on poor women as objects of a culture change campaign designed to create Puerto Rico's "new man."

Operation Bootstrap and Engineering the "Fever"

Beginning in 1947, the Puerto Rican legislature passed a number of important laws ushering in Puerto Rico's export-oriented industrialization program, Operation Bootstrap. Prior to that time, Puerto Rico's industrial program had been guided by elements of the Chardón Plan that encouraged government-owned manufacturing enterprises, such as cement and glass-producing companies. An earlier commitment to industrialization based on the use of local materials and markets, as well as to land reform and rural economic development, was now replaced with a vision of modernization based on foreign and domestic private investment, which the PPD encouraged through tax holidays, loan assistance programs, and wage and rent subsidies. In short, the initiation of Operation Bootstrap, with its emphasis on attracting foreign investment and export-oriented industrialization — commonly referred to today as the *maquiladora* model — made clear "that the intention of new policy was no longer social justice, even narrowly defined."[42]

In tandem with these changes in economic policy, the Puerto Rican government initiated a culture change campaign that focused in large part on creating Puerto Rico's "new man" by promoting mass migration to the United States, shifting its focus to urban rather than rural development, and, ironically, constructing an "official" Puerto Rican cultural tradition based on folkloric notions of rural life. Three new institutions were crucial in promoting this culture change and managing its consequences. The Bureau of Employment and Migration facilitated the relocation and integration of Puerto Rican migrants on the mainland. *Fomento Magazine,* the Economic Development Administration's (Fomento) official advertising medium, was used to attract foreign investors and promote tourism on the island. At the same time, the Institute of Puerto Rican Culture was charged with constructing and promoting "official" Puerto Rican culture.

The scope of these institutions reveals a comprehensive and integrated approach to "modernization" characteristic of postwar development strategies throughout Latin America that targeted specific social groups, such as women and peasants, transforming them into spectacles of a development project that "dictated the manner in which peasants, women, and the environment were apprehended." In Puerto Rico, women and the island's rural population were deliberately targeted not only in order to control and discipline them, but also to transform "the conditions under which [individuals] live in a productive, normalized social environment: in short, to create modernity."[43] In the case of Puerto Rico, modernity also entailed migration, both within Puerto Rico and to U.S. cities. *Pepinianos'* oral histories of this period employ a variety of metaphors for this migration, as migrants described themselves as "fugitives" or as victims afflicted by the "fever" that drove them to Puerto Rico's growing cities and even to places like New York and Chicago. The fever afflicting them was a deliberately engineered one, as government officials used powerful visual images, radio, and television to feed a fever soothed only by migration. Migrants' stories further encouraged the massive postwar migration to U.S. cities and conditioned subsequent displacements on the mainland. Taken together, migrants' stories and government complicity helped create a context in which migration became synonymous with notions of progress and modernity.

THE BUREAU OF EMPLOYMENT AND MIGRATION

By the late 1940s, U.S. and Puerto Rican policy makers revisited the possibility of promoting Puerto Rican settlement communities abroad by providing "proper" incentives and careful planning. Antonio Fernós-Isern, resident commissioner in Washington, D.C., advocated this position in a *New York Times* article in 1946. He cautioned that a migration "hemorrhage" could be prevented through state intervention, likening it to an "emergency 'bloodletting' scientifically carried out":

If the proper conditions are found to exist in any given place and the proper inducements are offered, emigration will of itself start to develop. . . . It may come to be an added source of income for [Puerto Rico] if the proper economic relations are maintained between the Island and the emigrant groups in their new settlement. . . . [Through such a plan] we could improve such conditions as are being created in the City of New York, we could help Puerto Rico to its feet, and we could bring about the development of wealth in New World areas where virgin soil and natural riches are just waiting for the hands of man, for enterprise and for vision.[44]

Such settlement communities in "New World areas" such as Brazil and the Dominican Republic were never founded. But Fernós-Isern's statement underscores two important elements of the planned migration strategy: how to encourage emigration and maintain links between the island and migrants in a way that would economically benefit the island through the investment of migrant capital; and second, how to "manage" this migration so as to promote the integration of migrants and diminish nativist backlash against these newcomers. On December 5, 1947, the Puerto Rican legislature passed Public Law 25 establishing the Bureau of Employment and Migration, the agency charged with managing Puerto Rican migration to the mainland.[45]

The stated purpose of the Bureau of Employment and Migration was to serve as an employment office that would help orient Puerto Rican migrants in their search for jobs in New York City, the location of the bureau's first mainland office in 1948 (which replaced the Puerto Rican government's Employment and Identification Office, established in the 1930s).[46] The officially "neutral" position of the Puerto Rican government on migration mirrored its stance on population control.

The government of Puerto Rico neither encourages nor discourages the migration of Puerto Rican workmen [sic] to the United States or any foreign country; but it considers its duty to be, in the case of any workman or groups of workmen who wish to move to the Continental United States or to other countries, for the purpose of securing lucrative employment, to provide the proper guidance with respect to opportunities for employment and the problems of adjustment usually encountered in environments which are ethnologically alien; and it is likewise its duty, through such guidance of Puerto Rican workmen who migrate to the United States and other countries, to endeavor to reduce to a minimum the natural problems of adjustment arising out of any migratory movement of this nature.[47]

The government's stated neutrality with regard to migration was disingenuous at best. By establishing institutions such as the Bureau of Employment and Migration in New York and eventually in Chicago (1949) and other U.S. cities, the Puerto Rican government actively encouraged migration to the mainland by facilitating settlement and employment, thus laying the groundwork for subsequent chain migration. In addition to providing "proper guidance" to secure employment, the bureau was also actively involved in promoting a positive public image of Puerto Rican migrants, particularly in cities like New York, where the growing Puerto Rican population had elicited public fear. Beginning in the late 1940s, the *New York Times*, *Life* magazine, and other local media published sensational accounts describing the "swarm" of Puerto Ricans in communities like East Harlem, which were "reeking of migrants" ready to avail themselves of New York's generous welfare programs.[48]

In response to nativist fears and hostility, the bureau — which was reorganized and renamed the Migration Division of the Department of Labor in 1951 — refashioned itself as an agency concerned largely with public relations, a point highlighted in the division's annual and monthly reports. The division's Information Section issued press releases, articles, pamphlets, and films to local media, such as the *New York Post* and the *Connecticut Herald,* to underscore the positive contributions of Puerto Rican migrants. It also collaborated with national magazines, such as *Time, Life, Esquire, People Today, Cosmopolitan,* the *New York Times Magazine,* as well as radio and television stations, such as NBC, CBS, and WNYC, in disseminating information about Puerto Ricans in the United States and the success of Puerto Rico's industrialization program. According to the Migration Division, public media were important vehicles for defusing the rising tensions in neighborhoods where Puerto Rican newcomers resided, such as the "virtual racial powder keg" in Washington Heights in November 1952. In that month's report, the division's director, American sociologist Clarence Senior, informed the main office that he and others were in the process of writing articles aimed at "curbing some of the hysteria about the number of Puerto Ricans in New York and the problems they are supposed to be causing," and concluded that "it will be necessary to conduct an intensive campaign on the West Side if we are to avoid serious trouble there," referring to escalating tensions between white ethnics and Puerto Ricans, dramatized years later in the 1961 film *West Side Story.* Manufacturing a positive public image was one of the Migration Division's highest priorities, and this was reflected in the agency's budget requests and reports, which "placed public relations at the top of the list of the agency's goals."[49]

Intervening in an increasingly tense racial/ethnic climate in New York City, the division also coupled its public relations campaign with a concerted effort to relocate and redirect Puerto Rican migrants away from New York and toward cities like Chicago. Unlike New York, where Puerto Rican *colonias* had been thriving since the 1930s, Chicago's Puerto Rican population was dispersed, as new migrants settled in a variety of neighborhoods — Chicago's Black Belt, Back of the Yards, and the downtown area — and lived among newly arrived southern blacks and Mexicans, Chicago's most recent migrants.

The division's efforts to redirect Puerto Rican migration to Chicago were in large part a response to a political and intellectual postwar milieu that emphasized acculturation and assimilation as vehicles of "Americanization" and modernization, an inheritance of Progressive Era theories of human flexibility and plasticity, which were key to what Eric Wolf refers to as the era of Liberal Reform.[50] Residential isolation based on ethnic affiliation was thought to invite divided loyalties and retard assimilation. And since the expanding postwar U.S. economy and Puerto Rico's industrialization program depended on a modernized, assimilated, and "Americanized" labor force, social scientists and government officials collaborated to promote a "modern" social life and work ethic in U.S. cities.[51] On the island, the division opened orientation centers that discouraged migration to New York City by warning islanders about the scarcity of jobs and adequate housing, and by providing information about new destinations outside the New York area. Chicago quickly became a popular destination for new migrants, who were encouraged by a number of factors, including films shown in orientation centers on the island and in New York. These media celebrated Chicago Puerto Ricans' success in acquiring stable jobs, building their own homes, and opening small businesses. Unlike New York Puerto Ricans, Chicago Puerto Ricans were praised for their ability to adapt — or integrate, according to officials at Chicago's Hull House — to their new environment.[52]

According to the division's monthly reports, from 1952 to 1953 there were more "jobs than applicants for jobs," and there was "almost 100 percent employment among Puerto Ricans in the Chicago-Calumet area." These accounts were dramatically different from those in New York, where concern about Puerto Ricans' growing dependency on welfare fueled nativist backlash.[53] Chicago Puerto Ricans, according to one report, "do not constitute a problem for the city."[54] In fact, they had become standard-bearers of "good" migrant behavior and were favorably compared to "bad" New York Puerto Ricans. Local politicians and media employed this "ethnic report card" approach, ranking Chicago Puerto Ricans at the top, with New York Puerto Ricans and American blacks at the bottom.[55] Division officials in the Chicago office noted clearly that there were few problems among Chicago Puerto Ricans and that "[the] main social problem with [Puerto Ricans in Chicago] has been those who have lived in New York City." Division reports provided a detailed account of a Puerto Rican man from New York who was jailed in Chicago; of another who, despite the division's attempts to locate stable employment for him, was unable to hold a job successfully; and of New York Puerto Ricans who were placed in good jobs and eventually quit them in order to return to New York.[56]

While the division firmly believed that one way to address the "Puerto Rican problem" in New York was to disperse its population by encouraging New York Puerto Ricans to settle elsewhere, nativist resistance to Chicago's newcomers presented its own problems, and the division's Chicago office spent much of its time working with city agencies and local media to prevent such antagonisms. Division officials noted in their 1953 annual report, for example, "For various weeks the difficulties that a great number of Puerto Rican workers in Chicago have encountered have served as headline [news] for the press and have constituted the principal news on the radio and television. In order to change public opinion in this case, we appealed to the city's resources, contacts that we have developed since this office was established."[57]

Manufacturing and disseminating a positive public image of Puerto Rican migrants became one of the Migration Division's most important functions. Architects of Puerto Rico's industrialization program believed that its success was contingent on continued emigration, a point division officials discussed extensively in their annual reports. At the end of his 1953–54 report, Clarence Senior clearly drew the connections among migration, public relations, and the success of the industrialization project:

Presently, although we believe that we have had some success informing the general public about Puerto Rico, we believe that we still have not begun to do all that is possible and that we should do. For this reason, recognizing the need to work in favor of the thousands of Puerto Ricans who reside in the United States and whose adjustment to the community depend, in part, on a better understanding of Puerto Ricans and the contributions they can make in the community in which they have chosen to live, the Division is formulating plans for a more extensive public relations campaign. This campaign's goal is to inform, principally, the continental public of the activities and contributions of Puerto Rico and Puerto Ricans who live in the United States. The Division is of the opinion that a campaign such as this would help all government agencies in the promotion of industrialization, tourism and all government programs and activities, moving to improve the standard of living of Puerto Ricans in Puerto Rico as well as in the United States. As a result, this will be one of the primordial activities of the Division in the years to come.[58]

The Migration Division's role in managing migration to the mainland clearly required intervention on a number of different levels in Puerto Rico and in U.S. cities: encouraging potential migrants through an extensive publicity campaign regarding opportunities abroad; educating migrants about favorable destinations and orienting them through the division offices on the mainland; helping to secure employment and adequate housing; and manufacturing and promoting a positive image of Puerto Rican migrants through local and national media. Perhaps more importantly, these activities facilitated a key shift in the Puerto Rican cultural landscape that transformed a largely rural, agriculturally based population into an increasingly mobile and urban labor force. While internal migration and proletarian labor were not new to Puerto Rican migrants, their rapid incorporation into industrial labor on the island and the mainland was indeed a novel social formation. This was cemented in part by the institutionalization of migration through a planned migration strategy to the mainland. On the island, two government agencies — the Economic Development Administration (Fomento) and the Institute of Puerto Rican Culture — were key in complementing the Migration Division's efforts to further Operation Bootstrap's success by promoting a new culture that would be more amenable to rapid industrialization in Puerto Rico and locating the discussion of culture squarely within the modernization discourse of Operation Bootstrap.

FOMENTO DE PUERTO RICO

Established as an executive agency in 1950, Fomento was responsible for promoting Puerto Rico's industrialization program by "conducting economic research, providing labor training and recruitment services," and ultimately attracting private investment to the island.[59] Fomento's role as the engine of economic development was further strengthened when the Puerto Rican government was reorganized, setting the stage not only for full implementation of Puerto Rico's industrialization program, but also for Puerto Rico's new political status in 1952 as a U.S. commonwealth, or Estado Libre Asociado. Like those of the Migration Division, much of Fomento's administrative energies were channeled into public relations at home and abroad to promote Puerto Rico's industrialization program and to attract foreign — primarily North American — capital to the island. During the 1950s, Fomento produced pamphlets, brochures, and articles in English that were used to "sell Puerto Rico to U.S. investors as an industrial and profit paradise."[60] Attractive, glossy advertisements distributed to U.S. businessmen promoted "Puerto Rico, U.S.A." as a safe and economically profitable environment and celebrated Puerto Rico's "Americanness," downplaying its "foreignness" in order to assuage U.S. businessmen's fears.

In addition to its English-based advertisement campaign, Fomento also produced an attractive magazine, *Fomento de Puerto Rico,* which showcased the different faces and moments of Operation Bootstrap with photos of industrial workers and articles by economists and policy experts optimistically assessing the challenges facing the industrialization program and the government's ability to meet them effectively. In its first issue, Teodoro Moscoso, Fomento's director, argued that Puerto Rico's industrialization program was unique and its success unprecedented: "I do not know of any other similar program that has taken place in an over-populated country that has achieved the concrete results that we have in Puerto Rico, except, possibly, Israel."[61] This characteristically optimistic tone conveys the prevailing ethos beginning in the 1950s: the unequivo-cal belief that modernization would solve all social and economic prob-lems in Puerto Rico. Culture and the creation of the new "modern man" were fundamental principles of this ideology of development and served as an important template for the magazine's content.

While the magazine focused primarily on new factories, expanding opportunities for workers, and improvements in the island's infrastruc-ture, some articles spotlighted the role of agriculture in the developing economy and the rise of women workers in the island's new industries. In short, Fomento's mission was to showcase Operation Bootstrap's efforts to "forjar una conciencia industrial" (forge an industrial con-science), a process that was regarded as a deeply patriotic act "that every good Puerto Rican should strive to achieve." Fomento encouraged this collective industrial conscience through education, training, and orien-tation campaigns and by using films, radio announcements, and bill-boards hailing the newest industrial projects and the industrialization pro-gram's progress. The ubiquitous image of the man on the wheel best captures Fomento's vision of modernity.[62]

Agricultural workers and women were the populations most in need of this new *conciencia industrial*; and *Fomento de Puerto Rico,* whose pri-mary audience was the emerging urban middle class on the island as well as foreign investors, provided revealing snapshots of this cultural shift. Many of the magazine's articles emphasized the need to train workers in order to improve the quality of the labor force. While Puerto Rico was poor in natural resources, these articles maintained, it was rich in surplus labor, one of the most important resources necessary for industrial devel-opment. This labor force was largely rural, although recent internal migration had resulted in a newly urban and proletarian labor pool with extensive experience in wage labor. Experience in wage labor, however, did not necessarily create an "industrial tradition," and one of Operation

Bootstrap's primary objectives was to do precisely that by incorporating rural surplus labor and women into industrial work. "The agriculturalist's task," one article maintained, was to keep pace with, and be a handmaiden of, industrial development:

In addition to increasing work opportunities for a greater number of citizens, industrial development permits residents in urban areas to become better clients for island agriculturalists. Industrialization balances the relationship between agriculture and industry more effectively, at the same time as it extends the economic horizon of urban and rural zones. . . . Agriculture, at the very least, must maintain the same rhythm of industrial advancement and expansion in order to firmly cement these [industrial] activities and make them permanent.[63]

Clearly, Fomento recognized the importance of agricultural work on the island, but industrial employment commanded higher wages and greater social status. Magazines, newspapers, and billboards consistently underscored an emerging modern sensibility that dismissed agricultural work as inferior, tedious, and an obstacle to progress, and in doing so contributed to the demise of the rural-based labor force.

Pepinianos' narratives of the 1950s echo *Fomento de Puerto Rico*'s accounts of this novel tension. Men who migrated during this time often reminisce that they had no choice but to migrate because "no había trabajo en San Sebastián" (there were no jobs in San Sebastián). When I asked them how this was possible, they clarified: "No habían trabajos industriales aquí" (There weren't any industrial jobs here). Working in *el campo* (the fields), these men suggested, was as good as having no job at all. Jorge Colosio's story illustrates this point vividly. In 1951, Jorge was recruited to work in Florida as a contract laborer. The recruiter promised that if he worked hard, he would make a lot of money working in a factory. But when Jorge arrived in Florida, he was sent to work in the fields alongside other Puerto Ricans and American blacks, who had also been told they would be employed as factory workers. After several months, Jorge and a handful of other Puerto Ricans decided to leave the farm for Chicago, where he was told he could make more money in a factory. "Why would I leave Puerto Rico only to work in the fields in Florida? Me huía de la caña" (I was fleeing from [having to work in] the cane), he explained, "porque era una vida muy dura, sacrificada, y triste" (because it was a very hard, difficult, and sad life).

Jorge fondly remembers his nine years in Chicago, but he also admits that it was a difficult time. He often felt powerless, unsettled, and nervous, and he compared his life with Sam Shepherd's in the movie *The*

Fugitive. He enjoyed that movie, he explained, because it was filmed in Chicago, and he recognized many of the city's famous landmarks. He also identified profoundly with Sam Shepherd, the innocent fugitive caught up in events beyond his control. "The only difference between me and Sam Shepherd is that he was fleeing Cook County, and I was fleeing from the cane." Migrating (*huyendose de la caña*) was a way for Jorge to exercise some control over his life, but he still felt vulnerable to powerful economic forces both on the island and the mainland.

Manny Vélez, who had lived in Chicago for more than twenty years before returning to San Sebastián in the early 1970s, echoed Jorge's sentiments, describing his decision to leave the countryside as catching a "fever" (*la fiebre*) that was contagious and infected many living in the area at that time. He smiled as he recounted his decision to leave first San Sebastián and eventually Puerto Rico:

> I don't know why I went [to Chicago]. I didn't really have to go there. There were others who really did have to leave, but not me. I think it was the fever. Yes, the fever to leave. People would return and begin to talk and, well, I thought I should leave . . . to get to know [a new place]. I had two jobs. I worked as an assistant in a movie theater, and I also worked as a woodworker in Aguadilla . . . . So when I decided to go to the United States, I talked with the director of the theater . . . who told me he didn't want me to go. "Why [are you leaving] when everything is going so well for you? Don't leave, because soon the [film] operator is old, and I want you to have his position . . . ." At that time, an operator made twenty-five dollars a week, which at that time, in 1949, that was good money. I was only earning twelve dollars a week. "I'll get everything you need," he told me. But the fever. . . . [He shakes his head and pauses.] He finally gave me three letters of recommendation and I left.

La fiebre led Manny first to Gary, Indiana, where he lived with an uncle who had helped pay his airfare. He worked at Carnegie Steel and eventually at U.S. Steel before moving to New York City to marry Ana Bosque, also from San Sebastián. According to Ana, she had also longed to live in the United States, so when Manny had migrated to Gary, Ana had decided to go live with her mother in New York, where she had lived until she and Manny moved to Chicago.

By 1953, Ana and Manny were living in Chicago's Lincoln Park neighborhood near Clark Street and North Avenue, and they moved several times within that same neighborhood. A few years later, when Manny entered the armed forces, Ana returned to New York City with her toddler son, where she stayed once again with her mother until Manny finished his military service and they all returned to Chicago. Manny and

Ana both worked a number of different jobs in Chicago — she and her sister worked in the Advance Transformers factory on Western and George Avenues; Manny worked in a factory, drove a taxi, and eventually served as a superintendent in the building where they lived before they returned to San Sebastián in the early 1960s. In retrospect, Ana and Manny laugh at how much they moved and how they eventually returned to raise their son and daughter in San Sebastián, a much better place to raise children, they assured me. "It was the fever," Manny repeated throughout our conversation, and Ana agreed. "It was the fever to leave."

This "fever" to "flee the cane" was not unique to residents of San Sebastián, but was part of larger demographic shifts that disproportionately afflicted the western central region of the island. After a steady population increase in San Sebastián through the 1940s, San Sebastián's population decreased by more than 5 percent in the 1950s, with the town's rural population dropping by 12 percent, a trend that also characterized neighboring municipalities whose economies depended largely on coffee production and the home needlework industry, both in serious decline. By contrast, the island population grew by 6 percent, and the San Juan metropolitan area grew by 27 percent, as women and men left rural communities in search of manufacturing jobs. Between 1950 and 1956, the number of workers employed in agriculture dropped by 30 percent, due largely to migration to the island's growing urban areas and the U.S. mainland.[64]

These rapid population changes were of considerable concern to officials in Puerto Rico's Department of Agriculture and Commerce, who noted in the 1953–54 annual report that "we must lament, and lament profoundly, that within the dynamic of economic and cultural development we have not paid sufficient attention to the importance of [agriculture]."[65] Two years later, the department noted that while this change was beneficial to the country in general, it had also "affected some agricultural zones, occasioning a temporary labor shortage in agriculture, especially in sugar, which continues to depend on abundant manual labor during the harvest."[66] The population decline in San Sebastián in the 1950s and 1960s is particularly striking because these decades are precisely what many *pepinianos* regard as "the golden years of the sugar industry." In 1953, for example, La Plata ground nearly half a million tons of sugar, and in 1956 more than 1,500 *colonos* were growing and processing cane, the highest number on record.[67] Ironically, these are also the beginnings of a severe labor shortage in San Sebastián, showing that migration was a response not to a lack of jobs in the region, but rather to a lack of industrial jobs, which were increasingly desired by Puerto Rican workers.

While the rural labor shortage was certainly troublesome for some government officials, it underscored the industrialization project's success in transforming *el jíbaro* into Puerto Rico's "new man." Within the first decade of Operation Bootstrap's implementation, the government's campaign to *forjar una conciencia industrial* had given rise to a new "industrial culture" that was a hallmark of modernization.[68]

This prevailing ideology of development, like the overpopulation discourse supporting it, was deeply gendered. Only a handful of articles in *Fomento de Puerto Rico* specifically mentioned the key role women played in the industrialization process. But since nearly a quarter of the labor force were women, many of the photos of diligent industrial workers featured women participating in a wide range of occupational tasks. Operation Bootstrap's first phase, in 1950–63, consisted primarily of light industry, electronic manufacturing, and textiles — all of which relied heavily on women workers. Women were easily incorporated into these new industries because so many of them had extensive experience in the needle trades both at home and in the factories. By 1935, more than half of all island women in the labor force were involved in home-based needlework, factory-based needle trades, and other factory employment, such as cigar and tobacco, thus contributing necessary income to cash-strapped households.[69]

With the expansion of textiles and needlework in the 1950s, factories drew on an experienced female labor pool. Women were easily incorporated into needle trade and electronics wage labor because of the belief that these occupations were a "natural" extension of their household skills. This "nimble fingers" argument was based on the assumption that women were "naturally" suited to quick, repetitive tasks and had the "delicate hand" needed for embroidery, cutting, and sewing, as well as work in the electronics industry, which required laborers to work on small, intricate parts.[70] Finally, like the rural population in general, women's incorporation into the labor force was seen — and promoted by official media such as *Fomento de Puerto Rico* — not only as a way for women to *superarse* (improve themselves) and assume more financial responsibility in the home, but as patriotic activity contributing to Puerto Rico's modernization.

Although Puerto Rico's industrialization program was contingent upon low-wage women's labor, the progress and modernization discourse was almost exclusively masculine. Working-class women's wage labor was discussed as novel and perhaps even a detrimental consequence of modernization. Like the prescribed role of agricultural workers in the modernization project, women's employment was considered auxiliary, a way for women to supplement men's "traditional" and more important role as economic providers. As in other modernization projects — in Malaysia, Mexico, and Colombia, for example — shifting gender ideologies were contested and often fraught with contradictions.[71] Again, *Fomento de Puerto Rico* reflected this ambivalence in its concern about the effect of women's wage labor on family structure and social order:

In the family, there is no doubt that this situation has produced a fundamental change in [family] relations and that there is occurring a mutation in the traditional household structure, where until recently the man had been the only provider and, as a result, the absolute lord and master. Today, the currents of modern life have taken women toward intellectual and economic emancipation. Complicating daily life even further, the woman, now capable of understanding other problems in addition to the home, has gone to the offices, has invaded the professional camps, and has made her own the new skills and techniques of industry.[72]

Clearly, on both an individual and a national level, modernity symbolized freedom: intellectual and financial freedom for women, and economic freedom and development for the nation. Operation Bootstrap was predicated on women's freedom from "traditional constraints" — family, land, and community — in order to achieve the greatest good: economic development. That same economic model now characterizes the "new global economic order" based on free trade, and transnational capital flows "free" from national borders. One of the clearest examples of this economic arrangement is the *maquiladora* model, which, as we have seen, was first implemented in Puerto Rico and whose success depended on "emancipated" women's labor. What was less clear to government officials and island elites in the 1950s, however, was the price of this "emancipation." Their anxiety about the cultural consequences of modernity fueled, in part, the creation of a cultural component to Puerto Rico's developmentalist ideology, later called Operation Serenity, and the establishment of the Institute of Puerto Rican Culture.

THE INSTITUTE OF PUERTO RICAN CULTURE

Government officials believed that changes in the Puerto Rican cultural landscape were necessary for the success of the island's industrialization program. But these changes were also of great concern to island officials and elites who debated the relationship between culture and modernization. From its inception, the PPD employed cultural symbols to cement its political power. The *pava* (a straw hat typically worn by *el jíbaro*) and the motto *Pan, tierra y libertad* (Bread, land, and liberty) were powerful symbols at the heart of the party's cultural nationalist project. They would later become an important part of its — and thus, Puerto Rico's — ideology of development. As Arlene Dávila points out, scholars of Puerto Rico have paid much academic attention to Operation Bootstrap's role in transforming Puerto Rico's social, economic, and political landscape, but they have frequently overlooked the importance of Operation Serenity, Operation Bootstrap's cultural complement. Operation Serenity addressed the growing concern about the relationship between culture and modernization and provided a spiritual anchor for the rural population — and, I would argue, women in particular — swept up in modernization's powerful currents. As Arlene Dávila notes:

Operation Serenity aimed to provide a sense of spiritual balance to a society threatened by the rapid social change caused by the new economic policies. The idea was to prepare the peasantry for modernity while protecting them from the devastating effects of materialism and consumerism, which were seen as threatening the moral basis on which Puerto Rican nationality was perceived to rest.

One of the ways government officials attempted to preserve Puerto Rico's moral and cultural foundation was by establishing the Institute of Puerto Rican Culture (ICP) in 1956, the official vehicle for constructing and disseminating Puerto Rican culture.[73]

The high optimism marking the initial stages of Operation Bootstrap was evident in *pepinianos'* stories about the era of *los populares* or *el tiempo de Muñoz Marín*.[74] Many of the people with whom I spoke characterized this period as one of plentiful opportunity. During this time, they explained, people were not afraid of "hard work" — which often included migration — and they were proud to be *puertorriqueños*. One politically active man from the town suggested that Muñoz Marín was the principal source of this new optimism and pride. As the primary architect of Puerto Rico's commonwealth status in 1952, Muñoz Marín negotiated what many *pepinianos* believed to be the perfect political arrangement between the United States and Puerto Rico. As a U.S. commonwealth, Puerto Ricans not only enjoyed many of the benefits of living in a U.S. state, but they were also able to maintain a critical, anti-imperialist stance and preserve their cultural and "national" integrity. Such an agreement, one man assured me, was proof that Puerto Ricans were more clever than *los norteamericanos* (North Americans) and contributed to the optimism that characterized the era of *los populares*. A bumper sticker popular in San

Sebastián in 1998, "Yo no tengo la culpa, yo voté Popular" (It's not my fault; I voted for the Populares), reveals not only a deep discontent with Governor Pedro Roselló and the ruling New Progressive Party (PNP), but also nostalgia for a time when Puerto Rican culture and *puertorriqueñidad* were embraced as a means to resist the Americanization of Puerto Rican values and culture. Ironically, most *pepinianos* unequivocally support U.S. economic involvement in the island, but they want economic involvement while preserving *puertorriqueñidad*.

These popular feelings were encouraged and shaped by the ICP and its culturalist policies. Drawing on already resonant cultural images like the *pava* and *el jíbaro*, the ICP deployed these precapitalist symbols to promote a folkloric culture based on the moral superiority of preindustrial lifeways and "traditional" rural values.[75] *El jíbaro* — the humble, hardworking, and fiercely independent and rebellious worker of the land — is the spiritual and moral symbol of Puerto Rican identity. He also embodies Puerto Rico's Spanish heritage, and consequently the nation's "whiteness," thus erasing the island's African roots and black identity.[76] *El jíbaro* is also always a male. He has no female iconic counterpart, a fact that reveals the gendered assumptions underlying Puerto Rico's ideology of development. This masculine symbol, however, does reveal much about gender and the ICP's cultural nationalist project: In the context of men's eroding economic power, a result of Operation Bootstrap's reliance on female labor, *el jíbaro* stresses men's cultural and spiritual power as an "authentic" symbol of national identity. In short, Puerto Rico's "new man" was actually the emerging female factory worker, but *el jíbaro's* soul — and the soul of the nation — was thoroughly masculine, embodying all of the pre-industrial moral virtues of an idealized past.[77]

San Sebastián, in this regard, embodied the balance of tradition and modernity encouraged by Operation Serenity. In January 1952, the island's principal newspaper, *El Mundo,* profiled rural municipalities, including San Sebastián, in a series of articles hailing their rich history, cultural traditions, and successful collaborative efforts in promoting the island's economic development. San Sebastián, according to these popular accounts, simultaneously embodied the virtues of "modernity" and "tradition." The rich agricultural tradition that uniquely defined the town, as well as its excellent paved roads, new highways, and lines of communication, guaranteed San Sebastián's continued importance to the island economy. Moreover, its deeply "modern" sensibility, arising from its unique history of Spanish urban development in the early nineteenth century, was celebrated by popular media, with *El Mundo* making the following observations: "San Sebastián has the privilege of being the first population in Puerto Rico to vigorously establish the urban planning principles that now form the basis of the modern law of planning in Puerto Rico. . . . [Urban] planning [in the form of maps and zoning], therefore, was not new for San Sebastián."[78] According to *El Mundo*'s editors, San Sebastián was "a symbol of the new Puerto Rico, one that sought to overcome its problems and difficulties, one that always looks ahead and, rather than walking in doubt, advances with a firm step toward success.[79] Puerto Rico's quest for progress lay therefore in striking a balance between appropriating "modern" values of technological and economic progress and preserving "traditional" values of a proud, agrarian, Spanish past.

While *El Mundo* painted an idyllic portrait of the harmonious marriage of progress and tradition, census data provide a more complicated image of modernization. During the 1950s and 1960s, due to substantial out-migration, San Sebastián's population dropped to pre-1940 levels.[80] While the architects of Operation Bootstrap might consider this fact an unequivocal example of the industrialization program's success, extensive and sustained out-migration harmed the town's economic base. In fact, San Sebastián's *colonos* entreated the Puerto Rican government during these years to act aggressively to remedy an acute labor shortage in agricultural production. In 1967, a group of *colonos* formed a committee and collaborated with the Labor Department on a plan that would recruit unemployed men and women to work in local agriculture.[81] Radio announcements and *autoparlantes* (cars riding through town with loudspeakers on top) were also used to advertise jobs on local farms, although the fever to migrate and find high-status industrial positions, rather than working in low-wage and arduous agricultural jobs, proved too seductive an alternative, and the town's population slowly decreased in the 1950s and 1960s.[82]

Older *pepinianos* recalled this period as one of extreme labor shortage. One *colono* from Saltos — a rural sector that produced much of the cane sold to La Plata — explained that he frequently picked up workers at designated locations and provided free lunches made by his wife as an added incentive. He admitted that the work was hard and wages were low compared to factory jobs and employment one could secure *afuera*. But as a small *colono,* he didn't have the resources that other larger landowners could invest in workers' wages and, as a result, he often operated at a loss. Like other *colonos,* he left San Sebastián in the 1950s and lived for a number of years *afuera* in Brooklyn, returning to San Sebastián in the mid 1960s with the dream of owning his own land and animals and raising crops. His return to Pepino — as for many who spent years living abroad — was extremely stressful, and he confided hesitantly that in the period shortly after his return, he often considered going back to Brooklyn. In the end, he remained in San Sebastián and has been relatively successful as a small agricultural farmer. Others were not so fortunate, engaging in a pattern of circular migration between San Sebastián and U.S. cities in search of stable employment. In the end, this *colono* explained, the government's participation in the recruitment effort was successful in attracting laborers from nearby towns to work in San Sebastián. But its success was short-lived.[83]

The discourse of progress, modernization, and the allure of urban living had a profound impact on San Sebastián's political, economic, and cultural life, as thousands of *pepinianos* caught *la fiebre* that led them to cities in Puerto Rico and the United States. Older return migrants frequently reminisce about their time *afuera*. Interestingly, these stories are told in an almost competitive fashion, as each narrator attempts to provide more shocking and exotic tales of life in U.S. cities: the different kinds of people with whom s/he came in contact, the various languages s/he learned to speak, and the cultural knowledge s/he acquired abroad. It is clear that while these return migrants often speak nostalgically of *los tiempos de* Muñoz Marín and industrialization, they also remember that life at that time was *dura* (hard), and the transition to urban living, while exciting, was difficult and often dangerous. Women and men frequently left San Sebastián alone and unmarried and returned years later married to *pepinianos* whom they had met abroad or to people from other towns in Puerto Rico. The architects of the industrialization program did not foresee the far-reaching consequences of migration and modernization. It was in *los tiempos de* Marín that disparate places like San Sebastián and Chicago became intimately — ideologically, socially, politically, and economically — linked. These links have developed over the years, and have continued to reproduce themselves into the present.

CHAPTER 3

"Know Your Fellow American Citizen from Puerto Rico"

When Jorge Colosio, Ana Bosque, and Manny Vélez arrived in Chicago in the early 1950s, they entered an urban landscape they had come to know through migrants' stories and media images that inundated Puerto Rican towns, inspiring residents to leave their homes, family members, and even jobs to live and work in American cities. By 1950, Chicago was home to more than three thousand Puerto Rican migrants, some who had arrived during the interwar period, although most were newcomers from after 1946. Postwar Chicago was also home to migrants and immigrants from the American South, Europe, and Mexico who had settled in the city decades earlier. In 1910, for example, over a third of Chicago's white population had immigrated from Europe and three-fourths had at least one immigrant parent. And between 1910 and 1920, the city's African American population more than doubled as a result of the Great Migration of black southerners.[1] White Appalachian migrants and Mexican immigrants also arrived in the early twentieth century, albeit in smaller numbers, making Chicago an unusually diverse city. Labor recruitment and contract labor were important catalysts in the explosion of Chicago's immigrant and migrant population. In the late nineteenth century, Polish laborers were recruited to work in labor-hungry steel mills, followed by Slovenian immigrants in the first decade of the twentieth century. During World War II, Mexican workers — seasoned migrants familiar with the recruitment circuit as a result of earlier contract labor agreements between the U.S. and Mexican governments, including the Bracero program beginning in 1942 — were recruited to work in Chicago's southern steel mills in order to remedy the wartime labor shortage.[2]

Thus, when Puerto Rican contract laborers arrived in 1946, they traveled a path familiar to many Chicago residents. Beginning in September of that year, Castle, Barton and Associates, a private Chicago-based employment agency, contracted several hundred Puerto Rican women and men to work in Chicago-area homes and factories. This labor recruitment to Chicago was an important element of the Puerto Rican government's planned migration strategy of encouraging emigration from the island in order to alleviate alleged "population pressures." Yet it was also an attempt to steer Puerto Rican migrants away from New York City, where local media actively campaigned against continued migration from the island, and to redirect them to places like Chicago; Lorain, Ohio; Gary, Indiana; and Milwaukee, Wisconsin, where Puerto Rican migrants could find employment in industry and agriculture. These contract laborers "provided the base from which sprang the Puerto Rican communities on the mainland."[3]

While the contract labor system successfully enlisted workers for Chicago's expanding postwar economy, it was also an abusive and largely unregulated arrangement. Deceitful recruiters would arrive in Puerto Rico with a promise of jobs that never materialized, or they would charge both the employer and the employee placement fees, and sell workers items critical to their relocation. Once employed, contract laborers often faced abuses by their employers as well. Shortly after the arrival of the first wave of Puerto Rican contract workers in Chicago, dozens of men and women wrote to the commissioner of the Insular Department of Labor detailing employer abuse, poor living conditions, violated labor contracts, and arbitrary deductions from workers' salaries. Although the commissioner's initial response was tepid at best, the Puerto Rican government subsequently intervened on the workers' behalf and, in doing so, ushered in a new era of island-Chicago ties designed to promote the full integration of Puerto Ricans into the cultural, economic, and social life of the city. Indeed, island and city officials were equally committed to Puerto Ricans' peaceful assimilation into Chicago, a process they hoped would ensure continued emigration from Puerto Rico and avoid the nativist hostility growing in New York City. Accordingly, they provided migrants with institutional support and encouraged them to create community organizations and engage in mainstream civic activities. These institutions also launched an extensive media campaign to educate service providers and city residents about their new neighbors, who were, after all, "fellow American citizens," a fact emphasized in the widely distributed pamphlet, "Know your Fellow American Citizen from Puerto Rico."[4]

This chapter explores the varying ways in which government officials in Chicago and Puerto Rico and local media have viewed Puerto Rican migrants in the city and the role these institutions have played in managing postwar migration to Chicago.[5] Beginning with the "Chicago Experiment" in 1946 and continuing today, Puerto Ricans have inhabited a variety of ideological spaces in Chicago's urban imagination. In what follows, I present the different ways Chicago Puerto Ricans have been constructed over time, arguing that these understandings are based on ideologies of gender, race, and class, and embedded in Chicago's shifting political economy. As Puerto Ricans' structural position has changed vis-à-vis the city's ethnic and racial others, so too has public opinion moved from celebrating Chicago Puerto Ricans as a model minority in the early postwar period to deriding them in the mid 1960s as slum dwellers mired in a "culture of poverty," and eventually as members of urban America's "underclass." These designations, I argue, rarely reflect the lived experiences of Chicago Puerto Ricans. Instead, they are labels that mystify entrenched racism in housing and employment, and ultimately municipal neglect, by providing facile cultural explanations of group success and failure in urban America.

Understanding Migrants in the City

As an immigrant city at the turn of the century, Chicago was a "natural laboratory" for social reformers, government officials, and Chicago School urban ethnographers concerned with a variety of emerging social problems. Progressive Era reformer Jane Addams, for example, pioneered the settlement house movement in Chicago as part of a "social housekeeping" campaign to improve immigrants' living conditions and provide them with "moral uplift." Local government and law enforcement officials dedicated themselves to "defending the city" against labor unrest and ameliorating Chicago's "vice problem," as immigrants and southern blacks poured into the urban landscape. And the University of Chicago's urban social scientists produced an impressive collection of ethnographic studies examining the contours of industrial life and modern urban America.[6]

Collectively, these groups shared a preoccupation with immigrants and the various "collisions, conflicts and fusions" occasioned by new people and cultures in urban America.[7] Chicago School sociologist Robert Park, for example, dedicated much of his work to theorizing the impact of migration on the individual migrant and the moral order of the city. Migration, he argued, encouraged two distinct but related behaviors characterizing modern urban dwellers: It threw the migrant into a state of "moral turmoil" that prevented him or her from fully belonging to either world, but, by living simultaneously in two different worlds, the migrant was more creative and intelligent than nonmigrants and was emancipated from "the traditional organization of society." As an enlightened and cosmopolitan individual, the "marginal man" acquired "an intellectual bias" that freed him from the "local proprieties and customs" that would normally confine his actions. Less positively, however, the marginal man was also in a permanent state of crisis, plagued by "spiritual instability, intensified self-consciousness, restlessness and malaise." In short, the marginal man embodied the processes of civilization and progress emerging from a fusion of distinct cultures.[8]

Park's theories about migrants were intimately related to another central concern of Chicago School ethnographers, namely the gradual process of assimilation, which they regarded as both a natural evolutionary movement and, more importantly, the sociological bedrock of civilization and progress. The moral and social order of the city depended on the peaceful assimilation of immigrants. It also depended on the full assimilation of mulattos, mestizos, Eurasians, and others of "mixed blood" who inhabited the liminal space between cultures, since "[all] our so-called racial problems grow out of situations in which assimilation and amalgamation do not take place at all, or take place very slowly."[9] Theorizing this process was not merely an academic concern. Indeed, the desire to assimilate and "Americanize" immigrants and newly urbanized non-immigrant groups, such as American blacks, Native Americans, and eventually Puerto Ricans, was partly fueled by the need for a disciplined, modern workforce to meet the demands of the expanding industrial city.[10] Yet it also reflected an emerging "liberal technocratic strain of the social sciences," which believed in bringing social science expertise to bear on domestic and foreign policy matters as a pragmatic way of overcoming obstacles to economic progress and rational urban planning. To that end, social scientists advised policymakers on the ways urban dwellers organized themselves, identified how values and cultural customs shaped the communities they constructed, and proposed various strategies to encourage the assimilation of those groups, whose communities might pose a threat to the city's moral and social order. For Puerto Ricans arriving in postwar Chicago, residential dispersal was regarded — and actively pursued — as the most effective way of ensuring the group's social integration and minimizing intergroup conflict, an approach that contrasted dramatically with the way policymakers and some of their academic advisors addressed mounting problems with the city's black residents, who were residentially segregated in the city's bursting black belt.[11]

Assimilationist thinking continued to define academic and policy approaches to migrants in postwar Chicago, and it clearly shaped the social milieu Puerto Rican contract laborers encountered in 1946. On September 24 of that year, the island newspaper *El Mundo* triumphantly announced the departure of a handful of women selected to work as domestic workers in Chicago. A photograph of the departing migrants, smiling and waving as they boarded an airplane, was prominently positioned on the front page of the newspaper, conveying the spirit of optimism that characterized this new era of mass migration to the United States. Modernization, the newspaper suggested, offered new and exciting opportunities to Puerto Rican workers, including air travel, job opportunities, and a new life for men and women *afuera* in American cities. *El Mundo* subsequently ran a series of articles highlighting the success of *domésticas* in Chicago, the enthusiasm this recruitment effort generated for implementing similar programs in other towns, and the city's positive response to its newest migrants.[12] Government officials quickly dubbed "the Chicago Experiment" a surprising success and embraced it as a model for public and private collaboration in addressing island and mainland labor problems. The Chicago-based employment agency Castle, Barton, and Associates spearheaded the recruitment effort as a way of remedying the city's "maid shortage," resulting from a national shift in women's employment from domestic to industrial work beginning in the early 1900s. This early migration was critical, sociologist Maura Toro-Morn argues, because it linked Chicago and Puerto Rico in "distinctively gendered ways."[13]

As *domésticas,* Puerto Rican women joined the ranks of paid domestic workers whose ethnic and racial composition evolved in relation to changes in immigration policy, shifting racial and ethnic hierarchies, and white women's expanded employment opportunities. In northern industrial cities like Chicago, for example, unmarried Irish, German, and Scandinavian immigrant women served as live-in domestic laborers at the end of the nineteenth and into the early twentieth century, until their numbers declined as a result of restricted European immigration during World War I and, eventually, increased employment opportunities for white women in the expanding industrial economy.[14] Consequently, black women from the American South, who "had always predominated as a servant caste in the South, whether in slavery or after," were increasingly employed as domestic workers in northern cities, although they were less likely to work as live-in domestics, opting instead for day work.[15] Unsurprisingly, the experiences of Puerto Rican *domésticas* reflected those of other immigrant and migrant domestic laborers. As live-in workers, for example, they exercised little control over their working hours, wages, and private lives, and they were also subject to the whims of employers, who could send them to work elsewhere with less than a day's notice. When possible, either through marriage or by securing alternative employment and housing options, many *domésticas* chose to leave employers' homes, sometimes breaching their original labor contracts.[16]

Puertorriqueñas' experiences as domestic workers also reveal, however, the racialized and gendered consequences of regional economic development, which certainly informed — and continue to shape — internal and international migration. Both African American and Puerto Rican women, for example, were recruited to work as live-in domestics in northern cities, a plan actively encouraged by local officials, who viewed their exodus as a way of alleviating pressing economic problems in their regions of origin. In the years following the Civil War, the Bureau of Refugees, Freedmen, and Abandoned Lands sought to reduce relief rolls in the South by convincing its representatives in Boston to "accept applications for 'colored girl servants'" whose transportation costs were covered by the bureau, which also promised to subsidize return fare for unsatisfactory employees.[17] Government officials in Puerto Rico also favorably regarded Puerto Rican women's labor migration and actively provided institutional support to sustain contract labor migration of both men and women after private efforts foundered. In both cases, local governments determined that economic development depended largely on their ability to mobilize young women of color as domestic labor migrants, a strategy presaging today's highly regulated state-sponsored labor recruitment programs, which involve thousands of domestic workers who comprise what Rhacel Salazar Parreñas calls the "international division of reproductive labor."[18]

The Chicago Experiment's initial success was soon tempered by widely publicized employer and employee dissatisfaction. In 1946 the Women's Bureau issued a report documenting *domésticas'* claims of being forced to work long hours for little pay with no time off. Their American employers cited domestics' "youthfulness" as one reason for their dissatisfaction, compounded by the women's "inexperience, lack of training, unfamiliarity with modern household equipment, and with customs and work tempo in the United States, inadequate prior health examination, [and] lack of funds and winter clothes."[19] *El Mundo* also reported on the problems of contract laborers in Chicago, citing a study by Elena Padilla and other Puerto Rican students at the University of Chicago, which detailed employer abuse, including labor violations and breached contracts, and petitioned the island government's involvement in the matter. By early January 1947, the president of the Puerto Rican Senate, Luis Muñoz Marín, commissioned Senator Vicente Géigel Polanco to investigate the plight of Puerto Rican workers and use his findings to amend existing laws regulating Puerto Rico's contract labor system.[20]

Upon his return to the island, Géigel Polanco reported to the Senate that the labor conditions were not "as bad" as unofficial reports had previously indicated. The Puerto Rican government could improve migrant workers' experiences, however, by implementing legislation to protect them abroad and allocating funds to improve their training in Puerto Rico. The problems in Chicago could have been avoided, he concluded, if laborers had been properly selected and trained before leaving Puerto Rico. This careful selection process was especially important, since emigration was increasingly regarded as an indispensable feature of Puerto Rico's development program, a point to which Géigel Polanco alluded in saying, "There is a good opportunity in Chicago to find work since there is no opposition by local labor unions. If we can arrange the emigration of the worker in a more effective manner, we will be doing a great service to Puerto Rico by reducing unemployment on the island."[21]

The Puerto Rican government responded to Géigel Polanco's report by immediately implementing two novel programs. In 1947, Puerto Rico's Department of Labor, in conjunction with the Department of Instruction's Vocational Education Division, established eight *centros domésticos* — domestic training centers — to prepare young women for housework in American cities.[22] According to Labor Commissioner Fernando Sierra Berdecía, the *centros* would offer a three-month course to "competently train" *domésticas* in household work tailored specifically to North American sensibilities. In addition to learning how to properly perform domestic chores, such as washing dishes, cleaning and arranging furniture, making beds, and answering the door, students would take courses in conversational English and child nutrition.[23] Government officials projected that these *centros domésticos* would train approximately 1,500 women annually and would meet North American demands for domestic workers for the next five years.[24]

Although the Puerto Rican government nominally reformed the contract labor system, their remarkably public emphasis on migrant preparation and training as a way of ensuring a smoother transition into the Chicago labor market, and ultimately into the city's civic life, betrayed a new approach to managing Puerto Rican migration that had long-lasting and deeply gendered consequences. On the one hand, policymakers were increasingly vocal about the advantages of encouraging young women's migration, since "aside from birth control, the most effective means of reducing the population of Puerto Rico is emigration, primarily women of child-bearing ages." More importantly, perhaps, it was believed that women's emigration would facilitate continued emigration since "[it] is obvious that girls, with their typically strong family loyalties, will send for their kin" and serve as "advance-guards which would make easy the entrance of late-comers."[25] On the other hand, these same policymakers and their academic advisors fixed their social engineering gaze more broadly on the particular behavior of migrants and the communities and institutions they created in their new environment, and involved themselves in ensuring that Puerto Rican migrants, like Robert Park's "marginal man" decades earlier, were on an evolutionary track toward assimilation that could easily be facilitated through proper orientation and training. Indeed, the Chicago Experiment was a defining moment in Puerto Rican labor and migration history, establishing a precedent for the island government's involvement in migrant life abroad. Thus, immediately following the creation of the island's *centros domésticos,* the Puerto Rican government initiated a second program, the Migration Division Office, dedicated to managing Puerto Rican migrants on the mainland.

Managing Migrants in the City

The Migration Division established its Chicago office in 1949 as the principal government entity responsible for managing Puerto Rican labor migration throughout the Midwest, especially in Ohio, Indiana, Illinois, and Wisconsin. Although the office was initially established to orient migrant workers and help them secure employment, promoting Puerto Ricans' gradual integration into their new social and cultural context quickly became the agency's principal goal. This assimilation frame provided the ideological foundation for the Migration Division's activities in the early postwar period. It also offered an analytic lens for understanding the apparent ease with which Chicago Puerto Ricans — supposedly in contrast to their New York counterparts and southern blacks in

Chicago — adapted to their new urban environment. Anthropologist Elena Padilla's seminal study comparing New York and Chicago Puerto Rican migrant assimilation, for example, found that Chicago Puerto Ricans were indeed assimilable, a phenomenon she attributed primarily to migrants' ecological distribution in the city.[26] Unlike New York Puerto Ricans, who resided primarily in *colonias,* Chicago Puerto Ricans were scattered over several neighborhoods, including the Loop, Back of the Yards, and Chicago's Black Belt, as a result of the city's racial and linguistic geography; the preponderance of contracted laborers, such as live-in *domésticas,* who resided throughout the city and suburbs; and the precedent set by residentially and socially integrated Puerto Ricans who had arrived during the interwar period. Padilla concluded that new Puerto Rican migrants could be expected to follow the same road to assimilation as long as families and unmarried adolescents did not predominate, since these social types integrated less readily into American society, which provided migrants with critical "social orientation for their behavior."[27]

While division officials clearly concerned themselves with Puerto Ricans' full integration into their host society, they were equally committed to manufacturing and managing a positive public image of Puerto Rican migrants in order to avoid the nativist backlash that had stymied Puerto Ricans in New York City. To that end, the Chicago division office collaborated with local government and community agencies to address problems involving Puerto Rican residents. Division officials, for example, worked closely with the Chicago Council against Racial and Religious Discrimination and Chicago's Public Welfare office to resolve work-related conflicts, and they responded to negative news reports about Puerto Rican workers through local radio and print media. They consulted frequently with researchers like sociologist Harvey Perloff from the University of Chicago and demographer Paul Hatt of Northwestern University in projects about integration, employment, and ethnic relations between Puerto Rican migrants and Mexicans in the city. The division also helped Northwestern University researchers collect data for a fertility study in Puerto Rico.[28] Finally, division officials advised Puerto Rican residents to establish community organizations and institutions that would address the needs of their growing community. Clearly, the Migration Division was deeply engaged in promoting Puerto Rican migrants' full assimilation and creating civic organizations that would "not get off on a tangent destructive to the ultimate goal of integration." But their activities were also aimed at creating a "dependable" (or perhaps docile) labor force, and ultimately, I would argue, circumscribing migrants' political independence, by actively supporting those civic organizations and institutions least likely to challenge the status quo.[29]

The office also used local radio and print media to disseminate a profile of "the Puerto Rican migrant" that stressed his/her industrious work ethic and ability to assimilate easily into the urban American environment. The division's February 1952 monthly report, for example, documented employers' concern about Puerto Rican workers' absenteeism, and their swift response in persuading local radio stations to air public service announcements stressing the importance of being responsible and reliable employees. The division also showed films such as *The Girl from Puerto Rico, The Crowded Island,* and *Pedacito de Tierra* in local community colleges and social service agencies and loaned them to city organizations like the Pan-American Council of Chicago as part of their education campaign.[30] When the *Daily News* published unflattering articles about Puerto Ricans in the city, division officials immediately mobilized Puerto Rican community organizations to "channel their energy in a constructive way." In response, the division director, Anthony Vega, wrote a letter to the editor that was "courteous and proper, but also firm" and sent a copy to all concerned organizations. This action led to two additional articles in the *Daily News* that were much more positive than the previous ones.[31]

Clearly, while the Migration Division's stated purpose was to "help individual adjustment and integration into the community where one resides," its principal focus was to promote a positive image of migrants and maintain a favorable working relationship with civic groups and government agencies.[32] An inventory of its print materials demonstrates that "between 60 and 70 percent of Migration Division press releases, articles, pamphlets and films in the middle 1950s appeared in English, addressed to a non–Puerto Rican audience."[33] Division officials also encouraged migrants to become actively involved in civic life as a way to advance the Migration Division's goals. Thus everything from blood drives ("Such efforts as obtaining blood donors among the Puerto Rican residents will maintain our good relations with the hospitals") to ethnic celebrations ("All of this activity has created much favorable publicity in all the city and has been a valuable organizing experience for the various Councils of the *Caballeros de San Juan* [the Knights of San Juan]") either promoted or detracted from the division's primary objective.[34]

The Migration Division office readily acknowledged its public relations campaign and admitted that such measures were fueled by two important and related phenomena: the desire to avoid the "racial powder keg" that characterized the experience of New York Puerto Ricans, and the need to manage the exodus of thousands of Puerto Ricans from the "overpopulated island" in order to ensure the industrialization program's success. The Division's annual report for 1955 noted:

[For] Puerto Rico migration has an important meaning, since it is common knowledge that migration, although voluntary, is an integral part of the program "Manos a la Obra" [Operation Bootstrap]. It is important because migration helps maintain a population index on a more or less stable level with its corresponding impact on employment and unemployment, in health, education and housing, etc. It is also important because it is a very important source of income for the economic life of the country.[35]

By acknowledging migration's critical role in Puerto Rico's industrialization program, the division not only betrayed the government's official position of neither stimulating nor discouraging migration; it also made clear that Puerto Rican migration and displacement was indeed a state-sponsored phenomena involving multiple sites and institutional actors working transnationally. Like the "Chicago Experiment," the Puerto Rican government's involvement in migrants' lives through the Migration Division was an important precursor to what scholars now refer to as the "new transnationalism."[36]

In its attempts to promote the peaceful integration of Puerto Rican migrants into Chicago's social life, the department made frequent and explicit comparisons of Puerto Ricans in New York and Chicago. Chicago Puerto Ricans were upheld as hardworking migrants, immune to the kind of violence, pathology, and welfare dependency that allegedly characterized their New York counterparts. Equally powerful, although not quite as explicit, were the ways in which Chicago Puerto Ricans were compared to racial and ethnic others inhabiting the city. Soon after their postwar arrival, mainstream newspapers and city agencies helped to reflect and shape a public image of Puerto Ricans as standard-bearers of hard work and "good" immigrant behavior. Between the late 1940s and the mid 1960s, they were popularly cast as the city's "model minority" and enjoyed this honorary status until June 1966, when the Division Street Riots erupted in the new Puerto Rican neighborhood. This journey from "model minority" to "underclass" has important political implications in that it reveals what constitutes "good" and "bad" ethnic groups. These designations continue to be salient instruments to identify and explain social problems as a product of culture rather than larger political-economic structures of inequality.

From "Model Minority" to "Underclass"

Everyone who has seen "West Side Story" or reads the papers or has seen Spanish Harlem in New York knows there is a "Puerto Rican problem."

He can talk knowledgeably about gang fights and knives and five Puerto Ricans hanging themselves in New York jails and all the other problems of the Spanish ghetto.

It has been printed and reprinted that more Puerto Ricans, sick of subway knifings and dirty air and dirty tenements, are going back to Puerto Rico than are coming to New York.

The surprising thing is that none of this is true in Chicago.

Chicago Daily News, June 5, 1966

While a number of scholars have argued that model minority rhetoric explaining Asian and Asian American success vis-à-vis U.S. blacks and Latinos has its roots in the Civil Rights Era, I argue that the postwar model minority tropes that elevated Chicago Puerto Ricans sprang from national anxiety about American families and gender ideologies.[37] As feminist scholars have noted, postwar family ideology rested largely on a new cult of domesticity that enshrined women's roles as selfless mothers and men as breadwinners. These iconic images of *the* American family were deeply raced and classed: Not only did they ignore white middle-class women's wage labor during the war, but they also erased poor and working women's continued formal and informal work and ignored the fact that some women — women of color as well as immigrant women — had long histories of wage labor and continued to work in postwar America.[38] Postwar mass media, especially television, were key to inventing and disseminating images of the American family as a harmonious domestic unit residing happily in segregated social spaces in the suburbs.[39] This postwar family ideology was a politically charged construct that celebrated proper gender roles, a robust work ethic, and strong family ties, values allegedly under assault by deviant sexualities, communism, and the anomie of urban life.[40] It was also the cornerstone of an emerging "model minority" trope in the 1950s.

In today's political and racial landscape, journalists, academics, and politicians invoke model minority rhetoric to explain Asian American educational and economic success. According to the model minority myth, Asian Americans possess unique cultural values — a strong work ethic, deference to authority, patience, and strong family ties — that have allowed them to succeed. And unlike poor blacks and Latinos, Asian Americans have allegedly done so with little government assistance. Asian American scholars have carefully documented the emergence of the model minority myth in the mid 1960s as a reaction to the Civil Rights movement and black and Latino political mobilization. Its persistence into the 1980s and 1990s, these writers argue, attests to the rightward shift in American racial politics since the late 1960s and the myth's appeal to deeply held beliefs of American liberal democracy, such as individualism and merit.[41] Both then and now, family ideology has been the tenuous foundation upon which this model minority rhetoric rests.

Beginning in the 1950s, national concerns about American families mapped onto Chicago's volatile problems of race and residential desegregation, complementary racial fears enabling Chicago Puerto Ricans to become the city's "model minority." Local news accounts prominently featured Puerto Rican migrants as hardworking family *men* who sent for their wives and families once they had established secure jobs and proper living arrangements in Chicago. Like European immigrants before them, Puerto Ricans allegedly hailed from close-knit families whose members were self-reliant, eager to work, and unwilling to receive public aid. A *Chicago Daily News* article in 1959, for example, spotlighted Cesar Rivera and Domingo LaBoy as "examples of good citizens among the Puerto Rican newcomers." The large number of family photos in LaBoy's home demonstrated his commitment to family both on the island and on the mainland, and Rivera was praised for being "very much the head of his family in the manner of the Spanish culture." In short, both men fit the profile of the Chicago Puerto Rican: "What kind of Puerto Rican comes to Chicago? The hardworking guy who isn't looking for a handout."[42]

By the late 1950s and early 1960s, Chicago media consistently praised its Puerto Rican residents for their strong families. One news article profiled the Medinas, a "model Puerto Rican family" whose social life centered on its large extended family and friends.

Most of the Medinas' social life centers around the family — more than one hundred relatives in Chicago — and Puerto Rican friends . . . . It is nothing for fifteen or twenty relatives to drop-in on one evening, to visit on the front porch or climb the additional flights to the Medinas' apartment. Occasionally the girls bring friends home from school . . . but usually they are Puerto Rican friends.[43]

Mainstream newspapers also emphasized the ways in which families — and, when necessary, local businesses — helped orient newcomers.

When a member of the family arrives every one of his kinfolk, blood or marriage, must be there to meet him. He must be taken in hand, housed where there is no room, and fed where there is nothing to eat. Finding work for the newcomer is a family project. Buying winter clothing (something unknown in tropical Puerto Rico) is another. If the family's resources are inadequate, the neighborhood lends its aid. The grocer, the bartender, and the beauty parlor operator relay bits of information on apartments and job openings.[44]

Such articles reified "the Puerto Rican family" as an unchanging cultural form. The accounts also elided the ideologically charged nature of upholding the Puerto Rican family as the standard-bearer for all families in the urban landscape. If all families behaved like these model families, the articles seemed to suggest, American households could avoid the social problems threatening to destroy the American family.

City agencies like the Mayor's Committee on New Residents affirmed these media portraits, underscoring the resemblance between the experience of Puerto Ricans and that of earlier immigrant groups. Despite unavoidable problems of "crowded slum housing, job difficulties, language trouble, prejudice and ghetto-living," Puerto Rican families were stable and organized "in the Spanish tradition."

Authority in the family resides in the male, the children are under his control, and the family group often comprises an extended clan of relatives. Relatives help each other because they are 'of the same blood' and children are almost always taken care of by the family and rarely are sent to an orphanage. Women are expected to be submissive, to restrict their activities to the home. Girls in lower class families usually marry young, and often they are content to live in a common law marriage without the benefit of civil or religious sanction.[45]

Such images suggest that Puerto Rican domestic groups were immune to the pathologies threatening the postwar American family. The celebration of their proper gender roles and strong kin ties also underscored the ways in which popular culture and social policy encouraged the postwar American family fantasy.[46]

In addition to being deeply family-oriented, Puerto Rican migrants were widely regarded as innocent, loving, and gentle people. Unlike "the Negro, Indian and Southern white" residing in Chicago, Puerto Ricans were described as dangerously naïve and vulnerable to unscrupulous business practices, such as faulty credit schemes.[47] According to police, young Puerto Rican men rarely caused problems, drank very little, and when they did get into trouble, one officer remarked, they usually fought among themselves: "They wander around in gangs of fifteen or twenty looking for their music. Every now and then a little trouble develops and knives come out. But they give me less trouble than a lot of the others."[48] According to the Mayor's Committee on New Residents, the little crime that did exist among juvenile or adult Puerto Rican men was "slum-conditioned, related to their cultural background (statutory rape) or their inadequate command of the English language (traffic violations)."[49] In short, the "dark-eyed, gentle people from the blue-ringed island" were remarkably different from Chicago's racial/ethnic others. One Puerto Rican man confirmed these observations, saying, "The Puerto Rican psychology is very different from, say, the Mexicans. They don't like to fight. Other Latins are more easily incited to violence. I never saw any mass movement interested in violence in Puerto Rico."[50]

Through the mid 1960s, Chicago media continued to compare Puerto Ricans to other ethnic groups, such as "hard-working" Irish, Polish, and Italian immigrants, and not-so-hardworking populations like the New York Puerto Ricans. Chicago's *Daily News* trumpeted Chicago Puerto Ricans as "an upbeat West Side Story": They were "peaceful and furiously ambitious" while New York *puertorriqeños* were violent, welfare-dependent, and involved in gangs. "If Horatio Alger were alive today," the article maintained, "*he* would sure be a [Chicago] Puerto Rican" (my emphasis). His industriousness, his level of self-analysis and his desire to "put roots here" resulted from the "modern Puerto Rican personality," which was "a mixture of Latin and North American characteristics."[51] This particular news account, like many others, spotlighted hardworking Puerto Rican men and the stable nuclear families they established, and portrayed women (rather incorrectly) solely as dutiful homemakers. This profile of the Puerto Rican migrant as a hardworking *man* not only erased women's migration experiences and work, but also served as a benchmark to distinguish "good" Puerto Rican migrants from "bad" ethnic others in the urban imagination.

Like its more recent incarnation, model minority rhetoric of the 1950s also highlighted cultural explanations for group success. As cultural hybrids, Puerto Ricans embodied the virtues of two distinct cultures — a patriarchal Spanish sensibility mixed with North American determination — which explained their impressive ability to overcome adversity. Chicago city officials were equally fascinated with this cultural spectacle:

Culturally, the Puerto Rican presents an interesting phenomenon. A thin layer of American culture is laid upon a strictly Spanish speaking background, and Puerto Rico may be called the melting-ground of two distinct cultures. This is visibly documented by the aged Spanish fortresses which once protected the harbor of San

Juan and only a little distance away, the tall chimneys of modern industrial plants, symbols of Puerto Rico's new association with industrial America. Both Spanish and English are taught and spoken and cockfighting and baseball are national pastimes. In short, when a Puerto Rican says goodbye to his native land, "he leaves a land as Spanish as avocados and as American as ice cream."[52]

Because Puerto Ricans were Latin *and* North American — they were, after all, American citizens, a fact agency documents and memos consistently affirmed — they successfully navigated between the Scylla and Charybdis of modern urban America: They nurtured strong families and communities without the provincialism or degraded ghetto living that allegedly characterized Chicago's black population. In this way, media representations of model Puerto Rican families clearly reflected important academic and policy concerns of the day. Acculturation theory and the vitriolic debates surrounding residential integration provided the backdrop against which this model minority image was constructed.

By highlighting Puerto Ricans' "Americanness" and their cultural values — patriarchal families, diligence, kindness, and strong family ties — city officials and local media provided white Chicagoans with a cultural antidote for their racial fears. Severe housing shortages in postwar Chicago exacerbated long-standing racial tensions between blacks and whites. The city's black belt overflowed, as blacks entered into formerly white neighborhoods like Oakland, Kenwood, Hyde Park, and Woodlawn.[53] Increased suburbanization in the 1950s helped to relieve the city's housing pressures, as middle-class whites relocated to new single-family homes in the suburbs. But for those whites remaining in the city, interracial friction over shared public spaces, such as parks and beaches, as well as often violent white protests against black residential integration, was almost commonplace.

White residents of South Deering and Hyde Park, for example, invoked cultural arguments to explain their resistance to black residents in their communities. Southern blacks were regarded as backward, while blacks from Chicago's ghettos suffered from "physical and . . . moral deterioration."[54] The prevailing assimilation theory, which affirmed the gradual cultural integration of "newcomers" into the larger white society, provided whites with academic ammunition to oppose black settlement in their neighborhoods on cultural rather than racial grounds. As whites in South Deering succinctly argued, they would oppose black integration in their neighborhood until blacks were "educated to behave and act like civilized people."[55]

According to U.S. racial definitions, most Puerto Ricans could not be regarded as "white," but media portraits of hardworking Puerto Rican families assured city residents that they were not black.[56] Being christened the modern Horatio Alger cemented the "model minority" status of Chicago Puerto Ricans. Yet it also subverted black claims of entrenched racism and racist social policy that kept black Chicagoans poor and segregated in the city's bursting ghettoes. Model minority rhetoric not only chastises ethnic/racial others for failing to achieve economic success, but it also smoothes over intragroup differences, ignores the ways in which racism shapes peoples' lives, and elides a more complicated reading of history. For example, at the same time as Chicago embraced Puerto Ricans as the city's model minority, government officials feverishly worked to repatriate unemployed Puerto Ricans to the island. While Chicago-based media virtually ignored these events, *El Mundo* provided extensive coverage of government plans to expel the city's "model citizens."

Like the mainland press, *El Mundo* favorably reported the ways in which Chicago Puerto Ricans differed from their New York counterparts. In March 1953, *El Mundo* ran an editorial referencing a *Chicago Sun-Times* article that praised Puerto Ricans working in Chicago. "These words constitute a welcome change in the panorama of Puerto Rican acclimation throughout the Continent," *El Mundo* assured its readers. Despite the large numbers of Puerto Ricans living in Chicago at the time, they did not seem to pose a problem. In fact, the editorial continued, "We celebrate the Chicago group's fine reputation . . . . This proves that our [people] can be successful in any of the large industrial or agricultural centers in the United States."[57]

One year later, these positive reports were replaced by a series of *El Mundo* articles documenting Chicago's housing shortage, Puerto Rican unemployment, and the city's plans to return unemployed migrants back to the island. For more than a week, *El Mundo* condemned Alvin E. Rose — Chicago's Public Welfare commissioner — and his plans to deny unemployed Puerto Ricans public aid and to use that money instead to relocate them in Puerto Rico. The editorial staff passionately denounced the city's racist actions, stating:

It is evident that the municipal authorities of the cold metropolis do not have a cordial attitude toward potential Puerto Rican migration to the city and want to discourage it by any means necessary . . . . We believe that we ought to combat prejudice in any form in which it might manifest itself, and we believe that the case of any Puerto Rican in Chicago, or anywhere else, deserves to be resolved according to its own merits and the circumstances surrounding it and not merely or prejudicially, because it has to do with a Puerto Rican . . . . To discriminate against [Puerto Ricans], or to treat them in a prejudiced fashion, is to deny United States citizens what has not been denied to foreigners of all other races who have migrated to the Nation.[58]

In an effort to improve strained relations, Alvin Rose went to Puerto Rico to discuss the situation with island officials. In Chicago, Clarence Senior, the national director of the Migration Division, organized a committee of twenty-eight local groups — including the Catholic Church, the Congress of Industrial Organizations, and the Migration Division's local office — to address the problem of minority unemployment in general and the relocation of unemployed Puerto Ricans in particular.[59] Despite these organized efforts, approximately one hundred Puerto Ricans were sent back to the island at that time. Following his visit to Puerto Rico, Rose announced that he was, in fact, quite happy with Chicago's Puerto Rican community and was confident that their situation would continue to improve. Returned migrants and island residents, however, were not so optimistic. An *El Mundo* editorial summarized the collective sentiment, asking why Puerto Ricans should be sent back to the island if the Irish and Italians were never sent back. "Are we, or are we not, American citizens?"[60]

The city's obsession with Puerto Rican residential patterns further betrayed its official narrative of model Puerto Rican migrants. The Catholic Youth Organization urged the city to investigate Puerto Ricans' residential patterns to determine if they were in fact failing to integrate, so that city organizations might "[revise their approach] in order to bring about such integration."[61] Similarly, the Welfare Council of Metropolitan Chicago actively prevented Puerto Ricans from settling in *colonias* or living exclusively with other Spanish speakers. They observed "the tendency for colonies of Puerto Ricans to grow within the city [and that] unless efforts are made to integrate these groups into the community as a whole, there will be a tendency for them to remain in these groups."[62] Such discussions were clearly informed by concerns about New York Puerto Ricans and Chicago School thinking that correlated residential integration with acculturation.

Finally, Chicago's Migration Division office documented various instances of discrimination against Puerto Ricans in employment, housing, and law enforcement, noting in its 1958 annual report:

The office confronted difficulties in communal situations; antagonisms on the part of the police against Puerto Ricans in Chicago; resistance by industrial and agricultural bosses as far as employing Puerto Ricans; social service agencies' lack of interest in handling cases involving Puerto Ricans; ignorance on the part of judges, lawyers, social workers, neighborhood groups, landlords, etc., with respect to Puerto Ricans and the recently arrived Puerto Rican; indifference on the part of government agencies about employment, housing, health, welfare, and delicate situations involving . . . their communities.[63]

The Division Office was particularly concerned by such problems, since they went beyond the expected intergroup conflict, such as problems between Italians and Puerto Ricans, which had been well documented.[64] Instead, division officials were confronted with the fact that Puerto Ricans also faced severe discrimination from government and city organizations, the same agencies that were publicly embracing Puerto Ricans as model citizens. Such reports clearly demonstrate two related problems with model minority rhetoric: It masks entrenched racism in city institutions by pitting minority groups against each other and focusing instead on dyadic instances of racism within these groups. It also obscures Puerto Ricans' true position in the racial hierarchy by subordinating ethnic/racial others to them. Rather than publicly denounce the city's racism, the Migration Division expressed its concerns internally in order to avoid public confrontation. In doing so, they were complicit in reproducing the myth of Chicago Puerto Ricans' painless assimilation, and delegitimized attempts to address discrimination and racism through political mobilization.[65]

Most scholars agree that model minority rhetoric stigmatizes both the group being praised and those who do not fit the model minority profile. It also relies on fantastic historical narratives that perpetuate the model minority's racial subordination while delegitimizing claims of racial inequality.[66] Furthermore, this myth relies on false claims about women, work, and family. Thus, while newspapers and government agencies praised Puerto Ricans for their patriarchal families and "Spanish" gender roles, city officials simultaneously expressed deep concern about Puerto Rican women's employment. Despite the model minority construction of Puerto Rican men as the indisputable heads of their families and of their wives as dutiful homemakers, historical and ethnographic evidence as well as women's life histories paint a very different picture. In short, Chicago Puerto Ricans' status as a model minority was short-lived precisely because it had very little basis in lived experience.

Madres Migrating on the Mayflower: Ideologies of Gender, Work, and American Families

In October 1996, I attended a banquet dinner sponsored by the East Chicago chapter of the National Conference of Puerto Rican Women (NaCOPRW). The event honored the "mothers of migration," the pioneering *madres* often overlooked in "official" histories of Puerto Rican migration to Chicago and nearby cities. Throughout the evening, daughters and granddaughters of the migration proudly shared their stories about the history of Puerto Ricans in this Chicago suburb, their parents' struggles to "give their children a better life," and, above all, the countless sacrifices their *madres* made both in Puerto Rico and on the mainland. One of the most striking moments of the evening was the presentation of awards honoring these women. The mistress of ceremonies introduced each woman with "Y la próxima madre . . ." (the next mother) and then read a brief biography, usually written by one of her daughters or granddaughters. For me, an eager participant-observer, these life histories were a gold mine of information. They detailed each woman's place of birth, her age, when she arrived in the Chicago area, the various American cities where she had lived before coming to the Midwest, an abbreviated labor history, and, finally, when and whom she married and the names and number of her children. The ceremony closed on an emotional note, with lighted candles for those *madres* who had died and one daughter bringing the audience to tears by singing "Wind beneath My Wings," which she dedicated to all the women honored that night. Acknowledging the audience's touching response, the NaCOPRW chapter president poignantly summed up the evening: "What we are all feeling is the emotion of feeling proud. That is how we should feel of ourselves and of all these women here tonight."

What was so remarkable about this evening was the organizers' ability to capture the complexity of these women's lives. Clearly, they were *madres*. But they were also pioneers of this city's Puerto Rican community. They worked in the local steel mills, ran their own businesses (boardinghouses, pawnshops, and bodegas), served as city employees, and frequently worked in the informal sector babysitting and selling homemade food and crocheted goods. And while the evening celebrated these women primarily as mothers, recognizing their productive labor also helps correct "official" histories of Puerto Rican migration that erase women's long and complicated labor history in Puerto Rico and Chicago.[67] Weaving together women's productive and reproductive roles in migrant narratives provides a more textured portrait of these women's lives and the communities they helped to create in postwar Chicago.

By the mid 1950s — the early years of Puerto Ricans' tenure as a model minority — the Migration Division Office was expressing deep concern about Puerto Rican women's ability to find secure employment in Chicago. In April 1952, the office documented a lack of employment for non–English speaking women who had been laid off by light industries. In

July, the office reiterated its concern about women's low levels of employment. Finally, that year's October report focused almost exclusively on women and the labor market, detailing how many had arrived at the division looking for work, the number of women successfully placed in jobs, and various division attempts to follow up on women they had referred for employment. Officials pointed out that this was exclusively a problem with female employment and underscored the need to teach women English so they would be able to secure jobs as office workers.[68]

The Mayor's Committee on New Residents later echoed this call for women to learn English. It also encouraged them to attend the Board of Education's Americanization classes. Like Mexican women in California decades earlier, Puerto Rican women were encouraged to learn English because of their role as mothers and homemakers.[69] But they were also singled out because of their long history of wage labor in Puerto Rico. According to the committee's report, women in general "have an excellent reputation with respect to their manual and finger dexterity. This has been particularly apparent in the case of Puerto Rican girls and women who are in great demand in the textile, clothing and related industries." Language and cultural education would only make them more attractive to local companies. To this end, the city offered classes at local elementary schools, a local high school, and even at the Cabrini Homes, where approximately one thousand Puerto Rican families lived.[70]

City planners' efforts to promote the employment of Puerto Rican women coincided with their embrace of Puerto Rican families as standard-bearers of the model American family. These surreptitious attempts to employ Puerto Rican women betray, however, the true race/class bias of postwar family ideology. As many feminist scholars have demonstrated, some women were always expected to work, and the prevailing gender ideology of the stay-at-home mom was deeply raced and classed, excluding poor and working-class white women and all women of color.[71] Puerto Rican women thus occupied an ambiguous ideological space in postwar Chicago. Like other poor and minority women, they were expected to work, but they were also upheld as the ideal of family and female virtue. Their propensity to work in the informal sector — caring for relatives' children or selling handicrafts, food, and clothes they made — often obscured their wage labor, thereby reproducing the myth of breadwinning fathers and nonproductive mothers, and reaffirming their popular image as mothers wholly dedicated to their nuclear families. As one woman explained to me when asked whether her mother ever worked, "My mother . . . she took care of us. She babysat. She never worked. She never worked. She always worked in the house. Because that is how my father was."

Unlike factory work or working on an assembly line, women's informal labor didn't challenge postwar gender ideology. In fact, it enabled Puerto Rican families to live the way white middle-class American families were supposed to live. While almost all of the women I interviewed earned income informally at some point in their labor histories, they also worked in factories making handbags, clocks, lamps, gloves, mattresses, and candy. They assembled automobiles, airplanes, bicycles, and furniture, and they also started their own businesses, like restaurants and clothing boutiques. Poor and working-class *puertorriqueñas* clearly worked in Chicago. Most had also been employed in Puerto Rico before leaving the island. In fact, some blamed their wage labor for strained male-female relations on the island and on the mainland. One newspaper article quoted a Puerto Rican man explaining that because women worked in Puerto Rico and men did not, "the rooster was no longer the rooster. Men were taking care of children. It was a tremendous loss of face. Men decided, 'I can't live here, my friends, my relatives are looking at me.' So they went to the States for work. Again, the man felt like the rooster."[72]

Such statements provide an interesting twist to contemporary ethnographic studies documenting the ways in which migration challenges "traditional" gender ideologies and erodes men's status and power. Patricia Pessar and Sherri Grasmuck's work among Dominican immigrants in New York, for example, shows that women resist men's attempts to return to the Dominican Republic because they fear losing autonomy gained largely through wage labor in New York.[73] Many of the women I interviewed also described *el sufrimiento* (suffering) of returning to the island after living and working in Chicago. Family and community pressure to stay at home, a renewed dependency on husbands because of inadequate public transportation, and limited job opportunities all contributed to women's dissatisfaction upon returning to Puerto Rico. Together, these narratives of migration, work, and gender ideologies draw in sharp relief how politically and ideologically charged poor Puerto Rican women's wage labor is. Almost fifty years after the model minority myth enshrined Puerto Rican women as dutiful wives, mothers, and homemakers, their reproductive and productive roles continue to be a politically charged terrain for activists, academics, and politicians. As for black Americans, Puerto Ricans' eventual membership in urban America's underclass rests, in large part, on faulty assumptions about women, culture, sexuality, and family ideology.

The Division Street Riots and the Emergence of Chicago's Underclass

One year after being christened the modern Horatio Alger, Chicago Puerto Ricans' status as a model minority was seriously challenged by the Division Street Riots in June 1966. On June 12, immediately following Humboldt Park's first Puerto Rican Day Parade celebration, a white police officer shot a young Puerto Rican man, Aracelis Baez. An already tense situation was further exacerbated by the police's use of attack dogs to subdue the crowd. On the surface, the three days of rioting were a reaction to a clear instance of police brutality. But as scholars and some community activists have recently argued, the riots — the Division Street Uprising, as it is popularly referred to by many in Chicago — were a response to a longer history of police abuse and economic and political marginalization of Puerto Ricans. The Division Street Riots stunned city officials, who had expected unrest in other Chicago neighborhoods, but not in the Puerto Rican community. Martin Luther King, Jr.'s protests in Chicago, marches demanding fair housing, and brutal repression of black militancy during the summer of 1966 all suggested that black ghettos — and not the new, quiescent Puerto Rican barrio — were the potentially volatile zones. According to the commissioner of the Chicago Commission on Human Relations, "There [was] no indication that something of this type could happen [in the Division Street area]. To say that we were surprised would be a big understatement."[74]

The Division Street Riots marked a radical shift in the history of Puerto Ricans in Chicago. The events impelled the creation of a number of community-based projects to address problems of poverty, housing discrimination, and police brutality among Puerto Ricans. Immediately after the riots, the city directed federal money from the government's War on Poverty program to Community Action Programs (CAP) in the Division Street area. In July 1966, the Chicago Committee on Urban Opportunity opened a multi-service center with Spanish-speaking staff on Division Street. CAP established the Neighborhood Youth Corps, more educational classes through special summer schools, new Headstart programs, and resources to help barrio residents with housing problems. The city also encouraged the police department to implement key changes, such as altering existing regulations about the use of police dogs, expanding the department's training program to include classes on Spanish language and culture, and offering special courses for Spanish speakers interested in joining the police force.[75]

The Division Street Riots were also key in transforming Puerto Rican community organizations into activism-oriented groups with a leadership interested in community development. The Spanish Action Committee of Chicago (SACC) and the Latin American Development Organization (LADO), for example, were formed following the riots and used boy-cotts, picketing, and demonstrations to protest the city's failure to provide important services in the barrio. In the three years following the riots, SACC picketed the Chicago Park District to create the Humboldt Park Recreation Committee. They pressured the Chicago Police Department to remove some officers from the Thirteenth District. And they also suc-cessfully resisted the Board of Education's redistricting efforts. Similarly, LADO developed community programs like the Pedro Albizu Campos Center for People's Health (a free health clinic), the Welfare Union (an advocacy group for public aid recipients), and perhaps most impor-tantly, the Ruiz Belvis Cultural Center, an organization committed to pro-viding free tutoring, English instruction, and classes in Puerto Rican art, music, and dance.[76]

The militant activism of the new Puerto Rican community organiza-tions helped politicize Chicago's street gangs. Beginning in 1967, the Young Lords Organization (YLO) — a group of largely second-generation Puerto Rican militants — focused their energies on community activism, particularly around issues of housing and urban renewal. In my fieldwork, people proudly pointed out that the YLO actually began in Chicago, and not in New York as many incorrectly believed.[77] Men and women for-merly involved with the YLO emphasize the multiracial coalitions they formed among poor people in Chicago. With the Black Panthers and the Young Patriots — a gang of poor Appalachian whites — the YLO protested the city's urban renewal plan, which displaced poor Puerto Rican, black, and white residents in West Lincoln Park. In late 1969, they took control of the Armitage Street Methodist Church, renaming it the "People's Church," and founded a day care center, a free health clinic, a cultural cen-ter, a newspaper, and a free breakfast program for neighborhood children. Throughout the 1970s, the YLO continued to be actively involved in com-munity politics, although, as many community activists have pointed out, federal and city repression of militant organizations in the late 1960s and 1970s weakened the YLO, as its members were imprisoned and harassed.[78] Many men and women formerly involved with the YLO are still involved in local community organizations and committed to using their history to encourage young Puerto Rican men and women to become involved in community activism.

Like the Black Power and Chicano movements in the late 1960s and 1970s, Puerto Rican activists increasingly articulated local community concerns in nationalist terms.[79] As Ana Yolanda Ramos-Zayas demonstrates at length, organizations such as the Puerto Rican Cultural Center (PRCC) link community-building projects to larger nationalist ideologies of Puerto Rican independence and draw on historical narratives of Puerto Rican nationalism from the 1930s to address contemporary problems. In Chicago, she argues, "Puerto Rican nationalism has become the instrumental political and cultural ideology formulated in community-building efforts among barrio activists and residents."[80] While the bridging of local and nationalist concerns is neither new nor exclusive to Puerto Ricans in Chicago, its pervasiveness in many grassroots community organizations, such as the Ruiz Belvis Cultural Center and the First Congregational Church, and the overwhelming popular understanding that committed community activists are almost always *independentistas* are particularly noteworthy.

Finally, the Division Street Riots were key in transforming the popular perception of Puerto Ricans as hard-working, peaceable, and furiously industrious people. News articles began to focus on the problems of gangs, drugs, welfare dependency, and violence that now, according to media accounts, characterized the community. Humboldt Park and West Town — the neighborhoods with the largest concentration of Puerto Ricans beginning in the late 1960s — were no longer quaint ethnic neighborhoods with diligent, noble migrants. Instead, they were portrayed as dangerous, decaying, and ruled by local gangs. Literary production, newspaper accounts, and policy debates reflect these changes on a national and local level. In *Humboldt's Gift,* Saul Bellow's main character, Charlie Citrine, laments the transformation of his former neighborhood into "what had become a tropical West Indies slum, resembling the parts of San Juan that stand beside lagoons, which bubble and smell like stewing tripe."[81] A news article shortly after the riots declared West Division Street "no man's street. It belongs to no one," and quoted a settlement house director saying, "Division [Street] is one of the most difficult streets of our city. It is one of those streets where the newcomer takes over without much trouble." Like the West Town community area in which it is located, Division Street was seen as riddled with juvenile delinquency, illegitimacy, and excessive public assistance.[82] And through the late 1970s, Chicago media focused — albeit sympathetically at times — on its "underfed, underemployed, poorly housed Puerto Rican community" and queried, "Language problems, lack of jobs, and massive cultural shock often shatter Puerto Rican families. The question is why is this the case now and not before?"[83]

Two nationally acclaimed books released in the 1960s offered possible explanations for these "new" problems in Chicago's Puerto Rican community, although they did not refer directly to Chicago Puerto Ricans. In *Beyond the Melting Pot*, Nathan Glazer and Daniel P. Moynihan declared that unlike other ethnic groups — specifically Jews, whom the authors repeatedly highlighted as a successful immigrant group — Puerto Ricans lacked "both a rich culture and a strong family system." They write:

The net of culture keeps up pride and encourages effort; the strong family serves to organize and channel resources in new situations. In both these aspects Puerto Rico was sadly defective. It was weak in folk arts, unsure in its cultural traditions, without a powerful faith . . . . Nor was there much strength in the Puerto Rican family.

Glazer and Moynihan elaborated on the problems of Puerto Rican families in New York by emphasizing that "broken families" tended to have more children and ended up on welfare, setting in motion an intergenerational culture of dependency. Like New York's black population, Puerto Ricans' cultural values explained their poor economic standing. And although their closing remarks appeared upbeat, if not meekly hopeful — "But the American nationality is still forming: its processes are mysterious, and the final form, if there is ever to be a final form, is as yet unknown" — it is clear that they believed culture, and not the state, was responsible for economic, social, and political outcomes.[84]

Anthropologist Oscar Lewis's *La vida* provided another narrative of broken Puerto Rican families. According to Lewis, many poor Puerto Rican families on the island and the mainland had developed a "culture of poverty" that was "both an adaptation and reaction . . . to their marginal position in a class-stratified, highly individuated, capitalistic society." Because "landless rural workers who migrate to the cities" were more likely to develop a culture of poverty than "migrants from stable peasant villages with a well-organized traditional culture," Chicago Puerto Ricans were prime candidates for participation in this new subculture. Among the many traits associated with the culture of poverty, the "lack of effective participation and integration . . . in the major institutions of the larger society" and a "relatively high incidence of the abandonment of wives and children" resonated most loudly with new media portraits of Chicago Puerto Ricans. Lewis believed that abolishing poverty in itself "may not be enough to eliminate the culture of poverty which is a whole way of life," although he was hopeful that revolution — "by creating basic structural changes in society, by redistributing wealth, by organizing the poor and giving them a sense of belonging, of power and of leadership" — might succeed in abolishing the culture of poverty.[85] However, Lewis regarded Puerto Ricans as lacking a revolutionary tradition, unlike Mexicans and Cubans, and as Laura Briggs notes, compared them unfavorably to Mexicans, characterizing the Puerto Rican poor as having "no knowledge of their own history . . . and far more deviant by virtually any standard." Such an assessment left little room for constructive policy interventions to ameliorate the plight of the Puerto Rican poor.[86]

Even though neither book specifically addressed Chicago Puerto Ricans, their broad popular appeal — like media images of New York Puerto Ricans decades earlier — almost certainly informed local perceptions of emerging urban problems.[87] Despite an expanding U.S. economy in the 1960s and 1970s, working-class Puerto Ricans — like poor blacks — lost jobs to the suburbanization of Chicago's manufacturing sector. Urban renewal plans in Lincoln Park also displaced poor blacks and Puerto Ricans, pushing them farther west into Humboldt Park and exacerbating both groups' already highly segregated residential patterns.[88] These political-economic shifts impoverished Chicago's Puerto Rican community, and the national racial backlash — which *Beyond the Melting Pot* helped usher in — blamed the poor themselves for their worsening economic conditions. As Steven Steinberg and Micaela di Leonardo have demonstrated, the white ethnic community ideology of family loyalty and strong neighborhoods emerged as the template to which poor urban minorities were compared.[89] If poor Puerto Ricans were only more like white ethnics, the logic goes, they would have intact families and strong communities, and they would lift themselves out of poverty.

A second riot in June 1977 and a wave of arson in Humboldt Park and West Town cemented Chicago Puerto Ricans' perceived participation in a "culture of poverty" and their eventual membership in America's "underclass" in the 1980s.[90] Beginning in 1975, local newspapers documented an alarming increase of fires in Humboldt Park. According to one account, from August 1974 to 1975, over four hundred fires were reported, mainly in the 0.5 square mile area between North Avenue and Division Street on the north and south and Western Avenue and California Street on the east and west.[91] Humboldt Park was described as an area "besieged," while residents accused landlords of paying Puerto Rican gangs to burn old houses they were unable to sell. One woman was quoted in a news article: "I think these slumlords are the ones we're dealing with.

They don't want to fix up the houses, they have just sucked the buildings dry." She then quoted a state legislator's response to the arsons: "Beautiful. Let the G.D. Puerto Ricans burn up the neighborhood. That's one way to get them out."[92] Chicago's *Daily News* criticized municipal neglect of Humboldt Park: "There are no special teams working in Humboldt Park, no special effort to control the seemingly endless fires. So the arsonists, uncounted and unconvicted, are free to continue burning. Nero fiddled while Rome burned, but no one seems to know who's playing the violin for Humboldt Park."[93]

Real estate developers certainly were not working to stop the burning. Instead, city government abetted developers' pursuit of exchange value by failing to investigate and prosecute those responsible for the 30 percent decrease in Humboldt Park's housing stock due to arson.[94] In fact, barrio residents, activists, and journalists all noted that while Humboldt Park burned — thereby expelling its poor Puerto Rican, black, and white residents — its eastern neighbor, Wicker Park, took off as "the hottest real estate market around." Young white professionals who "can't afford to buy in desirable locations elsewhere in the city" were turning to Wicker Park, a "heavily black and Puerto Rican [neighborhood], a dumping ground for welfare recipients, crime, garbage collection and sewage."[95] Housing pressures, Puerto Ricans' frustration with the city's failure to investigate years of arson in the barrio, continued police harassment, and their lack of political "clout" in city government all contributed to the outbreak of violence in June 1977. Unlike the Division Street Riots a decade earlier, these events demoralized an already weary community faced with rising unemployment, increased poverty, and sustained political marginalization. The "upbeat West Side Story" was now a "community without dreams" and a "troubled island without clout."[96]

Such images continued to define Humboldt Park for years to come. In 1997, for example, one journalist called it "hell's living room."[97] And while events in Humboldt Park and Puerto Ricans in general were practically invisible on English television stations, coverage in the Spanish news focused, in large part, on the problems with gangs and violence that "plagued" the Puerto Rican community. In late April of 1997, for example, a Spanish television station warned that "cuando sube la temperatura en Humboldt Park, sube la violencia" (when the temperature rises in Humboldt Park, the violence also rises). When English language print and television media did feature Humboldt Park in local news coverage, they focused almost exclusively on the divisiveness of nationalist politics and "terrorist activities" by Puerto Rican *independentistas* in Chicago, which, according to these media accounts, rendered Humboldt Park a dangerous political space as well. My G.E.D. students often complained that whenever the news was about Humboldt Park — or about Puerto Ricans in general — it was always negative. In class one day, Nelly López, a nineteen-year-old mother who grew up in Humboldt Park, expressed her frustration with a television news report: "I'm tired about them always saying bad things about Puerto Ricans, you know. That we're violent, gangbanging and doing drugs. That Humboldt Park is dangerous. It's not because we're Puerto Rican. It's poverty, you know. Sometimes we have to steal, do those things just to get by."

Unlike many politicians and academics, this student recognized the ways in which the economy — and not culture — shapes particular behaviors. A second-generation migrant, Nelly frequently discussed how the public perception of Puerto Ricans limited her employment possibilities. Echoing the findings of sociologists Joleen Kirschenman and Kathryn Neckerman, Nelly explained, "[Humboldt Park] is not dangerous. Why do they have to talk about us like that, you know? Because people see that and say, 'Oh, I'm not going to hire her, a Puerto Rican,' you know. Because of what they see."[98] Like many of my G.E.D. students, Nelly had worked in a number of poorly paid service sector jobs — serving at fast food restaurants, cashiering at dollar stores, and selling clothes in small neighborhood stores — and she often felt exploited in these jobs. One employer underpaid her on each paycheck. Another manager "worked me like a man," expecting her to work twelve-hour shifts with few or no breaks. Nelly felt compelled to quit still another job because she was afraid the storeowner would accuse her of stealing clothes lifted by the stores' patrons.

> N: I quit that job. . . . The main reason was because one day I was over there and some guy came in and it was around Christmas time, you know, and he came in and he just stuffed his coat with stuff . . . . And when I saw, in the back, if it was a wallet or a gun . . . he did it real slick, where nobody could see him. I didn't even catch him. But I knew when he walked out the store, he told me, 'Shut up. You better not even trip because I know you work here.'
>
> I: Was he white, black or Puerto Rican . . . ?
>
> N: He was Puerto Rican. So I quit, you know. Because I didn't want [my boss] to think I stole, you know. Because if he counts his merchandise, then, um, I didn't want him to know. I don't know, I felt like I failed, you know. But I wasn't gonna put my life for some clothes.
>
> I: You couldn't just tell him what happened?

N: [With a cigarette in her mouth, she shakes her head] 'Cause he was a real asshole, you know what I'm saying. So, you know, I just let it be.

Because Chicago is "the city of neighborhoods," "Humboldt Park" means "Puerto Rican" in the popular imagination. These racial/ethnic and spatial associations stigmatize Puerto Ricans and seriously limit their social and economic opportunities.

By criticizing the ways in which city institutions construct and reproduce dominant images of race and space that unfairly mark Puerto Ricans and Humboldt Park as dangerous, I do not wish to suggest that these communities do not have serious problems. Unemployment and poverty *are* pervasive among Puerto Ricans in the city. At 33.8 percent, Puerto Ricans have the highest poverty rate among Latinos (24.2 percent overall) and a slightly higher poverty rate than that of African Americans (33 percent).[99] Instead, I wish to highlight how local knowledge about a particular population is produced and imagined differently over time. The metamorphosis of first- and second-generation Puerto Ricans from a "model minority" to members of "the underclass" is related both to their position in the local economy and to the emergence of various ethnic others to replace them as standard-bearers of hard-working, furiously ambitious people.

Like blacks and other Latinos, Puerto Ricans have been disproportionately affected by economic restructuring in Chicago. Manufacturing jobs declined by more than half between 1947 and 1977, a trend that had a devastating impact on Latinos — particularly Puerto Ricans — who remained in low-paid jobs and industries. In contrast to Cubans and South Americans, Puerto Ricans and Mexicans have lower educational and average income levels and are concentrated in the low-wage service sector and as operatives.[100] Moreover, studies by the Latino Institute, the Chicago Urban League, and Northern Illinois University all demonstrate that none of the jobs requiring only a high school diploma — and not even all of those demanding some postsecondary education — pays a living wage for a family with dependent children.[101] According to the Latino Institute, more than 75 percent of Puerto Ricans are employed in those sectors of the economy. In short, while transnational investment and the loss of manufacturing jobs in the Chicago area have left Latinos in general much poorer than a decade earlier, Puerto Ricans specifically remain the most economically disadvantaged group in all Chicago.[102]

Public perceptions of Chicago Puerto Ricans have shifted dramatically over the past half-century. Like the political-economic contexts in which they are embedded, these images are constructed transnationally and are shaped in relation to real and imagined others in Chicago and abroad. As standard-bearers of hard work, loyal families, and strong communities, Puerto Rican migrants ascended to the model minority throne, which was based on ideological constructions of gender, family, and work that were race- and class-based. As Puerto Ricans' structural position has changed in Chicago, so too has public opinion, as politicians, academics, and journalists now perceive the "Puerto Rican problem" to be a product of excessive migration, pathological behavior, and poor family values. While academic and policy debates continue over the roots of immiseration on the island and the mainland, most experts agree that these problems are most appropriately understood transnationally. Such interpretations of deeply local issues attest to the long-standing and often conflictive transnational links connecting communities like Chicago to Puerto Rican towns and cities.

CHAPTER 4

Los de Afuera, Transnationalism, and the Cultural Politics of Identity

"El Pepino siempre llama" (Pepino always beckons), Mercedes Rubio quietly explained as we sat together in her small living room in Humboldt Park one cold October evening. "I was born in Aguadilla, but my parents were from Pepino. I was born August 1, 1951, delivered by a midwife — just like the Indians — right beside the sugarcane. I didn't go to school — well, I only went until I was ten years old. We were very poor. And even though I am still poor, compared to before, I live like a millionaire."

As Mercedes shared her life story with me, I was struck by how her narrative reflected the rhythm of her daily life with its quiet moments, unavoidable interruptions, interludes of resolution and calm, and even more periods of uncertainty and concern. One of nine children, she has moved between Chicago and San Sebastián at least four times since 1971, when she first left Pepino to live with a sister in Chicago. Each trip, she explains, "is like starting all over again. But if it all goes well for me, I'll stay a few years. Even if I lose everything, I do it for them. My children."

I met Mercedes and her family through Evelyn Trujillo, a thirty-one-year-old G.E.D. student from Humboldt Park. The Rubios were Evelyn's downstairs neighbors, and she had featured them in several in-class essays about her neighborhood and its people. One September morning, a student asked me about my ongoing research in Humboldt Park. When I explained that I was conducting interviews with people who had lived in Puerto Rico for varying lengths of time, including those who moved many times between Chicago and the island, Evelyn laughed, saying that I should talk with her downstairs neighbors. "You know the ones.

The ones that play the loud music." Even though Evelyn complained about the salsa music blaring from Mercedes's apartment day and night, the families were quite friendly and spent a lot of time together, a fact due largely to the friendship between Evelyn's younger daughter, Bianca, and Mercedes's children and grandchildren.

Their friendship was strengthened through the daily struggle of living in a neighborhood divided by feuding gangs and riddled with gunfire, and sharing a deteriorating two-story house near the corner of California and Armitage Avenues, near the border of Humboldt Park and Logan Square. Like many Puerto Rican families in the area, they battled with the landlord — usually unsuccessfully — to provide adequate heat in the winter; repair faucets, broken light switches, and windows; and rid the apartment of rats. Evelyn's husband, Frank, worked with Mercedes's husband and son-in-law to fix those things the landlord refused to repair. And Evelyn, Mercedes, and her oldest daughter, Yamila, often borrowed household items from each other or sent their daughters to each other's apartments with prepared food. Both families lived month to month, depending on public aid, income from the informal economy, and their husbands' sporadic wages as day laborers.

When I met Mercedes, one of her daughters had just graduated from Clemente High School, and the entire family was preparing to move back to San Sebastián. Their large extended family — twelve members total — shared the first floor and basement of the two-story house, and like Evelyn, Frank, and their two daughters, Mercedes's family lived in extremely cramped conditions. Yamila and her husband and their two children slept together in the basement, while Tamara (Yamila's younger sister) and her two children shared one bedroom, and Mercedes, her husband, and their youngest son slept in another on the first floor. The other two daughters slept on a neat, plastic-covered couch in the living room. Although the family was excited about returning to Pepino, Mercedes expressed a great deal of anxiety because she knew they would have to live with either her sister or her son's family until they could find their own place. The last time she was in San Sebastián, she lived in one of town's *caseríos* (public housing), but she was sure that she would not be as fortunate this time, given the limited availability of *caseríos*.

For Mercedes and other Puerto Ricans in Chicago and San Sebastián, moving between "dual home bases" is stressful and often fraught with uncertainty.[1] Most worry about where they will live, a reasonable concern given the paucity of affordable housing for large families in Chicago and the unavailability of public housing both in Chicago and in San Sebastián.

Others are concerned with whether they will adjust to their new environment and find stable employment. Like thousands of other poor and working-class Puerto Ricans, Mercedes's movement between Chicago and San Sebastián can be understood as a "flexible survival strategy" used by migrants to negotiate the changing political-economic realities circumscribing their lives and to enhance their economic status. Puerto Ricans living in Chicago, for example, may move to the island in search of a safer environment for their children and families or to improve their living conditions. They may subsequently return to Chicago for better health care, jobs, or schooling. The decision to move rests partly on migrants' assessment of which place offers the best opportunity to meet household needs, but it is also conditioned by decades of migration practices that have become woven into the fabric of Puerto Rican island and mainland communities.

The back-and-forth movement of Puerto Ricans has received critical attention from academics and policymakers interested in understanding the scope, causes, and consequences of this movement, which challenges traditional views of migration as a unidirectional phenomenon, offering instead a more complicated portrait of migrant life and practices that involves multiple dwellings and, at times, high rates of mobility. Some writers have argued that Puerto Ricans' circular migration is a disruptive process that prevents migrants and their children from establishing strong roots and attachments in local communities, labor markets, and institutions such as schools. Others have countered these claims, emphasizing the structural forces underlying these multiple movements, such as deteriorating labor possibilities as a result of economic restructuring in northeastern cities like New York or changes in minimum wage legislation in Puerto Rico in the 1970s. Still others have demonstrated that only a specific type of migrant engages in circular migration and that most are settled in particular communities. One study notes, for instance, that despite the absence of legal barriers, Puerto Rican migrants are less likely to engage in recurrent migration than are undocumented Mexican immigrants in the United States, who show surprisingly high mobility rates.[2] Over the years, public and academic attention to Puerto Ricans' circular migration — the *vaivén* tradition — has obscured the rootedness of the lives of most Puerto Ricans on the island and the mainland. Thus, while "ir y venir" (going and coming) has become an almost unquestioned cultural trope of the Puerto Rican nation, new work on Puerto Rican communities reveals that "quedarse y sobrevivir" — remaining and surviving — is perhaps a more appropriate way of describing the experience of most Puerto Ricans.[3] Indeed, most Puerto Rican migrants lead deeply local lives, although they do so transnationally, either by actively maintaining political, economic, and social links with another community or by nurturing affective ties connecting them with other places through ethnic celebrations, cultural events, sports, and even stories.

That the lives of so many Puerto Ricans continue to be bound up with events, people, communities, and imaginings from places they left long ago, or perhaps have never even visited, attests to the profound way in which state-sanctioned migration policies from decades earlier have shaped the social, economic, and political landscapes of Puerto Rican communities. The policies guiding Puerto Rico's industrialization program not only succeeded in globalizing the island economy; they also stimulated a variety of migration patterns and social practices that gave initial form to transnational social fields in which people "take actions, make decisions, feel concerns, and develop identities within social networks that connect them to two or more societies simultaneously."[4] Over time, these transnational social fields have matured through the active participation of migrants, returnees, and even nonmigrants whose daily practices in particular places and historically determined times intersect with "transnational networks of meaning and power" in the contested process of "place-making" — that is, the dynamic process whereby local meanings, identities, and spaces are socially constructed within hierarchies of power and difference operating at both a local and a global scale.[5] Place-making is a critical feature of transnational social fields: It is a process that locates transnational phenomena in "specific social relations established between specific people," while simultaneously providing a lens for analyzing instances of conflict, resistance, and accommodation among differently situated individuals and social groups that occur within transnational social fields. For example, community groups, labor unions, and grassroots activists may organize against the presence of global businesses — such as coffee shops or clothing stores — that "from above" threaten to transform a town's distinctive economic and social life. But they may also viciously resist the ways in which migrants, returning with different kinds of cultural knowledge and social remittances, challenge "from below" ideas of group membership, identity, and belonging.[6]

In San Sebastián, this process of place-making has been particularly conflictive since the 1960s, when both the town and the island experienced high levels of return migration. Over the past three decades, many *pepinianos* have echoed Mercedes Rubios's feelings about San Sebastián, saying that it always calls you back home. They have also discovered that returning "home" is not always easy. After years of living *afuera,* many *pepinianos* — particularly women and children — have a difficult time adjusting to their new life in rural Puerto Rico.[7] Return migrants are commonly derided as *Nuyoricans,* a culturally distinct group whose members are usually born and raised *afuera.* While most return migrants eventually overcome such a stigma, the idea of *los de afuera* — literally "those from the outside" or "outsiders" — continues to define membership in the Puerto Rican nation and is used as shorthand to refer to everyone from Dominican immigrants to *Nuyoricans* and "criminals" allegedly terrorizing the island. This *los de afuera* discourse is also employed in local community politics to resist the ways in which "progreso" (progress) threatens "authentic" or "traditional" Puerto Rican culture. Ultimately, these conflicts remind us that place-making within a transnational social field is fundamentally about power — the power to make place out of space, the power to decide who belongs and who does not — and that imagining and forming transnational identities is a historically contingent process circumscribed by power relations operating on local, regional, and transnational levels.

Return Migration to San Sebastián

When I began my fieldwork in San Sebastián, I went to live with my *tía* Cristina in Barrio Saltos. I was not sure at first if I would live with my *tía* and her family throughout my fieldwork or if I would eventually look for my own apartment in town, approximately two miles away. I quickly realized, however, that *despachar en la tienda* — serving customers in the store — was probably one of the best places for me to learn about the community's migration history, since almost all of the people frequenting Cristina's store have lived for a year or longer in a major U.S. city like New York, Newark, or Chicago. My *tía* soon convinced me that living with her would benefit us all. Not only would I be able to do my field research *para terminar la tesis* (finish my dissertation), but I would also be able to help in the store and *servir de compañía* (be good company) for her and my father's cousin, who also lived with Tía Cristi and her husband, Bernardino.

Like most of their neighbors, Cristina, Bernardino, and their two children had returned to San Sebastián in the 1960s after nearly two decades of living in New York City. Cristina had migrated alone to Brooklyn in 1945 and had worked in a garment factory while living with a maternal aunt until she could afford her own apartment, where her brothers and sisters eventually joined her. Shortly after her arrival, Cristina sent for six of her brothers and sisters — including my grandfather — to live with her in Williamsburg, Brooklyn, where much of the family continues to live today. In Brooklyn, Cristina married Bernardino Robles, also from

Pepino. And in 1964, they moved back to San Sebastián with their two children, residing with extended family until they were able to establish themselves in the town. Cristina and Bernardino lived the Puerto Rican dream: After living and working *afuera* for many years, they returned to their hometown, bought some land, built a home, and raised their children in Puerto Rico. They also built a *tiendita* next to their two-story home. In the course of many months of selling food, soda, beer, and shots of rum — and playing countless games of dominoes — I learned that *la tiendita,* like many institutions and homes throughout San Sebastián, is very much a product of the town's long and complicated migration history. It is also an important barrio institution that mediates transnational practices in a number of significant ways.

First and foremost, *la tienda* is a public gathering place for neighbors and friends. While it is primarily frequented by older men, teenage boys and young men mix with this older crowd to share stories, discuss politics, and play dominoes. It is also a customary final stop before one goes *afuera.* During my fieldwork and my tenure *despachando* at the store, every person who left to work and live in the United States spent time there the night before they were to leave. In addition to saying their goodbyes to friends and neighbors, they listened to stories and were given advice and money by my *tía* and anyone else who could afford it, "por si acaso" (just in case) anything went wrong. These discussions, it seemed, were always the most fun for the "old-timers," who enjoyed telling shocking stories of life in American cities and reminiscing about "los tiempos de antes" — the old days.

The *tienda* is also one of the first places one visits upon moving into the neighborhood, a place to meet neighbors and catch up with people one hasn't seen in years. Newcomers visit the store to buy food, use the phone, get information about the area, and initiate a good relationship with Cristina, who almost always provides food on credit despite the large, weathered sign in the store stating "No se fía bebidas alcohólicas" and "No se fía, ni preguntar" ("We do not sell alcohol on credit" and "There is no credit, do not even ask").

The *tienda* also provides critical services for family members, neighbors, and close friends: ready cash in emergencies, check cashing for older residents who are unable to go to *el pueblo* to do so, a place to sell or exchange locally grown fruits and vegetables for nonperishable goods, and a place to buy food and necessary household items on credit until one's check arrives at the beginning of the month. In short, the *tienda* functions as a kind of bank that operates on the basis of personal relationships and connects households in a web of reciprocal arrangements. For residents in Barrio Saltos, this kind of economic safety net is extremely important.

Like other rural municipalities in the island's central region, San Sebastián is quite poor. Its per capita income is one of the lowest on the island, a phenomenon some scholars have referred to as Puerto Rico's "deep regional inequality."[8] Cash-strapped households therefore often make ends meet by raising small animals and growing minor crops — *plátanos, guineos,* and a variety of tubers — for their own consumption or to sell locally. In this context, *la tiendita* emerges as an important economic institution for poor families who don't have banks, credit unions, or credit cards to carry them from month to month.

While working in the *tienda,* I met men and women who had lived *afuera,* returned, and frequently moved to the United States again for short periods of time. In this most appropriate space symbolizing the migration, they shared their stories with me about life in U.S. cities, the difficulty of return, and their dreams and hopes for the future. Although my research focuses specifically on these people's lives, census data suggest that their migration experiences are typical. Between 1970 and 1980, the population of San Sebastián increased by more than 20 percent, a remarkable demographic shift following two decades of population decline in the 1950s and 1960s. This trend, however, is not surprising, and in fact reflects population increases throughout the island. While return migration to the island began in earnest in the 1960s, it reached a peak in the 1970s and continued at a steady although diminished rate through the 1980s.[9] The life histories and stories of the residents of Barrio Saltos reveal myriad economic and noneconomic factors informing migration decisions. They also paint a complicated portrait of life in San Sebastián and the ways in which migration, identity, and the politics of place remain emotionally charged issues in their daily lives.

Return of the Native

> *This* coquí *represents the spirit of struggle of those* pepinianos *who leave their natural habitat in order to contribute from afar the best of their talents and their lives to the unfolding of history and the development of our dear land.*
>
> "El Coquí Pepiniano," a poem accompanying
> the bookmark and pin distributed to visitors
> by the Municipality of San Sebastián

As I began identifying barrio residents who had lived in Chicago, several men at the *tienda* insisted I speak with Carlos Arroyo, a deeply religious man who attended the local Adventist church. But Carlos's whereabouts were disputed by some men stopping in the store for an afternoon beer. "Carlos Arroyo? He's not here. *El anda pa' Chicago*" (He's over in Chicago). "He's here," another man replied. "He lives on the street with the Flamboyán on the corner." And the debate continued until a local schoolteacher offered to take me to meet Carlos to prove that he was indeed living in San Sebastián. This, of course, didn't settle the disagreement — I was told by some of the regulars in the store that they wouldn't believe Carlos was in town until I returned with an interview — but the discussion did highlight the mobile lives of the residents in Saltos. Neighbors take great pride in knowing who lives in the community, their extensive kin networks, and when people come and go. And they are not surprised when people move back and forth between San Sebastián and the United States, because *ir y venir* (coming and going) is embedded in the town's history. As the distinguished writer Luis Rafael Sánchez eloquently explains, the "airbus" carries a floating nation smuggling hope between two ports.[10]

When I finally did meet Carlos and his wife Nilda, they laughed at my description of the confusion about where they lived. Their family had in fact recently lived in Chicago, but they had been back in Saltos for almost three years. The neighbors probably assumed Carlos's recent visit to his sick mother in Chicago was "permanent," an understandable conclusion given that most people leaving the town usually buy either one-way or open-ended fares just in case they decide to stay.[11] Our first meeting appropriately coincided with the beginning of the 1998 NBA finals featuring the Chicago Bulls playing — and eventually defeating — the Utah Jazz. Luckily, we were able to watch the game in his home, since he had recently installed a satellite dish for this very purpose. I was immediately impressed by all the household objects signaling their links to Chicago: a large photograph of the city on the wall, Chicago Bulls memorabilia throughout the home (although, with Michael Jordan and the Bulls' international fame, almost everyone in the town wears Chicago Bulls hats, T-shirts, and jerseys, regardless of where they lived in the United States), and other trinkets stamped with "Chicago" and the city's recognizable skyline.

Carlos began his migration history by describing his life in San Sebastián before he moved to Chicago,

I was born in San Sebastián, in Barrio Guatemala, in the sector Central La Plata. We were very poor. The house where we lived, well, we closed the door with only a little rope. We didn't have doors like we now have today. I studied until the sixth grade — until the fifth grade here in Puerto Rico — and then in 1957 I went to Chicago. My father took me there supposedly for a vacation, which lasted until 1975 . . . . I was ten years old [when I left].

Carlos and another brother moved in with their father and his wife, leaving their mother and other siblings in San Sebastián. In 1960, his mother sold their house in Pepino to pay for airfare to Chicago, and they all moved into a small apartment on Milwaukee Avenue and Racine, then to an apartment on Chicago Avenue, where they lived until Carlos and Nilda married in 1966.

Like other return migrants I interviewed, Carlos and Nilda worked in a number of different factories in the Chicago area. In 1965, he joined his father and brothers at the Merrit Casket Company, but he quickly left to make more money at a nearby rubber factory, where he worked for almost four months. On November 11, 1965, Carlos went to work for the Teletype Corporation in Skokie, where he stayed until the factory closed in 1975. Nilda first arrived in 1965, when she was eighteen years old, and initially worked caring for her cousins' three children. This arrangement quickly soured, however, when Nilda, like many other im/migrants, discovered that the social networks on which she relied provided "grounds for cooperation but at the same time bred conflict."[12] She explains,

The first job I had was I took care of my cousin's three children while she [worked]. She was supposed to find a job for me, right? But time went by and she didn't find anything for me at the factory where she worked. My mom finally told me, "Look, your cousin tricked you. You'd better find another job yourself." So I went and found a factory job at night. A candy factory, the Holloway Company. I had a shift from 12 A.M. to 7 the next day. It was horrible because I was always tired. I would also eat some of the chocolates [she laughs] . . . . That was my second job . . . . After that, I wanted to find a day job, because that job was too hard. I went to work at Freddy Hope Lamps, a lamp factory, but I didn't speak English. The girls would ask me, "Do you speak English?" And I said, "Just a little bit." [She laughs again.] . . . When I would go to work, I looked like a model because I would do my hair, put on make-up and I looked like a model. I worked sanding wood, and I worked at a long table with a lot of black women who had liquor and would drink. The owner was an old man who finally took me out of there. He saw me, I was like a flower, he said, so he put me in a cleaner place working with a Japanese man named Frank . . . and I worked with [him] assembling lamps. It was a really nice job and clean. And I liked it a lot.

Nilda later worked at a plastics factory, the last job she had before she and Carlos married. After marrying and having children, Nilda worked sporadically in a number of clerical positions.

When I asked Carlos and Nilda why they returned to San Sebastián, they responded with what would soon become a familiar refrain among migrants: "We always thought we would return here to raise our children. The younger [they are], the easier [it is for them]." In Puerto Rico, it is a truism that the island is a better place to raise children. My first encounter with this virtually unquestioned belief was a conversation I had with a taxi driver the day I arrived to do fieldwork in Puerto Rico. As he drove me from the airport in Carolina to the nearby town of Río Piedras to catch a *carro público* to San Sebastián, he explained to me that Puerto Rico was the best place to raise children. It was okay to live in the United States in order to work and save some money. But the moment a couple has children, he assured me, they should return to Puerto Rico, where life is "menos complicada y más sana" (less complicated and healthier). When I asked him if he thought San Juan was safer and healthier than other American cities, he said yes, adding, "There is simply no comparison between the life here and *afuera*. In fact, it would be *irresponsible* for people to raise children *afuera* if they could come back and live in Puerto Rico." This sentiment was echoed by almost everyone I met and interviewed in San Sebastián, and it was one of the most popular explanations for a family's return.

When Carlos and Nilda decided to return to San Sebastián in 1975, Carlos came first and began looking for work. Although it was difficult finding work and a place for his family to live, he believed they were making the best decision for their children. When I asked why they decided to return to San Sebastián, Carlos replied,

> C: I believe that my roots called me back here. The family — well, I thought that it would be easier to find work here. We never really considered living in the metropolitan area [San Juan] because we thought that we were going to be faced with the same problems that exist in all big cities, like Chicago.
>
> I: And how did you — did you have problems when you were living in Chicago? Did that also [influence your decision to leave]?
>
> C: We didn't have problems per se. But we did have a vision for our children. And we wanted them to study in a better environment. For that reason, we wanted to come to the countryside.
>
> N: Yes, because here they had a place to play and everything.
>
> C: They had more room to run. And that's how it was. They grew up like little wild children. [He smiles.] In the open country they could go outside every day and there was no fear and it wasn't even slightly dangerous [*ni estaba calientito*]. And little by little, they were able to adjust well.

Carlos and Nilda's concerns are similar to those of parents in both San Sebastián and Chicago, who use migration as a strategy to protect their children from urban dangers — like gangs, violence, drugs, and over-crowded schools — which disproportionately affect residents in poor and working-class neighborhoods. Their decision also highlights the ways in which places like Chicago and San Sebastián are increasingly imagined as mutually exclusive spheres of productive and reproductive labor. As the taxi driver said, you go to the United States to work, but you live and raise your children in Puerto Rico.[13]

Like Carlos and Nilda, Juan and Carmen de Jesús were concerned about potential dangers in Chicago, and returned to San Sebastián in 1977 shortly after their three children were born. One of my father's cousins introduced me to Juan and Carmen one hot afternoon in March. They were *hermanos de la iglesia* (church brethren) who attended one of the growing number of evangelical churches in San Sebastián. As we sat in front of their small, neat home, Carmen, Juan, and their daughter Laura asked me questions about my family and Chicago, and they eagerly shared with me their stories about life *afuera* and in Pepino. As Carmen described her life in Chicago, she grew increasingly animated and repeated several times how happy she had been there. Her various factory jobs and extensive social network of family, friends, and neighbors provided a stable, rich life. But she suddenly became serious when I asked why they had moved back. "[We returned] because of the children, you know. It was best for our children." They were afraid that their son might have problems with gangs when he was older, she explained. So they bought some land in San Sebastián, cashed in Juan's profit shares from the paint company where he worked, and returned to Puerto Rico.

Angie Rubiani, a quiet woman in her early fifties whose husband, Rubén, is a regular at Cristina's store, also said their family returned once they had children. She liked Chicago, she explained to me one night, as we talked in the living room of her small wood house. The balmy, almost uncomfortably warm evening — pleasantly interrupted by the melodious songs of the *coquís* nearby — provided a fascinating contrast to her stories of the gray, bitter-cold Chicago winters that assaulted her daughters' frail health.

They were always sick . . . . The winter was very bad for them. And it was like, when one wasn't sick, the other was. The winter really affected them, you know? Problems with their throats, their ears. And my oldest even got bronchitis twice . . . . The doctor who treated them — no, not the doctor, it was the pharmacist. I would always see him because of my medical plan, he would see the girls and he told me to come back to Puerto Rico. For the girls' health.

When I asked her if they would have stayed if her daughters had been healthier, she shook her head, saying that their neighborhood and the local elementary school "se estaban dañando" (were deteriorating), and she was scared to send her kids to school. So in 1978 they moved back to San Sebastián, although Rubén returned to Chicago to work for six months before settling permanently with his family in Saltos.

What is striking about these and other narratives of return is the way in which people privilege concern about raising their children in explaining why they left Chicago. In fact, their stories are checkered with myriad reasons for return, including sick relatives in Puerto Rico, housing problems in Chicago, battles with depression exacerbated by long, isolated winters, and, not surprisingly, job loss. Thus, immediately after Carlos and Nilda explained that they wanted to raise their children in Puerto Rico, Carlos mentioned that he had been laid off after ten years of working for Teletype Corporation. This was the best time to move, he explained, since the company gave him a severance package that paid for airfare and allowed him to ship his belongings back to Puerto Rico. Juan similarly confided that he was afraid that the paint factory where he worked just before leaving Chicago might relocate, like other blue-collar jobs in Chicago at that time. These narratives of return, however, are consistent with a migration ideology that anticipates that people will return to Puerto Rico to live a better life. According to this logic, migration is an economically motivated decision to "mejorarse y progresar"(better oneself and progress), while return is largely informed by "place utility" and sentimental attachments to home and nation. The assumption is that one returns to Puerto Rico to retire or enjoy life after many years of hard work *afuera*.[14]

Migrants often feel the pressure to succeed *afuera* and return with enough money to buy land, build a home, own cars, and consume at a level commensurate with their new economic and social status. These pressures are reinforced by people's remarks and good wishes before one leaves. For example, the night before eighteen-year-old Willy left to work in Atlantic City, he talked with old-timers who had lived and worked abroad decades earlier. Not only did they congratulate him for leaving and being an example to the other youth, who are constantly reviled as lazy and ignorant of the honor of hard work, but they each patted him on the back, shook his hand, and said, "Suerte. Y vuelve con mucho dinero" (Good luck. And come back with a lot of money). Willy laughed nervously and assured them all that that was the idea. These interactions confirm other scholars' accounts of the social pressure migrants face to succeed abroad and alter their social status upon return. As Grasmuck and Pessar point out, the popular refrain "If things go well for you over there, write" not only reinforces the expectation of succeeding abroad, but it is also a key mechanism in mythologizing migrant success by erasing failures.[15]

Many *pepinianos* explained that they never adjusted to life *afuera*. In fact, they often compared themselves to the *coquí*, the tiny, melodious frog native to Puerto Rico that popularly represents "Puerto Ricanness." Like the *coquí*, I was repeatedly told, *true* Puerto Ricans cannot thrive outside of Puerto Rico. They might be able to live, *pero no cantan afuera* (but they don't sing outside). For that reason, many proudly reminded me, to really live your life, you must return to your native land. But for many, returning to San Sebastián is not easy. Although most of the people I interviewed had been back in the town for at least fifteen years, they recalled in vivid detail the difficulties they had faced in adjusting to life in San Sebastián again. Women and children were particularly clear about how they suffered during this transition. As I demonstrate below, these narratives reveal that migration is often a conflictive process, in which women and children contest and resist new gender and generational ideologies and culturally prescribed behaviors that circumscribe their lives.

The Suffering of Return

The past decade has witnessed a dramatic shift in migration research, as feminist scholars have theorized the role of gender in migration processes. As many of these writers have demonstrated, migration decisions are guided by kinship and hierarchies of power based on gender and generation within households and among migrant social networks, which are often sites of struggle and contestation. Return migration in particular raises troubling questions, since women frequently fear losing independence gained in the United States.[16] My research among return migrants in San Sebastián revealed similar concerns, as women described *el sufrimiento* (suffering) involved in returning to the island after living and working in Chicago. Family and community pressure to stay at home, a renewed dependency on husbands because of inadequate public transportation, and limited job opportunities all contributed to women's dissatisfaction upon returning to Puerto Rico.

Elena Rodriguez is the energetic pastor of an evangelical church who has lived in San Sebastián for more than twenty years. Born in Aibonito, in the southeastern region of Puerto Rico, Elena was raised in Chicago

with her nine brothers and sisters. At the age of seventeen, she married
Lolo. Shortly after they were married, they went to live in San Sebastián.
When I asked her if she wanted to return to Puerto Rico, she smiled and
said, "This is where the story begins! You cannot even imagine how much
I suffered in that change!" When she first arrived in Puerto Rico, she lived
with her mother-in-law for a month, while her husband remained in
Chicago with plans to eventually join her there. She explained:

I came to Puerto Rico before [my husband] to set things up. And in that month,
well, for me, that month was terrible for me, because there weren't the same facilities you could find [in Chicago]. When I began to stay in my mother-in-law's
house and she would say to me, "There's no water," . . . and I saw that the stores
were far away, that there weren't any stores close or pharmacies close . . . and
when one left the doctor's office worse than when they arrived . . . I saw all this
and I wrote a letter to my husband saying, "Send me a ticket home fast because
I'm leaving. I am not going to live here." . . . Well, he sent me [and our two chil-
dren] tickets and I left.

Shortly after Elena returned to Chicago, however, her sister-in-law died
in San Sebastián, and her husband decided it was best for them to return
to Puerto Rico to take care of his mother. Because they didn't have their
own home, they lived with Lolo's mother, which only made a difficult
transition worse.

You know the saying "Quien se casa, casa quiere" [Everyone who marries wants
a home]? And living in another's house, no matter how well they treat you, you
want your own home. I lived in a room next to the carport [marquesina] and I
already had two children, and I felt uncomfortable in my mother-in-law's home.
And seeing that there was never any water — I had to go with buckets to get water
from the neighbors. And carrying that water in order to do something to help my
mother-in-law. And my husband was only making sixty dollars a week. [With
that] we had to pay the bank, feed our children — it wasn't easy. And I'm telling
you, for me it was so traumatic. I cried every night because I wanted to leave.
Every night. And I told my compañero, "If you want to stay, you stay. But I'm leaving. I can't take this anymore." Because I saw how if my children got sick here —
in Chicago, [the doctors] took care of them quickly, but here I had to wait to be
called, sometimes almost three hours, while my children suffered from fever, pain,
and they still made me wait . . . . I finally wrote to my father . . . and I told him,
"Papá, send me tickets because I'm leaving. I'm going to leave my husband
because life here is full of suffering (muy sufrida) . . . ." This is how I lived. It was
so traumatic. And honestly, honestly, I cried to leave [Puerto Rico] for ten years.

Elena's husband begged her to stay, and he eventually convinced her to
use the money her father sent for tickets back to Chicago to begin build-

ing a home of their own. She stayed in San Sebastián, but regretted her decision for a very long time.

Like Elena, Nilda vividly recalls her difficult transition to life in San Sebastián. Even though she disliked the weather in Chicago, she preferred living there because life was easier in the city and there was more to do. They lived near museums and parks, and they had access to public transportation. She adapted to her new life in San Sebastián slowly, she explained, and she was much happier once they had their own home. She still complains, however, about the town's lack of public transportation, a common lament among almost all the women in the town. Unless one owns a car and knows how to drive, one has to depend on the town's *carros públicos,* which run irregularly until 2 P.M., and they often have to wait until drivers have a full car of five or six people before they go on their routes. Women complained bitterly about this new dependence on husbands, friends, and family, and were frustrated that these transportation problems limited their movement, largely confining them to their homes.

Women's isolation was further heightened by their failure to work outside the home, a remarkable difference from their lives in Chicago. When I asked women about their jobs on the mainland, they were extremely animated and provided great detail about all the places where they worked, what they enjoyed about their jobs, the people with whom they worked, and frequently the racial/ethnic politics of the workplace. In San Sebastián, their labor history changed dramatically. Nilda worked irregularly when she first arrived, but she decided to collect unemployment after she began to have back problems. Carmen also stayed at home collecting unemployment while her husband worked in a series of factory jobs in San Sebastián, Isabela, and Aguadilla. Angie has been employed sporadically since her return and currently cares for an old man, cleaning his house and cooking his meals. For some women, working outside the home became a necessary condition for agreeing to stay in Puerto Rico. Elena, for example, became very involved in her local church. She eventually studied to be a pastor and now leads her own community. And Yahaira, a young woman who, like Elena, was born in Puerto Rico but raised in Chicago, decided to stay in San Sebastián only after her husband agreed to help her open a small cafeteria in the town.

Women rarely complained about their new domestic roles when I asked them directly about how the demands and expectations in their households had changed upon their return to San Sebastián. Rather, they often explained that they enjoyed staying home to care for their children. But in daily conversations, they frequently expressed frustration with how much more difficult domestic tasks were in San Sebastián. In addition to the problem with water — which continues to be a problem even today — women complained that in Puerto Rico they had to cook more often, it required more time to buy food because of poor public transportation, and there were fewer entertainment venues. The women also noted that because their husbands earned less money and the cost of living was higher in Puerto Rico than in the United States, they had to be creative in stretching their money. These new responsibilities increased women's *sufrimiento* and prompted some to advise their sisters to resist their husbands' efforts to return to Puerto Rico. Elena explained to me one day:

It wasn't easy. After living in Chicago where you have your good job, and you would eat out on Fridays and maybe Saturdays too . . . and to come to Puerto Rico I had to get used to cooking breakfast, lunch, and dinner. . . . It wasn't easy. . . . After one has lived in Chicago, it's not easy to adjust to life here. . . . I would never tell anyone to come to Puerto Rico [to live]. No one, no one, no one. When my sisters would come to visit, [I would take them aside and tell them], "Don't come to Puerto Rico to live. Leave me here, it's okay since I'm more settled here now. . . . My husband is here and I have a house. . . . But I would advise you not to come to live in Puerto Rico."

Return migration influenced domestic arrangements, making housework less egalitarian. While none of the women explicitly discussed their husbands' willingness to share in domestic chores, they implied that housework was primarily their responsibility and expressed great discontent with the amount of housework they had to do and the fact that it usually involved more labor-intensive chores than in Chicago. In Chicago, most of the women worked outside the home and had more disposable income, allowing them a reprieve from some cooking duties. Their lack of wage labor in San Sebastián, as well as their husbands' reduced earnings, circumscribed the household's disposable income and contributed to women's feelings of being overwhelmed by domestic tasks.

While Elena, Yahaira, and Nilda admit that they eventually adjusted to life in San Sebastián and, in retrospect, believe it was the best move for them, they also describe their children's difficulty adjusting to life in San Sebastián. Language problems, different norms for dress, and the stigma attached to being *de afuera* alienated migrant children from their peers, especially in school. Yahaira worried about her son's performance in school because of his language acquisition. When I asked her if Tito had problems with other students, she assured me that he got along with everyone. Overhearing our conversation, Tito politely corrected his mother, saying in Spanish, "I like it here, I like being in the open air and everything. But at school they bother me. They call me 'the gringo.' Well, they used to call me that, because I didn't speak Spanish. I spoke English too much. I used to get really mad." Yahaira was surprised by her son's response and sympathetically added that there were certain words *she* still couldn't pronounce correctly, being English dominant. Then, slipping into English, she complained, "There are some things that I'll never get used to here. People are so *nosey* here. Everybody *quiere saber la vida de uno*" (wants to know about your life).

Language has long been a lightning rod for debates about Puerto Rican identity, culture, and nationalism. In the early twentieth century, a language policy that promoted English as the official language of instruction at all grade levels was a key feature of the Americanization campaign that sought not only to cement loyalty to the U.S. colonial project by inspiring "admiration for 'American' history, polity, and symbols," but also to "uplift" the Puerto Rican people, who were regarded as racially inferior and mired in a language and culture devoid of democratic vocabulary and ideals.[17] Mandatory English instruction in the schools was reversed in 1952, but debates regarding the extent to which Puerto Ricans should be bilingual, the social meanings attached to English and Spanish use, and the relationship among language and cultural and national identity continue to incite impassioned responses.

Not surprisingly, return migrants, whose social identities and linguistic practices challenge the assumption that *a* language corresponds to *a* culture, have become embroiled in these debates and represent for some the unsavory consequences of globalization and transnational living. According to linguistic anthropologist Ana Celia Zentella, island writers, intellectuals, and government officials have expressed profound concern about the ways in which return migrants and their use of Spanglish and code-switching — alternating Spanish and English words, clauses, and phrases — threaten Puerto Rico's linguistic, and therefore cultural, integrity. Puerto Rico's distinctive colonial history with the United States has reinforced the persistent coupling of Puerto Rican identity with the Spanish language, contributing to what Zentella describes as a belief held by many island intellectuals that "English has had a continuously deteriorating effect on the Spanish of Puerto Rico and that, as a result, Puerto Rico's national identity itself is being threatened."[18]

The presence of return migrants and transnational actors throughout Puerto Rico requires an understanding of citizenship and nation that transcends the island's borders, although many dismiss these challenges "from below" as illegitimate, a source of corruption and danger. Puerto Ricans also resist efforts to use language to mobilize ideas of nation "from above," a source of great debate. This became particularly evident in March 1998, when the U.S. Congress debated the Young Bill, the statist-backed legislation promoting Puerto Rican statehood. Almost every night in March, residents in Barrio Saltos argued in *tía* Cristina's store about Puerto Rico's political status and the PNP's attempts to forge *la estadidad jíbara* — the Creole state, based on the idea that Puerto Rico could become a U.S. state while maintaining its cultural and linguistic integrity. One evening, Gonzalo, an octogenarian who had lived for more than thirty years in Brooklyn and a loyal *popular,* asked me if I preferred to speak English or Spanish. When I told him I preferred to speak Spanish in Puerto Rico, he smiled and warned me, "If we vote for state-hood, they are going to impose English as the official language. And you know, I ask myself why. Why? If there are more countries that speak Spanish than English, why English? In the United States, wherever you go, people speak Spanish. Even the Chinese speak Spanish. They speak it badly *[mata'o]*, but they speak it."

The topic came up again the next night as I played dominoes at the store, but this time it generated a much more heated debate. My uncle Bernardino and Ramón, a regular at the store who eventually migrated to New Jersey as a temporary agricultural worker, agreed that there was no reason for English to be the official language in Puerto Rico. Another man who joined our domino game disagreed, saying that it was good for English to be the official language because it was the international lan-guage of trade, politics, and commerce. Ramón answered angrily, "Why don't the Americans just learn Spanish? Or why can't we just be bilin-gual?" To which the old man replied, "Just look at Canada. Over there, everything is in English and French, and look at how many problems they're having now," referring to problems surrounding Quebec's nation-alist movement. As in most discussions of politics and Puerto Rico's polit-ical status, the debate quickly degenerated, with the old man ending the argument by saying that the problem with "us Puerto Ricans" is that "we're not prepared" *(preparado)*: "If we accept English as the official lan-guage, we would be able to overcome our problems and better ourselves."

It is of particular interest that in these debates, language represents cul-tural authenticity. Adults who returned to San Sebastián as young chil-dren — especially as teenagers — still agonize over their ability to speak Spanish not only correctly, but with a Puerto Rican accent, very quickly, and with clipped endings. One thirty-seven-year-old man confided that he is self-conscious about speaking Spanish because he believes he still has an accent betraying his U.S. upbringing. When he first arrived from the Chicago area back in the 1960s, Wilson was teased constantly about his language skills, a painful memory that reinforced his resolve to stay and raise his children in Puerto Rico. In order to compensate for his linguistic failures, he devotes his free time to traveling around the island attending each town's cultural festival and learning everything he can about Puerto Rican history and folklore. It wasn't easy living in San Sebastián after growing up in the United States, Wilson admitted. But in an interesting twist, he and other adults who were once subjected to teasing now readily condemn today's youth, using the same racialized language of contamination, disorder, and pathology that was directed at them when they occupied a similarly ambiguous cultural position. Wilson, like other returnees and nonmigrants, believes that many of Puerto Rico's problems — and San Sebastián's in particular — can be attributed to *los de afuera*, outsiders who not only refuse to assimilate to life in Puerto Rico, but who dare to transform its cultural, social, and political-economic landscape as well.

Los de Afuera: Community, Culture, and the Politics of Identity

As I was typing my field notes one night, a family friend entered the room and started asking me questions about my computer, my research project, and the interviews I was conducting in the town. When I explained that I was interviewing people who had lived in Chicago and other North American cities, he offered to introduce me to some teachers at the school where he worked as a physical education teacher. He also mentioned that he had a thirteen-year-old student in his class who used to live in Chicago, and that his school, like many in San Sebastián, was filled with students from the United States but lacked the resources to provide bilingual educational programs and support services for these struggling students. When I told Rafael that I would be interested in meeting this student to talk about how he has adapted to life here, he quickly responded, "He hasn't adapted. That's the problem with these young kids *de afuera*. They don't want to adapt themselves to their new environment. They want *us* to adapt to *them*." Rafael explained that the student refused to speak Spanish and was indifferent to his teachers' warnings that he would fail unless he tried harder to do so. "He only says, 'I don't speak Spanish,' and that's it. He doesn't try to adapt or anything." "It must be very difficult for an adolescent to get used to a new environment," I offered. "You know, he's dealing with all the problems of being an adolescent, in addition to being in a new and different environment." Rafael answered in a slightly condescending way, "Of course. But even though the other students try to be cool with him, he just doesn't want to change. He wants everyone to change for him."

While I was not surprised by Rafael's comments, I was struck by the irony of his observations about *los que vienen de afuera*. Like Wilson and other young adults, Rafael was born in the United States but raised in Puerto Rico. And he too faced problems adjusting to his new life here, although he was much younger when he arrived in San Sebastián, a fact he admits made the assimilation process much easier for him. What was most striking about this conversation was actually how unremarkable it was. Other than discussions about Puerto Rico's political status, laments about *la juventud de hoy* (today's youth) and *los de afuera* were the most popular topics of conversations during my fieldwork in San Sebastián. People argued passionately about contemporary social problems and attempted to provide explanations for the cultural changes they witnessed. For them, drugs, crime, sexual promiscuity, and a disdain for work, family, and community were the unwelcome consequences of a transnational existence enabling *los de afuera* to dwell among them.

Narrowly defined, *los de afuera* refers to Puerto Ricans who currently reside on the island after many years of living in the United States. More broadly, the label popularly applies to Dominicans, *pillos* (criminals), *asesinos* (murderers), and anyone else who does not properly belong in the imagined circle-of-the-we of the Puerto Rican nation.[19] Like the term *Nuyorican*, *los de afuera* is usually employed pejoratively, connoting a culturally distinct group whose values, behaviors, language, and dress directly challenge dominant understandings of "authentic" Puerto Rican culture. This stigmatizing label also homogenizes an extremely diverse group allegedly responsible for contaminating, polluting, and corrupting national identity.[20] On both a local and a national level, *los de afuera* is used to define membership in the immediate and national community. It is also strategically deployed in local politics to resist the transnational flow of ideas, people, and capital that is believed to destabilize traditional understandings of community, identity, and place.

In San Sebastián, young Puerto Rican men and women who do not fit the expected norms of behavior, dress, and linguistic performance are immediately labeled *de afuera,* regardless of whether or not they have actually lived outside of Puerto Rico. Multiple piercings, hip-hop styles for men, and "provocative dress" for women are commonly regarded as markers of one's outside status and usually provoke pointed remarks by older barrio residents. On several occasions, *la tienda* became the arena for heated intergenerational conflicts between young and old men who regularly demonstrated their disdain for each other. Because Cristina's store was directly across from the basketball courts, young men playing basketball or hanging out around the courts would often cross paths with the old men drinking and playing dominoes at the *tienda*. These men — most of whom had lived *afuera* for varying lengths of time — consistently complained about how the young men dressed, the music they listened to, and their multiple piercings, attributing these behaviors to the negative influences they received while living in the United States. One evening when I was working in the store, I jokingly told a young man with multiple piercings that he shouldn't smoke because he'd die young. One of the regulars looked up from his beer and sneered, "Que se muera, no más! Mira cómo es! Déjalo que se muera!" (Let him die! Just look at him! Just let him die!). The young man looked surprised at the outburst, said something under his breath, and left the store. Some men playing dominoes witnessed the exchange and laughed. One man quickly commented, "La juventud de hoy está perdida. Vienen de afuera, vienen para acá y no hacen na" (The youth of today is lost. They come from the outside, they come here and they don't do anything).

The idea of "la juventud perdida" was a common lament. Older community residents prayed for them — "Roguemos por los jóvenes, tan metidos en el vicio, en la droga, en la prostitución" (Let us pray for our youth, completely lost in vice, in drugs, in prostitution) — complaining that the young people were vastly different from how they were when they were younger — "La juventud de hoy no es lo mismo de antes. Son perdidos, y no saben vivir la vida" (Today's youth is not the same as before. They are lost, and they don't know how to live their lives) — and accusing them of being lazy, unmotivated, and corrupted by life *afuera*. Over a game of dominoes one day, the topic emerged again, as two older men tried to convince me and another woman, Beba, that today's youth were worthless. Severino commented, "'Chacho! Estos jóvenes — yo diría que solo un 25 porciento de la juventud hoy en día son buenos. Jóvenes que valen la pena y que no están metidos en problemas — en las gangas, en la droga" (Man! These young people — I'd say that only 25 percent of today's youth are good. Young people who really are worthwhile and are not involved in problems — in gangs, in drugs). "Sí," Carlos added, "la juventud está perdida" (Yes, the youth are lost). When Beba protested that this surely was not true, that there had to be more than 25 percent of the youth who were worthwhile, she was corrected by Severino. "No, no. Mira, los jóvenes de hoy no trabajan! No saben trabajar. Cogen el welfare, los cupones. No saben trabajar como nosotros . . . por eso los jóvenes son bancarrota. Es el modernismo — el mundo moderno. Y es lo mismo que allá [en los Estados Unidos]" (No, no. Look, today's young people don't work! They don't know how to work. They collect welfare, food stamps. They don't know how to work like us . . . . That's the reason why the youth are a lost cause. It's modernism — the modern world. And it's the same over there in the United States).

Young men, according to these narratives, did not know the value of work, the *honra* (honor) of making money and living an honest life. Moreover, unlike the critics, who had also lived *afuera* for varying lengths of time, these young men had allegedly internalized the cultural values attributed to urban "ghetto" living and had brought them to the island: Gangs, drugs, and increased violence in Puerto Rico were blamed in large part on *los que vienen de afuera*.

Notions of "la juventud perdida" are extremely gendered. While young men were derided for their apparent refusal to be productive members of the community, women *de afuera* were blamed for their domestic failings: They were immodest, "locas" (wild), "fiesteras" (partyers), "enamoradas" (easily seduced), and responsible for failed marriages and the moral deterioration of the town. Young women's dress was a particular site of struggle and an important terrain upon which ideas about the nation, gender, and identity were enacted.[21] When I first arrived in San Sebastián, for example, one of my great-aunts took enormous pride in introducing me to her friends and neighbors. When she invited me to meet the men at the bakery across the street from her home, she pointed out that although I was born and raised *afuera,* I was not "una de esas locas de afuera. Miren cómo se viste" (one of those wild girls from the United States. Look at how she dresses). And she gestured to my front, highlighting my appropriately long skirt and conservative blouse. "Es como si fuera criada aquí, como en los tiempos de antes" (It's like she was raised here, like in the old days), she concluded.

Young women born and raised on the island who do not fit expected norms of dress and behavior are criticized for acting as if they were *de afuera*. "[My granddaughter] se viste como si fuera de Nueva York" (dresses as if she were from New York), a middle-aged woman complained to four of her friends while visiting from Bayamón in Cristina's store. The comment provoked an intense conversation among the five middle-aged women, each of whom had lived at least ten years in Brooklyn, Newark, New Jersey, or Chicago and had returned in the 1970s to live in San Sebastián and the San Juan metropolitan area, only to find that the "American" lifestyle and values they hoped to leave behind now reached and corrupted young island women. *Nueva York* and *de afuera* are part of a racialized sexual vocabulary of contamination and impurity used to describe women who defy culturally prescribed roles of dress, sexual behavior, and modesty. Like many young Chicanas and *mejicanas,* young Puerto Rican women are constantly watched, their bodies, dress, and sexuality policed by family members and neighbors.[22] An essential component of this policing is gossip, that "semi-private, semi-public talk" that, as anthropologist Roger Lancaster cleverly demonstrates, "can take up almost any subject and imbue it with significance." In the case of returnees and transnational migrants, however, gossip often serves a punitive function of further marginalizing those groups already stigmatized as other and hence imagined as being outside the Puerto Rican nation.[23]

Thus, when Melinda, a flashy young mother of three then living in New York, made several trips to San Sebastián within six months, it was rumored that she was there because she had AIDS and needed to rest in the quiet of San Sebastián. Although no one ever really *knew* whether or not she had AIDS, the fact that people believed she was dying from the still-stigmatized disease — she was very thin, pale (she arrived in the middle of the New York winter), and reportedly used drugs — fueled gossip about her sexual liaisons with *los jóvenes* and married men in the neighborhood. On many occasions, angry wives fought with their husbands at Cristina's store, accusing them of having sexual liaisons with "esa loca de afuera que tiene SIDA" (that wild girl *de afuera* who has AIDS). Melinda emphatically denied the accusations and blamed the town's provincialism for perpetuating the rumors in the absence of any evidence. Regardless of its veracity, the gossip (and marital strain) Melinda's presence provoked highlights again that women's bodies are a site of struggle and contestation, and that transnational migrants not only are blamed for culturally polluting the Puerto Rican nation, but are popularly regarded as diseased and capable of physically contaminating the body politic with AIDS and other diseases. Alberto Sandoval Sánchez notes that the metaphor of an "air bus" or an "air bridge" facilitating movement between Puerto Rican and U.S. cities has also become "a space of continuity and contiguity that makes possible the passage of those condemned by Puerto Rican society: the sick, the infected, the contaminated, the marginal."[24]

HIV/AIDS is unquestionably one of the most pressing problems facing Puerto Rican communities: The Centers for Disease Control report that Puerto Rico registers one of the highest rates of HIV/AIDS in the United States and Puerto Rican women are one of the fastest-growing sectors infected with HIV/AIDS in the United States. Yet how a public health crisis that transcends international boundaries is reframed as a problem imported by migrants and those already on the margins speaks to the way ideas of purity — racial, linguistic, sexual, cultural — are marshaled to "uphold the frontier allegedly separating the island from the United States, and islander elites from U.S./lower-class Puerto Ricans . . . [and to] distinguish 'real' Puerto Ricans from imposters."[25] These metaphors of contamination, sexual pollution, and corruption of the nation have also been applied to immigrants in the United States, particularly to Mexican immigrants, who, as Leo Chávez demonstrates in his study on popular images of U.S. immigration, have been "represented almost entirely in alarmist imagery" of crisis, bombs, disease, and invasion since the 1960s.[26] In both instances, women's bodies, sexual practices, and reproductive potential are the objects of disdain, fear, and even punitive social policy measures like California's Proposition 187 in 1994, which sought to deny publicly funded health care and education to undocumented immigrants and their children. Such draconian policy measures have not been adopted in Puerto Rico, but the discourse enveloping return migrants is of the same xenophobic cloth, although with an important caveat. As Frances Negrón-Muntaner explains, cultural, linguistic, and sexual "impurity" implies hybridity and ultimately replacement, since "given the nation-building narratives' concern with reproduction, a hybrid cannot produce; it is sterile."[27]

Young women are also criticized for being out too much, relying too often on relatives to care for their children, and not properly attending to their husbands. Invariably, people blame these problems on the unsavory influence of American popular culture and distinct gender ideologies threatening "traditional" Puerto Rican family values. As feminist scholars have aptly noted, women are expected to signify cultural tradition and are the contested terrain upon which nationalist projects and ethnic identity and self-respect are constructed, resisted, and reconfigured. For some Filipino immigrant parents in California, for example, their young daughters' bodies and sexual behavior serve to "assert cultural superiority over the dominant group" and to resist white society's disparagement of their racialized sexuality. Research among Indian immigrant families in New York City uncovers similar dynamics, where ideas of "tradition" and the "authentic immigrant family" are contingent on young women's chastity, and shows how these ideas are produced transnationally. Sociologist Yen Le Espiritu notes that while such strategies are indeed attempts on the part of racialized groups to assert moral superiority over oppressor groups, they are problematic because they reinforce "masculinist and patriarchal power" and unfairly circumscribe women's lives by imposing "numerous restrictions on their autonomy, mobility, and personal decision making."[28] When Puerto Rican women fail to live up to constructed norms of behavior or dress, they are punished and labeled *de afuera,* a process that demonstrates the ways in which a glorified Puerto Rican past depends on racialized constructions of women and motherhood.

Community concern with women's private and public behavior also reveals important intergenerational conflicts over shifting cultural values regarding gender and sexuality that are embedded in regional political economies. As ethnographer Caridad Souza has shown in her research among working-class *puertorriqueñas* in New York City, young women's reproductive work is critical to households whose survival depends on family and community solidarity through the exchange of goods and services, and the pooling of resources among numerous kin and non-kin households. In this context, young women are expected to remain *en la casa* — inside the home or family — for important material and cultural reasons: Without their reproductive work, adult women — mothers, grandmothers, and aunts — are easily overwhelmed by (and unable to meet) the reproductive and productive demands within their own households and their kin networks. Being *una muchacha de la casa* also means abiding by the cultural norms of respectability, chastity, and family honor valued by the community. To be *de la calle* — outside the home or, literally, on the streets — is to be transgressive, sexually promiscuous, and dangerous.[29] Because this good-girl/bad-girl dichotomy also maps onto dominant understandings of those who are *de acá* and *de afuera,* young women from the mainland are usually regarded with suspicion, as *de la calle,* until they prove themselves otherwise.

In short, the term *de afuera* reproduces an understanding of community that smoothes over heterogeneity and changes over time. It also stigmatizes those people whose economic marginalization obliges them to move for survival. As many of the town's residents quietly lament, jobs are scarce in San Sebastián. The closing of Central La Plata, the town's sugar refinery, in May 1996, in addition to recent factory relocations and layoffs, have left thousands of men and women unemployed. And despite organized attempts to resist plant closings, San Sebastián's unemployment rate hovers around 25 percent, a statistic that does not include workers underemployed in low-wage service sector jobs. Global economic restructuring has had a tremendous impact on San Sebastián. The 1998 repeal of Law 936 (which awarded tax exempt status to North American companies) and factories' increased reliance on temporary workers have heightened laborers' vulnerability. When I asked *pepinianos* if one could find work in the town, they answered tentatively that people could find *trabajitos* (little jobs) here and there. But as Rubén, one of the most vocal critics of *la juventud perdida,* pointed out, they were usually dead-end jobs, so even young people with college degrees — including his own daughters, who were trained in the sciences but unable to find employment in the area — would almost certainly have to *irse pa' fuera.*

Young people, however, often serve as convenient scapegoats for larger political-economic problems.[30] Older adults regard them as significantly different from earlier generations — usually lazier, unwilling to make sacrifices or delay gratification — and guided by a value system qualitatively different from that of their parents or grandparents. Much of today's intergenerational conflict in San Sebastián is certainly a result of generational distance and misunderstanding. Yet the past two decades have also witnessed key political-economic changes throughout Puerto Rico — and in San Sebastián in particular — that have prevented many young women and men from participating in the formal economy and leading the kind of life their forbears supposedly led, usually as migrants themselves. Some scholars have described Puerto Rico as a "post-work society," whereby the American government promotes a political-economic system that discourages wage labor and instead provides federal transfer payments as a way to help people survive while maintaining the political status quo.[31] Others have carefully documented how the various stages of Puerto Rico's industrialization program have differentially incorporated some workers and marginalized others since the 1950s.[32] Anthropologist Helen Safa, for example, notes in her research among female factory workers in western Puerto Rico that most believe it is easier for women than for men to find employment. For most young *pepinianos,* unemployment, migration, varied domestic arrangements, and marital strain have very little to do with poor values and being *de afuera* or *de la calle.* These problems are largely the product of the economic marginalization of Puerto Ricans both on the island and the mainland. In San Sebastián, however, the *los de afuera* trope reveals not only disdain for outside influence, but deep ambivalence concerning the consequences of a transnational existence.

"Progreso" and "Some Things We Don't Want to Talk About"

Shortly after the 1990 census statistics were released, San Sebastián's local newspapers ran a series of articles questioning their accuracy. The town's official population of 38,799 surprised many *pepinianos,* who estimated more than 50,000 residents, a number that "would have made us into a 'city,' qualifying for federal funds directly from Washington."[33] While some critics blamed census workers for undercounting both households and their members, others argued that the town's inadequate infrastructure — such as roads, highways, and government offices — prevented companies and factories from locating in the area and providing the jobs needed to attract new residents. According to the town's local newspaper, *El Pepino,* poor economic development was responsible for the town's slow growth.

If we recognize [the lack of infrastructure], we then understand that the population stagnation is a response to the economic stagnation of the last twenty years. Therefore, rather than blaming those who conducted the census, the reasonable [alternative] is to concern ourselves with providing adequate alternatives and developing the collective will necessary to achieve our goals for the town *[pueblo].* We must move from the lamenting stage to the stage of creating better goals that work for San Sebastián, which is to work for the present and the future of our children.[34]

While San Sebastián's "population stagnation" is debatable, these comments clearly reveal profound frustration with political-economic changes that were fundamentally altering the town's social, political, and cultural landscape. Return migration in the 1970s and the 1980s, which accounted for much of the 10 percent increase in the town's population, tremendously strained local schools already struggling with limited resources, overcrowding, and poor administration. Another town newspaper, *El Palique,* reported extensively on the rising problem of "U.S.-style" gangs and vandalism in the town.[35] The worsening crisis of the town's sugar refinery heightened this insecurity: More than half of San Sebastián's residents depended either directly or indirectly on La Plata, which generated approximately $17 million for the local economy. Layoffs, slowdowns, and the fear of plant closure threatened to ruin the town. All of these pressures predictably informed the town's mayoral elections in 1992. That year, PNP candidate Justo Medina successfully campaigned as the one most capable of bringing *progreso* to the struggling town.

Born in San Sebastián but raised in Perth Amboy, New Jersey (the city fondly referred to as "the little San Sebastián"), Medina is a controversial figure, embodying many of the ambiguities and contradictions characterizing the town. Not only is he the first PNP mayor in a town deeply loyal to *los populares,* he is also *de afuera,* a fact that, according to his critics, makes him unfit to be mayor. His "outsider status" was a flash point during the campaign, as his supporters defended him against charges of being "imported from Perth Amboy." As one writer in *El Pepino* pointed out,

Speaking of candidates imported from Perth Amboy only contributes to further dividing our people. In San Sebastián, those with more or less have had to abandon our small homeland *pepiniana* to look for work opportunities elsewhere. It is precisely the love for our town that makes us return. Who in *Pepino* has not traveled to Perth Amboy or some other place in the United States and does not have a relative or friend living outside of San Sebastián due to circumstances that prevent him from remaining here? Does this make a difference in the human quality of those who emigrate and later return?[36]

Soon after taking office, Medina was praised for quickly implementing important changes. He addressed the town's long-standing sewage problems and ordered the cleanup of the Guatemala River. He also improved garbage service and within two months closed a garbage dump the former mayor had failed to close in his four years in office. Medina made a number of cosmetic changes as well — painting the town plaza, the municipal building, and the medical center, as well as cleaning the streets — that delighted *pepinianos* and rekindled their civic pride.[37] In short, don Justo (as he is popularly referred to) was bringing long-awaited progress to Pepino.

While many continue to praise don Justo for his work, others are extremely critical. A key issue dividing people is a difference in their understanding of the meaning and consequences of *progreso.* On the one hand, *pepinianos* celebrate recent changes enhancing San Sebastián's reputation as a commercial center and assure me that "San Sebastián es un pueblo chico, pero estamos progresando" (San Sebastián is a small town, but we are progressing). When I asked Lina, a thirty-seven-year-old woman who lived in Brooklyn for many years, to describe San Sebastián, she focused on the changes she had witnessed over the past seven years. "There have been a lot of changes, there didn't use to be so many houses in this barrio [of Saltos], but now there are so many. The land is more expensive and they have made new highways. [San Sebastián] is town that is progressing [*progresando*]." Other women, especially return migrants like Elena, comment on the new stores and fast-food restaurants in town, explaining that it makes life easier for them. Being able to shop and consume in places that are familiar to them as a result of their time *afuera* helps to ease the transition to life in San Sebastián.

One evening in the store, Rubén and other regulars provided insight into the impact of recent changes by comparing contemporary changes with the 1960s and 1970s. "Hay gente con mucho chavo aquí" (There are people with a lot of money here), Rubén commented, quickly rubbing his thumb and middle finger together. This money comes not only from migrant remittances, they reminded me, but also from the town's long, distinguished history of sugar production. Although thousands of *pepinianos* left to work in factories rather than in sugar production, the town, its banks, and their children's education have all been financed, as one *colono* eloquently explained, "con el dinero de la caña" (with money from the cane). But this is not considered *progreso*. Instead, new infrastructure, opportunities to consume luxury goods, and North American chain stores symbolize the town's progress, now attributed largely to the mayor. "En estos últimos ocho años, han habido cambios bien grandes, un progreso enorme. Puentes nuevos, todo — todo nuevo" (In the past eight years, there have been big changes, enormous progress. New bridges, new — everything new), Rubén proudly explained. "Es el alcalde que viene de afuera" (It's the mayor *de afuera*), he said with a wink.

Others, however, are more cautious, wary of the effects of *progreso* on the town. The Asociación de Comerciantes, Empresarios y Profesionales del Pepino (Association of Merchants, Businessmen, and Professionals of Pepino), for example, actively opposes the proliferation of commercial centers and megastores in the town, arguing that they will destroy local businesses, which are unable to compete with them. In a series of articles and public hearings, the Asociación urged the mayor to advance a development plan that would protect small locally owned businesses by helping them secure low-interest loans and capital investment to improve production, and by endorsing only those companies and factories "netamente Pepinianas y netamente Puertorriqueñas" (completely Pepinianas and completely Puerto Rican). "The lack of a public policy directed to this end has permitted past and present projects such as the San Sebastián Shopping Center to develop at the expense not only of local commerce, but of the life and social livelihood of our community."[38] Notwithstanding these appeals, local government endorsed proposals to open a number of new commercial centers around the town beginning in 1994, hailing them as the cornerstone of San Sebastián's *renacimiento* (renaissance).[39] Local businesses have responded by appealing to residents' local pride, encouraging them to buy in stores "100 percent *pepinianas.*" "Buying in Pepino [for Christmas]," the editors of the town's cultural magazine assured its readers, "contributes to progress and the development of our economy. Back those who give us Life!"[40] True progress, according to these accounts, depends on loyalty, an organic community, and respect for tradition.

Entreaties to "buy local" coincide with the efforts of other *pepinianos* to resist the cultural changes occasioned by *progreso*. One prominent lawyer and *independentista* noted that the problem with progress as currently envisaged is its origin *afuera*. It is coercive and imperialist, replacing local traditions with a homogenized global culture *de afuera*. This, he assured me in a measured tone, is one of San Sebastián's greatest dilemmas.

The return of those who come and go between here and the United States is a problem. The mayor is a product of the migration. And you can see the impact return migration has had even on the highways. The mayors who migrated, who have been through that, don't make *small* streets or roads. When people return, they have a larger vision of the world: *big* projects, with *big* thinking that is metropolitan, even North American. *Big* cars, *big* streets . . . . It's a process that affects the vision of life here, of how we should do things here. [They believe] things should also be *big* here [like in the United States]. That big vision *[visión grande]*, it's not from here. It's from *there*. And those who return want us to consider their stay in the United States as a doctorate in life. They are the ones who know, who are always talking, who know from where the sun rises.

According to many *pepinianos,* this "visión grande" threatens the "traditional" cultural values and practices they believe characterize San Sebastián and make it unique. Since the 1950s, San Sebastián, its neighboring municipality Lares, and other towns of the central highland region have been popularly regarded as sites of authentic Puerto Rican culture, a folkloric identity advanced by the cultural programs put on by the Institute of Puerto Rican Culture beginning in 1955.[41] For more than thirty years, local community activists and cultural workers have promoted this image of the town by organizing cultural festivals and showcasing the cultural production of local artisans. These activists also played an important role in the island's "culture wars" in the 1980s, collaborating with the Comité Pro Defensa de la Cultura Puertorriqueña (Committee for the Defense of Puerto Rican Culture) and establishing a local chapter, the Comité Pepiniano Pro Defensa y Fomento de la Cultura Puertorriqueña (Pepiniano Committee for the Defense and Promotion of Puerto Rican Culture), to resist the "Americanization" of Puerto Rican cultural identity and to reinvigorate the town's cultural life, widely lamented as a "cultural desert."[42]

The rise of annexationist politics in the 1980s and 1990s further intensified these local efforts, as the PNP successfully enlisted a multiclass coalition on a national level to advance its goal of *la estadidad jíbara* (creole statehood). The island's deteriorating economic conditions in the 1980s — rising poverty, increased unemployment, and the shift from a labor- to capital-intensive economic model — contributed to the PNP's successful mobilization. *La estadidad jíbara* would not only preserve the island's cultural and linguistic integrity, it would also guarantee Puerto Rico full equality as a state, thereby relieving the island's poverty through fully extended federal funds.[43] Although the hope of economic and social progress helped to usher in the PNP and Justo Medina in 1992, many in San Sebastián remained suspicious of the idea of a creole state. Moreover, increased return migration in the 1980s heightened concerns about Puerto Rican cultural integrity. *Populares* and *independentistas* responded to these changes by denouncing the cultural impact of *progreso* and the inferior subculture *los de afuera* had introduced in the town. In December 1991, for example, *El Maguey* warned its readers that there were "many [Christmas] traditions that apathy, weariness, and/or 'progress' have allowed to disappear," and it encouraged *pepinianos* to hold fast to the "magical and beautiful experiences our forbears gave to us."[44] Cultural workers urged the municipal government to implement a cultural public policy celebrating "our social inheritance and our historical patrimony."[45]

For this reason, many residents of San Sebastián were extremely apprehensive of Justo Medina and his annexationist ideology. One example of his distinct vision was his backing of a new tabloid-size weekly, *El Progreso,* a newspaper that resembled the *New York Daily News* more than the town's tradition of modest publications, like *El Pepino, El Palique,* and *El Maguey.* Many *pepinianos* complained bitterly about these changes, accusing the mayor of using the paper as an unofficial vehicle for his administration and squeezing out the town's other print media, which frequently criticized him and his policies. Such tactics, one man assured me, were typical of *los de afuera,* and they lent support to rumors of don Justo's corrupt ways, including his alleged financial gains through illegal activities in Perth Amboy.[46]

"Mira," one forty-year-old New York–born man told me, "este alcalde que tenemos aquí, el vino de afuera. Igual que el alcalde de Aguadilla.

Pero él no trabaja nada para su pueblo. Este alcalde vino, trabajó sus cuatro añitos y se tiró para el alcalde. Y ganó. Vino y hizo su residencia y ahora es alcalde" (Look, this mayor we have, he came *de afuera*. The same as the mayor of Aguadilla [a nearby city]. But he doesn't work at all for his town. This mayor came, worked for four years, and ran for mayor. And he won. He came and established his residency and now he's the mayor). Not only was the mayor accused of buying the elections — a strategy local *populares* and *independentistas* claim is consistently employed by *los penenpes* (PNPs) on both local and national levels — but he is also believed to embody everything that is wrong with *los que vienen de afuera*: arrogance and *vendepatria,* disloyalty to the Puerto Rican nation.

A more recent example of this annexationist vision is don Justo's response to the Puerto Rican Telephone Company (PRTC) strike in the summer of 1998. On June 19, PRTC workers called an island-wide strike to protest the government's plans to privatize the phone company and sell it to the U.S.-based GTE. For several weeks, with much local support throughout the island, strikers demonstrated to call attention to the PNP's move to privatize the island's "national patrimony." In San Sebastián, telephone workers marched, picketed, and camped out by the PRTC office at the town's entrance. Medina's call for increased police presence in the town and his failure to support the strikers reinforced popular perceptions of him as an uncritical ally of the PNP. Most town residents, however, supported the strikers in spite of widespread disruptions in phone service, providing them with food, drink, and moral support. When I went to the strikers' tent to offer my support and talk with some of the *huelguistas* (strikers), they were initially wary, asking me to describe my research in the town. When I explained that my project focused on migration — a topic presumably unrelated to their cause — but that I was also interested in things unrelated to migration, one *huelguista* assured me that these events were inextricably linked to migration. He explained:

This strike, I think, has a lot to do with migration. The emigration of Puerto Ricans began with industry, when the industries arrived in the United States. With those industries in the United States, many agricultural workers left the fields to work in factories here and in the United States . . . . Workers today, we, well, we're becoming even poorer. And with privatization, it's even worse and makes it necessary to leave [Puerto Rico] to look for ways to live one's life. To look for something better *afuera*. To look for opportunities. Today, the situation of our workers is bad, although it's getting better. Yes, San Sebastián has two shopping [centers], but . . . . This strike has everything to do with migration.

While PNP leaders hailed privatization as economic progress, others were acutely aware of its negative consequences: job loss, economic insecurity, and heightened social vulnerability. *La telefónica,* they confided, was one of the few stable, well-paid jobs in Puerto Rico. With privatization, these jobs would certainly be lost, compelling people to search for employment elsewhere on the island or on the mainland.

My second visit to the picket line later that evening was even more inspiring. Under the makeshift tarp shelter housing the *huelguistas,* another telephone worker asked for my professional opinion "como antropóloga" (as an anthropologist) whether I believed the strike was "algo cultural," a cultural phenomenon: "O sea, tú crees que [the strike] es una expresión cultural?" (In other words, do you believe that the strike is a cultural expression?) When I confessed that I was not sure what he meant, he explained that by culture he meant a process of coming together in mutual understanding of a shared vision, to which I responded, "Then yes, I do think the strike is a cultural expression." Alejandro smiled and said, "I think it's very interesting that you say that. You're an anthropologist and you study culture. And you're here at the strike because you know that this is culture. But not everyone thinks the way you do." He then explained that earlier that weekend, the *huelguistas* had met with members of the Casa Pepiniana de la Cultura (CPC), the local cultural group in charge of organizing the up-coming Festival de la Hamaca.[47] Some of the telephone workers had asked the CPC to use the festival to officially endorse the strike. Many CPC members adamantly resisted, saying that the strike was a political matter, and that it was not right to use a cultural event to back a political movement. Alejandro laughed quietly, explaining,

[For them], it was not a cultural matter. But for us, this strike *is* culture. It is the soul of many people. This tent, for example, is a center of life. It is the heart and center of this strike and the heart and center for us, the *huelguistas.* Here you make friends, you break with the routine of daily life to come as another soul here, under this tent. The strike is a process, a search for all of us — a search to ensure jobs for all of us, [to ensure] just employment. *La telefónica* is not like Cellular One or other companies, who are only out to make a buck. [We] look to serve *al pueblo* [the people]. And only the government can oversee this . . . . We are on strike because we're at war, a war against privatization. *This is culture,* because this process, this strike has changed people's way of thinking, the way people think about workers. Here, with this strike, we have demonstrated that it is the workers who produce [and work] for the people, who produce for the country. This isn't only about the sale of the telephone company. It's about our nation.

Metaphors of war capture the sentiments of many *pepinianos* regarding their struggle against transnational capital, ideas, goods, and values. Many *puertorriqueños* believe that, unlike Cellular One, GTE, or other transnational corporations, the PRTC has an organic connection to *el pueblo puertorriqueño*. Defending it against the powerful forces of global capital easily became an allegory of resistance against colonialism, cultural imperialism, and economic marginalization.

It is striking that in these political struggles, real fears about the consequences of global capital in a small town are articulated through the discourse of *los de afuera* at the same time as residents praise the men and women who migrated in the 1950s and 1960s because they understood "la honra de trabajar" (the honor of hard work). In fact, the town's migrants occupy an ambiguous ideological and material space. On the one hand, they are celebrated and honored each year during San Sebastián's most important cultural events, the Festival de la Novilla in January and the Festival de la Hamaca in July. And residents proudly point out that the town was built not only through the labor of those working in sugarcane, but also through the years of struggle and sacrifice of migrants working in industrial jobs in the North. But that, a young, unemployed return migrant explained to me, was in "los tiempos de la migración, en los años cuarenta, cincuenta, y sesenta," in the years of the migration, in the 1940s, 1950s, and 1960s. Today the circulation of people is reviled, pathologized, and blamed for the political-economic consequences of inequality, domination, and unequal development.

This is precisely the "thing we don't want to talk about" in San Sebastián: the ways in which return migration and increased globalization have radically transformed the social, cultural, and political-economic landscape of the town. When I asked people about return migrants, I was usually regaled with stories about overcrowded schools, increasing delinquency and violence in the town, problems with gangs, and a "subculture" of deviant values, drugs, and unemployment. No one labeled him/herself as a migrant or a return migrant. In fact, some people were offended when I asked them to describe their experiences as return migrants. "Yo no soy migrante" (I'm not a migrant), insisted a sixty-year-old woman who had lived for more than thirty years in Brooklyn. She explained that *los migrantes* were the men and women engaged in seasonal agricultural work in the eastern United States. She had just happened to live for many years *afuera*. And when I asked the *independentista* lawyer about return migration, he smiled. "Es un tema de que no queremos hablar" (It's a topic we don't want to talk about), he said, handing me a book by way of explanation.[48] In it, one chapter, "Algunas cosas de las que no queremos hablar," discusses humorously and critically "la gente que va y viene de los Estados Unidos" (the people who come and go from the United States) and the impact this has on the town. While Pepín de la Vega (the anonymous author's nom de plume) assures his readers that he is primarily concerned about "los que se van de una forma y vienen de otra forma" (those who leave one way and return another), his musings betray the deep ambivalence of most *pepinianos* regarding their transnational lives and the ways in which migration, *progreso,* community, and culture come together in complicated and unexpected ways. As a fellow passenger ironically remarked in the *carro público* on my first trip to San Sebastián, the town's increased crime attests to its progress as a "real" city. "Ahora te asaltan en Pepino. Es otro signo que ya somos civilizados" (Now you can be assaulted in Pepino. It's another sign that were are now civilized).

For many *pepinianos,* transnationalism is not something to celebrate. Instead it is an unwelcome consequence of San Sebastián's long migration history and a global economy that continues to shape the town's social landscape. Transnational migration can surely be a vehicle to construct a counterhegemonic political space, as well as a strategic response to global economic restructuring.[49] But it is also a process that is resisted, contested, and reconfigured in communities deeply affected by the neoliberal economic policies that shape people's lives from above, such as privatizing companies that formerly provided steady and well-remunerated jobs, and replacing them with service industries that increasingly rely on a flexible labor force. These same communities may also resist changes that transnational actors impose from below, through their social remittances, new cultural and linguistic knowledge, and different values and ideologies. These cleavages not only reveal the ways in which ideas of the nation and citizenship are being challenged, but they also point to exciting possibilities for building meaningful communities and creating place in transnational settings that may ultimately include broader understandings of identity, belonging, and community.

CHAPTER 5

Gentrification, Intrametropolitan Migration, and the Politics of Place

As I arrived to teach my G.E.D. class at the Ruiz Belvis Cultural Center one spring afternoon, Eddie Vélez — a seventeen-year-old Puerto Rican/ Mexican student — asked if I would switch roles and tell him about my life for a change. "I know you know a lot about me," he said, with a characteristically wry smile. "Now I want to know about you and your family." For months, Eddie and I had been discussing his options for after he passed his G.E.D. Like many of my students, he was considering going into the military. I was encouraging him to go to college, telling him how smart he was, especially in math and science. Eddie admitted that for the first time ever he was actually enjoying school, partly because he realized that he was "good at it." When other students needed help or felt intimidated in math — which was almost daily — Eddie quickly volunteered to explain algebra, fractions, or geometry to them. This, I reminded him, only confirmed that he should continue his studies and become a teacher, the kind of teacher he never had while he was in school, as he said. But on that day Eddie was interested in understanding the roots of our ongoing disagreement about his future, so he asked me pointed questions about my parents, the schools I attended, and where my family lived.

"So when you were my age," he clarified, "your parents were buying a house." I told him that when I was sixteen, my family moved into our own home after years of renting houses and apartments in northern California. Eddie didn't seem interested in hearing about how I had moved frequently when I was younger. Instead, he wanted to compare our lives at his current age of seventeen. At that age, I was living in a house that my parents were buying, attending a good Catholic high school from which I would graduate with high honors, and like him, making postgraduation plans. But, unlike Eddie, I *knew* I was headed for college and that I would most likely move away from home to do so. It was just a matter of deciding, based on financial aid packages and scholarships, which one I would attend. This, I believed, was one of the most important differences between us. Eddie had a slightly different analysis.

"See, we come from completely different families," he concluded. "I move around all the time. Every four to five years. Now we have to move again. The landlady came upstairs the other day and started crying because she knows my brother is dealin'. They pass by the house and are whistling for him to come out. She's got kids. And she's scared. So now we have to move again. In our last place, we only lived there a year." Eddie smiled and paused, adding sadly, "Now we have to move again." Even though I wanted him to go to college rather than enter the military, Eddie explained, I had to consider how different our families and our lives really were. He moved around a lot, while I had lived in a stable household when I was his age. My family was supportive of my decisions, while his father, when he was drunk or high, asked him why he couldn't be more like his brother. Eddie looked at me and smiled. "My brother deals drugs and is in a gang. Why does he want me to be like him?" As the other students returned from break, Eddie concluded, "I just wanted to see how different my background is from your background," and we returned to the classroom to work on the day's math exercises.

Eddie's questions that day underscored my "outsider within" status.[1] As a middle-class Puerto Rican feminist researcher among poor and working-class *puertorriqueños* studying for their G.E.D., my students often reminded me of how class background shaped our understanding and expectations of each other. My role as their teacher accentuated this hierarchical relationship, which was also influenced by education and cultural capital. Eddie's inquiry into my background therefore reveals an important problem with multiculturalist thinking that exhorts ethnic minorities to serve as role models to urban youth. It ignores how one's social location — including class, gender, race, sexuality, and culture — shapes a diversity of outcomes within ethnic groups.[2] This kind of thinking also helps to reproduce the idea of a meritocracy in which those who work hard are justly rewarded. For Eddie, residential mobility is key to understanding one's social location. Living in one's own home provides residential security, freeing one up to pursue goals and dreams that are sidelined when one lives day-to-day, unsure of where one's family might be the next day.

Many poor and working-class Puerto Ricans in Chicago move a lot.

Although some of this movement involves return or circular migration to Puerto Rico, most of their mobility entails intrametropolitan migration. Like other economically marginal groups in the city, Chicago Puerto Ricans' housing options are severely limited. Federal cutbacks in community development and subsidized housing construction beginning in the 1970s, as well as municipal failure to maintain low-cost housing, have created a housing crisis for the city's poor and working-class population, which is forced to live in old housing stock, usually in overcrowded conditions. According to the Chicago Urban League, federal funding for low-income housing in Illinois has been cut by 87 percent since the 1980s, and despite state, local, and private efforts to meet the growing need for affordable housing, Chicago's housing crisis has become even more critical in the 1990s.[3]

Poor and working-class residents are also vulnerable to political-economic changes that "revitalize" formerly neglected urban areas, ultimately displacing them. The past decade's prosperity wave, witnessing almost unprecedented growth in middle-income housing construction and rehabilitation of the city's housing stock, has passed by many residents, particularly those shuttling between Chicago and Puerto Rico. In fact, neighborhoods like Humboldt Park, whose residents are largely Latino or African American and poor, have been virtually ignored by affordable housing projects and slated instead for the demolition of buildings, which are usually replaced by high-rent lofts and condominiums.[4] As one *puertorriqueña* remarked to me as we washed clothes at a Laundromat in Humboldt Park, "yuppies" and rehabilitated housing usually result in poor and working-class families getting priced out of their neighborhoods. Comparing her observations in Humboldt Park with the gentrification she witnessed in the Belmont area in the 1980s, she warned us, "Did you see those rehabbed houses on Humboldt Boulevard and Wabansia? When I saw they were rehabbing, I was like, 'Forget about it. We're out of here.'"

In what follows, I focus on the politics of place and the process of place-making in Chicago, another site within a transnational social field linking Puerto Rico to mainland communities. I look at poor and working-class *puertorriqueños'* extremely mobile lives and the factors impelling this intrametropolitan migration. Evictions, problems resulting from overcrowded living conditions, and domestic disputes contribute to Puerto Ricans' high residential mobility. But like poor whites, blacks, and other Latinos, Puerto Rican residents are also vulnerable to the politics of uneven development targeting their neighborhoods for urban "revival." Low-income residents in gentrifying communities are not only physically displaced by these political-economic processes, but they are also heavily policed by law enforcement officials charged with ensuring a "safe" space for new residents. Grassroots efforts to resist these changes are constructed transnationally, as community organizers strategically deploy cultural symbols to construct a "Puerto Rican space" that preserves neighborhood use value. These efforts to deter displacement through resistance, political mobilization, and coalition-building challenge an image of the underclass that emphasizes pathological behavior, presenting instead a portrait of agency and collective action among poor and working-class Puerto Ricans whose lives are circumscribed by the politics of uneven development that increasingly define the "global city" of Chicago.

Intrametropolitan Migration in the Near Northwest Side

With more than 750,000 Latino residents, Chicago is home to the third-largest and one of the most diverse Latino populations in the country. According to the 2000 census, more than a quarter of Chicago's population is now Latino, a demographic shift that has contributed to an increase in the city's population for the first time in fifty years.[5] Mexicans and Mexican Americans constitute by far the largest section of Chicago's Latino population, comprising 70.6 percent, with Chicago Puerto Ricans at 15 percent, followed by Guatemalans, Ecuadorians, and Cubans. Although 2000 census data suggest that residential segregation in Chicago has fallen significantly in the past decade — with twenty-seven of the city's seventy-seven neighborhoods indexing a distinct racial or ethnic majority, down from forty-four, according to 1990 census data — Latino housing advocates in the 1990s noted that 92 percent of Latinos were residentially segregated in approximately a third of the city's community areas.[6] Moreover, despite a long history of residential integration, Mexicans continue to be spatially identified with the south side (Pilsen and *La Villita*) and Puerto Ricans with the north side (Humboldt Park). Since the 1980s, however, these residential patterns have shifted, as Mexicans and Puerto Ricans have moved north and west in the city and have increasingly relocated to working-class Chicago suburbs like Cicero, Addison, and Waukegan, profoundly transforming metropolitan Chicago's ethno-spatial landscape.[7]

According to the 1990 census, more than 60 percent of Chicago's Puerto Rican population resided in West Town, Humboldt Park, and

Logan Square, the community areas composing the city's fabled Near Northwest Side. Although these neighborhoods are popularly imagined as "the Puerto Rican community," they are actually quite mixed. Small Polish bakeries and restaurants, established decades ago when Poles predominated, can still be found, now adjacent to Mexican *taquerías* and Puerto Rican *cafeterías* along Western Avenue and Division Street. Signs in liquor store windows advertising the sale of cold beer in English, Spanish, and Polish (*cerveza fría* and *sliwo piva*) further attest to the ongoing mix in these neighborhoods. The 1990 census, for example, showed that more than 50 percent of Humboldt Park's residents were black, and approximately 20 percent were Mexican or Mexican American. Logan Square's Puerto Rican population is the largest in the city, but this community area is also home to more than 21,000 Mexicans and Chicago's largest Cuban and South and Central American populations. And in West Town, Mexicans significantly outnumber Puerto Rican residents.[8] Despite Puerto Ricans' diminishing numerical presence, however, these neighborhoods — especially Humboldt Park — continue to be an important symbolic and material space for Chicago Puerto Ricans.[9] As Nelly López aptly noted in class one day, Humboldt Park is widely regarded as a place where one can consume Puerto Rican culture. "I take my kid to Humboldt Park for the food, the *piraguas* [shaved ice], you know. My kid sees lots of people — black, Mexicans, Polish. But I take him to Humboldt Park to see Puerto Rican culture." "Yeah," Eddie agreed. "Humboldt Park is the heart of Puerto Rican people in the city."

Humboldt Park is also one of the poorest community areas in the city. Only 21 percent of residents over the age of twenty-five have postsecondary education, compared with 41 percent citywide. With its unemployment rate hovering around 20 percent, more than a third of the families in Humboldt Park live below the poverty line, and the median family income ($21,296) is well below the city median. West Town and Logan Square's demographic profiles are slightly better, although they too suffer higher poverty rates than the city at large.[10] While all three communities register high rates of public aid, the majority of these impoverished households are working poor, with members employed full-time at low-wage jobs. One report by the Chicago Urban League, the Latino Institute, and the University of Northern Illinois found that Latinos are the group most likely to be working poor, with nearly 25 percent of Chicago Latinos living in poverty. Among the Latino poor, Puerto Ricans have the highest poverty rates in the city as well as the greatest percentage of female-headed households, making them one of the city's most economically marginalized groups.[11] These trends mirror national statistics, showing that in 1995, for example, Latino median family income dropped by 5.1 percent at the same time as it rose for every other American racial and ethnic group. Among the Latino poor, Puerto Ricans have the highest poverty rates in the city, as well as the greatest percentage of female-headed households, making them one of the city's most economically marginalized groups. In addition to enduring poverty and its attendant social problems, poor families in these communities are extremely mobile, engaging in intrametropolitan migration not easily captured by census data.

By intrametropolitan migration, I refer specifically to the movement of low-income city residents within the Standard Metropolitan Area of Chicago. Most of this movement occurs within neighborhoods or between contiguous community areas, but it increasingly includes relocation to economically distressed suburbs adjacent to the city.[12] I use the term *migration* here to highlight both the constraints and uncertainties of the high residential mobility of the poor and its structural similarity to movement across geopolitical borders. On the one hand, poor families move frequently to improve their living arrangements: a larger living space, a safer neighborhood, improved conditions of apartments. But they are also evicted by landlords, forced out by other family members (especially those who are doubled up), or leave as a result of domestic problems (divorce, breakups, abuse).[13] Like international migrants, intrametropolitan movers use networks of relatives and friends to find new housing in familiar or nearby neighborhoods, even if that means living in less than ideal circumstances. These short-distance moves allow household members' kin and social networks to remain intact, an important consideration for poor families who rely on established ties with nearby friends, family, and locally owned small stores to help "make ends meet."[14]

Neighborhood stores are critical to many women, whose long-standing relationship with the owners allows them to buy on credit while waiting for the next paycheck. This kind of reciprocity cements some women's loyalty to these stores and keeps them away from larger supermarkets, where goods may be significantly cheaper. One woman explained this seemingly irrational strategy: "You owe these [small] stores. Try to get something on credit from the big supermarkets when you don't have money. They don't give you credit. But the *bodegas,* when they know you, they do." Women invest great amounts of mental and emotional energy in cultivating these relationships and strategizing about how to maintain other networks critical to making ends meet.

Even when women and their families stay put, they still think about changing residence or finding a better place to live. Many people expressed a desire for a larger apartment to accommodate their families; they also hoped to move away from the violence associated with gangs and the drug economy operating in their neighborhoods. These conversations served as a popular topic of conversation at school, work, and home. Aida Rodríguez talked every day about her dream to move to a better neighborhood and a larger apartment. Her neighborhood was deteriorating rapidly, with young men dealing drugs in front of her house, and she worried particularly about gang members harassing her teenage son as he came and went. They also had a recurring problem with rats, which were so big that at night they resembled small cats lurking around her apartment building. Her cramped two-bedroom apartment was too small for her, her husband, and their five children, and she fought constantly with the landlord over necessary repairs. Evelyn Trujillo also talked about moving into a bigger space, citing problems with gangs and rats, and frustrations with her intransigent landlord. During class breaks, G.E.D. students swapped stories about their problems with landlords and overcrowding, shared strategies about how to get out of bad living arrangements, and discussed their fears of being evicted. And while few people actually moved — Aida, for example, didn't move into a bigger place until after I finished my fieldwork — their stories reveal how movement has become part of the fabric of their lives.

People's life histories were also filled with myriad stories about moving. In the fifteen years Juan and Carmen de Jesús lived in Chicago, for example, they moved twenty-four times: They first lived in pre–urban renewal Lincoln Park near the factories and warehouses where they were employed. They were evicted from several apartments after landlords sold their homes to private developers, and like many Puerto Ricans in the late 1960s and 1970s, they moved west to Humboldt Park, where they continued to move regularly in search of the "right place." They eventually bought a house with Juan's brother, where they lived until they left Chicago for San Sebastián in 1977.

Carlos and Nilda Arroyo laughed when they talked about how many times they moved within the same four-block area of Noble Square — at least six times, Carlos told me — and how they managed to always live on Erie Street, which allowed them to maintain their connections with extended family and friends. This became even more important after their children were born, because Nilda sporadically worked out of the house and relied heavily on kin and close friends for childcare. The proximity of these social networks was crucial. Loss of networks, in fact, informed the decisions of some first-generation migrants to return to Puerto Rico. Although Angie Rubiani told me that her main reason for returning to

San Sebastián was fear of neighborhood changes and the fact that Puerto Rico was a better place to raise children, she also emphasized the loneliness of being so far away from her sister, who lived in another part of Chicago. Similarly, Mercedes Rubio explained that when her older sister decided to return to Puerto Rico, Mercedes also left, because she relied on her sister for help with household tasks, childcare, and running errands. After a number of years in Puerto Rico, Mercedes returned to Chicago when her oldest daughter, Yamila, decided to move there in order to free herself from problems with her husband's family in San Sebastián and get better medical attention for her young son, who was born with medical problems.

When I asked Nelly López where she had lived as a child, she told a familiar story of high residential mobility.

> *N:* I grew up on Division and, um, I can't remember now. I think Cortez. And we moved a lot. . . . I grew up all over, and all over Humboldt Park. . . . I grew up moving everywhere because of all the problems with my mom and my stepfather. They fought a lot and we had to, like, move. Because the landlords would kick us out or, you know, too much fighting or people complained. [She pauses.] When I was seven years old, my stepfather, he got real bad abusing my mother. . . . And after that we were back and forth in shelters.
>
> *I:* How long were you in and out of shelters?
>
> *N:* Like for a year and a half. Like in one and a half years, we'd been in like five different shelters. And because my mom, she didn't want to lose us or nothing. She wanted to help us. So, in all the shelters they give you counseling. They help you financially. They helped my mom. And then my mom went back with him. So, when I was thirteen . . . she went back with him.

Nelly's narrative is not atypical. Of the women I knew and interviewed in Chicago and San Sebastián, most cited divorce and domestic abuse as the primary reasons for their frequent moves and sometimes homelessness, although few mentioned living in shelters.[15] Teenage pregnancy was another reason for young women's mobile living patterns. When Nelly learned she was pregnant at the age of fourteen, she went to live with her maternal grandmother in West Town, where she stayed until the baby was born. Starting a few months after his birth, she lived in various apartments, including one shared with her mother, while trying to support herself with occasional money from the baby's father.

Another student, Yvette Jiménez, a twenty-five-year-old mother of three, also described a highly mobile childhood exacerbated by an unexpected pregnancy. Soon after discovering she was pregnant, Yvette went to live with her sister and brother-in-law so that her parents would not find out. After residing with them for eight months, she returned to her parents' house with her newborn son and lived there for one year. When her parents temporarily moved back to Puerto Rico, Yvette refused to join them and lived with a cousin for a year. Tired of being uprooted and struggling to raise her son alone, Yvette turned to the baby's father for help. That, she says, was her biggest mistake.

I lived with my cousin. But then *pendeja* [stupid] Yvette [she laughs] was like, blind, because I swore I was in love with him, and I moved in with him and his parents. . . . I lived with them for a couple of years. And then when I, I was like, "I have to get out of here because I'm gonna kill you or you're gonna kill me or something's gonna go wrong." So we moved . . . I moved, I wanted to move out. I moved out with my cousin, and [the baby's father] wanted to stay with me. But he had his other girlfriends on the side, which I knew about. *Pero me hice la ciega* [I played blind]. I have no idea why. I still don't. So we found an apartment and we moved in together. But his parents didn't want to give me my son. They told me [they would give him to me] when we settled down, when we figured out what we wanted to do. *Then* they'd give me my son. Four years later, I was already pregnant and had my other son. . . . All I went through was struggle in those four years, trying to figure out where I was going to live, what I was going to do with myself, what I was going to do for my kids and this and that. And then I finally settled down into an apartment, I had my other son, and they still didn't want to give me my other son. I didn't get my son until he was five years old or six years old when he was all ready for first grade.

Like many circular migrants, Yvette was punished for her highly mobile life. Rather than helping her, her family blamed her for being uprooted and unstable, problems that were the result of larger structural forces that made these moves necessary. For the last two decades, Chicago's housing crisis for low-income residents has severely limited their residential options. The lack of decent and affordable housing continues to be one of the greatest problems facing poor working-class Latinos in the city.

Chicago's Housing Crisis and the Consequences of Growth Politics

Chicago's housing crisis is one of both affordability and availability.[16] In areas like the Near Northwest side, housing stock has dwindled since the

1970s, and overcrowding has increased dramatically, with almost a fifth of household members in Humboldt Park, West Town, and Logan Square living in overcrowded conditions.[17] In Humboldt Park alone, more than 6,500 housing units were lost in the 1980s and 1990s, and more than sixty buildings were slated to be torn down in the city's fast-track demolition program at the turn of the twenty-first century.[18] While the entire city suffered from federal and municipal cutbacks in subsidized housing projects and a concomitant rise in private residential development, Latino neighborhoods were particularly troubled: Of the 1,600 new units created by the Department of Housing in 1995, for example, approximately 5 percent were located in predominantly Latino community areas. These statistics are particularly troubling because these neighborhoods also experience some of the highest levels of gentrification in the city. Finally, Latinos have been systematically excluded from federally assisted housing programs in Chicago, a matter remedied only recently with a lawsuit against the Chicago Housing Authority (CHA) and the U.S. Department of Housing and Urban Development (HUD). Of the eighteen thousand Section 8 housing vouchers used in Chicago, for example, only three hundred were used by Latinos. According to Hipólito Roldán, president of the Hispanic Housing Development Corporation, "The CHA, which is a public body charged with providing affordable housing to those of certain income levels, has for many decades ignored the Latino community. Even though we are about 25 percent of the population of the city, we were less than 2 percent of the people living in public housing."[19]

Before this lawsuit, public housing had not been a viable option for most Latinos in Chicago. In the 1980s, Mayor Harold Washington, who was elected through a historic coalition of African American and Latino community leaders and voters, addressed the persistent housing problem facing Latinos by creating the Mayor's Advisory Committee on Latino Affairs. One of the committee's most important findings was the systematic exclusion of Latinos from CHA housing programs. Despite the committee's repeated efforts to negotiate a settlement with the CHA that would address the housing needs of Latinos, in 1989 they formed their own housing advocacy organization, Latinos United, which in 1994 sued HUD and CHA for discriminating against Latino families in need of public housing services. Within two years, Latinos United settled with HUD and CHA and implemented an aggressive $1.6 million campaign to inform Latinos of housing services available to them. CHA housing offices were opened on the north and south sides; they advertised in

Spanish news media the opening of a Section 8 waiting list; and CHA agreed to set aside 20 percent of its yearly vouchers for Latino families. Notwithstanding these groundbreaking changes in public housing, working-class and poor Latinos still face myriad housing problems.

In the face of such dim housing prospects, many low-income Latinos live in substandard housing, doubling up with family and friends in already overcrowded apartments. Aida's family, for example, lives in a cramped two-bedroom apartment with a moderately sized living room and kitchen. Three daughters share a bedroom only big enough for their bunk bed and one tall dresser. Aida and her husband share the other bedroom, and her two sons sleep on a mattress in the living room. On several occasions, Aida also had to make room for in-laws who were either homeless or in transition. Even though the doubling up was infrequent, it was extremely stressful for Aida and her children, who, because of safety issues, leave the apartment only to go to school or the store.

Families also double up in their own or rented two- and three-story homes. Yvette, for example, shares a two-story house with her mother-in-law and her sister and her family. Another Mexican woman, Guadalupe Vera, owns a three-story home near the border of Humboldt Park and Logan Square and has her two daughters, their husbands, and their five children living on the second and third floors. Guadalupe and her husband live on the first floor with an uncle, and they also rent a room to friends in need of inexpensive temporary housing. Twenty-year-old Lorena Santiago shares a two-story house with her husband's family in western Humboldt Park. She and her husband and baby live in the basement; her in-laws are on the first floor with their teenage granddaughter; and her sister-in-law and her family live on the second floor. Like many migrant households, these domestic units are extremely fluid, with kin and friends coming and going as they search for more permanent housing.

According to Carlos de Jesús, executive director of Latinos United, this pattern of overcrowding is common in Latino communities, largely a result of Chicago's continuing housing crisis for poor and working-class residents. On average, Latinos spend more than 75 percent of their monthly income on rent, a rate far exceeding what government standards rate as reasonable.[20] From 1980 to 1990, the median rent in the twenty-five Chicago community areas where more than 90 percent of the city's Latinos live increased by 135 percent, twice the rate of inflation and a third more than the average increase citywide. In addition, between 1980 and 1990, Chicago lost 42,000 units of housing, 46 percent of which was in Latino communities.[21]

Attempts to replace lost housing stock with affordable housing are frequently opposed by elected officials and neighborhood residents. In West Town, plans to build Erie Co-op, a multisite cooperative housing development for thirty families earning between $15,000 and $30,000 a year, was opposed by Alderman Jesse Granato, as well as by newcomers complaining that they already had too much low-income housing in the community. Not surprisingly, West Town — or Wicker Park — is currently one of the hottest real estate markets in the city; it is also one of the most rapidly gentrifying areas. These conflicts over affordable housing, fast-track demolition programs, and the rehabilitation of old housing stock are fundamentally struggles over neighborhood use versus exchange value and the nature of growth politics in the city.

For local elite groups — including developers, local businesses, transnational corporations, and real estate financiers — the city is a growth machine "that can increase aggregate rents and trap related wealth for those in the right position to benefit." According to this logic, the purpose of local government is to promote growth because it "strengthens the local tax base, creates jobs, provides resources to solve existing social problems, meets the housing needs caused by natural population growth, and allows the market to serve public tastes in housing, neighborhoods, and commercial development."[22] While some of these claims might be true for some times and places, it is clear that in most contexts the notion of "value-free development" is pure fantasy. Local growth is fundamentally about the social construction of place and attempts to enhance exchange value over use value in ways that sacrifice the majority and reward the few.[23]

One of the clearest examples of this struggle between use and exchange value is to be found in postwar urban planning policies promoting downtown development. In Chicago, these plans included a redevelopment strategy to rebuild the downtown Loop district, creation of a network of expressways and rapid transportation lines servicing the Loop, and construction of middle-class housing directly north and west of the downtown area. As part of the Chicago 21 Plan sponsored by the Chicago Central Area Committee — an umbrella organization of private businesses, including representatives from banks, newspapers, large department stores, and powerful downtown companies — the renewed focus on downtown economic development advanced a "corporate vision of Chicago in the twenty-first century" based on the transformation of the Loop into a regional, national, and now global financial and administrative center. Successful restructuring of the Chicago economy depended not only on public policies and expenditures favorable to corporate interests, but also on the development of a "buffer zone to protect the downtown investments from the growing number of poor and minority people living in Chicago's surrounding neighborhoods." Urban renewal in Lincoln Park in the 1960s and the gentrification of Old Town in the 1970s, and now of West Town, are consequences of these development projects. The displacement of impoverished Puerto Rican, white, and black residents from these areas, particularly Lincoln Park, attests not only to the devastating consequences of uneven development, but also to its westward expansion.[24]

Gentrification is one example of how the pursuit of greater exchange value disrupts life in poor communities. The term refers to an economic and social process whereby private capital (real estate firms, developers) and individual homeowners and renters reinvest in fiscally neglected neighborhoods through housing rehabilitation, loft conversions, and the construction of new housing stock. Unlike urban renewal, gentrification is a gradual process, occurring one building or block at a time, slowly reconfiguring the neighborhood landscape of consumption and residence by displacing poor and working-class residents unable to afford to live in "revitalized" neighborhoods with rising rents, property taxes, and new businesses catering to an upscale clientele. The language describing the main protagonists in these processes — "urban pioneers," "refugees," "migrants" — evokes feelings of danger, chaos, and disorder. It also implies hope, change, and optimism for communities formerly regarded as hopeless, uninhabitable, and untamed.[25] In these accounts, gentrification is a positive process revitalizing poor neighborhoods and allegedly improving the quality of life for all residents. City officials, developers, local media, and even some residents often welcome the consequences of gentrification, including declining crime rates, increased property values and municipal tax base, the arrival of city services, and upscale commercial activity. Yet some community activists and scholars have convincingly argued that gentrification is not a neutral process, but rather one that brutally displaces poor and working-class residents from neighborhoods where they have established rich networks of support among family, friends, and local businesses crucial to their material survival.[26] The struggles surrounding gentrification are ultimately about power and the social construction of space and how race, ethnicity, class, age, and gender fundamentally inform these changing meanings of place over time.

The gentrification of Wicker Park is a telling example of these tensions. Because one of the most powerful ways to claim place is to "give it a name," it is not surprising that new neighborhood toponyms have emerged in the gentrification process.[27] Wicker Park, for example, is a small neighborhood in the West Town community area home to trendy restaurants, shops, and vibrant nightlife, as well as to a handful of impressive greystone mansions composing the area's historical landmark district. Because Chicago is divided into both community areas and neighborhoods, which frequently overlap each other, people refer to where they live by using either community or neighborhood names. But because Chicago is *also* "the city of neighborhoods," with a very clear racial and ethnic geography, spatial designations are extremely political and even volatile. Thus, the Ruiz Belvis Cultural Center, located at the six corners intersection of North Avenue, Damen, and Milwaukee Avenue — the heart of gentrifying Wicker Park — is technically in West Town, according to the Centro's students, staff, and participants. However, young newcomers to the neighborhood — who are largely middle-class, educated, and white — refer to the area as Wicker Park. These linguistic conflicts anger the Centro's community activists, who have been fighting physical displacement for the last decade and who regard the name *Wicker Park* as a way to erase them linguistically. As one long-time organizer exclaimed during a meeting, "This is *West Town*. This isn't Wicker Park. First they try to kick us [the Centro] out, now they're trying to change our name, our identity!"

Another example of this linguistic twist is a conversation I had with a downstairs neighbor over breakfast one morning. Laura, a young, upwardly mobile *tejana*, told me that she actually enjoyed living in West Bucktown. When I corrected her, saying we actually lived in Humboldt Park, she looked quite shocked. "Humboldt Park? We live in West Bucktown. At least that's what it said in the ad for my apartment." And she was right. Classified ads announcing available apartments in the *Chicago Reader*, for example, rarely name Humboldt Park or West Town. Wicker Park, West Bucktown, and Logan Square are all more palatable names for the gentrifying areas where poor and "dangerous" ethnic and racial others still reside. Signs for new condominiums on Humboldt Park's eastern border with West Town also advertise luxury living in West Bucktown, soothing newcomers' racial fears.

Gentrification's name game is complemented by a new landscape of consumption.[28] The dollar stores, used furniture stores, *cafeterías, botánicas,* and small local grocery stores that once dotted Milwaukee Avenue are slowly giving way to cafés, stores, bars, and restaurants, like the Bongo Room, Soul Kitchen, and Celluloid. Unlike the upscale restaurants in the trendier and more expensive neighborhoods of Lincoln Park, Old Town, and Bucktown to the east, Wicker Park offers "New American cuisine" that reinforces the image of the neighborhood as an alternative space whose residents value "vernacular traditions," resist corporate interests and mainstream tastes, and boast of living in a neighborhood free (at least until recently) of global chain businesses like Starbucks. Thus social values and behaviors have become embedded in the neighborhood spatial environment.[29] The artists, actors, and students residing in Wicker Park participate in these new consumption patterns, not only as consumers but also as members of a willing labor force whose cultural capital allows them to navigate these roles easily. Although these restaurants generate economic activity and increase the area's exchange value, the profits do not trickle down to poor nonwhite residents, who are not hired to work in the neighborhood's new restaurants, stores, and boutiques. Thus, despite claims to the contrary, gentrification's economic benefits extend to only a select group of workers.

Ironically, Wicker Park's successful transformation from barrio to trendy enclave has made it increasingly difficult for the less affluent newcomers to remain in the neighborhood as the community's exchange value continues to rise. Within the past few years, the neighborhood's landscape of consumption and residence has shifted significantly, as newcomers, like working-class residents before them, are slowly priced out of an extremely tight housing market, and as the character of the neighborhood increasingly comes to mirror that of other urban spaces offering the kinds of restaurants, entertainment, food, and services favored by urban elites. The number of luxury lofts and condominiums has increased dramatically since the mid 1990s, with some apartments in Bucktown and Wicker Park becoming as expensive as the western areas of Lincoln Park. In the past three years, organizations like the Old Wicker Park Organization and West Town United have mobilized to resist this gentrification, claiming that increased rents and new construction have priced them out.[30] In these heated discussions, however, very little attention is paid to how organizations like the Centro and its students are affected by these changes. Groups like the Old Wicker Park Organization focus instead on preserving housing options for threatened white middle-class and upwardly mobile residents. In this extremely competitive race to maximize exchange value, coercion — economic, physical, and cultural — becomes one way to achieve this goal, and disrupts the lives of marginalized groups with very little power to resist these changes.

The Near Northwest Side Story

Traveling east from Humboldt Park to Wicker Park provides an important glimpse into the geography of gentrification. Just west of Western Avenue on Wabansia Street — the border between Humboldt Park and West Town — lie the elevated El tracks and the Bloomingdale Street viaduct, and below them, a row of old houses badly in need of repair. Next door are new luxury townhomes and lofts. Some of them have been converted from old housing stock, warehouses, and factories, others are new buildings with garages and private yards. Farther east, below the old Canadian railroad tracks, are long cement walls covered with boldly colored murals painted by neighborhood youth participating in the Mayor's Summer Youth Program. One mural features a young man holding a can of spray paint, posed ominously in front of a large shark with the word "CULTURA" — culture — written across it. Against a backdrop of the Puerto Rican flag, the message reads, "This mural is dedicated 2 all the sisters and brothers who hold pride in our culture and defend it. *Boricua, defiende lo tuyo* [Boricua, defend what is yours]."

Still farther east, just before the Ruiz Belvis Cultural Center, are more lofts and new buildings under construction and a sign advertising "an entire block of buildable land, residential or commercial." A billboard in front of elegant new townhouses reads, "Urban Gardens Townhomes. 2–3 bedrooms/2.5–3.5 bath. 5 signature floorplans; 2 car garage; open and luminiferous; private outdoor space; gated security courtyard; formal dining room, family room. From $249,000." More modest lofts ($199,000) lie just to the west on a new, unnamed street. And farther east, as you turn southeast on Milwaukee toward the six corners hub of Wicker Park, are more older buildings, warehouses, and closed factories with signs in their windows saying "For Lease" and "For Sale." The juxtaposition is truly remarkable.

As one stands in front of the Centro — with its brightly painted sign decorated with *vejigantes, maracas,* and *guiros* (Puerto Rican cultural symbols and instruments) above a front window displaying paintings and woodcarvings by local artists — it is clear why developers, the local alderman, real estate agents, and new upwardly mobile professional (and usually white) residents want the Centro to move: It is a risky space frequented by potentially dangerous young men and women who disrupt the new vision of the neighborhood. Since the 1980s, the Centro has resisted myriad attempts to displace them, including arbitrary zoning and building code enforcement; harassment by neighbors complaining about young men "hanging out" in front of the Centro; city fines levied against the Centro for inappropriate licenses; and phone calls, mailings, and periodic visits by private individuals and developers interested in buying the building where the Centro is located. The Centro's board has remained defiant, spending tens of thousands of dollars to remain compliant with shifting city licensing, building, and zoning codes. But like the neighborhood's working-class residents in the early 1980s, the Centro's staff, students, and other patrons are frequently harassed and intimidated by powerful interests, including law enforcement. Their narratives of gentrification's impact on their lives are sobering, and confirm David Harvey's contention that "the perpetual reshaping of the geographic landscape of capitalism is a process of violence and pain."[31]

The young men who study at the Centro and participate in its cultural programs are the most vulnerable to these demographic shifts and the attendant use of state power to protect the neighborhood's newest residents through surveillance and manipulation of young Puerto Ricans' bodies. In her excellent discussion of criminality and the exercise of state power in Brazil, anthropologist Teresa Caldeira provides similar examples of how the body — of both "alleged criminals" and "all categories of people considered in need of special control (including children, women, the poor and the insane)" — becomes the "locus of punishment, justice, and example in Brazil," as well as a legitimate field of interventions and manipulations unprotected by individual civil rights.[32] My male students often arrived in class tired, upset, and frustrated with the ways in which gentrification had transformed their daily routine. Police harassed them, stopped them randomly to question and frisk them, taunted them, and often engaged in unlawful procedures just to humiliate them. One twenty-one-year-old student, Leo Chacón, lived just west of the Centro and complained bitterly about the changes he witnessed in his neighborhood. "The whites," he explained, were moving into the neighborhood, and Latino homeowners were facilitating this process by "selling out," selling their homes to newcomers and then moving to the suburbs. Leo's new neighbors constantly called the police on him and his friends when they were hanging out in front of their own apartments and homes. Now, he explained, the police passed by routinely, and they had stopped Leo and other men frequently enough to know them by name. "'Where ya goin', Mr. Chacón? How are ya doin' today, Mr. Chacón?' The cops are always stopping me and trying to pin shit on me. I ain't done nothing. Ever since these white folks moved in, I can't even walk in my own 'hood."

Leo was not the only one to complain about how the police treated him. During my three years teaching and volunteering at the Centro, all of the young men with whom I worked had similar stories. As young men of color — most Puerto Rican, others Mexican or Mexican/Puerto Rican — they were clearly marked, embodying a profile targeted by law enforcement officials. During breaks, these young men complained bitterly about how the police treated them, and they were surprised to discover that they were all hassled by the same officers. One day, Leo and Marvin Polanco, an eighteen-year-old Puerto Rican student, described a particular Latino police officer and his white partner, who were known for harassing young men in the neighborhood.

> *M:* It was three guys, right. We were all Puerto Rican. And then . . . these cops . . . they were coming down Evergreen Street [in Humboldt Park]. They were going to stop some gang members, but then when they saw us, they came and stopped us. And we weren't even on the corner. We were like twenty or thirty feet away from the corner, right, and [this Latino cop] comes and stops us. "Hey, you guys" [lowering his voice to sound authoritative], "What 'cha doin'?" He starts checking us out, right, and then this guy, he said his name's Corona, and he comes and hits my friend on the chin. "Oh, why you tryin' to get smart," you know? My friend was like, "No, sir. I'm not tryin' to get smart." You know. And he gave him all the respect. And there was this white guy, right.
>
> *L:* His white partner, right?
>
> *M:* Yeah! And he came to me like, "What you ridin' on?" "I'm not ridin' nothin'," you know. He's saying I was gettin' smart with him. He started goin' like [he pokes his finger into his chest], you know? Real hard to me, pointing on my chest real hard. I'm like, "No, why are you doin' this," you know? He's like, "Shut up." I'm like, "You shut up." And he, the Hispanic one . . . he said, "Why you don't wanna respect us?" And I was like, "I respect everybody who respects me." [Leo huffs knowingly in complete disgust and then puts his hand out to Marvin.] You know what I'm sayin? [taking Leo's hand, and they shake]. So then, um, he hit my friend again. Then we made a report.

When other police officers arrived to take down Marvin's complaint, they asked for a description of the officer. But when Marvin described the officer, the officers dismissed their story, saying that no cops in their district fit that description. Soon after, the original two officers returned and began harassing Marvin again, this time for reporting them.

> *M:* The white guy, he told me, "You want me to take you by the Kings [opposition gang members from another neighborhood] so they could jump

you?" I'm like, "Go take me by the Kings. I got an aunt and uncle that live around there. You can do me a favor and drop me off." [Leo laughs.] And then he told me, "Oh, you want me to take you by such and such gang?" I'm like, "Go ahead. I got family there too. You're doin' me a favor." And he's like, "Gettin' smart?" and he pointed in my chest again. And I was like cryin' because it hurt. And I couldn't do nothin' about it.

L: Yes, you could.

M: I mean, 'cuz . . . [pauses] it's your word against a cop's, man. I mean, if you're a cop, man, I don't know. I don't care what anybody says, you understand? They're gonna win. You can't, you can't sue the government, man. I can't sue nobody.

Marvin's feelings were echoed by other men in the class. As I drove another G.E.D. student, Robby León, home one day, he told me similar stories. When I pulled into a grocery store parking lot near our homes, a police officer blocked the way, refusing to let me park in the lot. He just stared at Robby and me in my truck. When I began to roll down my window to say something to the officer, Robby stopped me, "No, just chill. That guy's an asshole. He knows me. That's why he's stopped there." After a few minutes, the officer slowly pulled out of the way, staring hard at Robby. "I can't believe that guy," I yelled. It was obvious that he was blocking me and I couldn't move. It was the first time I had experienced, albeit in a very minimal way, the mental games and taunting my students consistently described. "That guy [and some other cops] are real assholes. That guy made me pull down my pants in public. Why do you think I wear boxers?" I didn't know Roberto wore boxers, but I did know that like my other male students, he was the target of police harassment. They searched young women too, he explained, but you had to keep calm and know your rights. A woman officer tried to search his girlfriend once, but she refused because she knew that while she was on her porch, the officer needed a warrant, something I did not know. This kind of knowledge, he and my other students assured me, was one of their few defenses against police misconduct. It is also an example of how local knowledge is produced in a context of unequal power relations and subordination.

Law enforcement is a key component in the gentrification process. Like old buildings that are destroyed, gutted, and then rebuilt, gentrification reconfigures a neighborhood's racial and social landscape. In the urban imaginary, young brown and black men are discursively constructed as dangerous, threatening, requiring surveillance and punishment because they transgress norms of dress, class, and ethnicity. As Dwight Conquergood points out, "The discourse of transgression legitimizes official systems of surveillance, reform, enforcement, and demolition."³³ Another example of "legitimate" state surveillance is Chicago's anti-loitering law, which was ruled unconstitutional by the U.S. Supreme Court in 1999. Passed in 1992, the law resulted in more than 42,000 arrests of primarily young black and Latino men, who were charged with unlawfully congregating on the street with "no apparent purpose." In 1995, the Illinois courts suspended enforcement of the law, although police continued to use it to arrest and harass young men. Although the law's purpose was to fight Chicago's gang problem, it helped to reproduce a kind of racial profiling common in contemporary law enforcement that targets men and women based solely on skin color. Mayor Daley — one of the law's staunchest advocates — lamented the U.S. Supreme Court ruling: "We have to ask ourselves if it is constitutional for gang-bangers and drug dealers to own a corner. . . . [Everybody] knows that they aren't out there cooking hot dogs and studying Sunday-school lessons."³⁴

Increased policing of young men of color is one way to sanitize public space. Private businesses engage in similar activities, encouraging patronage from certain clients and discouraging others. This became particularly clear to me one day as I had lunch with Eddie, Nelly, and three other G.E.D. students at a popular diner we all frequented. I had brought my lunch that day but joined my students at their invitation. I entered the restaurant first and sat down at a table near the window, waiting for the others to get their food. Soon we were all sitting together, eating, laughing, and sharing stories, enjoying being together outside of the classroom. As we were getting ready to leave, Frankie, an eighteen-year-old Puerto Rican student, saw us in the restaurant and came in to join us, a Sprite in his hand. As soon as Frankie sat down, an owner whom I had come to know approached him aggressively, asking him what he thought he was doing sitting in his store with a soda he didn't buy there. Frankie had his headphones on, and he looked confused, removed his headphones, and asked the older man to repeat what he had said. By this time, the old man was livid and began screaming, "You get out of my store!" Stunned, Frankie stood up and walked out, mumbling, "This is messed up," and paced in front of the store window while talking to another student, Francisco. The man then turned to a woman who was sitting near us, grabbed her arm, and kicked her out as well. The woman screamed at him to let her go, and she stormed out of the store cursing at him in garbled English.

At this point, my students and I were visibly disturbed. "I'm never coming here again," Nelly said loudly. "He just lost himself a customer doing that." I then suggested to everyone that we should leave and finish our lunch in the Centro. As we walked out the door, I turned to the owner, who recognized me (I stopped at his store almost daily to buy fries), and said very calmly, "You know that student with the Sprite who you kicked out? Well, he's a student of mine and we came here to eat lunch; he was only in here to join me and the rest of the class." Before I could say any more, he started yelling at me in broken English, "You don't know! He comes in here and doesn't eat!" I yelled back that there were others with us who weren't eating food from his store, but he didn't bother to kick us out. He singled Frankie out for no apparent reason. "You get out of here! You are no kind of teacher! My daughter is a teacher, and you are no kind of teacher! You need to learn to control your students!" Control my students? From what? From sitting quietly with me and drinking a Sprite bought from a convenience store?

At this point, Nelly yelled back, "Don't you yell at my teacher! You show her respect!" The man screamed that I was no teacher and to get out of his store. As I left, I turned to him again, "You know, I tried to tell you calmly and I respected you. Why can't you respect me and my students?" He screamed at me again to leave. At this point, Eddie was moving closer to the counter where the man was. I grabbed Eddie's arm and we all left. "I was about to go off on that man," Eddie told me outside. "I was going to push all that stuff from the counter onto the floor. But I thought that wouldn't be a good idea." I agreed with him, congratulating him and the other students for keeping calm as we walked back to the Centro.

When Eddie saw Frankie, he told him breathlessly, "Dog, you missed it. You should have seen what happened." Nelly then explained that we had a fight with the man who kicked him out, and Frankie was really surprised. "Man, I ain't never going there again," Frankie said. "That man's all messed up." For the rest of the afternoon, we discussed what happened. We were all nervous, pumped with adrenaline, thinking of what we should have said to the man. "That was racism, I think," Nelly summed up, and we all agreed. Once we were a bit calmer, Eddie asked me, "Are you going to write this down?" "Of course I am," I answered. And all my students laughed. For me, this was data, a perfect example of how certain people — in this case, young Latino men who dress a particular way — are constructed as dangerous, undesirable, and threatening, and how these discursive practices have very real, material consequences. For my students, this was a common, albeit lamentable, incident reinforcing their marginalization in their own neighborhoods. It was no accident that Frankie was singled out and I was not. Gentrification discursively inscribes who is dangerous and who is a desirable customer, justifying rude treatment of those who appear to pose a threat, namely young, poor people of color.

The consequences of these gentrification processes are extremely gendered. Young women, for example, are less likely than men to be harassed by the police, but they do experience hostility from other city and neighborhood institutions. Many women I knew agonized over their interactions with city bureaucrats and other professionals because they felt marked linguistically, educationally, racially, and in terms of class. They sometimes asked me to accompany them to appointments, to make calls to city agencies for them, and at times, to attend their children's school functions in their place. I usually would do so, but I would also talk with them, explaining that they were perfectly articulate women who didn't have to be intimidated by others. That was easy for me to say, they told me, since I spoke proper English *and* Spanish. They were poor, sometimes relied on welfare, and barely had a high school education — targets of public derision.

One spring day, for example, Nelly asked me to take her to a lawyer's office in the Loop. Earlier that year, she and her boyfriend had been in a serious car accident, and she had recently been notified that her settlement check was ready for pickup. Nelly was extremely excited, telling me of her plans for the money. Her four-year-old son, Malik, sat between us in my truck and was just as excited as his mom, asking her if she would buy him new toys with the money. We both laughed as she reassured him that he would get new things too. Nelly wanted me to accompany her into the office, but by the time we arrived, Malik was asleep, and Nelly decided she could go in by herself, while I waited in the truck with her son.

When she returned half an hour later, Nelly was visibly upset. After subtracting lawyer's fees, charges for the ambulance, and other hidden costs, it came to less money than she had expected, and when she had tried to talk with someone in the office about this, she was ignored. "I hate going to places like that. I know they're rippin' me off because all they see when they look at me, you know — they think that I don't have any education, or I'm not educated. And they take advantage." As we drove back to her apartment in Logan Square, she fought back tears, telling me that she had been counting on that money to pay her bills. But the worst part of all was the humiliation she had experienced, feeling that she was "looked down on" for who she was.

She expressed similar concerns when looking for a new apartment. After many years of living doubled up with her mother, Nelly had to move. Things were getting tense in the overcrowded apartment they shared, and she needed to find a new place to live. For a month, Nelly attended class sporadically. When she finally did come to class, she explained that she was having a hard time finding an apartment she could afford in her gentrifying neighborhood. Landlords refused to return her calls, were not forthcoming when she tried to make appointments with them, and when she finally was able to see something, they showed her small, dingy apartments with paint peeling from the walls. One apartment didn't even have a back door. "I want to stay in the neighborhood where I am now," she said sadly. But this was looking increasingly more difficult with such high rent. All of this made her very depressed. When she finally did find an apartment, it was in an unfamiliar, largely Polish neighborhood in the western section of Logan Square. Even though it was a nice area, Nelly felt uncomfortable, judged, and at times invisible.

> N: If you go to a real nice neighborhood . . . you know, because I'm nappy-headed [she laughs nervously]. You know, they treat you like nothing . . . like they think you steal or like — suppose you buy a pack of cigarettes and they're $2.75, well, they'll count [the money] and assume something like, "Oh, well, this person looks like trouble," you know. This person's Puerto Rican. . . . In their mind, a spic or whatever.

> I: How do you know they think that? What do they do that makes you think they think that?

> N: Because [she laughs] I could tell because of the way they act. With an attitude, you know. Like . . . they can't even look at you. . . . I don't know how to describe it, but it's a look that I know. It's just — I'm a real nice person. People judge me like — maybe because I'm big . . . I'm like big-boned and I feel like people think that I'm mean. But I'm not. I'm real good. I'm a good person, you know. And I don't like prejudice . . . but . . . sometimes I *do* say something like, "I hate polacks." [She looks embarrassed and laughs nervously. I ask her why.] . . . Because they think of us as like real bad people. They think of Puerto Ricans as like — they don't know our history, you know? You know what I'm saying? They think they're white because they have blonde hair. And being white is no big thing, you know. . . . It's like [we're all] human beings. We all got mouths, eyes, . . . arms, and legs. Not all of us . . . none of us are perfect. You know, there's some people who don't got legs or whatever. But it's just like they treat you, like we're nothing. . . . I got an example. One day I was with my mom and we went to Walgreens. And my mom, she bought a pack of cigarettes . . . and my mom was like, "Can I have some matches?" And she was a Polish lady. And she looked at my mom and she got a pack of matches and she threw them at my mom. Okay? And . . . I don't know if I overreacted, but I grabbed her arm and I told her, "Don't throw the

matches at my mom, because you don't know who I am. You don't know who she is. Just because we're Puerto Rican doesn't . . . mean you have to discriminate." And she was like, "Do you want to talk to my manager?" And I go, "Yeah, I want to speak to your manager." And he was Polish.

I: So what did he say?

N: He was like, "Oh, there was nothing wrong. She didn't mean it. She was probably just in a hurry." I go, "There's nobody in the store barely!" . . . I told him, "I'll never [come] here again. And if I have any friends that come here, I'll never tell them to come here." It was on Belmont [Avenue]. You know, that upsets me. [She pauses.] Like around here, my neighborhood is 60 percent Polish. So, like, these people — not these people because I don't want to sound like a racist [she laughs]. But I feel like they look at us like nothing. They'll pass right by me. . . . I always say hello to little old men . . . these little old men that pass by. Not that I know them . . . but I always see them and say hi. And sometimes . . . somebody will pass by and I'll just smile and they look at me like, "Why are you even smiling at me? I don't like you." [She pauses.] . . . Lately I don't even smile. I just don't even look at people. I just keep on minding my own business.

Nelly's feeling of being invisible, judged, and uncomfortable in a new neighborhood is one reason why many women resist moving to new areas. In response, Puerto Rican women have come up with new housing options, like doubling up with other family members and close friends, periodically taking in boarders, and squeezing large extended families into smaller apartments in order to remain in neighborhoods where, over the years, they have cultivated rich networks of neighbors, stores, and small businesses that enable them to feed and clothe their families from month to month. Mercedes and her family, for example, could have found a bigger and better apartment farther west in the city, but she would rather stay in Humboldt Park, near her network of friends who provide companionship and financial and emotional help. When she returned to Chicago a year after moving to San Sebastián, she found an apartment around the corner from the neglected and deteriorating apartment where she had lived before. The dangerous but gentrifying neighborhood has an important use value for her that would be difficult to replace, and women like Mercedes have invested great amounts of time and energy in cultivating these relationships and figuring out where to buy basic foodstuffs based on price and quality.

Aida, for example, consistently talked about moving away from the *locura* (craziness) of her gang- and drug-ridden neighborhood, but she recognized the convenience of living in West Town and was proud of her economic strategies, which effectively stretched the household monthly income. "I buy my meat at Lorimar. I get my eggs and milk from Edmar's. And I can walk over to K-Mart, over on Milwaukee [Avenue]. I have everything I need right here." This was often a point of contention between her and her husband, Eli, who wanted to find a larger apartment farther west, away from their troubled neighborhood. But because Aida did not have a driver's license, she didn't want to be far from familiar stores and kin and friendship networks. "One day I'll get my house," she would say. "I'll get my license and my house, but not yet."

These creative strategies for remaining in one's neighborhood are frequently insufficient, however, and Latino families are increasingly forced to move farther west, into new and unfamiliar neighborhoods. According to 2000 census data, Hermosa, Avondale, and Belmont Cragin — the community areas just west of the Near Northwest Side neighborhoods — have indexed a dramatic rise in their Latino population of between 40 and 200 percent.[35] And although these new places may appear to be safer, more spacious, and quieter than their previous communities, women are faced with creating new support networks, learning to navigate unfamiliar surroundings, and becoming more dependent on automobiles — their own and those of friends and family — to get around the city. These changes may seem inconsequential, but they have a profound impact on women both emotionally and materially. The women must invest a lot of time to create relations that are critical for their households in the new neighborhoods. They are often more dependent on others for transportation as well. When *puertorriqueñas* do have their own cars, they rarely own them, instead paying a large portion of their monthly income in order to finance them, an increasingly common strategy among the poor, who rely on what Brett Williams calls the "fringe banking system" in order to get by.[36] Chicago's housing crisis has clearly had a profound impact on the lives of the city's most vulnerable residents.

Residents of the Near Northwest Side often express frustration with the changes occasioned by gentrification. They frequently say they are powerless against the police; against the negative stereotypes that people form about them based on their language, class, education, and phenotype (including skin color, hair, and facial features); and against the economic and political clout newcomers bring with them to their neighborhoods. Indeed, the poor believe they have little power in their lives, and gentrification only heightens their sense of impotence. Of course there are moments of resistance — young men using exceedingly polite language to resist police officers, knowing and claiming one's civil rights to circumvent unlawful police practices, refusing to leave one's neighborhood despite pressures from landlords and newcomers. But, as anthropologist Eric Wolf points out, structural power — the political-economic forces structuring the terrain of human activity — is often much harder to resist.[37]

La Casita and Other Community Strategies of Resistance

Since the early 1990s, community activists, neighborhood residents, and local businesses have organized on various fronts to resist the negative consequences of gentrification in Humboldt Park. They have done so largely by using history as an interpretive lens for understanding contemporary struggles and by linking local problems to broader questions of Puerto Rico's political status.[38] A popular bumper sticker featuring the Division Street flags with the words, "Aquí luchamos, aquí nos quedamos" (Here we fought, and here we shall remain), is an example of this intermingling of local and nationalist history. Not only is it a reminder of the 1966 Division Street Riots, but it also suggests a collective memory of displacement from Lincoln Park to Humboldt Park in the 1960s and a community determined to oppose further residential dislocation in the 1990s. The prominence of Chicago's Puerto Rican flag grounds these local struggles within a nationalist narrative that is also constructed transnationally. It is widely known and well documented that the most visible community activists in Humboldt Park are *independentistas*.[39] Not surprisingly, their use of history is frequently at odds with *estadistas,* who criticize nationalist heroes like Pedro Albizu Campos as terrorists and oppose activists' efforts to enshrine them in local celebrations and monuments. These struggles reveal important cleavages among Puerto Ricans that map onto nationalist politics regarding Puerto Rico's political status. Despite these intergroup conflicts, community organizers have effectively mobilized local support to resist further gentrification in their neighborhoods through cultural activities, public art, and creative organizing strategies drawing on interethnic coalition building. What follows are examples of how community residents have organized effectively around such issues.

PROTECTED HOUSING

In the fall of 1995, the Humboldt Park Empowerment Partnership (HPEP) distributed flyers throughout Near Northwest Side neighborhoods announcing "a grassroots movement of Humboldt Park institutions . . . dedicated to improving the life of the community surrounding the Park." An umbrella organization of more than sixty nonprofit community organizations, churches, block clubs, banks, and hospitals, HPEP organized public meetings to document residents' concerns about their neighborhoods. Their ultimate goal was to use the information from these forums to create a land use plan that would develop Humboldt Park in a way that would strengthen the community and protect low-income residents from being displaced by private developers. "Joining HPEP," the flyer announced, "is an act of self-defense." Together these community organizations aimed to create a healthier community and defend the residents against "speculation by outsiders who don't know or care about our people, institutions, or community."

To this end, HPEP encouraged people to stay in the neighborhood despite its problems, which was not an easy task since television and print media frequently provided sensational accounts of gang violence and made biblical references to a "Puerto Rican exodus" from Humboldt Park.[40] They lobbied the mayor's office for job training programs and for policy measures that would keep manufacturing jobs in the area. They organized demonstrations protesting city plans to place abandoned buildings on the fast track demolition program, pushing instead for rehabilitated housing for low-income residents. And they held meetings to inform people about developers' coercive tactics — instilling fear and exaggerating crime statistics — to get people to move. "Developers want Humboldt Park," according to Xavier Nogueras, HPEP chair. "The community is saying yes, we have our gang problems, but moving out is not the solution."[41]

After years of grassroots organizing and pressure on City Hall, the Chicago City Council designated parts of Humboldt Park a redevelopment zone, giving Puerto Rican alderman Billy Ocasio and HPEP control over land use. Under the new redevelopment plan, the city would appropriate nearly two hundred properties — most of them vacant lots — in Humboldt Park and give them to private developers pledging to construct affordable housing. The project included single-family homes, two-story residences, and designated green spaces, all in an effort to encourage home ownership among low-income families.[42]

Other groups, like Bickerdike Redevelopment Corporation, a nonprofit affordable housing developer in the Near Northwest Side, have also pushed for new units of affordable housing. Like HPEP, Bickerdike believes that home ownership and housing development are the most effective ways to resist gentrification.[43] The Chicago Mutual Housing Network has also joined the fray with the Humboldt Park Tenant Ownership Project, which would create 150 cooperative units for low- and middle-income families. And Latino housing groups, such as Lucha, Bohio, and Latinos United, have worked with these organizations to resist gentrification by facilitating home ownership, creating more affordable housing, and keeping Puerto Ricans, Latinos, and other working-class people in the neighborhood.

PASEO BORICUA

Efforts to protect low-income housing and provide more affordable housing options on the Near Northwest Side are part of a larger redevelopment plan designed to preserve a Puerto Rican presence in Humboldt Park by creating multi-ethnic coalitions across race and class, supporting local businesses, and promoting cultural development. To this end, the member organizations of HPEP worked with local political leaders and community activists to establish the Humboldt Park Empowerment Zone Strategic Plan in 1996. According to sociologist Nilda Flores-González, this economic initiative focused on the development of commercial strips "by attracting investors, particularly those from Puerto Rico who can provide products and services in high demand." A key component of this economic development plan was the creation of Paseo Boricua, "a mile-long stretch of Division Street between Western Avenue and Mozart Avenue that has been designated as the gate to the Puerto Rican community." Paseo Boricua is home to a number of Puerto Rican and Latino businesses — Mexican and Puerto Rican *panaderías* (bakeries), Puerto Rican restaurants, music stores, and gift shops — and more than half of the buildings are Latino- or Puerto Rican–owned. In addition to its vibrant commercial life, Paseo Boricua is adorned with culturally significant objects that animate the neighborhood with a distinctive Caribbean flavor and, perhaps more importantly, deploy cultural symbols and images in order to claim a Puerto Rican space and resist encroaching gentrification. *Placitas* with beautiful benches and little square cement tables for domino games adorn Paseo Boricua's sidewalks. And black metal plates engraved with cultural symbols representing Puerto Rico's *tres raíces* (three roots) — African, Taíno, and Spanish — alternate with Spanish-style lampposts resembling those found in *Viejo San Juan*. More recently, several stores along Paseo Boricua have renovated their storefronts to resemble colonial-era Spanish buildings commonly found in Old San Juan, and in 1997 *La*

Casita de Don Pedro, a small wooden house reminiscent of pre-industrial rural Puerto Rico, was built in an empty lot purchased and developed by Pedro Albizu Campos High School and Architreasures. With its manicured gardens and open area leading up the front porch, *la casita* provides a space for cultural activities, such as free *plena* and *bomba* workshops, presentations, and other community gatherings.[44]

The commercial activity and culturally significant objects lining Paseo Boricua lie between two fifty-ton steel Puerto Rican flags arching across Division Street at Artesian Avenue on the east and Mozart Street on the west. Inaugurated on Three Kings Day, January 6, 1995 — also the centennial celebration of the Puerto Rican flag — the Division Street flags are made of "a sinuous, overhead network of steel tubes . . . [that are] beguilingly airy: buoyant fancies of the highway, high-tech crocheting in welded metal, civic art, ethnic imagery and proud gateways to a neighborhood hungering for its place in the sun."[45] For many Puerto Ricans, these objects are an important source of cultural and national pride, not unlike the Chinatown gate near Cermak Road or the beautiful arch welcoming visitors to the Mexican neighborhood of La Villita. "I think [the Division Street flags] are sharp," Nelly explained in class, to the approval of her classmates. "It makes me feel proud. It's like we're noticed."

Paseo Boricua's importance extends beyond the Puerto Rican community in Chicago. As part of an economic development plan that joins cultural symbols to critical issues of affordable housing, residential security, support for small businesses, and services for neighborhood residents, Paseo Boricua has become an important model for other communities working to promote economic development in poor and working-class neighborhoods. In Puerto Rico, the Division Street flags and neighborhood have become almost as well known as El Barrio in New York City. Islanders wear T-shirts emblazoned with images of the Division Street flags, and while conducting my fieldwork in Puerto Rico in 1998, people often asked to see pictures of Paseo Boricua and wanted to know more about the Puerto Rican community there. These changes have rekindled ethnic pride and reaffirmed Humboldt Park's designation as the cultural, material, and spiritual center of Puerto Rican Chicago.[46] On a pleasant day, it is not uncommon to walk down *la Division* (a popular way of referring to this area) and see young children playing in front of stores or entering the Boriken Bakery, older men playing dominoes, and women pushing babies in strollers. Salsa music fills the air, drifting from cars and from the apartments above the businesses and stores along the street, while street vendors provide a vibrant street life, selling everything from clothing to savory *pinchos* (shish kebabs) and Mexican *paletas* (popsicles) — including, near the corner of Rockwell and Division Streets, an old man who religiously sells homemade coconut ice cream.

In order to preserve the neighborhood's use value, grassroots organizations like the Prairie Fire Organizing Committee have sponsored events, bringing together newcomers and long-time community residents to discuss how they can avoid the racial, class, and cultural tensions and residential dislocation characteristic of places like West Town and Wicker Park. Preliminary suggestions include property tax rebates for longtime homeowners and interethnic social activities to promote a stronger sense of community among neighborhood residents. While these efforts to avoid displacement are certainly a move in the right direction, they also require federal and local policies that provide residential security for low- and moderate-income residents, as well as progressive tax and zoning laws to protect neighborhoods from private developers.[47] Local elected officials, grassroots activists, and community leaders have organized to this end, although, as other scholars have shown, these moments of grassroots activism and multiracial coalition-building across class are "fragile and difficult to sustain over time."[48] These instances of collective action and political activism may be strengthened by linking the place-bound struggles of gentrification in the Near Northwest Side to shared issues of economic and political justice that transcend the neighborhood's boundaries, such as the ongoing struggle to expand public and affordable housing and improve local schools, while preserving community control and school reform.

THE FIGHT FOR CLEMENTE HIGH SCHOOL

Roberto Clemente High School — the second-largest Latino high school in the Chicago public school system — is located on Humboldt Park's eastern border. Despite the neighborhood's changing demographics, more than half of Clemente's Latino students are Puerto Rican and approximately 80 percent of its students are eligible for Title I funds.[49] Since the early 1970s, Clemente has emerged as a critical and contested Puerto Rican site, reflecting both national political struggles over the nature and implementation of multicultural school curricula and divisions among Puerto Ricans regarding Puerto Rico's political status. "Clemente is a symbol of cultural affirmation for us," a prominent *independentista* community leader explained one Friday evening. Indeed, its history attests to its importance in the lives of Puerto Rican residents in the city.

In 1973, students shut down then-Tuley High School, calling for the removal of its principal, demanding changes in the curriculum and building improvements, and pushing to rename the school after the famous Puerto Rican baseball player Roberto Clemente.[50] Fifteen years later, Clemente initiated an innovative school reform emphasizing a multicultural curriculum, parental involvement, and student-centered teaching practices. Despite its critics, the Clemente reform plan successfully reduced student dropout rates by more than 10 percent, and many of the ideas were implemented in other schools in the city. These reforms quickly came to a halt in 1996, however, when the Chicago Public Schools launched an investigation into mismanagement of funds.[51]

Clemente is also linked to a variety of community organizations in the Near Northwest Side. Pedro Albizu Campos Alternative High School, located in the Puerto Rican Cultural Center, used to be a Clemente satellite site, and it still maintains important institutional links with the school. Clemente hosts cultural programs, speakers, and other community events sponsored by neighborhood groups and open to the community. Organizations like Aspira and Vida/SIDA are connected to Clemente through its educational and counseling programs.[52] In addition to its symbolic importance, Clemente became an important space for people's material livelihood under school reform. Through the Parents' Institute, Clemente hired parents as tutors, office help, hall monitors, and mentors to address problems in the school. They also established a legal clinic with workshops instructing immigrants and parents on their rights in the school system, providing referrals to students with legal problems, and providing other services to parents.[53]

While most barrio residents are proud of Clemente High School — especially its fantastic murals boldly depicting Puerto Rican cultural and nationalist symbols along the outside wall along Division Street, its identity as *the* Puerto Rican high school, and its innovative programs affirming ethnic pride through a multicultural curriculum — they also worry about problems with gangs, school violence, high dropout rates, and low test scores, problems common in most Chicago public schools. Clemente's bold school reform program was one attempt to address these problems and provide radically different solutions. In 1995, the Chicago Public Schools administration placed Clemente on financial probation, and on academic probation in 1996.

On February 4, 1997, a front-page headline in the *Chicago Sun-Times* announced, "School funds used to push terrorists' release." The many articles that followed that day — and in the days and years since the story first unfolded — reported that between 1992 and 1995, Clemente High School misused Title I poverty funds, using the money to promote Puerto Rican independence, raise money for the campaign to release fifteen Puerto Rican political prisoners, and indoctrinate the students with anti-American ideas. *Independentista* teachers were accused of infusing the classroom with politics and of brainwashing students with anti-American ideas.

This was not the first scandal to hit Clemente. In 1995, the *Sun-Times* accused the school of misusing Title I monies, citing a list of illegitimate and arbitrary uses, despite the fact that some of these programs became models for other programs implemented by the school commissioner in other contexts.[54] For barrio activists, the attacks on Clemente were just another example of the community under assault. In 1984, FBI agents raided the Puerto Rican Cultural Center in search of explosives and evidence linking their leaders to the FALN (Armed Forces of National Liberation). In the summer of 1995, federal agents raided and eventually closed another Puerto Rican organization, the Humboldt Park Infant Mortality Initiative (HIMRI), claiming that it was housing terrorists. On the morning of that raid, community workers at the Ruiz Belvis Cultural Center had reason to believe that they would be raided as well. Lydia, one of the Centro's directors, warned Centro staff to be prepared — to have all paperwork in order, "just in case we're next." Like many barrio activists, the workers and volunteers at Ruiz Belvis have seen the FBI, COINTELPRO, and Chicago's "red squad" destroy community organizations by infiltrating their groups and using minor bookkeeping errors and building code violations to indict and eventually jail community leaders.

For those unfamiliar with the details of the political struggle, the Clemente scandal was bewildering. As I tutored Jesse Leyva in his parents' home one evening shortly after the story broke, his mother, Celia, turned up the volume on the television so that we could hear the "new developments" unfold on the Spanish-language news. "This is ridiculous," she later told me in an interview. "I think they're just tying to bring us down. That's what they are trying to do. You know, I don't think it's true what they're saying." "Why do you think they are trying to bring us down?" I asked her. "Because we're Spanish!" she said emphatically. "Because we're Spanish and probably . . . Clemente is just trying to help, you know."

Two of Celia's sons, including Jesse, had attended Clemente High School, but neither had graduated. She wasn't particularly invested in defending the school because, as she pointed out every time I arrived to tutor her son, who was studying for his G.E.D., they had failed her and her children. But she did believe that the Clemente administration and teachers were committed to improving the school. Like many Puerto

Rican parents, Celia believed that the attack on Clemente was part of a larger problem of discrimination against Latinos on both local and national levels. In Chicago, undercover sting operations had revealed widespread corruption in two largely minority police districts, and intense protests against police brutality in Latino communities had helped to uncover its pervasiveness in the city.[55] Nationally, California's Proposition 187 in 1994, welfare reform in 1996, and changes in immigration laws all had contributed to the popular belief that Latinos were under siege. "Por qué no nos quieren aquí?" (Why don't they want us here?), a young Mexican woman asked me one day as we washed our clothes at Paradise Wash. When I tried to explain, she turned away to continue folding her clothes. We Latinos all work hard, she said. Why wouldn't they want us here to work and improve ourselves? For many, the Clemente scandal was another example of how "they" didn't want "us" here.

Like the *mejicana* washing her clothes, barrio activists believed Latinos — and in the case of Clemente, Puerto Ricans in particular — were unjustly persecuted, and they used metaphors of war to describe this struggle. Before a board meeting one evening, a television producer from a local public channel dedicated to Puerto Rican programming came to community leaders at Ruiz Belvis to discuss the upcoming community forum on Clemente's future. "We're at war with the yuppies," he warned. "There is an invasion in this neighborhood like the one in Lincoln Park, *compañeros*." Everyone in the room agreed with him, with Lydia (Centro director) adding that although the problems at Clemente were complicated, one thing was clear: The Puerto Rican community needed to defend the school because it represented the political and cultural struggles won in the 1960s and 1970s. Retreat meant allowing Humboldt Park to become another Lincoln Park, since schools were an important anchor against the gentrification process. If you changed the schools, making them magnet schools, for example, you helped facilitate this gentrification process in the neighborhoods. "We need unity in the question of Clemente," Lydia said forcefully. And we need to understand, she continued, that this is about fighting for local power, local control of schools, and stronger communities.[56]

The metaphors of war continued at the Clemente community forum on May 3, 1997. With parents, students, Local School Council members, Chicago Public Schools (CPS) officials, and community activists all in attendance, the discussion opened with a performance by Son del Barrio, a nationally acclaimed salsa band made up of Clemente students.[57] With their opening song, Son del Barrio perfectly captured the benefits of smart, culturally grounded school reform. When they began their opening song,

"Vengo del Caribe; salsa con reggae traigo para ti" (I come from the Caribbean; salsa with reggae I bring to you), the audience was immediately captivated. The group was quite impressive, embodying the political economy of migration and culture through their mixing of musical genres, their interweaving of English and Spanish, and their challenging of stereotypes, with lines like, "Los Latinos somos inteligentes, no delincuentes" (We Latinos are intelligent, we're not delinquents). Their performance was impressive, setting the tone for the heated discussion that followed.

Representatives from the Latino Institute, Aspira, and the Local School Council opened the bilingual meeting by explaining that the purpose of the forum was to dispel the myths about Clemente and allow community members, students, and parents to express their concerns about the school's future. "If there were mistakes," Alina, the Aspira representative, calmly assured the audience, "we need to correct them and move ahead." The discussions and comments that followed were critical, yet respectful, but when Len Dominguez, the head of Clemente's probation team, refused to speak Spanish, there was an uproar. "If they understood me in Puerto Rico [when I spoke in both English and Spanish without simultaneous translation], then I am sure you will understand me here." His refusal to follow the agreed-upon format was a clear example of the administration's disdain for local control. It was also a subtle condemnation of Clemente's claims to cultural authenticity.[58]

The most powerful moment of the day, however, was an impassioned speech in Spanish by Ellie Lorenzo, a politically active *mejicana* whose daughter attended Clemente. She asked Len Dominguez and other CPS officials to explain Clemente's new enrollment plan, slated to be implemented the following year. As a concerned mother and committed member of the community, she wanted to know where the students diverted from Clemente would go, and admitted that she feared such a plan was another way to facilitate gentrification in the neighborhood.

Even though I am Mexican, I respect these [Puerto Rican] flags very much. This school is ours! And it lies between the two Puerto Rican flags. [City Alderman] Billy Ocasio fought for those flags. And they are a symbol to the yuppies that this is ours! If they're going to try to kick us out of here, I'll tell you now that there will be a big fight. We're ready for war, and the war is here!

By the end of Ellie's speech, people were on their feet, clapping, yelling, and chanting to keep and defend Clemente "as our own." Like the Division Street flags anchored nearby, Clemente High School is a symbol of resistance, defiance, and creating place.

The war metaphors surrounding the struggle for Clemente truly capture the daily lives of many Puerto Ricans living in the Near Northwest Side. They are patrolled, watched, monitored, and subjected to the violence of displacement, increased economic marginalization, destabilized communities, and substandard housing. The conflicts in neighborhoods like Humboldt Park, West Town, and Logan Square raise troubling questions about how to enhance neighborhood use value without sacrificing security and cultural integrity. These are some of the challenges facing many Chicago Puerto Ricans as they try to build safe, livable neighborhoods with accountable schools, affordable housing, and meaningful community. Yet equally critical is the way in which grassroots activists, elected officials, and community leaders engage in collective action so that their struggle for economic and political justice, which is grounded in a particular place, is not limited by neighborhood boundaries, but rather expands conventional ideas of community, place, identity, and belonging to include people who share common interests and concerns and who might otherwise be excluded.

Place-making in Chicago, like San Sebastián, is a deeply contested process, involving the power to determine the meaning and use of social space and the ability to define boundaries of inclusion and exclusion based on hierarchies of race, class, gender, sexuality, and culture. In both contexts, neoliberal economic policies have shaped the terrain in which place-making occurs, although they have done so in locally specific ways that provide opportunities and constraints distinctive to each place. The paucity of public housing for Latinos in Chicago and increased privatization of the city's housing market, for example, means that poor and working-class communities are vulnerable to revitalization projects that consistently displace them, forcing those with few economic resources to creatively strategize to meet their housing needs. Federal and municipal neglect of poor neighborhoods and families, coupled with a new "law-and-order state," exacerbates the precariousness of poor families who inhabit a landscape of risk and danger that includes law enforcement officials. The dwindling number of steady full-time jobs in San Sebastián requires people to cobble together formal and informal employment and creatively strategize to make ends meet as well. Many Puerto Ricans meet these challenges by constructing, participating, or at least maintaining and imagining transnational connections that become a critical part of how they understand themselves and the families and communities they hope to build.

CHAPTER 6

Transnational Lives, Kin Work,
and Strategies of Survival

In the preceding chapters, I have moved between San Sebastián and
Chicago, highlighting each community's migration history in order to
explore the origins of Puerto Rican displacement and illustrate how
regional and global political-economic processes have shaped migration
practices, gender ideologies, cultural and national identity, and local
struggles for place, as well as the various ways in which individual
migrants and their families have responded to these economic forces. One
way migrants have done so is by engaging in transnational practices that
provide social, economic, cultural, and emotional support to kin both in
the United States and in Puerto Rico. Recently, scholars have theorized
about these linkages, calling them transnational social fields, communities, circuits, and specifically in the context of parenting, transnational
motherhood. While there continues to be debate regarding the most
accurate label for transnational phenomena, there is broad agreement
among feminist scholars that women play an important role in creating,
maintaining, and reproducing transnational practices.[1] Women do this
through their productive and reproductive labor as migrants, their role in
caring for migrants' children, and their preservation of the links between
migrant and nonmigrant households.

For many poor and working-class Puerto Rican women and their families, transnationalism is a survival strategy. Some are highly mobile, moving frequently within a transnational social field; others actually move
very little, engaging instead in the transnational work of planning, strategizing, writing letters, making phone calls, and sharing resources that

links households together. Still others do not engage in what is usually regarded as transnational activity, yet they live their lives in what Sarah J. Mahler and Patricia R. Pessar describe as a "transnational cognitive space," wherein people imagine themselves as migrants or transnational actors and make decisions based on these imagined possibilities.[2] Aida Rodríguez was born in Chicago and has lived there almost her entire life, except for a brief time at the age of thirteen when her parents sent her to live in Puerto Rico, and the one year she lived with her husband and children in Brooklyn, New York. She does not visit Puerto Rico regularly, and her correspondence with family and friends on the island is episodic, motivated primarily by the possibility of sending her children (particularly her daughters) to Puerto Rico as teenagers if they begin to "get into trouble." Regardless of whether she actually sends her children to the island, she imagines this as a real possibility and makes decisions accordingly about strengthening particular kin and friendship networks in Puerto Rico. Considering this alternative soothes Aida, making her feel like she has some control over her life and the options she can provide for her children in a situation she consistently describes as chaotic, out-of-control, and unpredictable.

Mercedes Rubio's transnational practices, on the other hand, involve high levels of mobility and complex networks connecting her simultaneously to Chicago and San Sebastián. Mercedes moved between San Sebastián and Chicago three times between 1996 and 1998, and with each move, the composition of her household changed dramatically. In 1996, she lived in Chicago with four of her children, including her oldest daughter, Yamila, and her family. When she returned to San Sebastián later that year, she initially lived with her sister, subsequently with her son, his wife, and their child, before returning to Chicago with her two youngest children in 1997. Another daughter, Tamara, arrived in Chicago with her two children later that year, and they all lived together until Mercedes returned to San Sebastián in 1998 for an indefinite stay. Both Aida and Mercedes live transnationally, partly in response to the social conditions in Chicago that make raising and supporting families uncertain: the fear of gangs, inadequate neighborhood schools, and precarious housing options. Yet their activities and decisions also reflect their agency, shaped by their particular social situation as racialized women migrants strategizing to make ends meet.

In what follows, I continue to move between San Sebastián and Chicago to show a range of transnational activities and links, the nature of these ties, what they mean to the women who maintain and depend on them, and how, in this context, migration and transnational kin work have become culturally specific survival strategies employed largely by women. In Chicago, first-, second-, and third-generation Puerto Rican women migrants engage in these transnational practices, and they do so largely based on particular understandings of life "here" versus "there." For many women, urban life in Chicago, while providing a degree of liberation they believe is unavailable to them in rural Puerto Rico, is regarded as dangerous, uncertain, and severe — a vastly different life than that on the island. Cultural organizations, community leaders, and community-building strategies steeped in Puerto Rico's rural and folk traditions all serve to reinforce these contrasting visions of Chicago and Puerto Rico, although they cannot be understood merely in terms of a simple antinomy. Rather, ideas of Chicago and Puerto Rico are cultural categories through which we can understand Puerto Rican history and contemporary urban life produced in a context of colonialism, domination, inequality, and uneven development on the island and the mainland.[3]

Urban Life and Puerto Rican Folklore

Around the time local community leaders built *la casita* on Division Street, Mattel launched its new line of international Barbies. Puerto Rican Barbie is a light-skinned, dark-haired beauty dressed in a white peasant dress typical of iconic representations of the Puerto Rican *jíbara*. On the back of Barbie's box is her own narrative of Puerto Rican history and culture: what she and other Puerto Ricans eat, where they live, and even a brief discussion of Puerto Rico's political status. The Puerto Rican Barbie text ends with a quick pitch for tourism on the island, inviting all to visit her *en la isla del encanto* (the enchanted island) to enjoy Puerto Rico's unique — and apparently unchanging and rural — cultural traditions.

When I asked Aida if she knew about Puerto Rican Barbie, she became visibly excited, asking me how much it cost and where she could buy it. Like the other Puerto Rican women I knew, Aida had not heard of Mattel's new dolls. These Barbies were sold at pricey toy stores like F.A.O. Schwartz on Michigan Avenue, and not at the local K-Mart or other discount and dollar stores frequented by poor and working-class *puerto-rriqueñas*. When I told Aida how much Puerto Rican Barbie cost, she looked shocked and told me that she could easily buy several Barbies at K-Mart for that price. But a *Puerto Rican* Barbie would have been a special addition to her doll collection and to the collection of culturally significant objects adorning her home. Over the years, Aida has saved ashtrays, ceramic figurines, scenic pictures, coffee mugs, and painted plates with the words *Puerto Rico* or *La isla del encanto* emblazoned on them. These are cherished *recuerdos* (souvenirs) that show she is remembered fondly by family and friends traveling between Chicago and Puerto Rico and that embody her connection to the island. Displaying such *recuerdos* is a cultural performance common among migrants, who use these items to show that their lives "here" are interwoven with people and memories from "there."[4]

These *recuerdos* also symbolize and inscribe Puerto Rico and Chicago as culturally distinct places, one embodying nature, rural life, and a quaint pre-industrial life, and the other urban, industrial, and cosmopolitan. Migrants in San Sebastián, for example, prominently displayed spectacularly large posters of the Chicago and Manhattan skylines in their living rooms. They also had sports memorabilia — usually the Chicago Bulls or the New York Yankees — around their homes and wore T-shirts, caps, and shorts bearing the names of these teams. Pictures of *el coquí* — frequently wearing a *pava* (straw hat) — palm trees, and musical instruments like *maracas* and *güiros* decorated walls, entertainment centers, and coffee tables in Chicago homes. Puerto Rican Barbie easily fits into this dichotomous vision of the island and the mainland and reinforces the cultural, ethnic, and racial boundaries defining official representations of "Puerto Ricanness" and authentic Puerto Rican culture.

For Mattel, Puerto Rican Barbie — like her ethnically correct cousins — also presents interesting marketing possibilities for selling products that allow people to lay claim to racial and ethnic identities as consumers.[5] In the name of multiculturalism, this doll is an entrée into one segment of the nation's burgeoning Latino population, one of the fastest growing consumer markets in the country today, and one that is "targeted by . . . a vast network of advertising agencies and an entire marketing industry selling [Latinos] consumer products by addressing them as a common people and market."[6] Mattel's production, packaging, and distribution of cultural diversity through an international line of Barbies can be understood as what Arlene Dávila has identified as the "homogenization of a heterogeneous population" that increases Latinos' visibility in U.S. society simultaneously with "larger processes of partial containment and recognition of ethnic differences that are at play in other spheres of contemporary U.S. society, such as the level of politics and social and cultural policies."[7] This type of marketing strategy is an example of the danger in some multiculturalist thinking. It reifies culture, ignoring race and class differences, and preserves a "billiard balls" approach to culture that is extremely appealing to Americans eager to consume "authentic" cultural production.[8] It doesn't matter that most Puerto Ricans both on the island and the mainland are urban dwellers and are just as likely to eat hamburgers and pizza as *arroz con gandules.* Puerto Rican Barbie, like *la casita,* represents an authentic, pristine cultural past: before high unemployment, before migration, and before an alleged "culture of poverty" developed in Puerto Rican and American cities.

These images of rural Puerto Rico as a safe physical, cultural, and social space are extremely seductive. Throughout my field research in Chicago, second- and third-generation Puerto Ricans enjoyed telling me stories about their visits to the island or their plans to save money to take their families there one day. Aida frequently mentioned her short stay there as a young girl. And even though she is extremely critical of her parents' decision to send her away at such a young age — she was thirteen and was sent "against my own free will" — she remembers this time quite nostalgically. For her, Puerto Rico is like Eden, where the food is plentiful, no one goes hungry, and you can pick fruit off the trees when you wish. "You know, you can go out to your backyard and get *una china y un mango cuando te de la gana. Quieres un guineo? Corta allí* [an orange and a mango whenever you want. You want a banana? Just cut one there]. I was like, 'Man, *aquí nadie se muere de hambre'* [no one dies of hunger here]."

Yvette Jiménez recently visited Puerto Rico for the first time, and even though she is clear that she does not want to move there — "It was boring. I would never want to go there to live" — she dreams of taking her children there one day. "I told my sister," she said in an interview with me, "that if I don't make it to July of next year, if anything was to happen to me, my goal is just for my kids to go to Puerto Rico no matter what. I don't care if you have to put them on a plane *alone,* they're going to Puerto Rico. That's all I ask my sisters." When I asked her why it was important for them to go, she answered, "Well, that's how I see it. . . . That's all I ever want is for my kids, I want them to go to Puerto Rico so they can go, 'Yeah, I went to Puerto Rico. I don't remember much, but I *did* go to Puerto Rico.'"

These women's perceptions of Puerto Rico, Chicago, and homeplace are complicated and often contradictory, a fact that challenges the accounts of scholars who dichotomize women's migration experiences as a source of either liberation or oppression.[9] This is particularly true among second- and third-generation *puertorriqueñas,* who see the island not as a place of gender oppression, but rather as a refuge for themselves and their children. I was particularly surprised by this finding, since most of the women I interviewed in Puerto Rico talked exhaustively of the *sufrimiento* of return (as I discussed at length in Chapter 4). One reason so many Chicago *puertorriqueñas* regard the island as a refuge is their romanticizing of the island, an image consistently reinforced by cultural centers, community leaders, and middle-class islanders visiting Chicago, who portray Puerto Rico as an oasis from the supposed chaos and danger of urban life. In fact, many Chicago *puertorriqueñas* featured in this study had spent very little or no time in Puerto Rico, despite their strong attachments to the island. The women who had lived there or visited Puerto Rico regularly often downplayed their negative impressions of the island — usually described as boring, backward, and claustrophobic — once they had children and were worried about how to raise them. Remaining connected to Puerto Rico — or forging new ties with the island — allows these women to be active agents in creating safe, meaningful lives for their families in economically circumscribed circumstances. And while they are firmly rooted in their lives in Chicago, their decisions are deeply informed by a return ideology shaped not only by their own parents' attitudes and decisions, but by their own as well. Even if they never send their children, these women guard these ties as a way of coping with the danger and uncertainty of urban life in Chicago.

The Danger of Urban Life

For working-class Puerto Rican parents, urban life is *peligrosa* (dangerous), uncertain, and filled with violence, sexual danger, racism, and discrimination. This urban danger is clearly gendered, and migration is frequently viewed as a way to address actual and potential problems with children. For young women, sexual danger figures prominently in parents' concern about their daughters' future. Aida, for example, was sent to Puerto Rico when she was thirteen "para que no me dañara" (so I wouldn't be ruined). But you know," she told me, "we [young girls] almost always come back [to Chicago] and get in worse trouble than when we left." While critical of her mother's overprotective approach to raising her, Aida expresses similar concerns in raising her own teenage daughter and is afraid that she might "meterse las patas" (get pregnant). She spends much of her time strategizing about how to get her daughter out of this sexually dangerous environment before it is "too late."

Sending her daughter to live with an aunt in Puerto Rico is one option she has considered, although she is hesitant to do so because of her own experience.

Yvette's story is similar to Aida's, although Yvette was able to resist parental pressure to go to Puerto Rico by moving in with a cousin when she was fourteen years old, shortly after her first child was born. "I didn't want to go to Puerto Rico. I didn't know anyone in Puerto Rico. I didn't know *nothing* in Puerto Rico. I wanted to stay here and get school out of the way and whatever." Her older sister, Olga, however, was sent to the island while her parents fought, separated, and tried unsuccessfully to deal with the problems of Alma, their oldest daughter. Shortly after running away from home, Alma was returned by the Department of Children and Family Services, who threatened to put Yvette and her siblings in foster care if their parents were "unable to control them." Afraid that Child Services might take their children, the parents sent Olga to live with her maternal grandmother in Puerto Rico, and when she returned, she lived with an aunt and uncle while she finished school. Sending Olga — and trying to send Yvette and Alma as well — to live in Puerto Rico was one way for the parents to keep their adolescent daughters from getting into trouble and deal with an increasingly uncertain — and unstable — domestic living arrangement.

At the Centro, teenagers frequently told stories about parents threatening to send them back to Puerto Rico if they did not change their behavior. Sixteen-year-old Mari told one of the Centro counselors that her mother wanted to send her to Puerto Rico to get her away from her boyfriend, who had recently been shot by opposition gang members. The mother was afraid that Mari and her boyfriend were "too serious" and that something might happen to her if they continued to see each other. The only way to protect her daughter, she believed, was to send her to live in Puerto Rico. Mari, of course, did not agree. But teenagers generally have little power to convince their parents otherwise.

For young men, urban danger takes the form of gang violence, racial discrimination, and problems with the police. Parents frequently see migration as a strategy for protecting young men as well as young women, although in both cases children sent to live in Puerto Rico complain that these strategies are ineffective. Two teenage brothers dropped out of my G.E.D. class, for example, when they were sent to live with their maternal grandmother in Aguadilla after becoming involved with gangs. They eventually were allowed to return, they told me, because they continued to get into trouble in Puerto Rico.

Forty-five-year-old Celia Rivera explained that while gangs are certainly a problem, she believes that the police in Chicago pose an even greater danger for her son. "There's a lot of police discrimination here. A lot," she told me in an interview. Not only do the police stop her son and other young Latino men for little or no reason, but they fail to respond or respond much more slowly to complaints by "Spanish" people. "When Spanish — when Spanish have problems with Spanish, [the police] don't care. But if a Spanish would have a problem with a white person, they would go and get that Spanish or that black person wherever they're at. And that's how these police are. They don't like Spanish people *for nothin'*!" For this reason, she regards the police as one of the greatest threats facing her son. She fears his being stopped, harassed, questioned, and possibly physically harmed by what she and other Puerto Ricans believe to be a police force that discriminates and mistreats poor and working-class Latinos in Humboldt Park.

Finally, the danger of not finishing one's education prompts many parents to send children off to finish school in Puerto Rico because they believe the children have a better chance of doing so on the island than in Chicago public schools. A counselor at a local community organization told me that even though his father worked in a factory in northern Indiana, he was sent to school in Puerto Rico so that he would graduate. After finishing high school in Puerto Rico and serving in the armed forces, he returned to Chicago to work as a high school counselor. Parents like Mercedes echoed this concern. After her daughter, Josie, fought with a group of girls at Clemente High School, she immediately set in motion plans to send her back to Puerto Rico. Josie protested, saying that she wanted to finish high school in Chicago, and ultimately she was able to convince her mother to let her stay and finish her senior year rather than risk being held back by transferring to a school in Puerto Rico. Mercedes reluctantly agreed, but continued to express doubts about the safety of Chicago public schools and the impending decisions she would have to make about where to send her younger children for high school.

Clearly, not all parents are able to — nor do they choose to — send troubled or endangered children to live with relatives in Puerto Rico. It is important to note, however, that migration is imagined as a possible solution to problems with children and as a place that is fundamentally different from urban life in Chicago. Moreover, it is usually mothers who engage in this kind of emotional work, as they draw on kin networks in Puerto Rico that they have maintained and nurtured over time. In most cases, these women were enmeshed in similar transnational household strategies when they were younger. Some were sent to Chicago to help relatives with childcare or to look for employment; others were sent to Puerto Rico because of real or imagined urban dangers. These decisions are largely informed by visions of a safe, calm, and rural Puerto Rico. The island, nineteen-year-old Lorena Santiago insisted, is just a better place to live. "[You don't] worry about coming back home or the curfew [or] police, you know. . . . It's peaceful."

The power of these ideological constructions of Puerto Rico as opposed to the mainland became very real to me one night in San Sebastián, as I worked alone in my *tía* Cristina's store. By eight o'clock on most nights, the store was filled with older men playing dominoes, talking, and drinking beer and shots of rum. The basketball-playing *jóvenes* from across the street would also join the mix, drinking sodas, smoking, playing pool, or just sitting at the store counter to talk. It was often hard to carry on a conversation over the loud music from the jukebox, which exclusively played old Spanish ballads to which the *viejitos* would croon. However, on this particular evening, the store was filled with young girls and boys playing pool and speaking English. Someone had brought in a boom box blaring rap and hip-hop, and I soon realized that most of these *jóvenes* were unfamiliar to me. I asked Gero, one of the teens who frequented the store, where all these English-speaking kids came from, and he shot me a puzzled look, explaining that there are always *jóvenes de afuera* (young people from the United States) around the neighborhood. It was simply an interesting coincidence that they were all in Barrio Saltos — and now in the store — at the same time. Some came each summer; others came and went depending on problems at home and in school. This was very common, Gero assured me. In fact, one of the young men playing pool had run away from his foster home in Arecibo and was planning to camp out on the *cancha* (outdoor basketball court) until Social Services agreed to let him return to his mother in Passaic, New Jersey. After five years of being shuttled among different homes in Puerto Rico, Pablito wanted to go home to New Jersey.

When Cristina discovered that Pablito was sleeping on the benches of the *cancha*, she was quick to get his story, alert the neighbors of the situation, and do what she could to help him. After talking with Pablito myself and following numerous conversations with Cristina and her neighbors, I came to understand that his mother — like many of the mothers I knew in Chicago — had sent him to Puerto Rico in the hope that he would go to school, stay out of trouble, and ultimately be transformed in a new environment. He was originally sent to live with his maternal grandmother in San Sebastián, but as the summer months quickly turned into a year away from home, he became anxious and wanted to leave. "It was like [my mom] forgot about me or something." Almost predictably, living with his grandparents proved to be equally problematic, and after living with them for a year, Pablo went to stay in a series of homes throughout the island: first with his *abuelos'* neighbors as "un hijo de crianza," a familiar domestic arrangement in which children are raised by close family members or their friends; then in two group homes in San Sebastián, and most recently with foster parents in Arecibo. Tired of living in foster care and group homes, Pablo tried to convince Social Services to let him go home to his mother, but they refused his appeal. Pablito responded by running away from home again, believing that either agency officials would call his mother or she would somehow discover that her son was in trouble and come to Puerto Rico to bring him back to live with her in New Jersey.

As soon as Cristina assessed the situation, Pablito was enmeshed in the web of relationships that sustain economically precarious households in the barrio: Cristina prepared meals for him, allowed him to use the store's phone to make and receive calls, and contributed for the *carro público* to the airport in Aguadilla. Community members even gave him extra money for his trip, just in case he needed it. Cristina and her neighbors provided Pablito with the same kind of support that characterized inter-household relations in the neighborhood, which were based on reciprocity and exchange. And they did so mindful that they too had benefited from these networks and that many of their own children, grandchildren, nieces, and nephews had been — or one day might be — in a situation similar to Pablito's.

Parents are not alone in their belief in the transformative powers of rural living. In fact, they share their faith with a growing movement of government and nonprofit organizations dedicated to reforming troubled urban youth through outdoors programs that emphasize survival, cooperation, and the asceticism of wilderness camps. I came to know of these organizations one May evening as I worked in the store, after selling a can of soda to an African American man my age. Earlier in the evening, I had noticed Thomas playing basketball with two teenagers across the street and immediately took notice because all of the players were black and shouted to each other in perfect English. When Thomas asked me in his broken Spanish the price for a game of pool, I asked him in English where he was from, initiating a short but informative discussion of his work with Miracle Meadows, a West Virginia–based organization focusing on troubled youth. Thomas was a counselor for the program, and like the other staff members, he lived with a small group of teenage boys in a large house in the more remote hills of San Sebastián. Miracle Meadows, he explained, directs several homes in rural areas of the United States and Puerto Rico, and their goal is to provide a new, nonurban community and environment to help youth reorient themselves and transform their lives.

When I asked some of the store regulars whether they knew of this organization, they laughed knowingly, saying that Thomas must be part of "that dangerous religious sect" living in the "mansions and huge homes in Galateo," a nearby sector. When I asked them to explain, they repeated that it was a strange religious group that had a lot of money and didn't interact with the community. They lived isolated, mysterious, and therefore suspect lives. When I told them what Thomas had told me about his program, they were clearly uninterested but agreed with what the counselor and others firmly believed: Sending children to the *campo* (countryside) was a popular and effective strategy for dealing with wayward teens. Even though many of the old-timers complained about the proliferation of youth during the summer ("It feels like I'm in New York again," one man said disgustedly one day as he left the store, which was filled with English-speaking, hip-hop-listening youth), they all agreed that San Sebastián was a safe place for young people. As one social worker commented to me in an interview, "Sometimes just the mother's *fear* that her children will be lost to the streets makes her move to Puerto Rico or send them to live here with family. And it always has positive results."

While this kind of romanticizing of rural life, homeland, and *patria* is not necessarily new, it is important to examine the imaginary character of the idea of Puerto Rico as significantly "better" than Chicago. Evelyn Trujillo's husband, Frank, told me on several occasions how dangerous Puerto Rico is today. "If you're driving your car at night and the light turns red, in Puerto Rico," he told me, "you stop to look but then keep on going because of all the carjackings going on over there." The prevailing image of Puerto Rico as safe (because it is usually imagined as rural) and Chicago as *peligroso* creates a situation in which transnational migration is a plausible solution to problems with children. In this way, migration is neither disruptive nor indicative of a lack of commitment to life on the mainland, as some researchers would have us believe.[10] Instead, it reflects a sincere concern about the state of contemporary U.S. cities, as a result of deindustrialization and federal neglect of inner-city schools and neighborhoods since the 1960s, which disproportionately affect poor Puerto Rican youth.

Culturally (In)authentic Places

Urban communities are also imagined as culturally inauthentic places where an inferior or "Americanized" Puerto Rican culture thrives. This was a popular topic of conversation among many of the women I knew and interviewed, as they were quick to point out who is *really* Puerto Rican and the different ways in which they do or do not exactly fit the "authentic" Puerto Rican profile. As Aida explained to me, "My husband's cousin, she talks to you like a Puerto Rican. She doesn't got no accent, you know. *Yo no me crié así* [I wasn't raised like that] with the whole Puerto Rican culture. . . . I was raised with the American, an American — I'm an *Americanized* Puerto Rican." When I asked Aida what she meant by this, she replied, "Well, I'm of Puerto Rican descent, but I'm with the American culture more. You know, I guess, my Spanish ain't as great — as yours is, you know." I was completely shocked by Aida's comment, since I had also engaged in this I'm-not-really-authentically-Puerto Rican insecurity. Her assessment of what constitutes "authentic" Puerto Rican culture and identity is informed, in large part, by language and the ability to speak Spanish "correctly" — a piece of linguistic ideology that takes for granted that *a* language corresponds to *a* culture and that, in this case, "Spanish is equated with Puerto Rican values and English with American values in ways that objectify both language and culture."[11]

Interestingly, speaking Spanish well is not sufficient. For Aida and many others, children need to know how to speak *Puerto Rican* Spanish and be familiar with *Puerto Rican* culture and food. In an interview in Chicago, she explained that she tells her daughter that she is "being raised in the Puerto Rican culture. So, that's what you are. A Puerto Rican. . . . [Your cousin] is being raised with the Mexican culture. . . . He eats his tacos and his tortillas and all that. What do you eat? You don't eat *pozole*. He does. *Tú comes sancocho* [You eat beef stew]. You know. He eats *tamales,* you eat *pasteles.*" Aida added that going to Puerto Rico is a way to affirm her own — and her children's — cultural roots through knowledge of Puerto Rican history, language, culture, and food. She wants to send her children to Puerto Rico so they can see "*qué lindo es . . . cómo son la gente . . . las costumbres* [how beautiful it is, what the people are like, and the customs]. . . . I want [my kids] to know that they're Puerto Rican. We're not *American* Americans." When I asked Aida why this was important, she paused. "Why is that important?" she repeated. "To be honest with you? She smiled, lowered her voice, and continued,

Because, you know, *los puertorriqueños* is disappearing here in Chicago. It's becoming more of a *Mexican* place. Everywhere you go now, it's like, Mexican restaurants, Mexican owners and stores, you know. I don't see the Puerto Rican that much anymore. The only Puerto Ricans that you see are really up there, are the ones in Humboldt Park. And I love going to Humboldt Park because my kids, I like to take them there so they know that at least there's a piece of us here in Chicago — even though it's a little piece. Everywhere you go it's "La Villita." I'm not being a racist, but I feel, you know, if they got theirs, why can't we have ours? You know, we're not as bad as people think we are. Because I've seen, you know, Polish American people, I've seen them saying . . . that Puerto Ricans are troublemakers. Most of them are gangbangers. And that we're all good for nothin', you know. That we're — I remember one time we ran into this Italian man, he goes to the barrio, and I remember him saying, "Ah, you fuckin' Puerto Ricans, you know. All you guys, you're good for nothin'. You're troublemakers. You guys don't even know how to read."

The idea that Chicago was becoming "more of a Mexican place" was a common theme in my field research, and Puerto Ricans described these changes in cultural, economic, and political terms. While their reactions varied, ranging from serious anger and resentment to nonchalance, there was broad consensus that the "Mexicanization" of Chicago contributed to Puerto Ricans' increasingly marginal position in the city.[12] Unfortunately, these attitudes reflected a national anti-immigrant sentiment that characterized much of the 1990s and facilitated the passage of Proposition 187 in California in November 1994 and U.S. Congressional ratification of the Illegal Immigration Reform and Immigrant Responsibility Act in 1996, as well as the immigrant backlash through welfare reform in 1996.[13] Locally, the *Chicago Tribune*'s Mike Royko fanned nativist flames in February 1997 with his infamous column satirizing Chicago's Mexican community.[14] Echoing the dominant anti-immigrant rhetoric blaming Mexican workers for stealing "our jobs" or taking over "our schools," many Puerto Ricans worried that their economic marginalization contributed to prevailing stereotypes depicting them as lazy, dangerous, and on drugs. Aida explained:

I just get mad because a lot of people here . . . they think that's what we're about. Taking welfare, being in gangs. That's not right. Selling drugs. No. It's not. I don't think we've had our chance to progress, because everybody else has taken it. Everybody else has taken it. That's the way I see it. . . . You can't get a good job here. Why? Why? Because they [the Mexicans] come here, other people come here and get our jobs and then when we go to work, what is it? We got to earn what they are? When you know you're supposed to be earning more for the job?! I know . . . where my husband works, that's all you see there. Is Mexicans. You know . . . where he's working now, he's the only Puerto Rican working there. . . .

And my husband comes home and he says, "These Mexicans, you know." He's not being a racist because like now, they changed his hours. They turn around, he'll work from five o'clock in the morning to five o'clock in the afternoon. Come seven o'clock they'll call him and say, "Hey, get your butt to work now." [He'll work] through the whole night with two hours of sleep, 'til the next day. I tell him, "Hey, you don't have to be killing yourself for them." "No, but if the other guys do it, I have to do it. Otherwise, I won't get my hours and they'll get more hours and they'll work for anything, you know."

Like Aida, Nelly maintained that Mexicans "will work for anything," but she also believed this was an admirable cultural trait attesting to their exemplary work ethic. The irony in these discussions is that the widespread belief that Mexicans have contributed to Puerto Ricans' economic marginalization is based on Mexicans' marginal position with regard to citizenship. Many Puerto Ricans recognize that undocumented *mejicanos* are vulnerable both as employees and as residents living in an increasingly hostile society characterized by the nativist backlash in the 1990s. Yet by possessively investing in their own citizenship — in a way similar to white Americans' investment in the "resources, power, and opportunity" whiteness offer them — Puerto Ricans contribute to a discourse of illegality that further marginalizes Mexican immigrants and erects barriers of exclusion that prevent Puerto Ricans from seeing their shared social location with *mejicanos* and Mexican Americans in Chicago's racialized political economy.[15] In an effort to create an economic, social, political, and cultural space, many Puerto Ricans use citizenship to victimize, demonize, and marginalize Mexican immigrants who have been, and continue to be, allies in civil rights struggles.[16]

Puerto Ricans, for example, believe that Mexicans resent them because they are born American citizens. "To me it feels like [Mexicans] hate us because we don't need to get passports and we don't need to go through immigration and all that," Yvette told me one evening. At a party where Puerto Ricans and Mexicans were present, the topic of conversation turned to Puerto Rico's political status, with a young Puerto Rican man arguing passionately for Puerto Rican statehood, saying that Puerto Rico could become a U.S. state while maintaining its language and culture. Others argued against statehood, some advocating preserving Puerto Rico's current commonwealth status and others supporting complete independence. The young Puerto Rican man was not dissuaded, warning, "If Puerto Rico became independent, then we wouldn't be citizens. Can you imagine that? We'd have to all get *green cards!*" Everyone except the Mexican guests burst into laughter and commented that that was the most ridiculous thing they had ever heard. After the Puerto

Ricans regained their composure, there was an uncomfortable silence, as the two groups avoided eye contact and uncomfortably focused on the paper plates they held in their laps as they finished eating birthday cake.

This inter-Latino tension is usually subtle, frequently surfacing around issues of food, music, and other cultural traditions. Learning how to make white rice correctly or spending hours peeling, grating, and mixing green bananas and *plátanos* to make *pasteles* at Christmas and other special occasions is a small political act imbued with important cultural meaning.[17] Women are extremely conscious of the importance of these ritual and quotidian cultural activities and often brag about how well they perform them. In class, Nelly frequently remarked on how well she cooked and how she only prepared Puerto Rican food in her home. When we had class parties, she and other women eagerly showcased their talents by bringing in typical labor-intensive foods like *pasteles* and *empanadillas* and special desserts like *flan, tembleque,* and *dulce de papaya* (custard, coconut custard, and candied papaya). Inevitably, these celebrations provoked conversations about other holiday fare — *lechón asado, arroz con gandules* — and what different families prepared and ate on those occasions, a cultural performance engaged in by both women and men to show their Puerto Ricanness.

Aida, for example, loves to cook and prides herself on being one of the best in her family, a fact confirmed by all her kin. Holidays are particularly important cultural performances, although she is also proud of the daily expressions of *puertorriqueñidad* she sees in her children. She explained to me one day,

> One thing I always tell my kids, I wasn't born in Puerto Rico and I wasn't raised in Puerto Rico. But of the culture, of what I've learned, that's what I'll teach you. You know, we don't celebrate Three Kings Day. . . . We celebrate Christmas. And it's typical Puerto Rican food. You know, it's not American food. And you've got *pasteles y arroz con gandules* and the *parrandas* [typical Christmas singing and parties]. . . . My favorite music is salsa. . . . And Milly loves salsa. . . . My girls love the *novelas* [Spanish soap operas]. . . . And they ask them, you know, when they ask in the school, "What nationality are you?" "Oh, I'm Puerto Rican. I'm Puerto Rican, I eat rice and beans and *pasteles* and I eat all the Puerto Rican food." I don't eat meat loafs, or once in a while I'll make a lasagna for them. But that's a treat — that's something different. But *no los he criado — no quiero que sean muy americanos* [I didn't raise them — I don't want them to be too American].

Food, music, and language are all politicized activities among Chicago Puerto Ricans, especially for second- and third-generation migrants, who often worry that they are not "Puerto Rican enough." With all of its ethnic Others, Chicago is a place of great cultural ambiguity. In this context, Puerto Rican families — and within these families, almost exclusively women — use migration, food, and language to affirm the cultural integrity they feel is threatened by the forces of "Americanization" and "Mexicanization" they confront in schools, on television, and in their daily routine.

Such beliefs reveal serious obstacles to Félix Padilla's vision of "Latinismo," a pan-ethnic formation created by Puerto Rican and Mexican community leaders. They underscore the persistence of national identities, particularly in the context of economic uncertainty and competition over scarce resources, such as affordable housing, urban space, and secure employment. While nonprofit organizations, such as the Latino Institute and other pan-ethnic organizations, attempt to forge a Latino identity in order to address shared problems, this coalition-building is frequently strained and disguises inter-Latino conflict. These different conceptions of Latino and national identity also belie important class-based cleavages among Puerto Ricans in Chicago — white-collar professionals versus working-class and poor Puerto Rican residents — which map onto political positions with regard to Puerto Rico's political status and reveal the "development of a Puerto-Ricanness that [is] internally classed as well as externally underclassed."[18] This "Puerto-Ricanness" is also fundamental to working-class Puerto Ricans' perceptions of their cultural identity and integrity vis-à-vis ethnic others in the city.

When migration is not possible, Puerto Rican cultural centers and community organizations are seen as sources of "true" cultural knowledge. They are also popularly regarded as "cultural embassies" where one can go for help, information, and proper cultural orientation. A Puerto Rican woman in her mid thirties, for example, arrived at the Centro one day and asked me to help her identify Puerto Rico's national flower. I didn't have this information, but when my coworker told her it was the *amapola,* the woman smiled and said to her in Spanish, "That's what I thought it was too. But it's not. It's actually another flower." As we looked through encyclopedias and other books to find Puerto Rico's *true* national flower, the woman confessed hesitatingly that she was relieved that neither of us knew the answer.[19] If we, who worked in a Puerto Rican cultural center, didn't know the name of the flower, she told us, it was okay that she didn't possess this cultural knowledge either. She needed the information for her daughter, who was participating in the Miss Puerto Rico contest for Chicago's Puerto Rican Day Parade. "I got her into the contest because I am realizing that she is losing her culture. And that scares me," the mother confided. Getting her children involved in cultural activities was extremely important, so that they would not become "too American." It was also a way for her to lay claim to ethnic identity through her children's cultural knowledge and participation in cultural events. The work of culture is largely women's responsibility, and by encouraging her daughter to engage in these cultural events, the mother was helping to reproduce the notion that preserving cultural identity is a feminine province.

Children and parents, however, are often at odds about what constitutes authentic cultural identity. These intergenerational conflicts are most clear in cultural centers and during community events like the Puerto Rican Day Parade, revealing another transnational phenomenon: On both the island and the mainland, cultural production and national identity are sites of struggle and contestation. In this context, cultural centers — with their mandate to "defender la cultura" (defend the culture) — often take on the role of cultural gatekeepers, prescribing proper visual and musical representations of Puerto Rican culture and often backgrounding alternative cultural forms emerging from the varied life experience of second- and third-generation Chicago Puerto Ricans. While cultural workers acknowledge that young *puertorriqueños* listen primarily to rap, hip-hop, and freestyle music, they understand this as part of contemporary youth culture, which is heavily influenced by African Americans and other U.S. Latinos.[20] *Bomba* and *plena*, on the other hand (music once derided as "vulgar" and "lumpen"), are promoted as authentic cultural expressions, and young Puerto Ricans are encouraged to learn about these musical forms as part of their cultural education.[21]

Such gestures are certainly important, but they frequently inhibit discussion about the evolving nature of Puerto Rican culture, a fact that became particularly clear to me during an intergenerational artistic collaboration at the Centro. When Leo Chacón and a handful of students were recruited for a video project, they participated enthusiastically. Not only would they learn filming, editing, and production skills, but participation in the program also gave them the opportunity to interview important community leaders and to learn more about the history of the Centro and of Puerto Ricans' political struggles in the city. The students worked hard, putting in extra hours after class and polishing their speaking and writing skills. After finishing the video, they had to choose music for the opening and closing of the film. After much deliberation, the students chose a number of hip-hop songs they felt represented the history of struggle and defiance they had so carefully documented. When the students proudly showed the video to members of the Centro staff, many objected strongly to the musical choices, saying that a video about the Puerto Rican community required "Puerto Rican music" — meaning *jíbaro* music or *bomba* and *plena*, not rap or hip-hop. Predictably, this created an extremely painful conflict. Some students threatened to resign from the project if they were not allowed to use the music they had chosen. Others, like Leo, felt betrayed and erased, saying that this was "their video" and this was the music they and their friends listened to. The Centro staff members critical of the video defended their decision, arguing that in the context of cultural imperialism, it was important to *defender y promover* [defend and promote] Puerto Rican culture. As members of a cultural center, their job was to instruct young people in Puerto Rican history, politics, and culture, and to promote this knowledge through cultural programs, educational forums, and festivals.

Struggles over the meaning and nature of authentic Puerto Rican culture were also evident at festivals. Frequently an older crowd would gather to hear salsa from the 1960s and 1970s and *bomba y plena* at the main musical stage, while younger *puertorriqueños* spread out in the park, spontaneously forming small clusters around boom boxes blaring freestyle and disco music, as each person took a turn dancing in the middle of the group. These festivals, like the cultural centers and community institutions that help to organize them, are important sites for examining how national and cultural identity is deployed, contested, and reconfigured in a transnational setting.

Migration As Kin Work

Women's work is a recurring theme in these pages. We have seen how local and national governments encouraged women to participate in wage labor in order to meet the demand for unskilled workers in Puerto Rico and Chicago. I have also shown how their productive lives were often erased by local institutions — media, government agencies, and even ethnic organizations themselves — as they were reimagined in ways that fit prevailing ideologies of race, gender, class, and family. Until recently, community histories have ignored women's pioneering role in constructing and sustaining local and transnational communities, celebrating instead men's industrial wage labor.[22] Because women frequently migrated to do the reproductive work of other women — as *domésticas* for American families or for their female kin in U.S. cities — they are absent from dominant migration narratives that emphasize men's experiences of "fleeing the cane," or "buscando ambiente" — looking for something better. Women also succumbed to "the fever" of migration, but they did so largely through female networks, which, as scholars have noted, enmeshed them in webs of economic, affective, and moral indebtedness.[23]

These women-centered networks continue to be important for second- and third-generation *puertorriqueñas* in Chicago. As I have shown, women use them to avoid actual and potential dangers confronting their children. And because children and other family members lay claim to a cultural and ethnic identity through women's cultural work, *puertorriqueñas* draw on these networks to reaffirm cultural ties with the island. The time, energy, and emotional energy women devote to these networks demonstrate their important symbolic and material meaning. Together this work constitutes what Micaela di Leonardo has identified as the work of kinship.

Kin work includes "the conception, maintenance, and ritual celebration of cross-household kin ties, including visits, letters, telephone calls, presents, and cards to kin." It also involves the mental work required to sustain these interhousehold links and decisions to strengthen or neglect various kin ties. The transnational networks Puerto Rican women utilize and make available to their family members are sustained through their kin work. This is particularly evident around holidays, like Christmas and especially Mother's Day. In San Sebastián, the weeks leading up to Mother's Day witness a deluge of television and radio advertisements for gifts easily sent by mail. The town's post office extends its working hours until late in the evening the week before Mother's Day, and the wait to send packages is excruciatingly long. Glimpses of the packages held by the women waiting in these lines indicated that they were sending them to female kin in places like Chicago, Perth Amboy, Newark, and New York City.

Pepinianas were also remembered on this day, receiving large boxes, phone calls, and cards with money. When Tía Cristina asked me to drive her to town to get money orders, I was shocked to see the number of cards and the amount of money she was sending to female kin in New York and New Jersey. When I asked her why she was doing this — and expressed concern about the amount of money she was sending — she assured me that she would get as much or more in return. As the cards and packages rolled in, I realized that my *tía* was right. She received almost twice as much money for Mother's Day as she had paid out. This came in large part, she pointed out, from family members who had visited or sent their kin to live with her during difficult times. Sending her money — even if it was only twenty-five dollars — was a symbolic gesture of thanks and repayment, and it strengthened their relationship with her as well.

Women in San Sebastián also sent food — especially items typical of Puerto Rico, like fresh *gandules,* homemade cheese, and other special desserts — with family members traveling *afuera*. When I traveled home to New Jersey during my fieldwork, Tía Cristina sent fresh white beans, homemade cheese, candied papaya, and fresh *gandules* not only for me and my husband, but also for her niece in Newark and for other kin with whom my cousin would, in turn, share the food. Marixsa Alicea has documented that some women send entire meals with female kin and arrange for the meal be served to family members in Chicago.[24] This kind of work, she points out, creates an important sense of family that is nurtured through women's kin work.

Migration itself is also a type of kin work. Women may move to Puerto Rico or to the mainland to care for relatives when they are sick or in need of care. One of my G.E.D. students moved to Puerto Rico twice within two years to care for her sick mother. In San Sebastián, I met women and men who traveled frequently to Chicago and other cities to care for aging relatives. Like other kinds of kin work, these efforts are unremunerated and are culturally assigned largely to women, although men occasionally travel to care for family members abroad.[25] Women also help to bring sick kin to Chicago and serve as translators and liaisons with government agencies, as they file documents, meet with social workers, and secure important services.[26]

While mothers usually handle interhousehold labor, adolescent daughters are often charged with the reproductive work within the household. They help with cooking, cleaning, laundry, and childcare, freeing up their mothers to perform kin work that links their households with others.[27] When mothers are unable to migrate to fulfill their family obligations, they often send their daughters — or nieces if they live together. Adelina Santos, a thirty-five-year-old staff member at Ruiz Belvis, sent a niece to Puerto Rico to care for her grandmother until Adelina was able to get time off from work. And other women had long strategy sessions to decide who would be sent in the next crisis. Young girls were not often sent abroad, but mothers did rely on adolescent daughters and female kin to help them and sustain their networks. Just as children and other family members lay claim to particular identities through women's work, mothers strengthen and reinvigorate their kin ties through their children's work, migration, and relations with kin across households.[28]

I was made particularly aware of the importance of female-centered networks near the end of my fieldwork in San Sebastián, when I accompanied my *tía* to a neighbor's wake. In a small bedroom off the living room where the recently deceased lay, the widow's daughters — who lived scattered throughout Puerto Rico and the mainland — comforted their mother and assured her that they would care for her. My *tía* repeated their promises, telling her friend that she didn't have to worry about anything because daughters "siempre te cuidan" (always take care of you). Sons take care of their wives and belong to their families. But daughters always belong to you, remember you when they are *afuera*, and return to your side when you are old and sick and need them most. This was a familiar, and very sad, lament of my *tía*, who only has two sons and worries about who will care for her and her husband when they grow old. People recognize the power of these networks and increasingly depend on them in an era of political retrenchment and heightened uncertainty about the economy and government programs.

Chicago mothers confirm this view of daughters. Nelly used to say that she would love to have more children, but with one son already, she was not sure she was ready to have another baby. "If my son was a daughter, if I had a daughter now," she told me one day, "I think I'd have another kid now. That way she could help me out, you know." And Aida relies heavily on her daughters — particularly Milly, her oldest — to help her with household work. Popular culture — in both English and Spanish — reinforces and reflects these mother-daughter bonds through television, radio, and broadside advertisement. In Humboldt Park, a billboard for Western Union featured an attractive young woman next to a new but simple home with a bow tied around it and, below, the words "Lo que una buena hija hace" (what a good daughter does). Good daughters remember their mothers, send them money (via Western Union), and maintain their connections with home. Women do indeed live transnational lives, nurturing their ties with households abroad for economic, affective, and cultural reasons.

Other Strategies of Survival

Even though the connection to Puerto Rico has become an important way of dealing with problems in Chicago, Puerto Rican women generally "make ends meet" in deeply local ways. Most of these survival strategies involve making choices about the most reliable sources of support: husbands/boyfriends, the state, extended kin and friendship networks, or one's own children. And while women draw on all of these networks at different points, they prefer relying on their children, who, as mothers repeatedly intoned, "will always be there." When Aida and Eli were having problems, she would say that even if he were to leave her or if they separated, "yo siempre tengo a mis hijos" (I'll always have *my* kids). Nelly echoed Aida's faith in her children, proudly announcing that although her four-year-old-son, Malik, was close to his father, he was so attached to her that he insisted on following her even when she went to use the bathroom. Husbands and boyfriends come and go, she explained, but children are yours and they take care of you when they are older. For *puertorriqueñas,* public aid, being bilingual, and military service are important strategies in securing a better future for their children — "I don't want my kids to suffer like me" is a concern all share — and economic security for themselves after their children become self-sufficient.

PUBLIC AID

All of the *puertorriqueñas* I knew and interviewed relied on welfare for varying lengths of time. For many, this was a real source of shame; for others, public aid was a temporary strategy for dealing with their own or their partners' intermittent periods of unemployment, illness, or other family problems.[29] Regardless of their varying attitudes about welfare use, all of the women were extremely aware of dominant representations of public aid recipients and contemporary debates about "ending welfare as we know it." During our first interview, in a noisy coffee shop near her home, Aida forcefully denied that welfare was a crutch for poor women. "[The politicians] say that welfare is a way of life. How could it be a way of life? I get three hundred dollars a month for me and my five kids. That's not a way of life. That's not life at all." Lorena Santiago described feeling embarrassed about being on welfare, fearing that her three-year-old-son might soon become ashamed of her. She also described profound frustration with media stereotypes of women on welfare as lazy, unmotivated, and unwilling to work. These media accounts ignore her, and other women's, attempts to improve their lives. Tearfully, she explained her feelings about welfare and the public perception of those who use public aid:

I don't want people to look at [my son] and . . . you know, "His mother's on welfare. She's nothing," you know. Which is not true. I am trying so hard for my son. . . . If people only knew. I want to cry, I'm gonna cry [she looks at me, stops, and wipes her eyes]. So much people, well, Washington, they're saying that most of us, right? [she points to herself and me], we don't want to work, right? You gotta understand . . . I couldn't work. I have a reason. My baby was born sick, okay? I was gonna work. . . . I went to get a job. No — no job wants to pay my son's bills, you know what I'm saying? His bills are high. So I had no choice but to go on welfare. I had no choice at all. So right now I'm working for a better education so I could get a good job, so I could get a good insurance, so they could pay my son's [bills] — 'cause I just can't go to a hotdog stand and get me, you know, a job and expecting them to pay my son's bills. It's — I can't do that. So I want to get an education and show — and prove and show to *them* in Washington that I could make a difference, you know. That I am not like that. I'm not just sittin' in my house, just on my butt not doing anything, which is not true, you know.

Like Lorena, most of the women in my G.E.D. class used welfare while they prepared to take the exam, and made plans for more training once they passed the test successfully. Aida passed the G.E.D. in the spring of 1996, proudly attended the graduation ceremony at Malcolm X City College in June, and soon thereafter enrolled in classes at the Office of Neighborhood Technology in West Town. After finishing the certificate program, she began working at her children's high school, earning eight dollars an hour as a paid volunteer in their truancy program — the most money she had ever made. After twenty-four-year-old Emilia Lozano passed her G.E.D., she made plans to study to become a nurse's aid so that she could support herself and her six-year-old daughter, although Emilia was often discouraged by family and friends who told her that nursing was too demanding a career for her. This kind of discouragement was common among my students, male and female. They often came to class demoralized, frustrated, and confused about continuing their studies. "[My husband] Manny never asks me about school or nothing," Nelly complained at school one day. This was a concern echoed by many women, who struggled to study in the hope of eventually getting off of public aid. Lorena complained, "I can't study at home." Aida also suggested that her husband Eli might even be jealous that she was "improving" herself by getting the education he did not have.

Other family members worried that putting one's faith in education rather than public aid was too much of a risk. Adelina Santos described her struggles with family and public aid, expressing genuine surprise that she had eventually overcome the obstacles (erected by her mother, sisters, estranged husband, and the larger society) and secured steady employment as a secretary at Ruiz Belvis. After Adelina's husband left her to return to Puerto Rico, she tried several times to go to school, but repeat-edly postponed these plans because her youngest son was frequently ill. After taking classes at Wright Community College, she applied for a job and participated in Project Chance, a welfare-to-work program that pro-vides support — childcare, money for public transportation, and most importantly, a medical card — for women beginning new jobs. After a bad experience depending on her husband, Adelina didn't want to depend on anyone, including her female kin, even if that meant doing things "the hard way." She explained,

So, in January, I began to study at Wright College. I went to Wright College and I used to take my littlest one with me [on the bus] to classes. He was only three years old . . . . I didn't have a car, and I didn't wait for anyone in my family to tell me, "No, I'll take you to school." No. I didn't even really have any money for transportation because at the time I was getting public aid and, well, it was a big help to me, but it didn't help me to pay for everything. I had to stretch my money to pay for the bus. So, I would catch the bus with my littlest son. I would go to college that way. Then in May, I saw a poster [announcing] a position at Marshall Field's. I went and applied, and my family told me, "Don't go looking for work because you're getting [public] aid and with five kids, they give you a lot." I told them, "Look, as long as I am without work, public aid is fine for me. But when I can work, no. If I know I can work [and get a job] — and look, if the day comes when I am sick or old and can't work anymore, and they will have to help me out, then I believe they will gladly help me. Because I never took advantage [of the sys-tem], you know. I'm not going to stay in my house. Besides, I'm a woman used to working."

Adelina's insistence on making her limited money "stretch" to pay for bus fare rather than relying on well-intentioned family members is one of many choices she and other women make to assert their independence in a social and political-economic context that consistently limits their agency. This fear of depending on others was a recurring theme in the life history narratives of all these women. They worked hard for this inde-pendence, and in my interviews and daily interactions with them, they shared with me their dreams of being employed in respectable, well-paid jobs that were personally fulfilling and socially rewarding.

After detailing her long and unsatisfying job history, Nelly discussed at length her hopes for meaningful employment and financial independence.

> N: I want to get a job to satisfy me, where I'm gonna get somewhere. I don't want a job where I'm gonna be there for twenty years, you know, bustin' my ass. I want to get a job where I'm gonna work and enjoy it so that one day I can retire. That's the kind of job I want, you know. I want to do a

goodwill job . . . something good where I work in an office. I always wanted to work in an office with a computer. I always wanted to do that. This is my dream. My dream is to dress in a suit, like, you know, a nice suit. Nice skirt suit with high heels, walkin' downtown with my briefcase, go to my office. That's my dream . . . That's what I always wanted to do, you know.

I: Why? What does that mean?

N: I don't know. It feels like control. It feels like I'm not dependent on nobody. I'm independent, you know? And I look good in high heels [we both laugh]. So, I'm like, okay. I just want to work on my weight, you know, because I went to the doctor and he told me I was thirty pounds overweight. . . . I feel like I had a pause in my life. I wanted to make up with my son all the lost time — and do things that my mom never did for me. I want to bake for him. When it's Christmas, it's Christmas cookies. When it's Halloween, we do Halloween cookies. . . . I always want to have a tradition so that, you know, so he finds . . . when he gets older, being a man, being a father to his kids, you know, he does stuff like that. . . . Because I don't think there's anything wrong with a man that makes cookies and likes to cook. . . .

I: You said that, when you describe yourself as wearing high heels and walking with a briefcase and stuff like that, that it will make you feel independent and that you feel dependent now. Like, why do you feel dependent? Who do you feel dependent on?

N: Um, I feel dependent on Manny, 'cause when he gets paid, he has to give me money. I feel like a kid, you know, getting my allowance cause I feel like — I could be like, "No, honey, I don't need your money. I got my money," you know. Like [I could say to him], "Oh, you need twenty dollars? Here you go." That's how I want to feel. I want to feel like I have my own money. Like, my son, he has gym shoes, okay? [She laughs nervously.] They're real expensive. I have Payless gym shoes. And they're — I've had them for two years. . . . I got other shoes, I love to buy shoes . . . but I never have enough for a pair of gym shoes, you know, a good pair of them. . . .

I: Have you ever felt like that? That you have money and that you're independent?

N: I do, sometimes. I did. When I had a job. When I had a job I felt like that, you know, where I'm like, "Hey, this is my money," you know. . . . Over there in the dollar store, they paid me pretty good. Like $290. That $290 went so quick. Everybody got a present for Christmas, you know. 'Cause I spent my money. But I felt independent at the time . . . because it was *my* money. I worked for it. . . . It feels good when you work for your money.

After her son was born, Nelly received public aid and food stamps, and Manny helped with the bills. When she and Manny started living together three years later, Nelly got off of welfare, and together they lived on his wages as a gas station attendant until he lost his job. Reluctantly, she applied for public aid once again, but this time when Manny began working at another gas station, she stayed on welfare "just in case." "Ahh," she sighed with disgust. "I don't know. I want a job. I want a life, you know."

Because most women's husbands or boyfriends lack high school diplomas, their participation in the labor market is intermittent and tenuous. Their wages are also relatively low, and they rarely have medical benefits for themselves or their families.[30] For this reason, women resist depending on them for economic support, and when they do, they are usually very clear about what they expect their men to pay each month. For me, this was a very strange economic arrangement. Coming from a middle-class family where my parents both worked, paying bills from a joint checking account, I was not used to hearing partners specify who paid which bills each month. Yet this was common practice for these women. As I drove Aida home one day, she told me that she couldn't wait for her next paycheck, but that if she was short of money before then, she was sure Eli would help her out. But she was very clear that she did not want to make a habit of this, relying on him for money. "I take care of myself," she told me proudly. "I don't like to depend on him. I have my *dinerito y ya.*" Her welfare checks allowed her some economic independence, giving her a sense of control she didn't experience in other parts of her life.

In early 1997, Aida made a life-changing decision to get off welfare. Her job at the local high school was going well, and there were rumors that she was the top candidate for a full-time clerk position in the school office. Also, six months before, she and Eli had married, a step they had been debating for many years, and despite her reservations, Aida believed this was the right time "to move ahead." When I arrived at her home one March afternoon, she proudly showed me the official letter accompanying her last food stamp check stating that this was her final disbursement. When I asked her how she felt, she sighed, "It's scary. But I think they're right, you know. It can become a crutch." She added that now that she had her own money, she didn't need to depend on Eli, welfare, or anybody. She acknowledged that getting off welfare meant more insecurity and uncertainty, although she also stated that she was willing to take that risk.

Later that evening, she called Isis Malavé, a former G.E.D. student who was also in her early thirties and had recently stopped receiving welfare. We all talked excitedly, passing the phone back and forth and speaking loudly over the blaring television and salsa from the radio. Aida told Isis that she too was finished with welfare. "What do I miss the most?" I heard her say, repeating Isis's question. "Yes! *La tarjeta* [the Medicaid card]," and I could hear Isis agreeing that this was the scariest part of leaving welfare. Luckily, she told me later, she could still use the medical card for her children. This was her greatest concern. With her new job, she could pay the monthly bills without Eli's help, but medical expenses were a different matter. As long as welfare continued to cover her children, Aida felt some security in her decision. Besides, she reminded me, no matter what happened, she always had her children.

LANGUAGE

Many Chicago Puerto Ricans are obsessed with language. They worry that they do not speak Spanish correctly or with a "Puerto Rican" accent. And they are equally self-conscious about code switching, speaking in Spanglish, and being marked linguistically in English. Because language betrays one's class and educational position, many of my G.E.D. students avoided public speaking, and they were initially wary of me because, as Aida later pointed out, I "spoke good English *and* Spanish." I too participated in the language game, trying to shed my Mexicanized Spanish, acquired while growing up in northern California and living for a brief time in Mexico, for a more "authentic" Puerto Rican sound through deliberate inflections and by consciously adding an "L" sound at the end of words like *amor* (amol) and *trabajar* (trabajal), which seemed to give my words a more "Puerto Rican" lilt. Language, my Puerto Rican informants reminded me, creates boundaries of inclusion and exclusion. It is also a kind of capital desired not only for its cultural significance, but also for its economic promise.

There is broad agreement among Chicago Puerto Ricans that despite their economic, cultural, and social marginality, being bilingual gives them an edge over monolinguals in the city. Parents especially encourage bilingualism in their children, convinced that such skills make them more attractive in an increasingly competitive labor market. As we saw earlier, Aida stressed Spanish speaking at home, so that her children would remember they were "Puerto Rican" and preserve their cultural integrity. But she also believed that speaking both English and Spanish would increase their chances of securing stable jobs. She explained to me one day in her apartment:

I was telling Milly the other day, I said, "You know, Milly, they're teaching Mikey [a white neighbor] Spanish in school." And I told all my kids, "You know what?

It's important that you guys learn how to speak Spanish now. Because you see *los polaquitos y los negritos* [Polish and black Chicagoans], they're all gonna learn Spanish when you guys are looking for your jobs out there, and if you guys don't know Spanish, they're gonna get *your* jobs. Because they're requiring now to speak Spanish *and* English. . . . They're teaching mainly Spanish to *American* kids. And I told my kids, "You guys better learn Spanish, 'cause when you guys go and get your jobs in the future, you're not gonna get them. *They're* gonna get 'em. Because *they* know Spanish and *you* don't. And you're Puerto Rican? You should be ashamed of yourselves." I told them . . . and they understand. Now Jimmy [her oldest son] is getting into it now. He's getting into it more now. He's starting to speak a few words in Spanish.

Aida was extremely aware of U.S. debates surrounding bilingual education in public schools and the nativist backlash against such programs in places like California, although she understood this as anti-Mexican discrimination, to which she believed she and other Puerto Ricans were immune. She remained convinced that being bilingual would give her children an important edge over other young people, and she encouraged them to read, speak, and when possible, write in Spanish.

First-generation migrants in Chicago, however, encouraged their children to "defenderse en el inglés" (get along in English) and cited this as an important reason for remaining in Chicago. Aracelis and Juan Méndez, for example, moved several times between Chicago and Maunabo, Puerto Rico, in search of jobs, education, and medical attention. When Aracelis became sick in 1993, they returned to Chicago to seek treatment and decided to stay so that their children would grow up speaking English and Spanish. Aracelis explained,

We had two reasons to return to Chicago this time. My health. We came for a medical exam. And also because we wanted the kids, our children to speak English as well as they speak Spanish. So that one day in the future, they might have an easier time finding work or studying. We don't want them to go through the same things we have. . . . They teach English in Puerto Rico. But no matter how much grammar they teach — and half an hour a day every day is just not enough — it is not enough for one to really learn it. You can't know English as well as you do Spanish that way. And what we wanted was for them to know both languages equally well.

In three years of living in Chicago, she continued, her seventeen-year-old son, Abraham, had already learned more English than in all his years of school in Puerto Rico. His parents believed that these language skills would be invaluable to him in Puerto Rico because of the large number of North American companies looking to hire bilingual speakers. "People who are fluent in more than one language have more opportunities than those who only speak one," she assured me.

To underscore her point, Aracelis explained that the most successful people in Puerto Rico — including the governor at the time, Pedro Roselló — were educated in the United States and sent their children there to study as well. The only difference was that they had the economic resources to send their children to private schools in Puerto Rico where English instruction is stressed or to boarding schools in the United States, while people like her had to migrate to give their children these same opportunities. "The governor of Puerto Rico sends his children to study in the United States. . . . They attend private schools [in Puerto Rico]. When they finish high school, they send them here to study in the United States. . . . We don't have the resources to send them here. So we have to migrate with them. If we had the same opportunities as the governor of Puerto Rico — to send our kids here, we would just send them . . . but since we couldn't do that, we have to migrate for them."

Like a high school diploma, G.E.D certificate, or college education, bilingualism is a skill that can improve one's chances for a better life. And many women believe that by stressing these things with their children, they are helping the children avoid the difficulties they endured growing up. "What I've been through," Yvette once told me, "I don't want nobody to go through. Not even my worst enemy."

I wouldn't wish it on nobody. I wouldn't. I want my kids to have a better life than I had. It's not going to be perfect. They're not gonna be millionaires or nothin', but I want them to become *somebody*. I want them to be noticed as the way they are. Because anywhere I go, "O, tú eres la hija de Elba" [Oh, you're Elba's daughter]. No, I'm not. That's all we're known by. That's it. Or, "You're this person's sister," or that's all I'm known by. I don't want that for my kids. I want them to be known. "Oh, yeah, you're Andy, yeah." That's how I want my kids to be known. By who they are.

These women conveyed a profound urgency to improve their children's lives, partly because they depended on them. They also spoke hopefully, confident that through their collective sacrifice and hard work, their children would have easier, more meaningful lives.

THE MILITARY

Beginning at a very early age, military service becomes one of the most appealing and seemingly sure options for many poor and working-class families. Television advertisements, visits by recruiters in junior high and high school, and well-organized Junior ROTC programs offering financial incentives entice poor children to consider the military — rather than college — as an employment option after high school. Promises of money, free education, training, travel, discipline, honor, and respect seduce young men and women, although, as many of my students eventually discovered, these promises often prove elusive.

When Marvin Polanco first arrived in the G.E.D. program in January, he regaled me with stories about his experience in Lincoln's Challenge, a military boarding school for troubled youth near Champaign, Illinois. Shortly after he dropped out of Clemente High School, Marvin's mother signed him up for the five-month program, which promised to instill discipline, prepare him for the G.E.D., and pay him $2,200 after he successfully graduated. "But they tricked my mom," Marvin told me solemnly one day after class. He failed his G.E.D. exam: "The day I took the exam, they smoked me right before it," requiring him to exercise strenuously just prior to the test and leaving him exhausted, and he eventually discovered that he would receive barely five hundred dollars when he finished the program. "They try to brainwash you there," he volunteered another day. He also explained that he often feared for his safety while he attended the school. Between the physical discipline imposed by the officers and the danger of getting jumped by gang members participating in the program ("They're all down there: the Kings, Disciples. Even the KKK"), Marvin was afraid he wouldn't get out alive. After a few months, he ran away from the school and returned home, begging his mother not to send him back and promising to get his G.E.D. at Ruiz Belvis.

Many of my male G.E.D. students wanted to go into the military after they finished the exam. When they approached me about this, I encouraged them to consider enrolling in one of Chicago's city colleges and eventually transferring to either University of Illinois at Chicago or Northeastern University, both of which had programs specifically targeting incoming G.E.D. students. With the help of the Centro's counselors and staff, some of whom had successfully completed their G.E.D. and gone on to pursue university studies with the help of similar outreach programs, students were put in touch with representatives from these universities, given a tour of one of the city colleges, and sent on a campus visit to a small liberal arts college to whet their educational appetite. Michael Guzmán, one of the Centro's counselors, was extremely invested in pushing our students to consider college. A G.E.D. graduate himself and currently a student at Northeastern University, he had experienced firsthand the strong push towards military service and vocational training, and he worked tirelessly with Centro staff to provide the students with alternatives.

The "military debates" became a regular feature of class discussions, escalating to a heated discussion one day during art class. Amanda Vargas, the Centro's artist-in-residence, was working with the students when Eddie arrived late, announcing that he had met with an army recruiter who had explained to him that the G.I. Bill would pay for his college education. Eddie was seriously considering this option, and his enthusiasm spread to Frankie, who was also interested in joining the military. Soon a small group of women and men were asking Eddie questions and trying to see how they too could set up a meeting with the army recruiter. I was furious. I gathered the class together and asked them to think about why the military aggressively recruited them and other working-class people of color and not the predominately white and wealthy Northwestern University students I also taught. Initially stunned, my students responded passionately about the "honor of serving your country," telling me about their fathers, grandfathers, uncles, and brothers who had all served in the armed forces. They were angry with me for being upset and critical of what for many of them were small steps towards social and economic mobility. "My father and grandfather were in the army," Eddie insisted. "It's a good job. And that's what I need. I need to get out of my house and *away* from the drugs and get into a good place. I can't concentrate when I'm at home, you know. They're smokin', drinkin', and I can't concentrate. Even if I go to college, I still have to go *home*. Why do you think I work so many hours and *like* to come to school? I need to get out of that environment." The class was silent, and a few students nodded their heads. When I finally heard what Eddie was saying—what he had been trying to tell me for months now—I felt incredibly helpless and almost started to cry. His eyes were a little misty too.

After class, Eddie approached me again. "Look, if I go into the reserves, I go to boot camp, and then I go a weekend a month and then I go to school. Like DeVry [Technical School]. That's a good job, right? I can learn a job in the army—like cars—and then do the same thing in school. And then when I'm finished, *later*, when I have more *money*, I can go to college. It'll always be there, right?" I agreed that college would always be there, but that he needed to consider *all* of his options. If he was serious about the military, maybe we could speak with someone about an ROTC program that would pay for college now and train him to be an officer after he graduated. "I don't want you to make a decision without having all the information first," I told him. "I just don't want you to regret your decision later."

Eddie looked at me directly. "You know, my brother graduated from [an alternative high school], and they convinced him not to go into the military. Now he's gangbangin' and dealin' drugs. He's got no job, no education, and he could have gone into the military. I don't want that to happen to me." It finally hit me what he was trying to tell me. He was afraid his time was running out and that somehow, despite his best efforts, "the street" was going to get him. Like so many others — Aida, Yvette, Nelly, Lorena — Eddie was confronting power, the structural economic, social, racial, and educational forces circumscribing his daily life and his dreams. Facing this power, he felt desperate and insecure. At age seventeen, Eddie had not been arrested, was drug-free and in school, and realizing that this made him exceptional, he now feared that he too would fall into the patterns he saw in his family — drinking, drugs, gangs, and jail. Joining the military was like an amulet protecting him from the social and economic evils around him. Following Lila Abu-Lughod's call to view resistance as a diagnostic of how power operates in people's lives, I recognized that the economic and social forces structuring the lives of Chicago Puerto Ricans were almost all-powerful, leaving them feeling trapped and at times desperate.[31]

A few months after these "military debates," Aida asked me to drive her to the South Side to apply for the school clerk position she hoped to be offered. As we drove south on the Kennedy Expressway, squeezed in my pickup with her youngest son, Lolito, sitting quietly between us, she sobbed, telling me how she had packed Eli's things in some trash bags and was kicking him out. "Ya no puedo" (I can't do this anymore), she cried. "Prefiero morirme de hambre, faltar las cosas que sufrir más con él. No quiero sufrir más. Ya estoy cansada" (I would rather die of hunger, lack things, than suffer any longer with him. I don't want to suffer anymore. I'm just tired). As Aida cried, I didn't know what to say except that I would support her in any decision she made. After a few moments of silence, Lolito exclaimed happily, "Don't worry, mom. You still have us." Aida and I looked at each other, shocked. She had spoken in Spanish so he would not understand us, but of course he knew what was upsetting his mother. Following Lolito's lead, I added, "Yeah, she has all of you and me and Baron and Lenny and Simon," which made them both laugh because Lenny and Simon are our cats, whom Lolito loves.

That fall, Aida began a new job as the high school's office clerk. With a handsome salary, medical benefits for her and her children, and a little money put away in her first bank account, she felt more independent, secure, and extremely proud of all that she had accomplished. "You got your G.E.D., a job with good benefits, a credit union account. Now all you need is your driver's license," I kidded her one rainy October afternoon as I drove her to her mother's house. She and Eli eventually reconciled, although their relationship was never quite the same. Aida shared with me, once again, her plans to eventually buy a house. She talked incessantly of how proud she was of Milly for participating in her high school's Junior ROTC program. An 8 × 10 color photograph of Milly in her military uniform was prominently displayed on the crowded living room wall, and Aida also passed out wallet-sized photos of Milly to family and friends. Milly would graduate from high school at the end of the year. Then she would go to boot camp and start saving money for college. When I asked Milly why she wanted to go into the military, she said that she eventually wanted to go to school, but for now, she wanted to save money to help her mom "buy her house." When I suggested that going to college would help her get an even better job, where she could earn even more money, she smiled sweetly, saying that she really believed this was the best thing for her right now. Her mother needed her, depended on her, and she didn't want to let her down.

Aida actually had very mixed feelings about Milly's military service. On the one hand, the army provided economic security for both her and her daughter: Milly would have money to go to college, and she was more likely to avoid the kind of *sufrimiento* Aida had endured most of her life. On the other hand, Milly would be leaving home, and Aida would miss her terribly. Aida depended primarily on Milly, not only for economic support but, more importantly, for emotional sustenance. "He sufrido demasiado" (I have suffered too much), she told her cousin Mayra that afternoon, when I brought Aida to see her cousin and her mother, Magda. "No quiero sufrir más" (I don't want to suffer anymore). She then told Mayra about the problems she was having with Eli, and eventually the discussion turned to the women's children and their hopes for them. "I want to get my house next," Aida told us after bragging about Milly. She would graduate early and be one of the first women in her family to graduate with a high school diploma.

The pride Aida felt in Milly was mutual. "I'm really proud of Mami," Milly told me one day in her room. "You know, she studied hard, got her G.E.D., and she's making something of herself, you know." I agreed. Aida was truly an impressive woman with amazing children, incredible determination, and tremendous courage. Her children always told me how proud they were of their mother. As they should be. And so was I.

Like Aida, many working-class Puerto Rican women live transnationally as a way of surviving and caring for their families. They do so in a historical moment when traditional work venues — like industrial and factory labor — and government support (welfare, college financial aid services and programs) are dwindling and their productive opportunities are severely constrained. Chicago and island *puertorriqueñas* have responded to these political-economic changes by putting together elements of a kind of social and cultural citizenship that is deeply local, but with a transnational vision. This, as other scholars have noted, is not necessarily new; Puerto Ricans — as well as many others hailing from the Caribbean — have lived in two or more places for many generations. What may in fact be new, however, are the particular economies — one arguably a "postwork society" whose members rely heavily on slowly eroding federal subsidies; the other a postindustrial, global city — in which poor and working-class women seize and construct gendered economic and social opportunities for survival. Women's kin work — the largely unremunerated labor connecting households materially and symbolically — is essential to this transnational survival strategy, which sustains economically marginal households both on the island and on the mainland.

CHAPTER 7

Conclusion

Revisiting the Gender, Poverty, and Migration Debate

This book is an attempt to contribute to popular and academic debates about the "Puerto Rican problem" of persistent poverty and migration to the United States. I have used ethnographic and historical data to reveal how past and present migration has been a flexible survival strategy and to show the ways in which migrants have been apprehended by scholars, government officials, and media in Puerto Rico and the mainland. According to one account, Puerto Ricans' poor economic standing today is due largely to their circular migration patterns, which disrupt family life and schooling and weaken their attachment to local labor markets, relegating them to unskilled and poorly paid employment.[1] This argument fails to consider the larger historical context of Puerto Rican migration to American cities, including government efforts — both federal and local — to encourage migration while preserving economic, social, and political ties with island communities. This state-sanctioned migration strategy laid the foundation for the creation of ideological, economic, and affective links between cities like Chicago and San Sebastián that dramatically transformed both communities in unpredictable ways.

Planned migration was an important component of the developmentalist ideology that fueled Puerto Rico's industrialization program beginning in the late 1940s. According to this model, the island's economic development depended on the free flow of capital, goods, ideas, and people across geopolitical borders. As North American capital poured into the newly industrialized island economy, men and women migrated to Puerto Rico's burgeoning cities as factory workers. U.S. employers also

actively recruited Puerto Rican men and women to remedy labor shortages in cities like New York, Philadelphia, and Chicago. Government
officials hailed public and private efforts, like the "Chicago Experiment,"
which addressed the city's labor demands while relieving the island's population pressures by exporting young women workers. Policymakers
were particularly encouraged by the migration of Puerto Rican women,
since they believed it would reduce the rate of the island's population
growth, even while the women maintained economic connections with
island households and families through their remittances. These beliefs
were informed by ideologies of gender, class, family, and ethnicity that
continue to shape the dominant vision of Puerto Rican life in Chicago
today.

Puerto Rican migrants have occupied various ideological spaces, which
have shifted with the evolving American and regional economies and
racial hierarchies of Chicago and Puerto Rico. Their short-lived postwar
tenure as Chicago's model minority was directly related to their position
as recruited industrial and domestic workers gainfully employed in the
local labor market, as well as the construction by local media and government officials of a profile of hard-working Chicago Puerto Rican
migrants whose work ethic and family structure compared favorably to
ethnic and racial others, such as New York Puerto Ricans and poor
American blacks. As the city's manufacturing sector contracted in the late
1960s and 1970s, leaving many Chicago *puertorriqueños* unemployed and
poorer, their ideological position also changed and they entered the
national imagination as "slum-dwellers" mired in a "culture of poverty,"
and later as members of urban America's "underclass."

Chicago Puerto Ricans responded to these political-economic transformations in a number of ways. Like other Puerto Ricans in the United
States, many returned to the island during the 1960s and 1970s, motivated
by diminished employment opportunity on the mainland and improved
social and economic conditions on the island. In towns like San
Sebastián, they bought land, built homes, and found jobs in the new factories and even in the agricultural sector many had fled in the 1940s and
1950s. This return migration, however, was often difficult for women,
whose extensive labor experience in the United States had provided
them with economic and social freedoms sorely missed in their new lives
in rural Puerto Rico. The lack of reliable public transportation, cultural
norms of gendered behavior that confined women to their homes, and
limited economic opportunity all contributed to women's discontent
upon return. These observations confirm findings that migrant women

often resist men's attempts to return to their country of origin because it frequently means confronting a gender ideology that limits women's ability to work, socialize, and live the way they did in the United States. This return was also difficult for Puerto Rican children born and raised in U.S. cities, who not only faced linguistic and cultural obstacles to their integration into local communities, but were also targets of a fierce backlash against return migrants and of social opprobrium for not conforming to culturally prescribed norms of behavior, language, and dress.

Other *puertorriqueños,* however, remained in Chicago, establishing community organizations, cultural centers, and interethnic coalitions to advance school reform, protect low-income housing, and improve community-police relations. Many Puerto Rican community leaders have linked these local struggles to larger issues of Puerto Rico's political status and cultural nationalism. In their efforts to resist displacement caused by gentrification, for example, they have carved out a unique "Puerto Rican space" in the city's Near Northwest Side by deploying cultural symbols that inscribe a vision of Puerto Rico that is rural, folkloric, and nostalgic. These images of Puerto Rico also inform the attitudes of many Chicago *puertorriqueños* about the island and help to explain how return migration and transnational practices become part of a cultural strategy of survival. Because Puerto Rico is usually imagined to be rural and safe, sending troubled youth to the island is one way to deal with urban danger, economic uncertainty, and family problems.

While some Puerto Ricans continue to circulate between the island and the mainland — thereby further integrating the two economies — relatively few Puerto Ricans engage in this transnational movement. In fact, recent research reveals that very few migrants are multiple movers, and that most settle in a particular community. When migrants do engage in circular or transnational migration, they do so in order to take advantage of the broad social and economic networks that are part of their subsistence strategies, and they are usually successful in improving their occupational status through this process. These findings challenge earlier work suggesting that circular migration is commonplace, disruptive, and worsens migrants' socioeconomic position. Puerto Ricans' "mobile livelihoods" is a "productive survival strategy for many households on and off the island."[2]

My ethnographic data suggest similar trends. Chicago Puerto Ricans and *pepinianos* lead deeply local lives, although they do so transnationally. Of the people I met and interviewed in Chicago and San Sebastián, very few would be considered circular migrants, and their movement did little either to improve or worsen their economic condition. Instead, their migration addressed immediate problems — usually inadequate housing, illness, and children's problems in schools or with gangs. But migration was only one of many strategies for dealing with daily problems. Women in particular engaged in a variety of activities to "make ends meet." They worked in the informal sector, used public aid rather than relying on husbands and boyfriends, invested in their children by promoting bilingualism, higher education, and even military service as survival strategies. Through their kin work, women also maintained ties between households and kin on the island and the mainland. What is most striking about these transnational practices is how infrequently people actually move, a fact noted by other migration scholars, and one that points to the need to historicize different transnationalisms. In fact, these networks provide the security of knowing that migration is possible if necessary, while firmly grounding *puertorriqueños* in a particular community. In other words, transmigrants do, in fact, live either here or there.

These findings seriously challenge not only the "gender, poverty, and migration" thesis, but also underclass theory and some other approaches to transnational migration. Underclass theorists emphasize the disorganization of the poor and their social isolation, arguing that these are the key elements responsible for the persistent poverty of African Americans — and some would add, Puerto Ricans. According to this framework, the exodus of middle- and working-class families from "ghetto neighborhoods" created a vacuum of role models and basic neighborhood institutions, such as churches, stores, schools, and recreational facilities, which made possible the proliferation of "ghetto-specific" behavior. Left unchecked, these cultural traits — including out-of-wedlock births, teenage pregnancy, female-headed households, and weak labor-force attachment — became pathologies that are transmitted intergenerationally, reproducing the cycle of poverty.[3]

As I discussed earlier, whether Puerto Ricans fit this underclass profile has been the subject of much debate. In these pages, however, I have demonstrated that there is a high level of social organization among poor and working-class Puerto Ricans on the island and the mainland. Furthermore, like their African American working poor counterparts, Puerto Ricans in Chicago are deeply involved in community-based organizing.[4] The most serious problems facing both groups are not the lack of middle- and working-class role models in poor neighborhoods. Rather, Chicago *puertorriqueños* and African Americans continue to struggle to secure living-wage jobs — a result of economic restructuring as well as the racial-spatial discrimination that stigmatizes them as dangerous people from undesirable neighborhoods — and decent affordable housing, related problems often ignored by underclass theorists.

This book also challenges those transnational approaches to migration that uncritically celebrate transmigrants' nomadism, hybridity, and resistance to the global economy.[5] The contemporary romance with transnationalism both inside and outside the academy is particularly troubling, because it draws in sharp relief a double standard based on race/ethnicity, class, and gender. Private capital and popular culture celebrate the quick, unfettered, and easy transnational connections that have transformed our world into a global village, while the ebb and flow of displaced people, especially labor migrants and political refugees, is criticized and even violently resisted by nativist movements throughout Western Europe and the United States. Likewise, academic analyses of transnationalism frequently overlook the power inequalities involved in globalization and the fact that very few benefit from late capitalism's technological innovations. The highly mobile lifestyles of international elites — who may or may not inhabit a global ethnoscape — is pathologized when laborers and poor people engage in these practices, and this lifestyle is used to explain their economic and social marginalization.

In this book, I have provided a historical and political-economic context in which to understand the origins and consequences of state-sanctioned migration, displacement, and the ways in which people in disparate places like Chicago and San Sebastián continue to be connected through the transnational flow of capital, people, and ideologies. By revealing the mechanisms of power that have structured the terrain of activity of migrants and their children, and their myriad responses to this power, we can see how poor and working-class *puertorriqueños* create meaningful lives in marginal circumstances and under conditions not of their own choosing.

Notes

Preface

1. *Pepinianos* is a popular way to refer to people hailing from the town San Sebastián de las Vegas del Pepino, or simply El Pepino. Aware of the gender bias involved in language use, throughout this book I use terms like *pepinianos, Latinos,* and *puertorriqueños* when referring to both men and women, and *Latinas, puertorriqueñas,* and *pepinianas* when referring to just women.

Chapter 1: Introduction

1. Except for those of public officials, all names in these pages are pseudonyms.

2. Briggs 2002a, 116.

3. Pantojas-García (1990) refers to the industrialization model as "capital importation" and argues, "Today these strategies are known as the Puerto Rican model, the industrialization by invitation model, the Asian model, or the *maquiladora* model. But it all started with Operation Bootstrap" (61). Pioneering work on women and the international division of labor helped to reveal these important connections. See, for example, Fernández-Kelly 1983; Nash and Fernández-Kelly 1983; Leacock and Safa 1986; and Benería and Sen 1981.

4. Pantojas-García (1990) argues that Puerto Rico's overpopulation discourse beginning early in the twentieth century is an important piece of the "developmentalist ideology" guiding the island's industrial policies. Briggs (2002a) makes a similar argument, stating that postwar overpopulation discourse concerned with "overpopulating, working-class mothers came to undergird development policy" (110). For a feminist analysis of Puerto Rican economic

history and women's wage labor, see Acevedo 1990; Baerga 1993; A. Ortiz 1996; Whalen 1998a, 2001.

5. In her research on migration from San Lorenzo and Salinas, Puerto Rico, to Philadelphia, Whalen (2001) makes a similar argument, providing a thorough account of gender and postwar economies.

6. Segal 1987; Richardson 1989.

7. Duany 2002, 13.

8. See Villa (2000) for discussion of the consequences of geographic displacement on Chicanos' spatial practices and literature.

9. Ayala's study of social structure and property ownership in Vieques shows that U.S. military expropriation in Vieques occurred in a context of extreme land concentration that began during the early-twentieth-century sugar plantation economy and continued in naval land concentration, which "dislocated the sugar economy of Vieques without providing alternative means of development for the population, which was 'reconcentrated' in the central section of the island." (2001, 37). McCaffrey's ethnography of popular protest in Vieques also documents past and present dislocation of civilian residents on the island and notes that, contrary to the belief that military bases economically benefit the communities surrounding them, in Vieques, as in other communities around the world, the "legacy from military occupation has been stagnation and poverty" (2002, 11).

10. History Task Force 1979; Sánchez-Korrol 1994.

11. Bonilla 1994; Ellis, Conway, and Bailey 1996; Rivera-Batiz and Santiago 1996.

12. Meléndez 1993, 15-17.

13. For studies of the socio-economic impact of return migration, see Hernández-Álvarez's pioneering work (1967); as well as Ashton 1980; Bonilla and Campos 1986; Bonilla and Colón Jordán 1979; Cordero-Guzmán 1989; Enchautegui 1991; Muschkin 1993; and Torruellas and Vázquez 1982. Zentella (1990) and Negrón-Muntaner (1997) provide important analyses of language and culture in relation to return migration; and Vargas Ramos (2000) provides a thorough discussion of return migration and political participation in Aguadilla.

14. The idea of circular migration was first advanced by Juan Hernández Cruz (1985) and employed by other scholars of Puerto Rican migration, including Rodríguez 1993; Ortiz 1993; Torre, Rodriguez Vecchini, and Burgos 1994; Duany 2002; Ellis, Conway, and Bailey 1996; Kerkhof 2000.

15. Alicea (1990) writes that many Puerto Rican migrants create dual home bases on the island and the mainland, a process that allows them to "maintain social and psychological anchors in both the United States and Puerto Rico" and belong simultaneously to several dwellings (14). See also C. Rodríguez 1993; Meléndez 1993b; and Ortiz 1993 for a discussion of circular migration.

16. Tienda and Díaz 1987; Chavez 1991.

17. Duany 2002, 235. See also Alicea 1990, 1997; Ellis, Conway, and Bailey 1996; and Rodríguez 1993 make similar arguments about the use of migration as an important survival strategy. See also Olwig and Sorenson 2001 for a more elaborate discussion about mobile livelihood practices among global migrants.

18. Kearney 1995, 548. See also Smith 2001 for a critique of globalization theories and the conflation of *transnationalism* and *globalization*.

19. Guarnizo and Smith 1998, 3.

20. Massey 1999, 35. Examples of these approaches to migration include Lee 1966; Portes and Borocz 1989; Portes and Rumbaut 1990.

21. Glick Schiller, Basch, and Blanc 1992.

22. Examples of this work include Oscar Handlin's classic *The uprooted* (1973 [1951]) and John Bodnar's (1985) *The transplanted: A history of immigrants in urban America.*

23. Glick Schiller, Basch, and Blanc (1995) define transnational social fields as a set of dense migrant contacts and social networks across borders that have become institutionalized. Levitt describes them as the "social connections and organizations that tie [migrants and nonmigrants] to one another," creating a border-spanning arena enabling migrants, "if they choose, to remain active in both worlds" (2001, 8).

24. Guarnizo and Smith 1998, 11.

25. Notable exceptions include Schein's work (1998) on Miao in Minnesota; Kibria's work (1993) on Vietnamese immigrants in the United States; and Parreñas's research (2001) on transnational mothering among Filipino families.

26. "Profile of the Foreign-Born Population in the United States: 2000," Current Population Report, U.S. Census Bureau, December 2001. Opinions regarding the "Latinization" of the American sociocultural landscape range widely from hopeful celebration to dismal Malthusian forecasts of social disaster. See Davis 2000; E. Morales 2002; Suro 1998; and Brimelow 1995 for examples of these divergent visions.

27. Vélez-Ibáñez 1996, 19. Cantú's (1995) work also provides a poignant account of the meaning and experiences of the U.S.-Mexican border and binational families, and is part of a substantial literature on Mexican binational kinship and households predating contemporary transnational approaches to migration studies. See Álvarez 1991; Guarnizo 1994; Ho 1993; Hurtado 1994; Palerm 1991; Vélez-Ibáñez 1993, 1996.

28. See, for example, De Genova and Ramos-Zayas's (2003) work on Puerto Ricans and Mexicans in Chicago as an example of this tension. Bourgois (1995) provides similar examples of Puerto Rican/Mexican tensions around issues of citizenship.

29. Writing about the boundary between the United States and Mexico, Kearney analytically distinguishes between borders and boundaries to underscore "the lack of correspondence between the borders and boundaries of the nation-state," as well as the emergence of identities that transcend "official spatial and legal bounds" (1991, 53, 70). This distinction is especially useful for understanding the ways in which Puerto Ricans' migration practices involve the crossing of multiple borders within a particular nation-state.

30. Duany 2002, 294.

31. Conservative policy analyst Linda Chavez (1991), for example, bemoans Puerto Ricans' poor economic, cultural, and moral performance, saying that they

have "been smothered by entitlements, which should serve as a warning to other Hispanics," like Mexican immigrants and "even the illegal alien," whose hard work and sacrifice — twin values allegedly unfamiliar to most Puerto Ricans — have enabled them to improve their economic position over time (152). She further suggests that the privilege of American citizenship has been wasted on Puerto Ricans, who have been "showered with too much government attention, but of the wrong kind." She writes, "Citizenship, which should have enhanced Puerto Rican achievement, may actually have hindered it by conferring entitlements, such as welfare, with no concomitant obligations. The state has functioned too much like an anonymous *patrón*, dispensing welfare checks that allowed recipients to avoid the responsibilities of autonomous adults" (159).

32. Bourgois (1995) describes mounting tension between Mexicans and Puerto Ricans in El Barrio (the East Harlem section of Manhattan), increased Puerto Rican violence against Mexicans in the neighborhood, and both sides' willingness to construct and accept racist stereotypes of each other. When Bourgois asks one undocumented Mexican immigrant why "an articulate, native-born, fluent-English speaker" who is Puerto Rican cannot find a decent-paying job, the Mexican immigrant responds by blaming Puerto Ricans for being "stupid," wanting only to make "easy money," and failing to make the most of their privileged position as American citizens — including being fluent in English (130). Smith (1998) documents similar frustration among Brooklyn Ticuanenses — natives of Ticuani, a small town in Puebla, Mexico — who attribute Puerto Ricans' and African Americans' failings to their "bad" culture and poor communities (211).

33. This is not to downplay the fact that the INS is one of the most powerful and visible agencies of state power for undocumented immigrants. Instead, I wish to build on a vast literature that investigates alternative ways of understanding migrants' economic vulnerability and exploitability, such as Chávez 1992; Lamphere, Stepick, and Grenier 1994; Rodríguez and Hagan 1992; and Vélez-Ibañez 1996. Heyman (1998), for example, seriously challenges claims that the INS is complicit in controlling and disciplining immigrant labor. "The increment of exploitability," he writes, "which probably does benefit employers, is not obviously sought by cohesive capitalist elites, but rather is the result of a complex political process" (173). A key component of these political processes is racialized "anti-laborer prejudice" that easily lends itself to the kind of xenophobia currently characterizing American society (174). Seen from below — that is, analyzing INS enforcement practices — it is clear that migrants' exploitability is a result of specific enforcement practices and "immigrants' relatively successful conspiracies to avoid the law," driven largely by this racialized nativism (173). Hector Delgado (1993) makes a similar observation about the role of the INS in disciplining immigrant labor, observing that, contrary to popular perceptions, they do not interfere with the union-organizing of undocumented workers. In fact, many workers do not actively fear the INS. Also see Gledhill (1998) for an analysis of how trade policy, such as NAFTA (the North American Free Trade Agreement), has an important effect on labor market conditions and the structuring of the economic and social livelihood of migrants.

34. Lowe 1996, 5. Similar experiences have been documented by Espiritu (2001) in her work among second-generation Filipinos in California, Kibria (1993) regarding Vietnamese families, and Tuan (1998) for Chinese and Japanese Americans. Waters (1996) draws similar conclusions in her research among Caribbean youth.

35. Glenn 1999, 5.

36. For two excellent reviews of the literature on women and migration, see Pedraza 1991 and Pessar 1999.

37. Gurak and Kritz 1982.

38. Diner 1983; Glenn 1986.

39. For examples, see Grasmuck and Pessar 1991; Hondagneu-Sotelo 1994; Menjívar 2000; Pessar 1986.

40. Mahler 1999; Mahler and Pessar 2001; Menjívar 2000. Cantú (2003) argues that sexuality is a dimension of power that shapes and organizes migration and settlement (261).

41. See Alicea 1997; Colen 1995; Hondagneu–Sotelo and Ávila 1997; Ho 1993; Parreñas 2001.

42. Di Leonardo 1992. Alicea (1997) provides an excellent discussion of women's kin work in sustaining Puerto Rican transnational practices and feelings of belonging.

43. Menjívar 2000, 174. Feminist scholars, such as Alicea 1997; Toro-Morn 1995; Torruellas, Benmayor, and Juarbe 1996; Benmayor, Torruellas, and Juarbe 1997; and Whalen 2001, have provided rich ethnographic and historical accounts of Puerto Rican women's border-spanning and cross-household economic strategies. And Hondagneu-Sotelo 1994; Mahler 1995; Menjívar 2000 have explored the gendered dimensions of immigrant network instability and tension.

44. Menjívar 2000, 2. Hagan 1998; Kwong 2001; Rodríguez and Hagen 1992; Zavella 2001 make similar arguments about the need to analyze immigrant social networks within the larger political and economic context and the experiences of poverty in which they are embedded.

45. See Olwig 1997; Ong 1999; Massey 1994.

46. Based on her extensive research on Nevis and Nevisian migrants, Olwig (1997, 1999) argues that many West Indian migrants are oriented not primarily to their place of residence but rather to their homes and communities of origin, which necessitates substantial back-and-forth movement. She describes this process as "rooted mobility (1999)." Acknowledging these often far-flung cultural sites, she exhorts anthropologists to engage in field research that expects neither a self-contained, localized social unit nor an entirely fluid, imagined, and mobile world. Instead, we should attend to the "cultural sites which have emerged in the interstices between local and global conditions of life" (1997, 35). Her call echoes that of William Roseberry and other anthropologists committed to political-economic approaches to anthropology that engage "the emergence of particular peoples at the conjunction of local and global histories" and power (Roseberry 1989, 49).

47. Valerie Matsumoto (1996) describes a similar experience, explaining that her curiosity about her family's history and her "naive fascination with the workings of ethnic networks and their meaning for those who participate in them"

informed her decision to study Asian American history and focus specifically on a Japanese American community (165). A third-generation Japanese American who grew up in a predominately Mexican American town, she expresses some of the same feelings of being an outsider as I felt while conducting research in Chicago and San Sebastián: In many ways, she was an insider, but she was also an outsider. Zavella (1993) makes similar observations about this insider/outsider dilemma in her analysis of ethnic identity construction among working-class Mexican American women.

48. San Sebastián, which covers approximately 71 square miles, is bordered by Isabela and Camuy to the north, Lares to the east, Las Marías to the south, and Moca to the west. While the town is an important commercial center, it is by no means a large city, a fact hotly disputed since the 1990 census when, according to local politicians, the municipality's population was undercounted and failed to meet U.S. federal standards for a city. The closest cities to San Sebastián are Aguadilla to the north and Mayaguez, the largest city in western Puerto Rico, to the west.

49. See Vargas Ramos 2001.

50. See Sennett and Cobb 1972. Smith (1997) makes a similar observation about poor families in Chicago decorating their homes in such a way as to hide their class status.

51. This idea of role models is advanced by a number of scholars who maintain that one way to ameliorate the "ghetto-specific" behaviors and "nihilism" allegedly characterizing America's African American underclass is to encourage class-integrated communities, where professional and middle-class blacks may serve as role models. See Wilson (1987) and West (1993) for examples of this work. I would like to thank Caridad Souza for discussing the problem of role models with me.

52. Joseph (1996) describes patriarchal connectivity as the patriarchal relational construct of self — or the relational sense of personhood — used to define and understand people as they are linked to others (108).

Chapter 2: "Fleeing the Cane" and the Origins of Displacement

1. San Sebastián ranks seventh in terms of the total market value of agricultural products sold and fourth and eighth in the value of crops and the value of livestock and poultry, respectively. USDA statistics, available at www.nass.usda.gov/pr/municipios/sansebastian.html.

2. El Grito de Lares refers to the uprising in the town of Lares, primarily by creoles (island-born descendents of Spanish immigrants) demanding independence from Spain. According to Olga Jiménez de Wagenheim, whose research meticulously covers the events, by midnight of September 23, 1868, the first day of the uprising, the rebels had "taken over the municipal seat of government, deposed the Spanish officials, and carried them off to jail along with the major Spanish merchants of the area. They declared Puerto Rico independent, installed

a provisional government, abolished the *libreta* system, and offered freedom to any slave joining the rebel cause" (1993, xiii). This armed struggle for independence was short-lived, but, as Wagenheim notes, the rebels' failure to liberate the island does not diminish the significance of the Grito de Lares, which has "grown in importance for an increasing number of Puerto Ricans since the 1930s" (xiii).

3. U.S. Census Bureau, *Census of Population and Housing 1990*. Rivera-Batiz and Santiago (1996) note that Puerto Rico's deep regional inequality "follows closely along metropolitan/nonmetropolitan lines. Most of the *municipios* with the lowest per capita income were in nonmetropolitan areas" (83).

4. "Desastre económico para San Sebastián," *El Palique,* October/November 1981.

5. Whalen 2001, 19. For a more general history of coffee production in nineteenth-century Puerto Rico, see Bergad 1983. Santiago Méndez (1988) provides a detailed examination of coffee production in late-nineteenth-century San Sebastián. The following narrative of coffee and sugar production and regional economic development draws on Santiago Méndez 1988; Rivera Montalvo 1993; and Whalen 2001, esp. pp. 19–25.

6. Santiago Méndez 1988, 176, 9.

7. Santiago Méndez 1988, 183, 185; Whalen 2001, 19–20.

8. Santiago Méndez 1988, 133

9. Mintz 1956, 338, 315, 348, quoted in Whalen 2001, 22; Quintero Rivera 1978, 71; 1988, 130. For a more extensive discussion of the political economic transformation of Puerto Rico from 1900 to 1930, see History Task Force 1979; Dietz 1986; Clark 1930; Quintero Rivera 1978; Picó 1988; Perloff 1950; Santiago-Valles 1994; González-Cruz 1998.

10. Rivera Montalvo 1993, 14; Santiago Méndez 1988, 133.

11. Rivera Montalvo 1993, 28–29, 26.

12. Whalen 2001, 23.

13. Whalen 2001, 63.

14. Silvestrini 1986, 248; Safa 1995; Whalen 2001, 63. For a discussion of women needleworkers in Puerto Rico and the Caribbean in general, see Baerga 1984, 1993; Boris 1996; A. Ortiz 1996.

15. U.S. Census Bureau 1940, *Characteristics of the Population, No. 2.*

16. Rivera Montalvo 1993, 89, 68.

17. Dietz 1986, 127–28.

18. History Task Force 1979, 118. For a more detailed discussion of Puerto Rico and the New Deal, see Lewis 1963; Mathews 1960; Stinson Fernández 1996. Both Mathews (1960) and Lewis (1963) argue that U.S. policymakers' enthusiasm to implement recovery strategies in Puerto Rico stemmed from their vision of a planned economy that would continue to expand in the years to come. Lewis argues further, however, that this new emphasis on social and economic development rather than political development was key in cementing the island's dependence on the mainland. See Lewis 1963, 123–42.

19. Lewis 1963, 125.

20. Puerto Rico Policy Commission 1934, 1. See also Descartes 1972 [1947],

185–87; Lewis 1963, 125–31; Pantojas-García 1990, 36–37; Picó 1988, 252–54; Stinson Fernández 1996, 121–23.

21. Lewis 1963, 125; Dietz 1986, 150–58; Pantojas-García 1990, chapters 2 and 3. In 1938, Luiz Muñoz Marín and other reformers founded the PPD, winning their first elections in 1940 and ushering in the era of the *populares* in Puerto Rico. Pantojas-García provides a detailed account of the consolidation of the PPD, their ascent to power and the ideological foundations of the party, which he identifies as "developmentalism."

22. Puerto Rico Policy Commission 1934, 1.

23. Whalen 2001, 27–28; Rivera Montalvo 1993, 49.

24. Puerto Rico Policy Commission 1934, 2, emphasis added. It is also important to note here that both Rexford Tugwell (later to become governor of Puerto Rico) and Eleanor Roosevelt, who visited the island in 1934 to assess the socioeconomic conditions of Puerto Rico and aid in the construction of New Deal strategies for the island, were in favor of including a birth control program as an integral part of the Chardón Plan. See Dietz 1986, 150; and López 1985, 28.

25. López 1985, 31–32.

26. Briggs 2002a, 90, 91.

27. In Ramírez de Arellano and Seipp 1983, 17.

28. Both Dr. José Lanauze Rolón, a socialist, prominent physician from Ponce and founder of La Liga para el Control de la Natalidad de Puerto Rico, and Muñoz Marín admired Margaret Sanger's work in the United States, although, as Briggs notes, the island birth control movement was not North American in origin. Rather it began "under the auspices of the Puerto Rican Socialist Party — before most places on the mainland (outside of New York City) even had an active birth control movement" (2002a, 90). Lanauze and others did, however, seek Sanger's support for the Liga, which quickly became the object of much opposition and criticism from the Catholic Church in Puerto Rico and the United States. Muñoz Marín demonstrated his belief in Sanger's views by stating in a 1922 article: "Let us take [our island] out of poverty by reducing the number of mouths to be fed, the number of feet to be shod, the number of bodies to be clothed, the number of children to be educated. How? By following with due seriousness the doctrines held by Mrs. Sanger in the U.S." (Ramírez de Arellano and Seipp 1983, 17).

29. As a social movement, eugenics was shaped by scientific advances in Mendel's laws of genetic characteristics and the rise of chromosome theory in the late nineteenth and early twentieth centuries. By the late 1920s, race and class fears fueled eugenic movements in Europe and the United States, the most obvious examples being the fusion of Germany's eugenics with anti-Semitism in the creation of National Socialism and the proliferation of sterilization laws in the United States, which targeted primarily "the poor (and often black) inmates of institutions for the feeble-minded." See Stepan 1991, 21–34, 135, and chapters 2 and 3 for the history of the eugenics movement in Latin America.

30. In Ramírez de Arellano and Seipp 1983, 20.

31. Briggs 2002a, 93–94. According to Briggs, the birth control clinic in San Juan was opened by Violet Callendar, a nurse trained in a Harlem clinic supported

by Margaret Sanger's Birth Control Clinical Research Bureau. Feminist leader Rosa González founded the clinic in Lares, and Dr. Manuel Guzmán Rodríguez, supported by Sanger, Protestant missionaries, and local women's groups, helped establish a clinic in Mayaguez (Briggs 2002a, 94).

32. In 1936, funds for birth control clinics and programs through PRERA, FERA, and PRRA (Puerto Rican Reconstruction Administration) were frozen due to intensive lobbying by U.S. Catholic bishops. See López 1985, 32.

33. The Association of Maternal and Child Care had close links with the U.S. eugenics movement and was funded in large part by the heir of Procter and Gamble, Dr. Clarence Gamble, who espoused eugenicist views and supported extreme birth control programs for impoverished women not only in Puerto Rico, but in Appalachia and the American rural South as well. In the two years of the association's operation, approximately five thousand women were served by providing access to a number of experimental birth control methods, such as spermicidal jellies, foams, and creams (rather than diaphragms, which had previously been advocated by island nurses and social workers), birth control options he believed the poor were more likely to use. See López 1985, 35–37; Ramírez de Arellano and Seipp 1983, 51–55; and Briggs 2002a, 102–108. Under Act 116, doctors were legally allowed to sterilize women who were mentally diseased, epileptic, or otherwise "unfit." Act 136 added an explicit class dimension to legal sterilization, subjecting poor women to sterilization procedures as well. A number of court battles ensued in the United States regarding Act 136, culminating with the repeal of the section of Act 136 that allowed for eugenic sterilization of poor women, although, as Ramírez de Arellano and Seipp point out, doctors were frequently able to circumvent the law by using health problems endemic in poor women as an excuse to continue sterilization (50).

34. Mass 1977, 69. Economist Amartya Sen (1997) refers to such policies as the "override" view of family planning, "since the family's personal decisions are overridden by some agency outside of the family — typically by the government of the country in question (whether or not it has been pressed to do so by 'outside' agencies, such as international organizations and pressure groups)" (92). He contrasts the "override" approach with the "collaborative" approach — one based on "expanded choices and enhanced security, and encouraged by open dialogue and extensive public discussions" — in dealing with population problems and argues that efforts to reduce population growth tend to promote family planning programs focusing on individual decisions and actions rather than on economic and social development that effectively reduces fertility rates.

35. Arturo Escobar (1995) locates growing concern about population at this time within "the new discourse of development" in postwar America. He points out that while Malthusian preoccupation with population existed much earlier with regard to Asia, from 1945 to 1955 academic and political attention shifted to Latin America and topics such as the relationship between economic and population growth, culture, and birth control. He argues that, like prevailing discourses on race and racism, "the discourses of population were being redeployed within the 'scientific' realm provided by demography, public health, and popula-

tion biology. A new view of population, and of scientific and technological instruments to manage it, was taking shape" (35). See also Ann Anagnost (1995) for a discussion of the different ways in which the population discourse informs various understandings of China's modernization project and "China's failure to progress in history" (24).

36. Williams 1977.

37. Jorge Duany, personal communication.

38. Hatt 1952, 193. While Hatt argued that overpopulation was not an adequate explanation for poverty in Puerto Rico, he and other social scientists involved in fertility and family studies at the time continued to advocate aggressive family planning strategies to reduce the island's population and facilitate economic growth.

39. Dietz 1986, 282–89. See also History Task Force 1979, 33–63 for a more extensive discussion of Malthusian versus Marxist theory in the case of Puerto Rico.

40. López 1985, 45.

41. See Boris's important work (1996, 33–54) on women in the needle industry during the New Deal era. Baerga (1984) provides an incisive analysis of the relationship between women's needlework and reproductive work as key to household economies of sugar workers. See also González 1993 and Hernández Angueira 1993 for more on the history of needlework in Puerto Rico, its origins, and its relationship to needlework in the United States.

42. Dietz 1986, 210. The name Operation Bootstrap was not adopted until 1950, but laws such as the Industrial Incentives Act of 1947 and the Industrialization Tax Exempt Act of 1948 laid the necessary foundation for the project prior to 1950. The following narrative is based on Baver 1993, chapter 2; Dietz 1986, 187–215; and Pantojas-García 1990, chapter 3.

43. Escobar 1995, 156.

44. Quoted in Lapp 1990, 38.

45. This law was passed based on the recommendation of the governor's Emigration Advisory Commission to create an emigration office to regulate and oversee Puerto Rican migration to the mainland.

46. The principal function of the Employment and Identification Office was to provide identification cards to prove Puerto Ricans' U.S. citizenship in order to secure employment in the city. See Lapp 1990, 38.

47. Introduction, Public Law 25, Commonwealth of Puerto Rico, Migration Division Employment Section Manual, cited in Lapp 1990, 72.

48. Lapp 1990, 5. Interestingly, debates regarding Puerto Ricans and welfare use continue today.

49. Migration Division, *Informe anual,* 1953–54, 22; Migration Division, *Monthly Report,* Nov. 1952, 2; Lapp 1990, 206–207. Beginning in the late 1940s, Clarence Senior collaborated extensively with the Puerto Rican government in their industrialization program, and eventually with the island's emigration policy. He wrote a number of books on Puerto Rican migration, including *Puerto Rican emigration* (1947), *The Puerto Ricans of New York City* (1948), and *The Puerto*

Rican journey: New York's newest migrants (1950) with C. Wright Mills and Rose K. Golden. He also served as a consultant to the Migration Division and eventually worked as chief of the division until 1960 (Lauria Pericelli 1990, 409–410).

50. Wolf 1974, 252. Wolf further argues that Liberal Reform era's emphasis on human plasticity and flexibility was a reaction to Social Darwinism. Boas's work in physical anthropology was key in promoting antiracist approaches to race and culture that were linked to Social Darwinism.

51. Orin Starn (1986) argues that the War Relocation Authority's internment of Japanese Americans during World War II and their promotion of residential dispersal after the war was informed in large part by prevailing ideas about nationalism, assimilation, and acculturation, and that U.S. anthropologists — seen as "scientists of culture" — provided their expertise in these wartime and postwar efforts. For more on the legacy of Progressive Era social reformers and Chicago School urban social science, see Hannerz 1980 and di Leonardo 1998.

52. Lapp 1990, 160–61.

53. Migration Division, *Monthly Report,* Aug. 1952, 1; Sept. 1952, 1.

54. Migration Division, *Informe anual,* 1953–54, 45–46. All of the Migration Division's annual reports were written in Spanish, while the monthly reports were submitted in English. All English translations of these documents in this book are my own.

55. Di Leonardo employs the phrase "ethnic report card" in her work on Italian Americans in northern California (1984, 96).

56. See Migration Division, *Monthly Report,* Mar. 1951, 1 of Chicago Report.

57. Migration Division, *Informe anual,* 1953, 45.

58. Migration Division, *Informe anual,* 1953–54, 55–56. See also the Migration Division's annual reports for 1954–1955 and 1955–1956 for more discussion on the relationship between the work of the division and the success of the industrialization program.

59. Pantojas-García 1990, 70; Whalen 2001, 28.

60. Pantojas-García 1990, 71.

61. Teodoro Moscoso, 1951, "Sobre la industrializacion: Sus metas y problemas actuales," *Fomento de Puerto Rico* 1, no. 1 (October): 3.

62. In the April 1955 issue, Samuel E. de la Rosa noted, "Helping to forge an industrial conscience on an island with an essentially agricultural tradition such as Puerto Rico is the work to which every good Puerto Rican should dedicate himself in this great nation of ours." "Forjando una conciencia industrial," 1955, *Fomento de Puerto Rico* 11, no. 2 (April): 9–11.

63. "La tarea de los agricultores," 1952, *Fomento de Puerto Rico* 1, no. 2 (January): 17–19.

64. Whalen 2001, 40, 39, 43.

65. *Informe anual,* 1953–54, 3.

66. *Informe anual,* 1956–57, 8.

67. Rivera Montalvo 1993, ix, 128.

68. This idea of industry-as-culture was debated in *Fomento de Puerto Rico* and in *Revista del Instituto de Cultura Puertorriqueña,* the official magazine of the

Institute of Puerto Rican Culture (ICP). See "Cultura e industria," 1956, *Fomento de Puerto Rico* 3, no. 2 (April): 30–31; "Reflexiones sobre la industrializacion en Puerto Rico," 1958, *Revista del Instituto de Cultura puertorriqueña* 1, no. 1 (Oct.– Dec.): 19–21; and "La industrialización y sus consecuencias," 1959, *Revista del Instituto de Cultura Puertorriqueña* 1, no. 1 (Oct.–Dec.): 49–50.

69. Ríos 1993, 92; Silvestrini 1986, 248. See also Acevedo 1990 for a gender analysis of the trajectory of Operation Bootstrap and women's differential incorporation into the labor market throughout the program's three phases.

70. See A. Ortiz 1996; Acevedo 1990; Baerga 1993; and Safa 1981, 1995 for a more elaborate discussion of gender ideology and women's employment in Puerto Rico and the Caribbean. For non-Caribbean examples, see Warren and Bourque 1991; Nash and Fernández-Kelly 1983; Fernández-Kelly 1983; Leacock and Safa 1986; Lamphere 1987; Lamphere et al. 1993; and Zavella 1987.

71. Safa (1995) explores this ambivalence and concomitant contradictions as women's industrial wage-labor often replaces men's in export-led industrialization in the Caribbean.

72. "La mujer puertorriqueña en el programa de industrialización," 1954, *Fomento de Puerto Rico* 1, no. 10 (Jan.): 24–26.

73. Dávila 1997, 34–37.

74. Literally, "the time of Muñoz Marín," referring to the first elected governor, who oversaw the initial stages of Operation Bootstrap. *Los populares* refers to members of the Partido Popular Democrático, or PPD.

75. The peasant and the countryside are popular images of continuity with a rural past. Much of the early urban studies scholarship invokes these images in analyzing the evolutionary movement from *Gemeinschaft* to *Gesellschaft*. See di Leonardo 1998; Ferguson 1992; Hannerz 1980; and Williams 1973 for more analysis of the rural/urban antinomy in literature and anthropology.

76. Dávila 1997, 72.

77. Idealizing precapitalist and "traditional" lifeways in the context of rapid modernization is not uncommon. In the case of India, Chatterjee (1989, 1993) argues that the contradictory pulls of nationalist ideology are resolved in part by making a clear distinction between material and spiritual cultural spheres. According to Chatterjee, nineteenth-century Indian nationalists maintained that "not only was it undesirable to imitate the West in anything other than the material aspects of life, it was even unnecessary to do so, because in the spiritual domain the East was superior to the West. What was necessary was to cultivate the material techniques of modern Western civilization while retaining and strengthening the distinctive spiritual essence of the national culture" (1989, 623). How gender is incorporated in these complicated nationalist projects varies widely and is inflected with class and race as well, as in the case of India's nationalist project, which embraced the image of the "new woman," who was superior to Western women and low-class "traditional" Indian women. Donna Guy's work (1991) on prostitution, gender, and nationalism in late-nineteenth- and early-twentieth-century Argentina provides another important portrait of the ways in which gender and class are central to nation-building projects and the definition of citizenship and moral virtue.

78. "Alcalde termina programa de mejoras públicas," *El Mundo,* Jan. 18, 1952.

79. Editorial, *El Mundo,* January 18, 1952.

80. According to the 1950s census, the population of San Sebastián was 35,376. In 1960 and 1970, it dropped to 33,451 and 30,175, respectively. In 1940, the population was 30,266.

81. The plan also proposed targeting school-age children as workers, who would receive special permission to work in the cane fields during the harvest when abundant labor was most needed.

82. See Rivera Montalvo 1993, 129–55, for a more detailed discussion of this committee and its results. See also Department of Labor, "Proyecto piloto de la caña," 1967–68.

83. It was not until much later that the government implemented a more aggressive policy, including wage subsidies, reliable transportation, and transportation stipends, to help struggling small farmers. Such changes have been important in remedying the agricultural labor shortage in the region.

Chapter 3: "Know Your Fellow American Citizen from Puerto Rico"

1. Grossman 1989, 162; Hirsch 1998 [1983], 16. Hirsch notes that while the arrival of southern blacks in Chicago between 1910 and 1920 represents the largest *percent* increase of the city's black population, the greatest increase in absolute numbers occurred during the 1940s and 1950s.

2. Maldonado 1979, 106; Kornblum 1974, 12–13; García 1996; Arredondo, in press.

3. Maldonado 1979, 103.

4. The Office of Puerto Rico in Washington D.C. issued the pamphlet to social service agencies and charity organizations throughout Chicago. The work of scholars and policy advisors like sociologist Clarence Senior were critical in this campaign to educate city residents in New York and Chicago about Puerto Rican migrants. One of Senior's most important books, *Strangers, then neighbors: From pilgrims to Puerto Ricans* (1961) is an example of the island government's efforts to promote a "neighborly" relationship with Americans.

5. Parts of this chapter appear in Pérez 2001.

6. Alejandro Portes (1978) argues that the study of immigrants is the foundation of modern urban social science in the United States. Examples of the work produced by University of Chicago social scientists (or Chicago School ethnographies) include Park 1928; Park and Burgess 1921; and Thomas and Znaniecki 1927. Other notable Chicago School ethnographies are Zorbaugh 1929; and Park, Burgess, and McKenzie 1925. The notion of "defending the city" comes from Hannerz's (1980, 20) discussion of the May 1, 1886, Haymarket Square Riots and the monument commemorating the role of law enforcement in the affair. See Drake and Cayton (1993 [1945], 55–57) for a discussion of Chicago's "vice problem" in the first two decades of the twentieth century. The following discussion of the importance of Chicago School sociology is based largely on Ulf Hannerz (1980), esp. chap. 2; and Persons (1987).

7. Park (1928) identifies migration as one of the most decisive influences in "the history of mankind." He writes, "The forces which have been decisive in the history of mankind are those which have brought men together in fruitful competition, conflict, and co-operation. Among the most important of these influences have been — according to what I have called the catastrophic theory of progress — migration and the incidental collisions, conflicts, and fusions of the people and cultures which they have occasioned" (882).

8. Park 1928, 887, 888, 893. According to Park, the European Jew was the consummate marginal man: "[The Jew] was a man on the margin of two cultures and two societies, which never completely interpenetrated and fused. The emancipated Jew was, and is, historically and typically the marginal man, the first cosmopolite and citizen of the world. He is, par excellence, the 'stranger,' whom Simmel, himself a Jew, has described with such profound insight and understanding in his *Sociologie*. Most if not all the characteristics of the Jew, certainly his pre-eminence as a trader and his keen intellectual interest, his sophistication, his idealism and lack of historic sense, are the characteristics of the city man, the man who ranges widely, lives preferably in a hotel — in short, the cosmopolite" (892).

9. Park 1928, 890.

10. In the 1930s, for example, E. Franklin Frasier emphasized black Americans' cultural rather than social assimilation. See di Leonardo (1998, 84–90) for more on race and ethnic politics of the Progressive Era, political economy, and the role of Chicago School sociologists.

11. Hirsch 1998 [1983]; Venkatesh 2000.

12. "Emigrantes van a trabajar en Chicago," *El Mundo*, Sept. 24, 1946. Less than a month after *El Mundo*'s initial report, the paper ran an article titled, "Domestics of color will be taken to Florida: Puerto Rican women workers would work in Miami and other southern cities" (*El Mundo,* Oct. 18, 1946). This piece foregrounded the unequivocal success of domestics in Chicago and the plans of Castle, Barton, and Associates to open an office in Miami and send a representative to Ponce to select domestic workers. Interestingly, previous press regarding domestics' emigration did not specify "de color." See also Whalen (1998a) and Toro-Morn (1999) for more on women contract laborers in Philadelphia and Chicago, respectively.

13. Toro-Morn 1999. Mary Romero (1992) points out that at the turn of the century, "industrialization was creating a shortage of household workers. The industrial expansion of the late nineteenth century increased employment options for women. Just as male servants turned to new occupations, women also left domestic service as soon as the job market expanded" (60).

The *Chicago Herald American* was the first Chicago newspaper to profile a recently arrived Puerto Rican *doméstica*. Titled "Puerto Rican maids: Successful experiment," the article featured Rosa Garcia, an eighteen-year-old woman who quickly became "the pride of the household and the envy of the neighborhood" (Oct. 5, 1946).

14. See Diner (1983) for a discussion of Irish domestics at the turn of the century. Marks (1989, 128–131) and Grossman (1989, 257) discuss black women's

domestic labor as one employment alternative both in the South and in northern cities after the Great Migration.

15. Hondagneu-Sotelo 2001, 14. Drake and Cayton point out that black women were less likely to work as live-in domestics in the North, opting instead for day work (1993 [1945], 242–47). Similarly, Puerto Rican female live-in domestics decreased with increased migration to the city.

16. Maldonado 1979, 114; Toro Morn 1999.

17. Katzman 1981, 204.

18. Parreñas 2000. Hondagneu-Sotelo (2001) discusses contemporary issues of Latina domestic workers in the United States.

19. Toro-Morn 1999, 53.

20. "Géigel partió en una mission especial ayer," *El Mundo* Jan. 3, 1947; Maldonado 1979, 114–15. Laws regulating contract labor can be traced back to 1919; they were amended in 1936 and, as a result of Géigel Polanco's investigation, again in 1947.

21. "Géigel presentará enmienda la ley de emigración obrera," *El Mundo,* Jan. 24, 1947.

22. "Crearán centros domésticos para entrenar mujeres en trabajo del hogar," *El Mundo,* Aug. 28, 1947.

23. Centers would be located in the municipalities of San Juan, Arecibo, Aguadilla, Ponce, Mayaguez, Caguas, Guayama, and Humacao and would follow a specialized curriculum: "The courses would be three months and would include the following areas: Conversational English, and training in the following domestic chores: washing kitchen utensils, cleaning and arranging furniture, making beds, polishing china and silver, answering the door, cleaning and scrubbing the floors, serving meals, taking messages, changing bed sheets, preparing lists for the laundry, operating appliances needed to execute household chores, childcare and child nutrition, and elementary culinary arts." *El Mundo,* Aug. 28, 1947.

24. Ibid. Toro-Morn (1999) also discusses the island's domestic training schools and refers specifically to the *Labor Information Bulletin*'s May 1948 report outlining the history of the "Caguas Project." For a detailed discussion on the creation of domestic centers and female contract labor, see also Whalen 1998a.

25. Donald J. O'Connor, memorandum to Manuel Pérez, commissioner of labor, "More on job procurement on the mainland," May 13, 1947, quoted in Maldonado 1979, 105; Toro-Morn 1999, 116; and Whalen 1998a, 214.

26. As a Puerto Rican graduate student in anthropology at the University of Chicago, Padilla engaged in pioneering field research not only among Puerto Ricans in Chicago, but also in New York and Puerto Rico. She was the only Puerto Rican researcher who collaborated with Julian Steward and his students on the People of Puerto Rico Project beginning in 1947. Her study of Nocorá, a state-run sugar plantation, was one of many community studies in the important — and unjustly neglected — *People of Puerto Rico* (1956). In 1958 she also published *Up from Puerto Rico* (1958), a study of Puerto Rican settlement in New York.

27. Padilla 1947, 101. Padilla's concern with Puerto Ricans' proper "social orientation" reveals her Chicago School theoretical grounding and Park's influence,

in particular, on her intellectual development. He also believed that "proper train-ing and orientation" ensured migrants' easy assimilation into their host society (Park 1928).

28. This nexus of University of Chicago researchers and Puerto Rican gov-ernment officials has important historical precedents. Rexford Tugwell, governor of Puerto Rico from 1941 to 1946, was also a professor at the University of Chi-cago, and Jaime Benítez, one of the founders of the Center for Social Science Research at the University of Puerto Rico in 1945, was a University of Chicago student. The University of Chicago, as well as Columbia, Harvard, and M.I.T., enjoyed important institutional links with the Center for Social Science Research that also allowed their researchers intimate connections with island government officials.

29. I want to thank Michelle Boyd for her observation of the division's com-plicity in muting migrants' political independence. Lapp's work (1990) supports this claim, noting that shortly after the Puerto Rican nationalist shooting on the U.S. Congress, Clarence Senior lamented that the event would "set [the divi-sion's] work back a long time," and that "the man on the street too often is found saying, 'Why don't we give them their independence so that they won't come here and menace us anymore.'" *Monthly Report,* Mar. 1954, quoted in Lapp 1990, 212–13). For details about the division's work with the Chicago Council against Racial and Religious Discrimination and Chicago's Public Welfare Office, see *Monthly Report,* Jan. 1952, 1; and *Informe anual,* 1953–54, 45. See also *Monthly Report,* Sept. 1953), 1, for a discussion of Paul Hatt's Northwestern University fer-tility study; and *Informe anual,* 1953–54, 45, for details on the University of Chicago's study on Puerto Ricans in the city. See *Informe anual,* 1955–56, 20; and *Monthly Report,* Apr. 1952, 2, about the importance of forming community organ-izations whose goals promote integration and assimilation.

30. See *Monthly Report,* Feb. 1951, 2, for details regarding radio announcements. And see *Monthly Report,* Nov. 1951, 1, and *Monthly Report,* Oct. 1953, for more information on the division's collaboration with city organizations and commu-nity agencies to show films about Puerto Rico. Both *The Girl from Puerto Rico* and *The Crowded Island* were produced by the Migration Division as part of its cam-paign to produce a positive image of Puerto Ricans on the mainland. When *Crowded in Paradise* — produced in collaboration with *Fomento de Puerto Rico* — was first released in New York, no Broadway theaters wanted to show it because "according to them, 'If we show a film that is favorable of Puerto Rico and the Puerto Ricans, many Puerto Ricans will attend our theater and that will send our clients away.' Just this one event demonstrates the need to distribute this film widely" (*Informe anual,* 1955–56, 12–13).

31. *Informe anual,* 1955–56, 102.

32. In its annual report for 1953–54, the division reaffirmed its mission: "This Division helps directly or indirectly those Puerto Ricans who come to the United States with their work plans, education, social well-being, to secure identification and establish themselves as American citizens and orient them in their rights and responsibilities in the community. It also helps individual adjustment and inte-

gration into the community where one resides with the direct cooperation of civic entities and public and private agencies so that they are better able to understand Puerto Ricans and recognize the valuable contribution they make and can make to the economies in the areas where they live and work" (1).

33. Lapp 1990, 207.

34. Los Caballeros de San Juan was the principal social organization among Puerto Ricans in Chicago of the 1950s and 1960s. Padilla (1987) argues that its importance was more institutional than cultural. He writes, "The significance of Los Caballeros de San Juan among Puerto Ricans was first of all institutional, and only secondarily a matter of cultural transmission and/or perpetuation as in the anthropological sense. Los Caballeros presented the primary means by which Puerto Ricans began to structure a self-conscious community for ethnic advancement and betterment. . . . The embryo of what was to later become a diverse Puerto Rican community had its inception in the growth of Los Caballeros" (126). In its 1955–56 annual report, the division explains at length the positive consequences of the first Día de San Juan celebration, concluding, "This positive but not essential activity that helps us to create a more favorable environment without having to spend either time or money is one example of how we apply our concept of 'the economy of effort,' allowing other groups and organizations as much responsibility they are able, or can be encouraged, to assume (101). See also *Monthly Report*, Dec. 1951, 1, for more on blood donations and positive hospital relations among Puerto Rican residents in Chicago.

35. *Informe anual,* 1955–56, 117.

36. One of the distinguishing features of the "new transnationalism" is government involvement in the lives of migrants abroad and the extension of some citizenship rights to diasporic communities (Glick Schiller, Basch, and Blanc 1992).

37. Several excellent works document and analyze the various ways in which model minority rhetoric has been used since the mid 1960s. See Lee 1996; Fong 1998; Kim 1993, 1999; and Prashad 2000 for a discussion of the rise of model minority rhetoric in the 1960s and its emergence in the 1980s and 1990s.

38. For examples of this work, see Coontz 1992; Glenn 1986; Zinn and Dill 1994.

39. Williams 1999, 85–86.

40. Coontz (1992) points out that rigid family and gender roles in postwar America converged with Cold War anxieties to further sanctify the family as the bedrock of American liberal democracy: "A 'normal' family and vigilant mother became the 'front line' of defense against treason; anticommunists linked deviant family or sexual behavior to sedition" (33).

41. Lee (1996) points to Hernstein and Murray's *The bell curve* (1994) and D'Souza's *The end of racism: Principles for a multicultural society* (1995) as key texts invoking the model minority to explain Asian American versus black and Latino academic success. Kim (1993) provides a more thorough political context for understanding current model minority morality plays, linking public policy discourse with academic perspectives about race, poverty, and family values. Prashad

(2000) makes an excellent critique of how the model minority discourse implicates South Asians in the United States as well as its larger political, economic, and academic context.

42. "Puerto Ricans are eager to work, want no handouts," *Chicago Daily News*, Aug. 11, 1959. See also "Puerto Ricans adding Latin culture to Chicago," *Chicago Sun-Times*, Mar. 1, 1953, for another example of media praise for Puerto Rican migrants in Chicago.

43. "Los Medinas, a model Puerto Rican family," *Chicago Tribune*, Sept. 17, 1961, quoted in Padilla 1987, 74.

44. "The Puerto Rican families in Chicago," *Chicago Tribune*, Jan. 24, 1968, quoted in Padilla 1987, 76.

45. Mayor's Committee on New Residents 1960, 5.

46. Williams (1999, 70–71; 85–89) discusses how popular media reinforced ideas of an authoritative male head of household, a profile Puerto Rican families fit and advanced in 1950s Chicago. Interestingly, the praise of Chicago's patriarchal Puerto Rican families was a regionally specific phenomenon informed largely by the city's race politics and political economic dynamics. Whalen's (1998a) work on Puerto Ricans in postwar Philadelphia paints a quite different portrait, whereby Puerto Rican families were criticized for their patriarchal family arrangements and the popular perception of Puerto Rican women as submissive, and therefore poor mothers.

47. "Puerto Ricans eager to work . . . ," *Chicago Daily News*, Aug. 11, 1959. See also *Informe anual*, 1961–62, 211–13, for more discussion of the division's concern about credit schemes. Padilla (1987, 60) also mentions the portrayal of Puerto Ricans as gentle, loving people, but regards it solely as "another major source of prejudice against Puerto Ricans." I agree that profound racism informed these characterizations, but it is also important to analyze the ways in which these portrayals are also used to denigrate other groups, such as blacks, Native Americans, and poor whites in the city.

48. Quoted in *Chicago Sun-Times*, Mar. 1, 1953.

49. Mayor's Committee on New Residents 1960, 8.

50. According to the article "Chicago's Proud Puerto Ricans," *Daily News*, June 5, 1965, this quotation is an example of Chicago Puerto Ricans' capacity for self-analysis.

51. Ibid. In 1953, the Catholic Youth Organization (CYO) shared similar concerns about Puerto Ricans in Chicago versus New York. In a memo to the Welfare Council of Metropolitan Chicago, CYO officials explained why it was important to conduct a study of the city's Puerto Rican population: "In general, and very importantly, such a study will point out the many problems faced by this group which day by day is rapidly increasing and which may be facing the same situation which confronts New York City at the present time. *Chicago certainly does not want to allow such a situation to get out of hand as it has in New York City*" (Sept. 21, 1953, quoted in Martinez 1989, 109, emphasis added).

52. Mayor's Committee on New Residents 1960, 5. The description "as Spanish as avocados and as American as ice cream" is from "Know your fellow American

citizen from Puerto Rico," a document distributed by the Office of the Common-wealth of Puerto Rico. The "Know your fellow American" pamphlets were read-ily available at the Migration Division Offices and were distributed to organiza-tions working with Puerto Rican migrants. According to a 1950 United Charities of Chicago interdepartmental memo, for example, supervisors issued copies of this pamphlet to district secretaries and departmental supervisors because "it should be of interest and help to the staff in working with Puerto Ricans who come to the United States" (United Charities of Chicago, May 31, 1950, Bulletin 204, quoted in Martinez 1989, 11).

53. Hirsch 1998 [1983], 4. Hirsch carefully describes the ways in which federal and local governments financed and facilitated the creation of Chicago's ghettos: "Indeed, the real tragedy surrounding the modern ghetto is not that it has been inherited but that it has been periodically renewed and strengthened. Fresh deci-sions, not the mere acquiescence to old ones, reinforced and shaped the con-temporary black metropolis (9).

54. Quoted in Hirsch 1998 [1983], 182.

55. *South Deering Bulletin,* Sept. 5, 1955, quoted in Hirsch 1998 [1983], 186.

56. Harden (2003) demonstrates that Japanese Americans in postwar Chicago also complicated notions of race and the city's fabled black/white color line. Like Puerto Ricans, Japanese Americans were used as a benchmark to compare the suc-cesses and failures of Chicago's black population

57. "Puertorriqueños en Chicago," *El Mundo,* Mar. 26, 1953. Of course, the unspoken assumption is that myriad problems in New York raised serious questions as to whether Puerto Ricans could live and work successfully in the United States. It is also clear that *El Mundo* editors believed that these were human capital prob-lems that could be remedied by training migrants: "The better prepared those who leave our country to acclimate themselves on the Continent, the easier it will be to achieve such success. We must continue encouraging the work of orientation and [establishing] networks. And we must continue to insist that the future emigrant is given here all opportunities to acquire adequate English dominance."

58. Editorial, *El Mundo,* Feb. 4, 1954. For more reaction to events unfolding in Chicago, see *El Mundo,* Feb. 3, 4, 6, 8, 9, 12, 1954.

59. "Boricuas en Chicago: Preside comité ha de ayudar a grupos minoría sin empleos," *El Mundo,* Feb. 8, 1954. The committee emphatically denounced the city's actions and pointed out that this was not a *Puerto Rican* problem but rather one that affected all ethnic groups. Bishop Shiel maintained that if Chicago Puerto Ricans were having problems, they should be resolved in Chicago and not in Puerto Rico. Similarly, the CIO spokesman asserted, "This is a national problem. And we should hope that city money is available for all in equal pro-portion." This kind of coalition-building is quite remarkable and deserves further academic attention.

60. "Carta de Chicago" *El Mundo,* Feb. 12, 1954.

61. "By indicating the areas of concentration we can determine if the group is becoming localized or whether it has integrated into different communities. Although efforts have been made to have them live in different communities,

there is no factual information on this matter." Catholic Youth Organization memo to the Welfare Council of Metropolitan Chicago, Sept. 21, 1953, quoted in Martinez 1989, 109.

62. The Welfare Council of Metropolitan Chicago minutes, April 9, 1954, Chicago Historical Society, quoted in Ramos-Zayas 2003, 48.

63. *Informe anual,* 1958–59, 132

64. Padilla (1987, 61) cites the *Saturday Evening Post*'s November 5, 1960 sensational news article depicting Chicago Puerto Ricans as killers and detailing their fights with the city's Italian population. Also, the famous Broadway musical *West Side Story* permanently etched Puerto Rican–white ethnic American rivalry into the American popular imagination.

65. Lapp explains that the Migration Division continually downplayed instances of racism and discrimination against Puerto Ricans, recasting these problems as cultural differences (1990, 124). I believe that such thinking reflected larger academic interpretations of urban problems in the late 1950s and 1960s and deeply informed the Migration Division's response to clear instances of racism in Chicago. *El Mundo,* again, reported strained relations between Puerto Ricans and police. In August 1958, a group of Puerto Ricans asked Governor Muñoz Marín to intervene in escalating ethnic conflicts and their poor relationship with the police. Muñoz Marín responded by going to Chicago the following month and meeting with the mayor and heads of social service agencies. In a meeting with Mayor Daley, Muñoz Marín praised Chicago for its long history of receiving immigrants from around the world and mentioned that Puerto Ricans were harassed by police with comments like "Go back from where you came from." He remarked, "If all were to follow the police order to return from where one came, Chicago would be in a very bad position." Rather than denounce police behavior, Daley quipped, "[By that logic], I guess I would have to leave too." Quoted in "Alcalde Daley: Ofrece a Muñoz ayuda a boricuas en Chicago [Mayor Daley: Offers to Muñoz help to Puerto Ricans in Chicago]," *El Mundo,* Sept. 6, 1958.

66. Kim (1993) lays out three ways in which the model minority myth perpetuates Asian American racial subordination: "It encourages Asian Americans to compare their status with that of other racial minorities, obscuring the persistent socioeconomic gap between themselves and whites; it exaggerates Asian Americans' prosperity and downplays their socioeconomic needs and problems; and it conceals anti-Asian racism behind a veil of essentializing praise" (12).

67. Examples of this erasure include landmark texts such as History Task Force 1979; Bonilla and Campos 1986; Padilla 1987. Works by Toro-Morn 1999; Alicea 1997; A. Ortiz 1996; Whalen 1998a, 2001; and Baerga 1993 have foregrounded gender in their examination of migration and work. As Caridad Souza has insightfully noted, canonical texts in Puerto Rican labor and migration history would look very different if women's productive and reproductive labor had been seriously considered (2001, personal communication).

68. *Monthly Reports,* Nov., April 1951; *Monthly Reports,* July, Oct. 1952; *Informe anual,* 1955–56, 96–97.

69. G. Sánchez (1994) provides an excellent analysis of Mexican women and Americanization programs in California in the Progressive Era. Such programs,

he argues, were a reaction to increased Mexican immigration at the turn of the century and an attempt to encourage immigrants to "conform to the American industrial order in a prescribed manner" (284). Arredondo (in press) makes a similar point about Mexicans in Chicago in the 1920s and 1930s.

70. The Migration Division documented one thousand Puerto Ricans in Cabrini Homes in 1959–60. *Informe anual,* 1959–60, 160; Migration Division memo to the Welfare Council of Metropolitan Chicago, July 22, 1953, quoted in Martinez 1989, 112; Mayor's Committee on New Residents 1960, 16–25.

71. For examples of this work, see Glenn 1986; Zinn and Dill 1994; A. Ortiz 1996; Ruiz 1993.

72. "Chicago's Proud Puerto Ricans," *Daily News,* June 5, 1965.

73. Several U.S.-based ethnographies document the ways in which women's wage labor challenges gender hierarchies and complicates gender ideologies with regard to family and housework. See Zavella 1987; Lamphere 1987; Lamphere, Stepick, and Grenier 1994; Pesquera 1993; Grasmuck and Pessar 1991.

74. *Chicago Daily News,* June 13, 1966, quoted in Padilla 1987, 149. The dominant perception of Puerto Ricans as docile, innocent, and naive — in addition to city concern about urban unrest in black communities in places like Harlem, Watts, and Detroit — contributed to a misapprehension of the state of race relations in Chicago. Moreover, the truism that Chicago's race problem — and its fabled color line — is purely black and white redirected government attention away from escalating tensions in nonblack areas. Mayor Daley conveniently blamed "outsiders" for fueling the riot (Royko 1971, 152). And while Padilla (1987, 149) cites police superintendent Orlando W. Wilson explaining his recent investigation into racial tensions in Puerto Rican and Mexican communities in the city, it is clear the city didn't give serious attention to longstanding complaints about housing discrimination, police brutality, and poor social services in those areas.

In his scathing portrait of Mayor Daley in *Boss,* Mike Royko sums up the city's treatment of its Puerto Rican population, underscoring their fear of Martin Luther King Jr.'s influence on poor minority communities in the city. He writes, "City Hall didn't bother to extend the usual ethnic courtesies to the Puerto Ricans. When they held their big festival in a local park, Daley and one of their aldermen didn't attend. The other aldermen's contribution was a stern warning to the festival organizers to not invite civil rights speakers. Because [Puerto Ricans] were undemanding and docile, they were cuffed around regularly by the police. The traffic policemen used the Puerto Rican neighborhood to dump their quota of tickets. Few of the policemen assigned to the district spoke Spanish. The Police Department didn't hire many Puerto Ricans because of the minimum height requirements" (151–52).

75. Mayor's Committee on New Residents 1966, 14–17.

76. Padilla 1987, 166–67; Ramos-Zayas 2003; López 1994, 23–24. Lapp describes a similar transformation from civic groups organized mainly around town clubs to activist-oriented groups among New York Puerto Ricans as well. This shift helped to diminish the New York Migration Division Office's influence in barrio politics beginning in the late 1960s.

77. Ramos-Zayas also documents this pride in the *Chicago* origins of the YLO

(2003, 53, 252 n. 14). For demographic reasons, New York's Puerto Rican community is usually believed to be the progenitor of all militant movements. Community activists in Chicago consistently refer to the fact that not only did the YLO begin in Chicago, but most of the political prisoners recently released lived and were politically involved in Chicago, not New York. Recent writing and oral histories about the YLO across the United States all refer to the importance of the Chicago YLO in inspiring similar grassroots efforts in cities like Philadelphia and New York. See Morales 1998; Guzmán 1998; and Whalen 1998b.

78. Padilla 1987, 120–23; Browning 1970. At Centro Cultural Ruiz Belvis, community activists often compare instances of repression against Puerto Rican grassroots institutions in the 1990s — such as the FBI raid and closing of the Humboldt Park Infant Mortality Reduction Initiative (HIMRI) in 1995, the political scandal at Roberto Clemente High School in 1997 (see Chapter 5), and the city's random enforcement of building and zoning codes at the Centro — to the era in which Chicago's Red Squad and COINTELPRO infiltrated community organizations and arrested and harassed their leaders.

79. Examples of work exploring this history include Rodolfo Acuña, 1974, *Occupied America: The Chicano's struggle toward liberation*; Rudolfo Anaya and Francisco A. Lomeli, 1989, *Aztlán: Essays on the Chicano homeland*; David Gutiérrez, 1995, *Walls and mirrors: Mexican Americans, Mexican immigrants, and the politics of ethnicity*; William Van Deburg, 1992, *New day in Babylon: The black power movement and American culture*; Philip Foner, ed., 1995, *The Black Panthers speak*; Alan Anderson, 1986, *Confronting the color line: The broken promise of the Civil Rights Movement in Chicago*.

80. Ramos-Zayas 2003, 4.

81. Quoted in "Puerto Ricans' area of agony," *Chicago Sun-Times,* June 12, 1977. The journalist correctly points out how nostalgic invocations of Humboldt Park's "better days" are largely fantasy, since it is the same neighborhood profiled in Nelson Algren's (1946) crime drama *The man with the golden arm.*

82. Studs Terkel's acclaimed *Division Street* (1966) paints quite a different picture, celebrating instead the ways in which the diversity of Division Street reflects the strengths and virtues of postwar America.

83. "Latins finally winning attention here," *Chicago Daily News,* Feb. 24, 1972; and "The Puerto Ricans," *Chicago Tribune,* May 5, 1975.

84. Glazer and Moynihan 1963, 88, 117–22.

85. Lewis 1966, xliv, xlv, lii.

86. Briggs 2002b, 90.

87. Steven Steinberg points out that *Beyond the melting pot* received the 1963 *Saturday Review of Literature*'s Anisfeld-Wolf award for bettering intergroup relations (1995, 11). Micaela di Leonardo documents the breadth of Oscar Lewis's popular appeal (1998, 115–16): *La vida* won the National Book Award for nonfiction in 1967, and his articles appeared in *Harper's, Commentary,* and *Redbook.* Laura Briggs also emphasizes the breadth of *La vida*'s appeal, noting that it was priced well below many "serious" books of the time and eventually released as "an inexpensive paperback edition — intending, and finding, a wide audience" (2002b, 89).

88. According to Massey and Denton (1993, 12, 144–46), Puerto Ricans in the

United States are the only Latino group to live in highly segregated communities similar to those of black Americans. It is for this reason that some scholars argue that Puerto Ricans, like African Americans, allegedly develop "underclass communities" and their concomitant pathologies. See also Squires (1991, 15) for a discussion of the racialized impact of the suburbanization of Chicago's manufacturing sector.

89. Di Leonardo 1998, 89–98; Steinberg 1995, 107–19. Both authors reveal that the white ethnic community construct is a largely fantastic claim of the past.

90. In *The truly disadvantaged* (1987), William Julius Wilson argues that structural changes in the urban economy have given rise to an urban underclass characterized by persistent poverty, high rates of female-headed households, and the social pathologies found specifically in "ghetto communities" (6). Although Wilson specifically identifies poor, residentially segregated African Americans as members of the "underclass," several scholars have employed the construct to understand poverty — and its concomitant behavioral pathologies — among Puerto Ricans. See Chavez (1991) and Tienda (1989) for similar discussions. Massey and Denton (1993) also discuss the fact that Puerto Ricans are the only Latino group to develop "underclass communities," meaning hypersegregated residential patterns rather than a set of values, behaviors, and domestic arrangements. For critiques of the underclass concept, see Reed 1992; di Leonardo 1998, 112–27; and Steinberg 1997. Moore and Pinderhughes's edited volume (1993) provides a discussion of Latinos and the underclass debate. Oscar Lewis's 1960s "culture of poverty argument" largely informs William J. Wilson's "underclass" notion in the 1980s, although, as some scholars have argued, the former argument was far more progressive. See di Leonardo 1998, 112–21; and Reed 1999, 186–90.

91. "Arson blitz is destroying changing area of the Northwest Side," *Daily News,* Sept. 6, 1975.

92. "Humboldt area besieged: A life of arson terror," *Daily News,* Sept. 8, 1975.

93. "Four hundred fires in year and few suspects," *Daily News,* Sept. 11, 1975.

94. Within a thirty-two-block area, almost one third of the housing stock was lost to arson in eight years. "Humboldt Park: 'Community without dreams,'" *Chicago Tribune,* May 1978. The events on Humboldt Park's eastern border are a clear example of the conflict between use and exchange value of city space. As Logan and Molotch (1987) elegantly demonstrate, place — and cities more generally — is socially constructed and subject to intense competition between "residents, who use place to satisfy essential needs of life, and entrepreneurs, who strive for financial return" (2).

95. "In Chicago, it's Wicker Park," *Chicago Sun-Times,* July 22, 1973.

96. *Chicago Tribune,* April 24, 1977; "Humboldt Park: 'Community without dreams,'" *Chicago Tribune,* May 1978; "Humboldt Park: Troubled 'island' without clout," *Chicago Tribune,* June 12, 1977.

97. Gene Wojciechowski, "Digging Dennis, just one of the kids," *Chicago Tribune Magazine,* March 16, 1997.

98. Using extensive interview data with Chicago employers, Kirschenman and Neckerman (1991) demonstrate the ways in which race, class, and city geography inform employers' hiring decisions. See also Souza (2000) for a discussion of the

negative stereotypes of Puerto Ricans in both academic and policy discussions; and Rodríguez (1997) for more on images of Latinas/os in the American media.

99. Latino Institute 1995. These rates are also consistent with national trends of Puerto Rican poverty in the U.S.

100. Betancur, Cordova, and Torres point out that despite the economic success of Cubans and South Americans, their wages according to the 1980 census still approximated those of Puerto Ricans and Mexicans rather than that of whites (1993, 130). The 1990 census, however, paints a very different picture, demonstrating a widening gap between Puerto Ricans and other Latino groups in terms of average income, employment rate, and poverty level.

101. "Jobs that pay: Are enough good jobs available in metropolitan Chicago?" Working Poor Project, November 1995. See also "When the job doesn't pay: Contingent workers in the Chicago metropolitan area," March 1995.

102. See Ranney and Cecil (1993) for a detailed analysis of the impact of transnational investment on women, Latinos, and blacks in the Chicago metropolitan area; and the Latino Institute's 1994 profile of Latinos in Chicago.

Chapter 4: *Los de Afuera*, Transnationalism, and the Cultural Politics of Identity

1. Alicea 1990.

2. Duany 2002, 234–35. He bases these findings on a study surveying four communities in Puerto Rico in the summer of 1998. The surveys used were adapted from those used in the Mexican Migration Project (MMP) of 1999 at the University of Pennsylvania and the University of Guadalajara, which were designed by a research team led by Douglas Massey. Comparing his findings with that of the MMP, Duany reported that only 13 percent of Puerto Ricans who had moved abroad were multiple movers, compared with nearly 44 percent of all migrants in the MMP study (22).

3. I would like to thank Isa Vélez and Patricia Zavella for helping me to clarify this point. Alicea 1997; Bourgois 1995; Glasser 1997; Ramos-Zayas 2003; Rúa 2001; Souza 2000; Stinson-Fernández 1994; and Whalen 2001 are examples of research focused on specific Puerto Rican communities on the mainland.

4. Glick Schiller, Basch, and Blanc-Szanton, 1992, 2.

5. Smith 2001, 106, 144; Massey 1994.

6. Smith and Guarnizo 1998.

7. Kerkhof (2000, 144) makes similar observations about children's difficulty in adjusting to life in Puerto Rico.

8. Francisco L. Rivera-Batiz and Carlos E. Santiago (1996) have noted this regional inequality, arguing that the income gap between municipalities on the island is increasingly polarized. "This inequity," they write, "follows closely along metropolitan/nonmetropolitan lines. Most of the *municipios* with the lowest per capita income were in nonmetropolitan areas" (83).

9. Rivera-Batiz and Santiago 1996, 55.

10. L. Sánchez 1994, 22. Popular references to "la guagua aérea" — the airbus — reveal the ease and frequency with which Puerto Ricans move between the island and the mainland, although such metaphors background the rootedness of people's lives in particular communities. Acclaimed writer Luis Rafael Sánchez explores the complexity of this movement in a provocative and humorous way in *La guagua aérea* (1994).

11. A travel agent in San Sebastián pointed this out to me in an interview. She also said that of the three most popular destinations — New York, Chicago, and Newark — most travelers went to Newark en route to Perth Amboy, New Jersey, the city many *pepinianos* refer to as the mini–San Sebastián on the mainland.

12. Menjívar 2000, 174. Menjívar's research among immigrant women from El Salvador provides important analysis of the conflicts, cleavages, and limits to immigrant social networks, the ways in which gender shapes them, and the prevailing "structures of opportunities" in which these social networks are embedded. Hondagneu-Sotelo 1994; Kibria 1993; and Mahler 1995, 1999 also provide critical attention to the conflicts surrounding immigrant social networks.

13. Alicea (1997, 619) makes similar observations, explaining that Chicago Puerto Ricans regard the island as a site for investment (buying land and a home, for example), recreation, and a safe place to raise children, while American cities are productive sites for work and reliable social services. Using Goldring's work (1992) among Mexican transnational families as an important comparison, Alicea explains that this differentiation of social space is largely a result of global and political restructuring.

14. Ellis, Conway, and Bailey (1996) describe four categories of return/circular migration: those who return because of the labor market, "tied" migration (a move precipitated by a partner's migration or family need), to improve place utility (a better place to live due to improved housing or preferred climate and culture), and other reasons, such as religious or political reasons.

15. Grasmuck and Pessar 1991, 92. Works by Goldring 1998; Levitt 2001; and Mahler 1995 explore similar issues of migrant success and the social pressures they face in sending communities. It is important to note here the difference between the kind of advice given to Puerto Rican migrants and that given to other Latin American immigrants bound for the United States. Because Puerto Ricans are American citizens and do not have to navigate the bureaucratic — and sometimes illegal — waters of international migration, my observations of old-timers' advice and even light-heartedness regarding migration is striking compared to other scholars' accounts of warnings and *consejos* (advice) given to Mexican and Central American immigrants. See Chávez 1992; Hondagneau-Sotelo 1994; Mahler 1995; and Menjívar 2000.

16. Examples of this work include Grasmuck and Pessar 1991; Goldring 1998; Hagan 1998; Hondagneu-Sotelo 1994; Levitt 2001; Mahler 1999; and Menjívar 2000. Research on the gendered dimensions of return migration include Grasmuck and Pessar 1991; Levitt 2001; and Pessar 1986.

17. Negrón-Muntaner 1997, 259; Urciuoli 1996, 47–48.

18. Zentella 1990, 85. The literature on language, bilingualism, and Puerto

Rican cultural identity is extensive. Notable examples of this work include Flores 1993; Flores and Yúdice 1983; Zentella 1990, 1997; Negrón-Muntaner 1997; and Urciuoli 1991, 1996.

19. The conflicts arising from return migration provide an interesting counterpoint to Anderson's notion of an imagined community (1983) and point to the different ways in which this imagined community is constructed differently over time. Here I have borrowed from David A. Hollinger's notion of "the circle of the 'We'" (1993) to discuss how different groups are included and excluded in popular understandings of the nation.

20. Many scholars have carefully documented the ways in which returnees and Spanglish-speaking Puerto Ricans on the island and the mainland are charged with corrupting Puerto Rico's linguistic integrity. Citing island writers, intellectuals, and government officials, Zentella (1990) reveals widespread concern for the deterioration of the Spanish language. Puerto Rico's distinctive colonial history with the United States has reinforced the "consistent identification of Puerto Rican identity with the Spanish language." As a result, "many of the island's intellectuals and others believe that English has had a continuously deteriorating effect on the Spanish of Puerto Rico and that, as a result, Puerto Rico's national identity itself is being threatened" (85). Negrón-Muntaner (1997) masterfully maps the gendered politics of language onto enduring debates regarding Puerto Rican identity, nationalism, and migration. For some island academics and politicians, bilingualism is often a metaphor for "ambiguity, cultural disorders, and political passivity." Similarly, defenders of the Spanish First legislation — an attempt to make Spanish the official language of government in Puerto Rico — regard bilingual Puerto Ricans on the island and the mainland as "a race of *tartamudos* [stutterers], unable to communicate either in English or Spanish." She writes, "For many intellectuals on the island, U.S. Puerto Ricans serve as a 'futuristic' projection of what all Puerto Ricans will/have become: culturally 'impure' or hybrid, racially *mestizo* and bilingual (that is, having two 'national' loyalties). The notion of 'hybridity' is important since given the nation-building narratives' concern with reproduction, a hybrid cannot reproduce; it is sterile. The possibility that the elite's destiny will be explicitly tied to the U.S. diasporas (the *hampa*) or be displaced by the 'lower classes' partly fuels these groups' writing off of two-thirds of the Puerto Rican population" (279). Kerkhof (2001) makes similar observations about the struggle over language and Puerto Rican return migrants as well.

In addition to linguistic corruption, return migrants are also popularly regarded as diseased, physically contaminating the body politic with AIDS and other diseases. A controversial *New York Times* article described the migration between Puerto Rico and New York as an "air bridge" transporting sick and polluted migrant bodies. "New Yoricans *[sic]*," are blamed, according to the article, for importing AIDS from the mainland, further cementing their marginal status (quoted in Sandoval Sánchez 1997, 203). Sandoval Sánchez writes, "The metaphorical construct of an 'air bridge' constitutes a space of continuity and contiguity that makes possible the passage of those condemned by Puerto Rican society: the sick, the infected, the contaminated, the marginal (IV drug users, homosexuals, gay tourists, prostitutes)" (203).

21. Goldring (1998) argues, for example, that migration often leads to "disagreements over meanings" within a transnational community, and that women's dress is an important site of struggle that is contested both directly and through gossip.

22. Zavella 1997, 396.

23. Lancaster 1992, 71–72. In his hilarious account of how community gossip successfully uncovered the true origin of his sudden illness, Lancaster demonstrates the form and function of gossip in a Managua neighborhood. It is both useful and playful, he writes, and binds people together in a web of economic and noneconomic relationships. Gossip in San Sebastián functions quite similarly to Lancaster's accounts of Managua, although it also marginalizes those groups who are the popular objects of gossip.

24. Sandoval Sánchez 1997, 203. Sandoval Sánchez also notes that the high incidence of AIDS among Puerto Rican men and women has created a new kind of migration: "The pattern is the following: Those who get infected in Puerto Rico come to New York and other U.S. cities for treatment. As American citizens they can get on a plane and qualify for Medicaid in the United States. And those who are in a terminal state go back to Puerto Rico to die with their families and to be buried in their native land" (1997, 202).

25. Negrón-Muntaner 1997, 280. Centers for Disease Control, Division of HIV/AIDS Prevention, HIV/AIDS Surveillance Report, December 2001, vol. 13, no. 2.

26. Chávez 2001, 260.

27. Negrón-Muntaner 1997, 279. For more on how *mejicanas* are implicated in the discussion of immigration, reproduction, and nativism, see Hondagneu-Sotelo 1995.

28. Espiritu 2001, 415, 416; Das Gupta 1997, 574. Other important examples of feminist analysis of nationalism and nation-building projects include di Leonardo 1984; Chatterjee 1989, 1993; Kaplan, Alarcón, and Moallem 1999; Grewel and Kaplan 1994.

29. Souza, 2002, 35. Behar (1993) also discusses this dichotomy of female respectability and women's attempts to resist and subvert such designations to claim power and a place on the street. This duality of street and home and female respectability exists throughout Latin America and among U.S. Latinos as well.

30. Zentella 1990, 91.

31. López (1994) argues that as a result of the most recent technological innovations and global restructuring, an important shift has occurred in which "those who can work, work too much, entering into forms of multiskilling and double shifts, while the majority become deskilled, disqualified, overly-trained and redundant" (112). In this context, Puerto Rico has, once again, become another living laboratory to examine the "strategies of coping with a post-work society and experiments in ambivalent postmodern sensibility" (ibid). This postwork society, she argues, is the product of a colonial political-economic relationship with the United States that originally promoted export-led industrialization, but more recently has "ceased to be oriented toward economic growth and turned instead toward a redistributive role in sustaining basic consumption and the standard of

living of the population" (116). López notes that in 1991 U.S. transfer payments totaled almost $5 billion and the gross national product was a little more than $5.5 billion, figures buttressing unconfirmed reports that only one in ten islanders does not receive transfer payments (ibid). While the idea of a postwork society is certainly a debatable one, her arguments do underscore how different the island's economy is now from that of the 1950s and 1960s, when many of the old-timers migrated and returned from working *afuera*.

32. See Safa 1995; Acevedo 1990; and Ríos 1993 for a discussion of gender and Puerto Rico's industrialization program.

33. *El Pepino* 3, no. 34 (June 1991); 3, no. 31 (Feb. 1991).

34. *El Pepino* 3, no. 34 (June 1991).

35. *El Palique*, no. 33 (Nov.–Dec. 1981); no. 34 (Dec. 1981); no. 50 (Aug. 1983); no. 63 (Dec. 1984). The town's newspaper, *El Palique*, circulated from 1977 to 1987. In November 1987, new editors and writers launched *El Pepino*, which circulated through the 1990s.

36. *El Pepino* 4, no. 40 (Sept. 1992).

37. *El Pepino* 4, no. 45 (April 1993).

38. *El Progreso*, November 22, 1994; *Comercio*, Sept. 1995.

39. Beginning in May 1996, *El Progreso* featured several articles about "the death and resurrection of San Sebastián" and the town's *renacimiento*. See *El Progreso*, May 11, 1996; Aug. 9, 1996; Sept. 13, 1996.

40. *El Maguey*, Dec. 1994.

41. In the early 1950s, during the crucial early years of Puerto Rico's industrialization program, *El Mundo* ran a series of articles spotlighting San Sebastián and its long, distinguished cultural history. The ICP's cultural programs reinforced these notions of the central highland region — San Sebastián included — as the cradle of Puerto Rican culture, embodied most clearly in *el jíbaro*. As Arlene Dávila points out, this symbol of resistance and freedom has been used by the island's literary elite since the nineteenth century, but the ICP is responsible for embracing it as an integral component of Puerto Rican national identity (1997, 63). A recent example of San Sebastián's importance in the island's cultural imaginary is an article in *El Nuevo Día* describing the town's rich cultural traditions, evident in the Festival de la Novilla, part of the annual *fiestas patronales de San Sebastián*, which are celebrated in honor of the town's patron saint each January. I would like to thank Miriam Jiménez Román for bringing this article to my attention. *El Nuevo Día*, Jan. 17, 2000.

42. In an article about Radio Pepino, a local radio station, writers at *El Palique* quoted Ricardo Alegría, ICP director, saying that the island's mass media was a "cultural desert" lacking intellectual and cultural content. *El Palique* leveled a similar charge against the town's mass media as well as the town's general cultural health. See "W.F.B.A. Desierto Cultural," *El Palique*, no. 27 (March–April 1981).

As Dávila demonstrates, the island's "culture wars" emerged largely out of political struggles among the PNP, the PPD, and the PIP with regard to Puerto Rico's political status and competing visions of "national culture." In 1979, the

PNP — the ruling party from 1976 to 1980 — established the Administración para el Fomento de las Artes y la Cultura (Administration for the Promotion of Art and Culture, AFAC), an umbrella organization "whose mission was to consolidate all artistic and cultural activity within a single government body" (1997, 44). AFAC's emphasis on "universal culture" — read by many as "high" culture — was the cornerstone of the PNP's cultural policy to expand Puerto Rican culture beyond the ICP's vision of autochthonous and folkloric culture. These disagreements about culture, according to Dávila, are volatile issues deeply embedded in competing political ideologies vis-à-vis the island's political status: "In the colonial context of Puerto Rico, this kind of universalist idea has always had dangerous implications because culture remains the most important basis for defining Puerto Rico's national identity. Most Puerto Rican intellectuals saw the ICP as the guardian of Puerto Rican culture and the vehicle for defending it against the threat of Americanization. Any threat to the institute was taken as a threat to Puerto Rican nationality" (1997, 46).

43. Meléndez and Meléndez 1993; Pantojas-García 1990; Dávila 1997; Baver 1993.

44. *El Maguey,* no. 4 (Dec. 1991).

45. *El Maguey,* no. 38 (March–April 1992).

46. These rumors were never proven, and put in sharp relief the different ways in which *los de afuera* are consistently maligned as deviant, immoral, and corrupt. Gutiérrez-Nájera (2003) observes similar conflicts about progress and modernity among residents of Yalálag in Oaxaca, Mexico, as they debate these issues transnationally.

47. El Festival de la Hamaca is an "invented tradition" of San Sebastián (Hobsbawm and Ranger 1983; Roseberry and O'Brien 1991) that has been remarkably successful. The CPC organized the first Festival de la Hamaca in 1982, and since that time, it has attracted islanders and international tourists interested in the town's fabled *hamaqueros,* whose beautiful hammocks — much to the joy and surprise of the *hamaqueros* and the town — now command a hefty sum.

48. The anonymous *Desde la 111: Algunos aperitivos y un plato fuerte* sardonically reflects on daily life and politics in San Sebastián. The author uses the pen name Pepín de la Vega, Peón del Pueblo, referring to the billboard character greeting visitors entering the town along Highway 111.

49. Kearny 1991, quoted in Smith and Guarnizo 1998; Glick Schiller, Basch, and Blanc 1995.

Chapter 5: Gentrification, Intrametropolitan Migration, and the Politics of Place

1. Borrowing from Collins's notion of the "outsider within" (1991), Zavella (1993) discusses important ethical questions facing "insider/outsider" feminist researchers navigating the power relations in which they are implicated.

2. Zavella 1991, 314.

3. Dehavenon 1996, xviii; Slayton 1987.

4. See "Humboldt Park residents want buildings salvaged," *Chicago Tribune,* Oct. 20, 1996; "The neighborhood as we know it?" *West Town Tenants Union Newsletter,* fall 1997; "To build or not to build," *Chicago Reader,* Feb. 5, 1999.

5. U.S. Census Bureau 2000; Pam Belluck, "Chicago Reverses Fifty Years of Declining Population," *New York Times,* March 15, 2001; Gary Washburn, "Hispanics Increase City's Population," *Chicago Tribune,* March 15, 2001.

6. According to Carlos de Jesús, the executive director of Latinos United, a housing advocacy group, of Chicago's seventy-seven community areas, twenty-three have a Latino population of 20 percent or more. Two other areas do not meet the 20 percent threshold, but register more than ten thousand Latino residents. See also community area profiles in Chicago Fact Book Consortium, *Local community fact book: Chicago metropolitan area, 1990.*

7. Carlos de Jesús, personal communication. Census data for 2000 on Latinos in Chicago suburbs confirm these demographic shifts. The Latino population in Cicero, for example, climbed from 37 to 77 percent between 1990 and 2000, and from 23 to 45 percent in Waukegan. See Gary Washburn, "Hispanics increase city's population," *Chicago Tribune,* March 15, 2001; and Teresa Puente and Bob Kemper, "Urban area isn't only place Latinos make mark," *Chicago Tribune,* March 15, 2002. Paul Cuadros's superb articles in the *Chicago Reporter* document white backlash against Latinos in Chicago's suburbs: "Racial change takes to suburbs," June 1993; "Numbers game: Zoning laws hit Latinos in suburbs," Dec. 1993; and "Suburban housing inspectors crack down on Latinos," Sept. 1995.

8. Chicago Fact Book Consortium, *Local community fact book,* 86–94.

9. As Ramos-Zayas (2003) points out, Puerto Rican nonprofit and grassroots community organizations, largely concentrated in these neighborhoods, are an important springboard for Puerto Rican upward mobility.

10. According to 1990 census data, Humboldt Park, West Town, and Logan Square are included in Chicago's low- and moderate-income community areas. See Immergluck (1994).

11. Chicago Urban League, Latino Institute, and Northern Illinois University 1994; Latino Institute 1995.

12. Cicero and Waukegan are the best examples of economically distressed suburbs, although Waukegan, a working-class suburb, is actually located on the other side of wealthy and exclusive northern suburbs like Lake Forest. See Nelson (1988) for more on the concept of intrametropolitan migration.

13. Several scholars have noted the poor's high residential mobility. See especially Fitchen 1996; Conquergood 1992; Edin and Lein 1997; Nelson 1988; Liebow 1993.

14. Edin and Lein (1997) provide a thorough inventory of poor mothers' strategies to fill the gap between monthly income and expenditures. They include cash contributions from boyfriends, absent fathers, and female kin — their own mothers and siblings — as well as in-kind contributions, like babysitting. Stack's classic work (1974) also documents network-based survival strategies based on mutual exchange among poor black mothers on welfare: Kin — including fictive

kin — shared meals, borrowed and loaned money, and helped with babysitting and household chores. My work among poor and working-class *puertorriqueñas,* as well as Souza's research among young Puerto Rican women in Queens (2002), reveals similar survival strategies not only among single mothers, but also among married women and those living with boyfriends.

15. Valerie Polakow's work (1993) provides detailed histories of poor women, their high residential mobility, and how these women and their children fell into homelessness.

16. Córdova 1991, 37. The following discussion of the effects of growth politics and gentrification on the lives of working-class Puerto Rican youth is further elaborated in Pérez 2002.

17. Chicago Fact Book Consortium, *Local community fact book* (1995, 86–94). In 1995, 25.8 percent of Chicago's Latinos lived in overcrowded conditions compared to 6 percent citywide. These alarming statistics — and the city's growing Latino homeless population — prompted the creation of the Latino Task Force against Homelessness, a coalition of community organizations operating out of Chicago's Coalition for the Homeless. While Latinos account for less than 10 percent of Chicago's homeless population, Latino task force Director Jose Landaverde points out, "When you have 10 to 15 people in a one-bedroom apartment, they are homeless. When they're making $4.25 an hour, they're likely to be homeless." "Task force fights Latino homelessness," *Streetwise,* Oct. 11, 1999.

18. "Humboldt Park residents want buildings salvaged," *Chicago Tribune,* Oct. 20, 1996.

19. "CHA and HUD aim aid to Chicago Latinos," *Extra,* July 17, 1997. See also Taylor 1988.

20. According to Córdova (1991), government guidelines suggest that households should not pay more than 30 percent of their income in housing. "In the city of Chicago, 36.8 percent of all renters pay 'excessive' housing costs, in a city where 19.2 percent of households are below the poverty level. Utilities and additional costs of housing make it increasingly difficult for the low- and moderate-income household to rent, let alone buy, property (37). A recent HUD study reveals that in this era of unprecedented economic growth, the housing affordability gap is worsening. The *New York Times* reported HUD's findings that 5.4 million low-income families pay more than fifty percent of their income for housing or substandard units, a 12 percent increase since 1991. Quoted in Eric Alterman, "Still with us," *The Nation,* April 24, 2000.

21. Carlos de Jesús, personal communication.

22. Logan and Molotch 1987, 50, 85.

23. Logan and Molotch (1987) argue that while growth politics may indeed help declining cities and, if kept under control, benefit large groups of people even in growing cities, in most cases "growth is at best a mixed blessing and the growth machine's claims are merely legitimating ideology, not accurate descriptions of reality" (85). This is certainly true in Chicago, where local media and politicians hail the last decade's real estate market boom for "improving" deteriorating neighborhoods like Humboldt Park and West Town (or Wicker Park) and ignore the

threat to these communities' use value for poor and working-class residents. See "Realty values on a roll in Humboldt Park," *Chicago Sun Times,* Nov. 15, 1991; "West Town: A community that works," *Sun Times,* Aug. 12, 1984; "Council committee labels Wicker Park a landmark," *Sun Times,* March 26, 1991.

24. Betancur, Bennett, and Wright, 1991, 203–204; Nyden and Wiewel 1991; Bennett 1989. Betacur, Bennett, and Wright argue that the Chicago 21 Plan was in fact a blueprint for "a fortress city. It aimed to redevelop the land that circled a blooming service sector downtown for middle- and upper-class residents" (204).

25. Regarding the language surrounding gentrification, Neil Smith writes, "The language of revitalization, recycling, upgrading and renaissance suggests that affected neighborhoods were somehow devitalized or culturally moribund prior to gentrification. While this is sometimes the case, it is often also true that very vital working-class communities are culturally *de*vitalized through gentrification as the new middle class scorns the streets in favor of the dining room and bedroom. The idea of 'urban pioneers' is as insulting applied to contemporary cities as the original idea of 'pioneers' in the U.S. West. Now, as then, it implies that no one lives in the areas being pioneered — no one worthy of notice, at least" (1996, 32–33). See "Wicker Park — Regentrification victim?" *Sun Times,* May 4, 1980; and "Wicker Park residents fight pressures to sell homes," *Sun Times,* Sept. 19, 1980, for examples of the various descriptions of gentrifiers.

26. Abu-Lughod 1994; Conquergood 1992; Muñiz 1998; Smith 1996; Williams 1988, 1996.

27. According to Sevcenko (2001), the success of the Loisaida's movement to resist gentrification and displacement of working-class residents, including Puerto Ricans, rested largely on its ability to define and name "the barren terrain before someone else did" (296). Aponte-Parés (1998) also provides important examples of claiming space and place among *puertorriqueños* in New York City, and Boyd (2000) provides another Chicago example of place-naming and changing meanings of space and identity in Chicago's Bronzeville neighborhood.

28. Zukin 1991, 212, 202. Brett Williams (1988) analyzes television as another landscape of consumption and demonstrates the ways in which these shifts in programming signal important demographic changes.

29. Zukin (1995) details how urban elites appropriate symbols of multiculturalism and inscribe them into the built environment to convey particular tastes and values, critical elements of a city's symbolic economy. See also Pellow (2001) and Valle and Torres (2000) for examples of how social values and behaviors are embedded into urban spatial environments.

30. These tensions were starkly revealed in the summer of 2001, when Wicker Park residents protested MTV's filming of *The Real World* in the neighborhood. See Pérez 2002 for a discussion of this struggle and the ways in which young Latinos are implicated in the gentrification process.

31. Harvey 1990, 72. For an excellent analysis of these dynamics in another Chicago neighborhood involving other ethnic and racial groups, see Conquergood 1992.

32. Caldeira 2000, 367–368. See also Roberts 1997 and Aponte-Parés 2001 for analysis of the racialized body and the social construction of place.

33. Conquergood 1992, 135.

34. Quoted in "Chicago expresses annoyance but understanding over decision on loitering," *New York Times,* June 12, 1999 (late edition).

35. Flores-González (2001) documents the following increases from 1990–2000: Hermosa 41.6 percent; Avondale 99.6 percent; and Belmont Cragin 198.1 percent.

36. The American poor's increasing reliance on the fringe banking system includes using pawn shops, check-cashing businesses, and rent-to-own stores to supply themselves with basic necessities, and securing homes and cars with high-interest loans, a strategy that has enriched some of the nation's largest financial institutions while burdening the poor with high-cost debt. Williams 2001, 99. See also Hudson 1996.

37. Wolf 1990.

38. The various organizations involved in securing affordable housing in Humboldt Park are an important exception here. They do invoke local Chicago history — the displacement of Puerto Ricans from Lincoln Park with 1960s urban renewal — but unlike the Puerto Rican Cultural Center, the Ruiz Belvis Cultural Center, and other community organizations grounded in Puerto Rican nationalism and *independentista* politics, they organize along common interests of housing, job security, and development in Humboldt Park.

39. Many Puerto Rican residents participating in the cultural centers' activities and festivals were indifferent to their politicized agenda, although at times it did become an issue as some worried what this association would mean. This was particularly clear in the wake of the Roberto Clemente High School scandals in 1997, in which the school was accused of misusing federal poverty funds in order to support the "terrorist" activities of Puerto Rican nationalists, and the 1995 closing of HIMRI because of its alleged terrorist activities. See Ramos-Zayas 2003 for a detailed analysis of the bridging of local and nationalist politics in Humboldt Park.

40. See "Éxodo boricua de Humboldt Park," *La Raza,* Aug. 10–16, 1995, for one example of these media accounts.

41. Quoted in "Humboldt Park residents back plan to keep community viable," *Chicago Tribune,* Feb. 14, 1999.

42. "Humboldt power play: Small group holds lots of sway," *Chicago Tribune,* Aug. 1, 1999.

43. "To build or not to build," *Chicago Reader,* Feb. 5, 1999. See also *West Town Tenants Union Newsletter,* fall 1997, for more details on local efforts to resist gentrification on the Near Northwest side.

44. Flores-González 2001, 13, 15. See also "Auge comercial en la calle Division," *Éxito,* June 11, 1998.

45. "Urban gateway," *Chicago Tribune,* June 4, 1995.

46. Ramos-Zayas (2003) argues that community activists are deeply invested in resisting displacement because their material livelihood depends on it. "It was possible that workers at community-based institutions, vendors who sold their wares from rolling carts, and owners of ethnic-specific businesses would not find a place in the institutions newly located in the barrio — fancy hospitals and proliferating coffee shops that were 'not created for Puerto Ricans'" (211–12).

47. As Williams notes (1996), new residents should work against displacement, but the "brutality of dislocation" requires concrete policy measures, including greater tenant security; zoning laws protecting affordable housing; federal enforcement of the Community Reinvestment Act and increased regulation of banks' lending practices; progressive tax policies, such as adding tax credits; and the decommodification of the speculative housing market (160–62).

48. Goode 2001, 366. Gregory's research on community and race politics in Queens reveals similar struggles to sustain a broad vision of shared interests across race, class, and community boundaries. Gregory 1998, 213–15.

49. Latino Institute 1997.

50. Padilla 1987, 93.

51. "Scandal school sees reform ideas copied," *Catalyst,* Oct. 1996.

52. Ramos-Zayas 2003.

53. "Clemente plan has roots in seventies protests," *Catalyst,* Dec.1992.

54. Wilfredo Cruz, "All politics is local," *In These Times,* April 14, 1997; Kari Lydersen, "Scandal-ridden school struggles within the politics of the Puerto Rican community," *Streetwise,* Sept. 29–Oct. 12, 1998. See also Ramos-Zayas 2003, 112–21.

55. See Don Terry, "Chicago police officers indicted in extortion scheme," *New York Times,* Dec. 21, 1996 (late edition); Editorial, *Chicago Sun-Times,* Jan. 15, 1997; "More Austin cops face arrest," *Chicago Sun-Times,* Jan. 12, 1997; "Cop scandal spreads," *Chicago Sun-Times,* March 19, 1997.

56. See Flores-González 2000 for more on the early battles around Clemente High School.

57. Son del Barrio was a perfect example of the positive results of Clemente's school reform. Because it focused largely on cultural and political instruction, writers, speakers, and musicians from Puerto Rico and Mexico were invited into the school to give workshops. Son del Barrio emerged from these exchanges. See Ramos-Zayas 2003, 101–102, for more on Son del Barrio.

58. By refusing to speak in Spanish, Dominguez seemed to suggest, "If they can understand me in Puerto Rico, where authentic Spanish speakers reside, then all of you mixed up, inauthentic Latinos should understand me as well." As Ramos-Zayas discusses at length, issues of cultural authenticity in Puerto Rican Chicago are important sites of struggle around issues of nationalism and national belonging (2003, 31–33).

Chapter 6: Transnational Lives, Kin Work, and Strategies of Survival

1. Work on gender and transnational households and communities includes Alicea 1997; Ho 1993; Hondagneu-Sotelo and Ávila 1997; Mahler 2001; Parreñas 2001. Although Ho (1993) discusses the "internationalization" of kinship and "international families" rather than "transnational" practices, I believe her analysis of kinship networks, migration, and gender is an important one, drawing our attention to women's creative strategies in balancing productive and reproductive work in migration.

2. Mahler and Pessar 2001, 447.

3. These cultural categories can also be understood as part of invented traditions, as discussed by Roseberry and O'Brien (1991).

4. Duany 1994 and Levitt 2001 make similar observations about the ways in which transmigrants use objects to show their connectedness to different places.

5. Elizabeth Chin (1999, 2001) provides an excellent analysis of the marketing and consumption of ethnically correct dolls. She notes that despite the toy industry's alleged intention to make minority children feel more comfortable by providing them with toys that look like them, they are interested less in "the unbearable whiteness of Barbie" than in tapping into minority consumer markets (1999, 310).

6. Dávila 2001b, 411. It is also no coincidence that Chicago is one of Mattel's markets for Latina Barbies, since according to the 2000 census one in four Chicagoans and one in ten Illinois residents are Latino. This is indeed a very large and young consumer market.

7. Dávila 2001a, 8.

8. Wolf's *Europe and the people without history* (1982) is arguably one of the most important works debunking a "billiard balls" approach to history, which treats cultures as distinct, bounded units that bump against each other but do not intermingle.

9. Alicea 1997, 614.

10. In an infamous opinion piece in the *New York Times,* Tienda and Díaz 1987 argued that circular migration was a key factor in mainland Puerto Ricans' poverty in that it created weak attachments to labor markets and communities.

11. Urciuoli 1996, 5

12. A number of my informants talk, at length, about the "Mexicanization" of Chicago and admit that they make racist comments about Mexicans. This placed me in an extremely difficult position both academically and politically as I tried to understand why many of them echoed the racist views held by mainstream society, which also regarded Puerto Ricans as racially inferior and dangerous. It became clear, however, that many informants were responding to real effects of deindustrialization in Chicago, such as economic displacement, growing immiseration, the decline of real wages, and intense competition for adequate housing and a dwindling number of well-paid jobs. This is not to suggest that their racism is acceptable or that it can be excused. Rather, it is important to contextualize these comments to see how economic insecurity and competition for scarce resources are inextricably linked to racist beliefs and practices, and how, as Goode and Maskovsky note, "Economic restructuring and changes in state policies create new pockets of poverty, transform social relations among the poor, and create new boundaries and tensions between the poor and other groups, within and across various axes of difference" (2001, 16). Elsewhere (Pérez 2003) I discuss how Puerto Rican women construct their gendered ethnic identities in relation to Mexican women in Chicago.

13. Proposition 187 required hospitals and schools to deny services to all undocumented persons and families. In the same spirit, the U.S. Congress passed the Illegal Immigration Reform and Immigration Responsibility Act in 1996,

which doubled the number of border patrol agents, mandated the construction of a triple wall surrounding some U.S./Mexican border crossings, and among other measures, implemented harsher punishments for multiple illegal entries (Heyman 1998, 165). These anti-immigrant policies were part of a larger rightward shift in American politics beginning in 1994 that witnessed a renewed emphasis on "personal responsibility" and punished the poor and immigrants — both legal and undocumented — through draconian legislation, including the 1996 welfare reform. See Sánchez 1997 and Perea 1996 for a discussion of the "new nativism" and its historical antecedents. See Souza (2000, 25–26) for more on the conservative backlash of the 1990s — including the 1994 publication of *The contract with America* — and its impact on welfare reform and other policy measures

14. According to Royko, the column was a satire of presidential hopeful Pat Buchanan and his call to provide greater INS security along the Mexican-U.S. border. See "Did Buchanan wimp out on Mexico?" *Chicago Tribune,* Feb. 27, 1996. Many Puerto Ricans quietly applauded Royko's remarks, saying that it was about time someone "stood up and told the truth about the Mexicans in the city." Puerto Rican community leaders, on the other hand, unequivocally denounced Royko and marched in solidarity with thousands of Mexican and Mexican American residents, leaders, and community organizations to protest the piece and demand Royko's dismissal or resignation, which never occurred.

15. Lipsitz 1998, viii; De Genova and Ramos-Zayas 2003.

16. Some scholars have noted that marginalized groups, in an effort to create a space — economic, political, social, and cultural — for themselves, victimize and demonize other marginal groups. In effect, the competition for scarce resources — which in the case of Chicago includes access to decent affordable housing, well-paid jobs, and good schools — divides potential allies, i.e., Mexicans and Puerto Ricans. See Bourgois 1995; Gledhill 1998; Smith 1998; and Zavella 2001 for their discussion of citizenship and inter- and intra-group conflicts.

17. In her discussion of Zumbagua life, Weismantel (1996) notes that in racially polarized Andean society, quotidian practices are political acts of Indian resistance to a national culture hostile to indigenous ways. Women are implicated in these daily acts of resistance in intimate ways, since they "often come to embody a threatened cultural heritage" (307).

18. Ramos-Zayas 2003, 117. See also Padilla 1985 for a discussion of the contingent construction of Latinismo in Chicago.

19. The national flower is the Puerto Rican hibiscus, or *flor de maga.*

20. Rivera (1997) persuasively argues that rap music has existed and evolved in Puerto Rico and among mainland Puerto Ricans for more than a decade. Her observations about its proliferation among poor island youth hold true for poor Chicago Puerto Ricans, who are also viewed as threats to society. By association, their music "is frequently perceived as a musical expression that promotes juvenile delinquency" (243). She also argues that attempts to rigidly define Puerto Rican culture as a bulwark against cultural imperialism smoothes over the fact that such designations are "mostly defined through the perspective of dominant social actors" (246).

21. Flores 1993, 95. Flores's essay provides important historical context for con-

temporary debates about "true" Puerto Rican culture. He notes that historically *bomba* and *plena* were denounced as vulgar and low culture by island elites, a view resurfacing with the naming of Puerto Rico's Fine Arts Museum after Rafael Cortijo, "the street musician par excellence, the unlettered, untutored promulgator of *bomba y plena*" (94). Dávila (1997) documents how *bomba* and *plena* — Afro-Puerto Rican musical and dance genres — are only marginally considered to be appropriate representations of Puerto Rican culture. White, peasant-centered cultural representations continue to define "officially" true Puerto Rican culture. For more discussion about the relationship between *bomba y plena* and hip-hop, see Flores 2000 and Rivera 2003.

22. Alicea (1997) and Toro-Morn's (1995) pioneering work are important examples of gender-focused research among Chicago Puerto Ricans. See also Whalen (2001) and Sánchez-Korrol (1994) for gender-focused historical research in Philadelphia and New York City, respectively.

23. Olwig (1993) notes that among Nevisian migrants, women maintain strong affective and economic connections with home communities, since these women rely on women-centered networks for money to migrate and for childcare while they are away. By nurturing these networks, migrant women ensure that their children are cared for, but they are also often constrained economically by sending remittances back to the island to sustain these households. Ho (1993) observes similar dynamics among Afro-Trinidadians in Los Angeles, who also belong to "international households" through childminding and sending remittances home. Alicea (1997), Toro-Morn (1995), and Whalen (1998a) have uncovered similar dynamics among Puerto Rican women in Chicago and Philadelphia who migrate to engage in productive and reproductive work while preserving important links with home communities, and Ellis, Conway, and Bailey (1996) examine these dynamics among Puerto Rican women "tied circulators."

24. Alicea 1997, 611

25. Di Leonardo 1992, 248, 249. Di Leonardo also notes that women tend to engage in this work not only for their own family but also for their husband's extended kin network, something I also observed among migrants in San Sebastián and Chicago. Alicea (1997, 612–13) makes similar observations about how women's migration is key to sustaining transnational households.

26. Aida often discussed this work as "knowing my rights," and she prided herself on being able to navigate government agencies effectively to get what she knew she was entitled to "as an American citizen." Although other women were not as explicit as Aida, her comments confirm Benmayor, Torruellas, and Juarbe (1997) in their important research among poor Puerto Rican women in El Barrio. "These women," they write, "made concrete claims on the social structures that oppressed them and affirmed their own cultural codes of rights and entitlement," which the authors refer to as "cultural citizenship" (153). See also Torruellas, Benmayor, and Juarbe (1996) for more on New York Puerto Rican women and visions of work and family.

27. Souza 2002, 35. Souza further argues that adolescent women's participation in household chores marks their transition from child to adult.

28. According to Alicea (1997), the work of kinship across geopolitical borders

also requires women to create a sense of familiarity among people who rarely see each other. Children are key in engendering these feelings of belonging. She writes, "Migrant women who brought their U.S.-born children to visit relatives in Puerto Rico, for example, introduced their children to longtime friends as relatives rather than as acquaintances. They expected their children to treat these fictitious kin with both respect and familiarity" (611).

29. Torruellas, Benmayor, and Juarbe (1996) make similar arguments about how New York *puertorriqueñas* understand public aid. They write, "[Puerto Rican women] did not consider becoming welfare recipients as a strategy for cheating the state but as one that enabled them to continue to exercise what they considered their reproductive and social responsibilities" (188).

30. See Torruellas, Benmayor, and Juarbe (1996, 194) for a discussion of these dynamics among New York Puerto Ricans.

31. Abu-Lughod 1990.

Chapter 7: Conclusion

1. Tienda and Díaz 1987; Chávez 1991; see also Rivera-Batiz and Santiago 1996.

2. Duany 2002, 234.

3. Wilson 1987, 56, 61, 137–38; Tienda 1989; see also Nicholas Lehman's article "The other underclass: Puerto Ricans in the U.S.," *Atlantic,* Dec. 1996.

4. See Bennett and Reed (1999) for a discussion of social organizations in Cabrini Green and a critique of Wilson's underclass model. For other important works challenging underclass ideology, see Reed 1992; Williams 1992; Steinberg 1997; di Leonardo 1998. Goode and Maskovsky (2001, 14) make a similar argument that poverty studies in general often erase the fact that politics and collective agency are an integral aspect of poor people's daily lives. Aponte-Parés (1999); Cruz (1998); Ramos-Zayas (2003); and Torres and Velázquez (1998) all emphasize the vibrant past and present of Puerto Rican community organizing in U.S. cities, providing an important counterpoint to underclass theorists' attempts to blame Puerto Ricans' poor economic standing on poor values, culture, and social disorganization.

5. As Gledhill (1999) points out, there is good reason "for not making 'the transmigrant' a universal hero of resistance in the face of disillusionment with former heroes, such as the working classes or post-colonial subalterns . . . [since] many of those who leave Mexico for the United States are seeking individualistic solutions to their problems, and live lives that are full of tensions with other categories of Mexican migrants and other subaltern groups across the border" (232).

Bibliography

Archival Collections

The Center for Puerto Rican Studies Library and Archives, Hunter College, City University of New York. Historical Archives of the Puerto Rican Migration to the United States, the Migration Division of the Department of Labor, Commonwealth of Puerto Rico

Informe anual, 1952–62
Monthly report, 1952–62

Newspapers and Periodicals

El Comercio, 1995–96 (Private Collection, San Sebastián)
Fomento de Puerto Rico, 1951–56 (Colección Puertorriqueña, University of Puerto Rico, Río Piedras)
El Maguey, 1991–97 (Private Collection, San Sebastián)
El Mundo, 1942–86 (Catalog, Colección Puertorriqueña, University of Puerto Rico, Rio Piedras)
El Palique, 1977–87 (Private Collection, San Sebastián)
El Pepino, 1987–96 (Private Collection, San Sebastián)
El Progreso, 1994–97 (Private Collection, San Sebastián)

Works Cited

Abbad y Lasierra, Iñigo. 1959. *Historia geográfica, civil y natural de la isla de San Juan Bautista de Puerto Rico*. Río Piedras: Editorial Universitaria.

Abu-Lughod, Janet L. 1994. *From urban village to East Village: The Battle for New York's Lower East Side.* Cambridge, Mass: Blackwell.

——. 1999. *New York, Chicago, Los Angeles: America's Global Cities.* Minneapolis: University of Minnesota Press.

Abu-Lughod, Lila. 1990. The romance of resistance: Tracing transformations of power through Bedouin women. *American Ethnologist* 17 (1): 41–55.

Acevedo, Luz del Alba. 1990. Industrialization and employment: Changes in the patterns of women's work in Puerto Rico. *Demography* 18 (2): 231–55.

Acosta-Belén, Edna. 1986. *The Puerto Rican woman: Perspectives on culture, history and society.* New York: Praeger Publishers.

Alicea, Marixsa. 1990. Dual home bases: A reconceptualization of Puerto Rican migration. *Latino Studies Journal* 1 (3): 78–98.

——. 1997. "A chambered nautilus": The contradictory nature of Puerto Rican women's role in the social construction of a transnational community. *Gender & Society* 11: 597–626.

Álvarez, Robert R. 1991. *Familia: Migration and adaptation in Baja and Alta California, 1800–1875.* Berkeley: University of California Press.

Anagnost, Ann. 1995. A surfeit of bodies: Population and the rationality of the state in post-Mao China. In *Conceiving the new world order: The global politics of reproduction,* edited by Faye D. Ginsburg and Rayna Rapp, 22–41. Berkeley: University of California Press.

Anderson, Benedict. 1983. *Imagined communities: Reflections on the origin and spread of nationalism.* London: Verso.

Aponte-Parés, Luis. 1998. What's yellow and white and has land all around it? Appropriating place in Puerto Rican *barrios.* In *The Latino studies reader: Culture, economy, and society,* edited by Antonia Darder and Rodolfo Torres, 271–80. Malden, Mass.: Blackwell Publishers.

——. 1999. Lessons from *el barrio* — The East Harlem Real Great Society/Urban Planning Studio: A Puerto Rican chapter in the fight for urban self-determination. In *Latino social movements,* edited by Rodolfo Torres and George Katsiaficas, 43–77. New York: Routledge.

——. 2001. *Outside/In:* Crossing queer and Latino boundaries. In *Mambo Montage: The Latinization of New York,* edited by Agustín Laó-Montes and Arlene Dávila, 263–386. New York: Columbia University Press.

Appadurai, Arjun. 1990. Disjuncture and difference in the global cultural economy. *Public Culture* 2 (2): 1–24.

——. 1991. Global ethnoscapes: Notes and queries for a transnational anthropology. *Recapturing anthropology: Working in the present,* edited by Richard G. Fox, 191–210. Santa Fe, N.M.: School of American Research Press.

——. 1996. *Modernity at Large: Cultural dimensions of globalization.* Minneapolis: University of Minnesota Press.

Arredondo, Gabriela. In press. Cartographies of Americanisms: Mexicans in Chicago, 1917–1939. In *Geographies of Latinidad: Mapping Latina/o Studies into the twenty-first century,* edited by Matt García, Marie Lerger, and Angarad Valdivia. Durham, N.C.: Duke University Press.

Ashton, Guy T. 1980. The return and re-return of long-term Puerto Rican migrants: A selective rural-urban sample. *Revista/Review Interamericana* 10 (1): 27–45.

Ayala, César J. 2001. From sugar plantations to military bases: The U.S. Navy's expropriation in Vieques, Puerto Rico, 1940–1945. *CENTRO: Journal of the Center for Puerto Rican Studies* 13 (1): 22–41.

Baerga, María del Carmen. 1984. Wages, consumption and survival: Working-class households in Puerto Rico in the 1930s. In *Households and the world economy,* edited by Joan Smith, Immanuel Wallerstein, and Hans Deiter Evers. Beverly Hills, Ca.: Sage Publications.

———. 1993. *Género y trabajo: La industria de la aguja en Puerto Rico y el Caribe Hispánico.* San Juan, Puerto Rico: Editorial de la Universidad de Puerto Rico.

Baerga, María del Carmen, and Lanny Thompson. 1990. Migration in a semi-periphery: The movement of Puerto Ricans and Dominicans. *International Migration Review* 24 (4): 656–83.

Basch, Linda, Nina Glick Schiller, and Cristina Szanton-Blanc. 1994. *Nations unbound: Transnational projects and the deterritorialized nation-state.* New York: Gordon and Breach.

Baver, Sherrie L. 1993. *The political economy of colonialism: The state and industrialization in Puerto Rico.* Westport: Praeger Press.

Behar, Ruth. 1993. *Translated woman: Crossing the border with Esperanza's story.* Boston: Beacon Press.

Behar, Ruth, and Deborah A. Gordon. 1995. *Women writing culture.* Berkeley: University of California Press.

Benería, Lourdes. 1982. *Women and development: The sexual division of labor in rural societies.* New York: Praeger.

Benería, Lourdes, and Gita Sen. 1981. Accumulation, reproduction and women's role in economic development: Boserup revisited. *Signs* 7 (2): 279–98.

Benmayor, Rina, Rosa M. Torruellas, and Ana L. Juarbe. 1997. Claiming cultural citizenship in East Harlem: "Si esto puede ayudar a la comunidad mía . . ." In *Latino cultural citizenship: Claiming identity, space, and rights,* edited by William V. Flores and Rina Benmayor, 152–209. Boston: Beacon Press.

Bennett, Larry. 1989. The declining politics of party and the rise of neighborhood politics. In *Unequal partnerships: The political economy of urban redevelopment in postwar America,* edited by Gregory Squires, 161–77. New Brunswick, N.J.: Rutgers University Press.

Bennett, Larry, and Adolph Reed Jr. 1999. The new face of urban renewal: The Near North Redevelopment Initiative and the Cabrini-Green neighborhood. In *Without Justice for all: The new liberalism and our retreat from racial equality,* edited by Adolph Reed Jr., 175–214. Boulder, Colo.: Westview Press.

Bergad, Laird. 1983. *Coffee and the growth of agrarian capitalism in nineteenth-century Puerto Rico.* Princeton, N. J.: Princeton University Press.

Besson, Jean. 1993. Reputation and respectability reconsidered: A new perspective on Afro-Caribbean peasant women. In *Women and change in the*

Caribbean: A pan-Caribbean perspective, edited by Janet Momsen, 15–37. Bloomington: Indiana University Press.

Betancur, John J., Deborah Bennett, and Patricia Wright. 1991. Effective strategies for community economic development. In *Challenging uneven development: An urban agenda for the 1990s,* edited by Philip W. Nyden and Wim Wiewel, 198–224. New Brunswick, N.J.: Rutgers University Press.

Betancur, John J., Teresa Cordova, and Maria de los Angeles Torres. 1993. Economic restructuring and the process of incorporation of Latinos into the Chicago economy. In *Latinos in a changing U.S. economy,* edited by Rebecca Morales and Frank Bonilla, 109–32. New York: Sage Publications.

Bodnar, John. 1985. *The transplanted: A history of immigrants in urban America.* Bloomington: Indiana University Press.

Bonilla, Frank. 1994. Manos que sobran: Work, migration and the Puerto Rican in the 1990's. In *The commuter nation: Perspectives on Puerto Rican migration,* edited by Carlos Antonio Torre, Hugo Rodriguez Vecchini and William Burgos, 115–49. Rio Piedras: Editorial de la Universidad de Puerto Rico.

Bonilla, Frank, and Ricardo Campos. 1986. *Industry and idleness.* New York: History and Migration Task Force, Centro de Estudios Puertorriqueños, Hunter College.

Bonilla, Frank, and Héctor Colón Jordán. 1979. "Mamá, Borinquen me llama!" Puerto Rican return migration in the seventies. *Migration Today* 7 (2): 1–6.

Borges-Méndez, Ramón. 1993. Migration, social networks, poverty and the regionalization of Puerto Rican settlements: Barrio formation in Lowell, Lawrence and Holyoke, Massachusetts. Special issue on Puerto Rican migration and poverty. *Latino Studies Journal* 4 (2): 3–21.

Boris, Eileen. 1996. Needlewomen under the New Deal in Puerto Rico, 1920–1945. In *Puerto Rican women and work: Bridges in transnational labor,* edited by Altagracia Ortiz, 33–54. Philadelphia: Temple University Press.

Boserup, Ester. 1970. *Women's role in economic development.* New York: St. Martin's Press.

Bourgois, Philippe. 1995. *In search of respect: Selling crack in El Barrio.* Cambridge: Cambridge University Press.

Boyd, Michelle. 2000. Reconstructing Bronzeville: Racial nostalgia and neighborhood redevelopment. *Journal of Urban Affairs* 22 (2): 107–22.

Bowles, Chester. 1955. Introduction to *Transformation: The story of modern Puerto Rico,* by Earl Parker Hanson. New York: Simon and Schuster.

Bretell, Caroline. 1987. *Men who migrate, women who wait: The demographic history of a Portuguese parish.* Princeton, N.J.: Princeton University Press.

Briggs, Laura. 2002a. *Reproducing empire: Race, sex, science and U.S. imperialism in Puerto Rico.* Berkeley: University of California Press.

———. 2002b. *La vida,* Moynihan, and other libels: Migration, social science, and the making of the Puerto Rican welfare queen. *CENTRO: Journal of the Center for Puerto Rican Studies* 14 (1): 75–101.

Brimelow, Peter. 1995. *Alien Nation: Common sense about America's immigration disaster.* New York: Random House.

Browning, Frank. 1970. From rumble to revolution: The Young Lords. *Ramparts* (October): 19–25.

Bryan, William S. 1899. *Our islands and their people.* St. Louis, Mo.: Thompson Publishing Company.

Buijs, Gina. 1993. *Migrant women: Crossing boundaries and changing identities.* Oxford: Berg.

Burns, Leland S. 1984. Harvey S. Perloff (1915–1983): A tribute. *Urban Studies* 21: 217–18.

Caldeira, Teresa P. R. 2000. *City of walls: Crime, segregation, and citizenship in Sao Paulo.* Berkeley: University of California Press.

Cantú, Lionel. 2003. A place called home: A queer political economy of Mexican immigrant men's family experiences. In *Perspectives on las Américas: A reader in culture, history and representation.* Edited by Matthew C. Gutmann, Félix V. Matos Rodriguez, Lynn Stephen, and Patricia Zavella, 259–73. Malden, Mass.: Blackwell Publishers.

Cantú, Norma. 1995. *Canícula: Snapshots of a girlhood en la frontera.* Albuquerque: University of New Mexico Press.

Cardona, Walter. 1985. *San Sebastián: Notas para su historia.* San Juan: Offset Printing.

Carrion, Arturo Morales. 1983. *Puerto Rico: A political and cultural history.* New York: W.W. Norton & Co.

Chaney, Elsa M., and Mary García Castro. 1989. *Muchachas no more: Household workers in Latin America and the Caribbean.* Philadelphia: Temple University Press.

Chant, Sylvia, ed. 1992. *Gender and migration in developing countries.* New York: Belhaven Press.

Chatterjee, Partha. 1989. Colonialism, nationalism and colonized women: The contest in India. *American Ethnologist* 16: 622–33.

———. 1993. *The nation and its fragments.* Princeton, N.J.: Princeton University Press.

Chávez, Leo R. 1992. *Shadowed lives: Undocumented immigrants in American society.* Fort Worth, Tex.: Harcourt Brace Jovanovich College Publishers.

———. 2001. *Covering immigration: Popular images and the politics of the nation.* Berkeley: University of California Press.

Chavez, Linda. 1991. *Out of the barrio: Toward a new politics of Hispanic assimilation.* New York: Harper Collins.

Chicago Fact Book Consortium. 1995. *Local community fact book, Chicago metropolitan area, 1990.* Chicago: University of Illinois Chicago.

Chicago Urban League, Latino Institute, and Northern Illinois University. 1994. *Working poor families in the Chicago metropolitan area.* Chicago: Chicago Urban League.

———. 1995. *When the job doesn't pay: Contingent workers in the Chicago metropolitan area.* Chicago: Chicago Urban League.

———. 1995. *Jobs that pay: Are enough jobs available in metropolitan Chicago?* Chicago: Chicago Urban League.

Chin, Elizabeth. 1999. Ethnically correct dolls: Toying with the race industry. *American Anthropologist* 101 (2): 305–21.

———. 2001. *Purchasing power: Black kids and American Consumer culture.* Minneapolis: University of Minnesota Press.

Clark, Victor. 1930. *Puerto Rico and its problems.* Washington, D.C.: Brookings Institute.

Colen, Shellee. 1995. "Like a mother to them": Stratified reproduction and West Indian childcare workers and employers in New York. In *Conceiving the new world order: The global politics of reproduction,* edited by Faye D. Ginsburg and Rayna Rapp, 78–102. Berkeley: University of California Press.

Collins, Patricia Hill. 1991. *Black feminist thought: Knowledge, consciousness, and the politics of empowerment.* New York: Routledge.

Colón, Alice. 1994. Puerto Rican women in the middle Atlantic region: Employment, loss of jobs, and the feminization of poverty. In *The commuter nation: Perspectives on Puerto Rican migration,* edited by Carlos Antonio Torre, Hugo Rodriguez Vecchini, and William Burgos, 255–85. Rio Piedras: Editorial de la Universidad de Puerto Rico.

Conquergood, Dwight. 1992. Life in Big Red. In *Structuring diversity: Ethnographic perspectives on the new immigration,* edited by Louise Lamphere, 95–144. Chicago: University of Chicago Press.

Coontz, Stephanie. 1992. *The way we never were: American families and the nostalgia trap.* New York: Basic Books.

Cordero-Guzmán, Héctor. 1989. The socio-demographic characteristics of return migrants to Puerto Rico and their participation in the labor market, 1965–1980. Master's thesis, University of Chicago.

Córdova, Teresa. 1991. Community intervention efforts to oppose gentrification. In *Challenging uneven development: An urban agenda for the 1990s,* edited by Philip W. Nyden and Wim Wiewel, 25–48. New Brunswick, N.J.: Rutgers University Press.

Cruz, José E. 1998. *Identity and Power: Puerto Rican politics and the challenge of ethnicity.* Philadelphia: Temple University Press.

Das Gupta, Monisha. 1997. "What is Indian about you?" A gendered, transnational approach to ethnicity. *Gender and Society* 11 (5): 572–96.

Dávila, Arlene. 1997. *Sponsored identities: Cultural politics in Puerto Rico.* Philadelphia: Temple University Press.

———. 2001a. *Latinos Inc.: The marketing and making of a people.* Berkeley: University of California Press.

———. 2001b. The Latin side of Madison Avenue: Marketing and language that makes us "hispanic." In *Mambo Montage: The Latinization of New York,* edited by Agustín Laó-Montes and Arlene Dávila, 411–24. New York: Columbia University Press.

Davis, Mike. 2000. *Magical urbanism: Latinos reinvent the U.S. big city.* London: Verso.

De Genova, Nicholas, and Ana Y. Ramos-Zayas. 2003. Latino rehearsals: Racialization and the politics of citizenship between Mexicans and Puerto Ricans in Chicago. *Journal of Latin American Anthropology* 8 (2): 18–57.

Dehavenon, Anna Lou. 1996. Doubling up: A strategy of urban reciprocity to avoid homelessness in Detroit. In *There's no place like home: Anthropological perspectives on housing and homelessness in the United States,* 51–66. Westport, Conn.: Bergin and Garvey.

Delgado, Héctor L. 1993. *New immigrants, old unions: Organizing undocumented workers in Los Angeles.* Philadelphia: Temple University Press.

Department of Labor, "Proyecto piloto de la caña," 1967–68.

Descartes, S. L. 1972 [1947]. Historical account of recent land reform in Puerto Rico. In *Portrait of a society,* edited by Eugenio Fernández Méndez. Río Piedras: University of Puerto Rico Press.

Dietz, James. 1986. *Economic history of Puerto Rico.* Princeton, N.J.: Princeton University Press.

di Leonardo, Micaela. 1984. *The varieties of ethnic experience: Kinship, class and gender among California Italian-Americans.* Ithaca, N.Y.: Cornell University Press.

——. 1991. Habits of the cumbered heart: Ethnic community and women's culture as invented tradition. In *Golden ages, dark ages: Imagining the past in anthropology and history,* edited by William Roseberry and Jay O'Brien. Berkeley: University of California Press

——. 1992. The female world of cards and holidays: Women, families and the work of kinship. In *Rethinking the family: Some feminist questions,* edited by Barrie Thorne with Marilyn Yalom, 246–61. Boston: Northeastern University Press.

——. 1995. White ethnicities, identity politics and baby bear's chair. *Social Text* 41 (winter): 165–91.

——. 1998. *Exotics at home: Anthropologies, others and American modernity.* Chicago: University of Chicago Press.

Diner, Hasia. 1983. *Erin's daughters in America: Irish immigrant women in the nineteenth century.* Baltimore, Md.: Johns Hopkins University Press.

Drake, St. Clair, and Horace R. Cayton. 1993 [1945]. *Black metropolis: Negro life in a northern city.* Chicago: University of Chicago Press.

Duany, Jorge. 1994. Quisqueya on the Hudson: The transnational identity of Dominicans in Washington Heights. New York: Dominican Research Monographs, City University of New York, Dominican Studies Institute.

——. 1997. Para reimaginarse la nación puertorriqueña. *Revista de Ciencias Sociales* 2: 10–24.

——. 2000. Nation on the move: The construction of cultural identities in Puerto Rico and the diaspora. *American Ethnologist* 27 (1): 5–30.

——. 2002. *The Puerto Rican nation on the move: Identities on the Island and the mainland.* Chapel Hill: University of North Carolina Press.

——. Forthcoming. Between the nation and the diaspora: Migration to and from Puerto Rico. In *Migration: A global view,* edited by Maura Toro-Morn and Marixsa Alicea. Westport, Conn.: Greenwood Press.

Edin, Kathryn, and Laura Lein. 1997. *Making ends meet: How single mothers survive welfare and low-wage work.* New York: Russell Sage Foundation.

Ellis, Mark, Dennis Conway, and Adrian Bailey. 1996. The circular migration of

Puerto Rican women: Towards a gendered explanation. *International Migration Quarterly Review* 34 (1): 31–64.

Enchautegui, María. 1991. *Subsequent moves and the dynamics of the migration decision: The case of return migration to Puerto Rico*. Ann Arbor: Populations Studies Center, University of Michigan.

Escobar, Arturo. 1995. *Encountering development: The making and unmaking of the third world*. Princeton, N.J.: Princeton University Press

Espiritu, Yen Le. 2001. "We don't sleep around like white girls do": Family, culture, and gender in Filipina American lives. *Signs: Journal of Women in Culture and Society* 26 (2): 415–40.

Ferguson, James. 1992. The country and the city on the Copperbelt. *Cultural Anthropology* 7 (1): 80–92.

Fernández-Kelly, Patricia. 1983. *For we are sold, I and my people: Women and industry in Mexico's frontier*. Albany: State University of New York Press.

Fitchen, Janet M. 1996. Poverty and homelessness in rural upstate New York. In *There's no place like home: Anthropological perspectives on housing and homelessness in the United States,* edited by Anna Lou Dehavenon, 1–18. Westport, Conn.: Bergin and Garvey.

Fitzpatrick, Joseph. 1971. *Puerto Rican Americans: The meaning of migration to the mainland*. Englewood Cliffs, N.J.: Prentice Hall.

Fleisher, Belton. 1961. Some economic aspects of Puerto Rican migration to the U.S. Ph.D. diss., Stanford University.

Flores, Juan. 1993. *Divided borders: Essays on Puerto Rican identity*. Houston, Tex.: Arte Público Press.

———. 2000. *From bomba to hip hop: Puerto Rican culture and Latino identity*. New York: Columbia University Press.

Flores, Juan, and George Yúdice. 1993. Living borders/*Buscando América*: Languages of Latino self-formation. *Social Text* 24: 57–84.

Flores–González, Nilda. 2000. "From radicals to terrorists": The evolving image of Clemente High School. Paper presented at the Puerto Rican Studies Association meeting, October 27, Amherst, Mass.

———. 2001. "Paseo Boricua:" Claiming a Puerto Rican Space in Chicago. *Journal of the Center for Puerto Rican Studies* 13 (2): 8–21.

Foner, Nancy. 1978. *Jamaica farewell: Jamaican migrants in London*. Berkeley: University of California Press.

Fong, Timothy P. 1998. *The contemporary Asian American experience: Beyond the model minority*. Upper Saddle River, N.J.: Prentice Hall Press.

Forni, Floreal. 1971. *The situation of the Puerto Rican population in Chicago and its viewpoints about racial relations*. Chicago: Community and Family Study Center, University of Chicago.

Freedman, Robert. 1950. *Recent migration to Chicago*. Chicago: University of Chicago Press.

García, Juan R. 1996. *Mexicans in the Midwest, 1900–1932*. Tucson: University of Arizona Press.

Gayer, Arthur D. 1938. *The sugar economy of Puerto Rico*. New York: Columbia University Press.

Georges, Eugenia. 1992. Gender, class and migration in the Dominican Republic: Women's experiences in a transnational community. In *Towards a transnational perspective on migration: Race class, ethnicity and nationalism reconsidered,* edited by Nina Glick Schiller, Linda Basch, and Cristina Szanton Blanc, 81–99. New York: New York Academy of Sciences.

Gil-Bermejo, Juana. 1970. *Panorama histórico de la agricultura en Puerto Rico.* San Juan: Instituto de Cultura Puertorriqueña

Glasser, Irene. 1996. The 1990 decennial census and patterns of homelessness in a small New England city. In *There's no place like home: Anthropological perspectives on housing and homelessness in the United States,* edited by Anna Lou Dehavenon, 19–34. Westport, Conn.: Bergin and Garvey.

Glasser, Ruth. 1997. *Aquí me quedo: Puerto Ricans in Connecticut.* Middletown, Conn.: Connecticut Humanities Council.

Glazer, Nathan, and Daniel P. Moynihan. 1963. *Beyond the melting pot: The Negroes, Puerto Ricans, Jews, Italians, and Irish of New York City.* Cambridge, Mass.: M.I.T. Press.

Gledhill, John. 1998. The Mexican contribution to restructuring U.S. capitalism. *Critique of Anthropology* 18 (3): 279–96.

——. 1999. Official masks and shadow powers: Towards an anthropology of the dark side of the state. *Urban Anthropology* 28 (3–4): 199–251.

Glenn, Evelyn Nakano. 1986. *Issei, Nisei, warbride.* Philadelphia: Temple University Press.

——. 1999. The social construction and institutionalization of gender and race: An integrative framework. In *Reinvisioning gender,* edited by Mayra Marx Ferree, Judith Lorber, and Beth B. Hess, 3–44. Thousand Oaks, Ca.: Sage Publications.

Glick Schiller, Nina. 1999. Transmigrants and nation-states: Something old and something new in the U.S. immigrant experience. In *The handbook of international migration,* edited by Charles Hirschman, Philip Kasinitz, and Josh De Wind, 94–119. New York: Russell Sage Foundation.

Glick Schiller, Nina, Linda Basch, and Cristina Szanton Blanc. 1992. *Towards a transnational perspective on migration: Race, class, ethnicity and nationalism reconsidered.* New York: New York Academy of Sciences.

——. 1995. From immigrant to transmigrant: Theorizing transnational migration. *Anthropological Quarterly* 68 (1): 48–63.

Goldring, Luin. 1992. Blurring borders: Community and social transformation in Mexico-U.S. transnational migration. Paper presented at New Perspectives on Mexico-U.S. Migration Conference, University of Chicago, October 23–24.

——. 1998. The power of status in transnational social fields. In *Transnationalism from below,* edited by Michael Peter Smith and Luis Eduardo Guarnizo, 165–95. New Brunswick, N.J.: Transaction Publishers

González, Lydia Milagros. 1993. La industria de la aguja de Puerto Rico y sus orígenes en los Estados Unidos. In *Género y trabajo: La industria de la aguja en Puerto Rico y el caribe hispánico,* edited by María del Carmen Baerga, 59–81. San Juan: Editorial de la Universidad de Puerto Rico.

González-Cruz, Michael. 1998. The invasion of Puerto Rico: Occupation and resistance to the colonial state, 1898 to the present. *Latin American Perspectives* 25 (5): 7–26.

Goode, Judith. 2001. Let's get our act together: How racial discourses disrupt neighborhood activism. In *The new poverty studies: The ethnography of power, politics, and impoverished people in the United States,* edited by Judith Goode and Jeff Maskovsky, 364–98. New York: New York University Press.

Goode, Judith, and Jeff Maskovsky. 2001. Introduction to *The new poverty studies: The ethnography of power, politics, and impoverished people in the United States,* 1–34. New York: New York University Press.

Grasmuck, Sherri, and Patricia Pessar. 1991. *Between two islands: Dominican international migration.* Berkeley: University of California Press.

Gregory, Steven. 1998. *Black Corona: Race and the politics of place in an urban community.* Princeton, N.J.: Princeton University Press.

Grewal, Inderpal, and Caren Kaplan, eds. 1994. *Scattered hegemonies: Postmodernity and transnational feminist practices.* Minneapolis: University of Minnesota Press.

Grossman, James R. 1989. *Land of hope: Chicago, black southerners, and the great migration.* Chicago: University of Chicago Press.

Guarnizo, Luis. 1994. Los Dominicanyorks: The making of a binational society. *Annals of the American Academy of Political and Social Science* 533: 70–86.

Guarnizo, Luis Eduardo, and Michael Peter Smith. 1998. The locations of transnationalism. In *Transnationalism from below,* edited by Michael Peter Smith and Luis Eduardo Guarnizo, 3–34. New Brunswick, N.J.: Transaction Publishers.

Gurak, D., and M. Kritz. 1982. Dominican and Colombian women in New York City: Household structure and employment patterns. *Migration Today* 10 (3–4): 249–71.

Gutiérrez-Nájera, Lourdes. 2003. Tripping over stones and falling in the streets: Migration and conflicting notions of progress and movement among Yalaltecos. Paper presented at the 24th International Congress of the Latin American Studies Association, Dallas, Texas, March 28.

Guy, Donna. 1991. *Sex and danger in Buenos Aires: Prostitution, family and nation in Argentina.* Lincoln: University of Nebraska Press.

Guzmán, Pablo. 1998. *La vida pura:* A lord of the barrio. In *The Puerto Rican movement: Voices from the diaspora,* edited by Andrés Torres and José E. Velázquez, 155–72. Philadelphia: Temple University Press.

Hagan, Jaqueline. 1994. *Deciding to be legal: A Mayan community in Houston.* Philadelphia: Temple University Press.

———. 1998. Social networks, gender and immigrant incorporation: Resources and constraints. *American Sociological Review* 63: 55–67.

Hagan, Jaqueline, and Néstor P. Rodríguez. 1992. Recent economic restructuring and evolving intergroup relations in Houston. In *Structuring diversity: Ethnographic perspectives on the new immigration,* edited by Louise Lamphere, 145–71. Chicago: University of Chicago Press.

Halfacree, Keith. 1995. Household migration and the structuration of patriarchy: Evidence from the USA. *Progress in Human Geography* 19 (2): 159–82.

Handlin, Oscar. 1973 [1951]. *The Uprooted*. Boston: Little Brown.

Hannerz, Ulf. 1980. *Exploring the city: Inquiries toward an urban anthropology*. New York: Columbia University Press.

Hanson, Earl Parker. 1955. *Transformation: The story of modern Puerto Rico*. New York: Simon and Schuster.

Harden, Jacalyn D. 2003. *Double Cross: Japanese Americans in black and white Chicago*. Minneapolis: University of Minnesota Press.

Harvey, Brett. 1993. *The fifties: A women's oral history*. New York: Harper Perennial.

Harvey, David. 1990. *The condition of postmodernity*. Oxford: Basil Blackwell Press.

Hatt, Paul. 1952. *Backgrounds of human fertility in Puerto Rico: A sociological survey*. Princeton, N.J.: Princeton University Press.

Hayden, Dolores. 1995. *The power of place*. Cambridge, Mass.: M.I.T. Press.

Hernández-Álvarez, Jose. 1967. *Return migration to Puerto Rico*. Berkeley: University of California Press.

Hernández Angueira, Luisa. 1993. El trabajo feminino a domicilio y la industria de la aguja en Puerto Rico, 1914–1940. In *Género y trabajo: La industria de la aguja en Puerto Rico y el caribe hispánico*, edited by María del Carmen Baerga, 83–102. San Juan: Editorial de la Universidad de Puerto Rico.

Hernández Cruz, Juan. 1985. Migración de retorno o circulación de obreros boricuas? *Revista de Ciencias Sociales* 24: 81–109.

——. 1994. *Corrientes migratorios en Puerto Rico*. San German: Universidad de Puerto Rico, San German.

Heyman, Josiah McC. 1998. State effects on labor exploitation: The INS and undocumented immigrants at the Mexico–United States border. *Critique of Anthropology* 18 (2): 157–80.

Hill, Reuben, J., Mayone Stycos, and Kurt Book. 1959. *The family and population control: A Puerto Rican experiment in social change*. Chapel Hill: University of North Carolina Press.

History Task Force. 1979. *Labor migration under capitalism: The Puerto Rican experience*. New York: Monthly Review Press.

Hirsch, Arnold. 1998 [1983]. *Making the second ghetto: Race and housing in Chicago, 1940–1960*. New York: Cambridge University Press.

Ho, Christine. 1993. The internationalization of kinship and the feminization of Caribbean migration: The case of Afro-Trinidadians in Los Angeles. *Human Organization* 52: 32–40.

Hobsbawm, Eric, and Terrance Ranger. 1983. *The invention of tradition*. New York: Cambridge University Press.

Hollinger, David A. 1993. How wide the circle of the "We"?: American intellectuals and the problem of the ethnos since World War II. *American Historical Review* 98 (April): 317–37.

Hondagneu-Sotelo, Pirrette. 1994. *Gendered transitions: Mexican experiences of immigration*. Berkeley: University of California Press.

——. 1995. Women and children first: New directions in anti-immigration politics. *Socialist Review* 25 (1): 169–90.

——. 2001. *Doméstica: Immigrant workers cleaning and caring in the shadows of affluence*. Berkeley: University of California Press.

Hondagneu-Sotelo, Pirrette, and Ernestina Ávila. 1997. "I'm here, but I'm also there": The meaning of Latina transnational motherhood. *Gender & Society* 11: 548–71.

Houston, Marion F., Roger G. Kramer, and Joan Mackin Barrett. 1984. Female predominance in immigration to the United States since 1930: A first look. *International Migration Review* 18 (4): 908–63.

Hudson, Mike. 1996. *Merchants of Misery.* Monroe, Maine: Common Courage Press.

Hurtado, Aída. 1995. Variations, combinations, and evolutions: Latino families in the United States. In *Understanding Latino families: Scholarship, policy, and practice,* edited by Ruth E. Zambrana, 40–61. Thousand Oaks, Ca.: Sage Publications.

Immergluck, Daniel. 1994. Against the tide: A closer look at economic change in Chicago's low- and moderate-income neighborhoods. Chicago: Woodstock Institute.

Joseph, Suad. 1996. Relationality and ethnographic subjectivity: Key informants and the construction of personhood in fieldwork. In *Feminist dilemmas in fieldwork,* edited by Diane L. Wolf, 107–21. Boulder, Colo.: Westview Press.

Kaplan, Caren, Norma Alarcón, and Minoo Moallem, eds. 1999. *Between woman and nation: Nationalisms, transnational feminisms, and the state.* Durham, N.C.: Duke University Press.

Katzman, David. 1981. *Seven days a week: Women and domestic service in industrializing America.* Chicago: University of Chicago Press.

Kearney, Michael. 1986. From the invisible hand to visible feet: Anthropological studies of migration and development. *Annual Review of Anthropology* 15: 331–361.

———. 1991. Borders and boundaries of state and self at the end of empire. *Journal of Historical Sociology* 5: 52–74.

———. 1995. The local and the global: The anthropology of globalization and transnationalism. *Annual Review of Anthropology* 24: 547–65.

Kerkhof, Erna. 2000. *Contested belonging: Circular migration and Puerto Rican identity.* Ph.D. diss., University of Utrecht, The Netherlands.

———. 2001. The myth of the dumb Puerto Rican: Circular migration and language struggle in Puerto Rico. *New West Indian Guide* 75 (3–4): 257–88.

Kibria, Nazli. 1993. *Family tightrope: The changing lives of Vietnamese immigrant communities.* Princeton, N.J.: Princeton University Press.

Kim, Claire Jean. 1993. Model minority compared to whom?: Myths, hierarchy and the new convergence on race. Unpublished manuscript.

———. 1999. The racial triangulation of Asian Americans. *Politics and Society* 27 (1): 105–38.

Kirshenman, Joleen, and Kathryn Neckerman. 1991. "We'd love to hire them, but . . ." : The meaning of race for employers. In *The urban underclass,* edited by Christopher Jencks and Paul E. Peterson, 203–32. Washington, D.C.: Brookings Institute.

Kornblum, William. 1974. *Blue collar community.* Chicago: University of Chicago Press.

Kwong, Peter. 2001. Poverty despite family ties. In *The new poverty studies: The ethnography of power, politics, and impoverished people in the United States,* edited by Judith Goode and Jeff Maskovsky, 57–78. New York: New York University Press

Lamphere, Louise. 1987. *From working daughters to working mothers: Immigrant women in a New England industrial community.* Ithaca, N.Y.: Cornell University Press.

Lamphere, Louise, Alex Stepick, and Guillermo Grenier, eds. 1994. *Newcomers in the workplace: Immigrants and the restructuring of the U.S. economy.* Philadelphia: Temple University Press.

Lamphere, Louise, Patricia Zavella, Felipe Gonzalez, with Peter B. Evans. 1993. *Sunbelt working mothers: Reconciling family and factory.* Ithaca, N.Y.: Cornell University Press.

Lancaster, Roger. 1992. *Life is hard: Machismo, danger, and the intimacy of power in Nicaragua.* Berkeley: University of California Press.

Lancaster, Roger, and Micaela di Leonardo, eds. 1997. *The Gender/Sexuality Reader: Culture, history and political economy.* New York: Routledge.

Laó, Agustín. 1997. Islands at the crossroads: Puerto Ricanness traveling between the translocal nation and the global city. In *Puerto Rican jam: Essays on culture and politics,* edited by Frances Negrón-Muntaner and Ramón Grosfoguel, 169–88. Minneapolis: University of Minnesota Press.

Lapp, Michael. 1990. Managing migration: The migration division of Puerto Rico and Puerto Ricans in New York City, 1948–1968. Ph.D. diss., Johns Hopkins University.

Latino Institute. 1994. *A profile of nine Latino groups in Chicago.* Chicago: Latino Institute.

———. 1995. *Facts on Chicago's Puerto Rican population.* Chicago: Latino Institute.

———. 1997. *Select facts on Roberto Clemente Community Academy High School.* (Fact sheet prepared for community hearings on Clemente Community Academy.) Chicago: Latino Institute.

Lauria Perricelli, Antonio. 1990. A study in historical and critical anthropology: The making of the people of Puerto Rico. Ph.D diss., Department of Anthropology, New School for Social Research.

Leacock, Eleanor, and Helen I. Safa, eds. 1986. *Women's work: Development and the division of labor by gender.* Westport, Conn.: Bergin and Garvey.

Lee, Everett. 1966. A theory of migration. *Demography* 3: 47–57.

Lee, Stacey. 1996. *Listening to Asian American youth.* New York: Columbia University Press.

Levine, Barry. 1987. *The Caribbean exodus.* New York: Praeger.

Levitt, Peggy. 2001. *The transnational villagers.* Berkeley: University of California Press.

Lewis, Gordon K. 1963. *Puerto Rico: Freedom and power in the Caribbean.* New York: Monthly Review Press.

Lewis, Oscar. 1966. *La Vida.* New York: Random House.

Liebow, Elliot. 1993. *Tell them who I am: The lives of homeless women.* New York: Free Press.

Lipsitz, George. 1998. *The possessive investment in whiteness: How white people profit from identity politics.* Philadelphia: Temple University Press.

Lockwood, Victoria S. 1993. *Tahitian transformation: Gender and capitalist development in a rural society.* Boulder: Lynne Reinner Publishers.

Logan, John, and Harvey Molotch. 1987. *Urban fortunes: The political economy of place.* Berkeley: University of California Press.

López, Adalberto. 1980. *The Puerto Ricans: Their history, culture, and society.* Cambridge: Schenkman Publishing Company.

López, Clara. 1997. LADO: The Latin American Defense Organization. *Diálogo* 2: 23–24.

López, Iris. 1985. Sterilization among Puerto Rican women: A case study in New York City. Ph.D. diss., Graduate School of Arts and Sciences.

———. 1987. Sterilization among Puerto Rican women in New York City: Public policy and social constraints. In *Cities of the United States: Studies in urban anthropology,* edited by Leith Mullings. New York: Columbia University Press

López, Maria Milagros. 1994. Post-work selves and entitlement "attitudes" in peripheral postindustrial Puerto Rico. *Social Text* 38 (spring): 111–33.

Low, Setha. 1996. The anthropology of cities. *Annual Review of Anthropology* 25: 383–409.

Lowe, Lisa. 1996. *Immigrant acts: On Asian American cultural politics.* Durham, N.C.: Duke University Press.

Luque de Sánchez, María Dolores. 1977. *La ocupación norteamericana y la Ley Foraker (La opinion pública puertorriqueña), 1898–1904.* Río Piedras, Puerto Rico: Ediciones Universitaria.

Mahler, Sarah J. 1995. *American dreaming: Immigrant life on the margins.* Princeton, N.J.: Princeton University Press.

———. 1998. Theoretical and empirical contributions toward a research agenda for transnationalism. In *Transnationalism from below,* edited by Michael Peter Smith and Luis Eduardo Guarnizo, 64–100. New Brunswick, N.J.: Transaction Publishers.

———. 1999. Engendering transnational migration: A case study of Salvadorans. *American Behavioral Scientist* 42 (4): 690–719.

Mahler, Sarah J., and Patricia R. Pessar. 2001. Gendered geographies of power: Analyzing gender across transnational spaces. *Identities* 7 (4): 441–59.

Maldonado, A. W. 1997. *Teodoro Moscoso and Puerto Rico's Operation Bootstrap.* Gainsville: University Press of Florida.

Maldonado, Edwin. 1979. Contract labor and the origin of Puerto Rican communities in the United States. *International Migration Review* 13: 103–21.

Maldonado-Denis, Manuel. 1972. *Puerto Rico: A socio-historic interpretation.* Translated by Elena Vialo. New York: Vintage Books.

———. 1976. *The Emigration dialectic: Puerto Rico and the USA.* New York: International Publishers.

Manning, Caroline. 1933. *The employment of women in Puerto Rico.* Washington, D.C.: U.S. Department of Labor.

Marks, Carole. 1989. *Farewell, we're good and gone: The great black migration.* Bloomington: Indiana University Press.

Martinez, Manuel. 1989. *Chicago: Historia de nuestra comunidad puertorriqueña.* Printed by author.

Martinez, Ruth E. 1982. Socioeconomic reintegration of return migrants to Puerto Rico. Ph.D. diss., Columbia University.

Mass, Bonnie. 1977. Puerto Rico: A case study of population control. *Latin American Perspectives* 24: 67–77.

Massey, Doreen. 1994. *Space, place and gender.* Minneapolis: University of Minnesota Press.

Massey, Douglas. 1986. The settlement process among Mexican immigrants to the United States and prospects for assimilation. *Annual Review of Sociology* 7: 57–85.

———. 1990a. The social and economic origins of immigration. *American Academy of Political and Social Sciences* 510 (July): 60–72.

———. 1990b. Social structure, household strategies, and the cumulative causation of migration. *Population Index* 56 (1): 3–26.

———. 1999. Why does immigration occur?: A theoretical synthesis. In *The handbook of international migration,* edited by Charles Hirschman, Philip Kasinitz, and Josh De Wind, 34–52. New York: Russell Sage Foundation.

Massey, Douglas, J. Arango, G. Hugo, A. Kouaouci, A Pelligrino, and J. Taylor. 1993. Theories of international migration: A review and appraisal. *Population and Development Review* 19 (3): 431–66).

Massey, Douglas S., and Nancy C. Denton. 1993. *American apartheid: Segregation and the making of the underclass.* Cambridge, Mass.: Harvard University Press.

Mathews, Thomas G. 1960. *Puerto Rican politics and the New Deal.* Gainesville: University of Florida Press.

Matos-Rodríguez, Félix V., and Linda Delgado. 1998. *Puerto Rican women's history: New Perspectives.* Armonk, N.Y.: M.E. Sharpe.

Matsumoto, Valerie. 1996. Reflections on oral history: Research in a Japanese American community. In *Feminist dilemmas in fieldwork,* edited by Diane L. Wolf. Boulder, 160–69. Colo.: Westview Press.

Mayor's Committee on New Residents. 1960. *Puerto Rican Americans in Chicago.* Chicago: Chicago Commission on Human Relations.

———. 1966. *The Puerto Rican residents of Chicago: A report on an open hearing, July 15 and 16.* Chicago: Chicago Commission on Human Relations.

McCaffrey, Katherine T. 2002. *Military power and popular protest: The U.S. Navy in Vieques, Puerto Rico.* New Brunswick, N.J.: Rutgers University Press.

Meléndez, Edwin. 1993a. *Los que se van, los que regresan: Puerto Rican migration to and from the United States, 1982–1988.* Political Economy Working Paper Series #1. Centro de Estudios Puertorriqueños, Hunter College, City University of New York.

———. 1993b. The unsettled relationship between Puerto Rican poverty and migration. *Latino Studies Journal* 4 (2): 45–55.

Meléndez, Edwin, and Edgardo Meléndez. 1993. *Colonial dilemma: Critical perspectives on contemporary Puerto Rico.* Boston: South End Press.

Méndez Liciaga, Andrés. 1925. *Boceto histórico del Pepino.* Mayaguez: La Voz de la Patria.

Menjívar, Cecilia. 2000. *Fragmented ties: Salvadoran immigrant networks in America.* Berkeley: University of California Press.

Mills, C. Wright, Clarence Senior, Rose Kohn Goldsen. 1950. *The Puerto Rican journey: New York's newest migrants.* New York: Russell and Russell Press.

Mintz, Sidney. 1956. Cañamelar: The Subculture of a Rural Sugar Plantation Proletariat. In *The people of Puerto Rico,* edited by Julian Steward, 314–417. Urbana: University of Illinois Press.

———. 1985. *Sweetness and power: The place of sugar in modern history.* New York: Penguin Books.

———. 1996. Enduring substances, trying theories: The Caribbean region as *oikoumene. Journal of the Royal Anthropological Institute* 2: 289–310.

———. 1998. The localization of anthropological practice: From area studies to transnationalism. *Critique of Anthropology* 18 (2): 117–33.

Moore, Joan, and Raquel Pinderhughes. 1993. *In the barrio: Latinos and the underclass debate.* New York: Russell Sage Foundation.

Morales, Ed. 2002. *Living in Spanglish: The search for Latino identity in America.* New York: St. Martin's Press.

Morales, Iris. 1998. Palante, siempre palante! The Young Lords. In *The Puerto Rican movement: Voices from the diaspora,* edited by Andrés Torres and José E. Velázquez, 210–27. Philadelphia: Temple University Press.

Morales, Rebecca, and Frank Bonilla. 1993. *Latinos in a changing U.S. economy.* London: Sage Publications.

Morokvasic, Mirjana. 1984. Birds of passage are also women... *International Migration Review* 18 (4): 886–907.

Moscoso, Teodoro. 1989. *Land tenure and social classes in Puerto Rico.* Unpublished manuscript.

Muñiz, Vicky. 1998. *Resisting gentrification and displacement: Voices of Puerto Rican women of the barrio.* New York: Garland Publishers.

Muschkin, Clara G. 1993. Consequences of return migrant status for employment in Puerto Rico. *International Migration Review* 27 (1): 70–102.

Nash, June, and María Patricia Fernández-Kelly, eds. 1983. *Women and men and the international division of labor.* Albany: State University of New York Press.

Nash, June, and Helen Safa. 1986. *Women and change in Latin America.* New York: Bergin and Garvey.

Negrón-Muntaner, Frances. 1997. English only jamás but Spanish only cuidado: Language and nationalism in contemporary Puerto Rico. In *Puerto Rican jam: Essays on culture and politics,* edited by Frances Negrón-Muntaner and Ramón Grosfoguel, 257–86. Minneapolis: University of Minnesota Press.

Nelson, Kathryn P. 1988. *Gentrification and distressed cities: An assessment of trends in intrametropolitan migration.* Madison: University of Wisconsin Press.

Nyden, Philip W., and Wim Wiewel. 1991. *Challenging uneven development: An urban agenda for the 1990s.* New Brunswick, N.J.: Rutgers University Press.

Oboler, Suzanne. 1995. *Ethnic labels, Latino lives: Identity and the politics of (re)presentation in the United States.* Minneapolis: University of Minnesota Press.

Olwig, Karen Fog. 1993. The migration experience: Nevisian women at home and abroad. In *Women and change in the Caribbean,* edited by Janet H. Momsen, 150–66. Bloomington: Indiana University Press.

———. 1997. Cultural sites: Sustaining a home in a deterritorialized world. In *Siting culture: The shifting anthropological object,* edited by Karen Fog Olwig and Kirsten Hastrup, 17–38. London: Routledge.

———.1999. Caribbean place identity: From family land to region and beyond. *Identities* 5 (4): 435–67.

Olwig, Karen Fog, and Kirsten Hastrup. 1997. Introduction. In *Siting culture: The shifting anthropological object,* edited by Karen Fog Olwig and Kirsten Hastrup, 1–14. London: Routledge.

Olwig, Karen Fog, and Nina Nyberg Sorenson, eds. 2001. *Work and migration: Life and livelihoods in a globalizing world.* New York: Routledge.

Ong, Aihwa. 1987. *Spirits of resistance and capitalist discipline.* Albany: State University of New York Press.

———. 1999. *Flexible citizenship: The cultural logics of transnationality.* Durham, N.C.: Duke University Press.

Ortiz, Altagracia. 1996. *Puerto Rican women and work: Bridges in transnational labor.* Philadelphia: Temple University Press.

Ortiz, Vilma. 1993. Circular migration and employment among Puerto Rican women. *Latino Studies Journal* 4 (2): 56–70.

———. 1996. Migration and marriage among Puerto Rican women. *International Migration Review* 30 (2): 460–84..

Padilla, Elena. 1947. Puerto Rican immigrants in New York and Chicago: A study in comparative assimilation. Ph.D. diss., Department of Anthropology, University of Chicago.

———. 1958. *Up from Puerto Rico.* New York: Columbia University Press.

Padilla, Felix. 1985. *Latino ethnic consciousness: The case of Mexican Americans and Puerto Ricans in Chicago.* Notre Dame, Ind.: University of Notre Dame Press.

———. 1987. *Puerto Rican Chicago.* Notre Dame, Ind.: University of Notre Dame Press.

———. 1993. The quest for community: Puerto Ricans in Chicago. In *In the barrios: Latinos and the underclass debate,* edited by Joan Moore and Raquel Pinderhughes, 129–48. New York: Russell Sage Foundation.

Palerm, Juan Vicente. 1991. Farm labor needs and farm workers in California, 1970–1989. Unpublished report for the State Employment Development Department.

Pantojas-García, Emilio. 1990. *Development strategies as ideology: Puerto Rico's export-led industrialization experiment.* Boulder, Colo.: Lynne Reinner Publishers.

Park, Robert. 1928. Human migration and the marginal man. *American Journal of Sociology* 33: 881–93.

Park, Robert, and Ernest Burgess. 1921. *Introduction to the science of sociology.* Chicago: University of Chicago Press.

Park, Robert, Ernest Burgess, and Roderick McKenzie. 1925. *The city.* Chicago: University of Chicago Press.

Parreñas, Rhacel Salazar. 2000. Migrant Filipina domestic workers and the international division of reproductive labor. *Gender & Society* 14: 560–80.

———. 2001. Mothering from a distance: Emotions, gender, and inter-generational relations in Filipino transnational families. *Feminist Studies* 27 (2): 361–90.

Pastor, Robert. 1985. *Migration and development in the Caribbean: The unexpected connection.* Boulder, Colo.: Westview Press.

Pedraza, Sylvia. 1990. Immigration research: A conceptual map. *Social Science History* 14: 43–67.

———. 1991. Women and migration: The social consequences of gender. *Annual Review of Sociology* 17: 303–25.

Pellow, Deborah. 2001. Cultural differences and urban spatial formation: Elements of boundedness in an Accra community. *American Anthropologist* 103 (1): 59–75.

Perea, Juan. 1996. *Immigrants out: The new nativism and the anti-immigrant impulse in the U.S.* New York: New York University Press.

Pérez, Gina M. 2001. "An up-beat West Side Story": Puerto Ricans and postwar racial politics in Chicago. *CENTRO: Journal of the Center for Puerto Rican Studies* 13 (2): 47–68.

———. 2002. The other "real world": Gentrification and the social construction of place in Chicago. *Urban Anthropology* 31 (1): 37–68.

———. 2003. "Puertorriqueñas rencorosas y mejicanas sufridas": Gendered ethnic identity formation in Chicago's Latino communities. *Journal of Latin American Anthropology* 8 (2): 96–125.

Perloff, Harvey. 1950. *Puerto Rico's economic future: A study in planned development.* Chicago: University of Chicago Press.

———. 1957. *Education for planning: City, state and regional.* Baltimore, Md.: Johns Hopkins University Press.

Persons, Stow. 1987. *Ethnic studies at Chicago.* Chicago: University of Chicago Press.

Pesquera, Beatríz M. 1993. "In the beginning he wouldn't even lift a spoon": The division of household labor. In *Building with our own hands: New directions in Chicana Studies,* edited by Adela de la Torre and Beatríz Pesquera, 181–95. Berkeley: University of California Press.

Pessar, Patricia. 1982. The role of households in international migration: The case of U.S.-bound migrants from the Dominican Republic. *International Migration Review* 16: 342–62.

———. 1986. The role of gender in Dominican settlement in the United States. In *Women and change in Latin America,* edited by June Nash and Helen Safa. South Hadley, Mass.: Bergin and Garvey.

———. 1999. Engendering migration studies: The case of new immigrants in the United States. *American Behavioral Scientist* 42 (4): 577–600.

Picó, Fernando. 1988. *Historia general de Puerto Rico.* Río Piedras, Puerto Rico: Huracán.

Polakow, Valerie. 1993. *Lives on the edge: Single mothers and their children in the other America.* Chicago: University of Chicago Press.

Portes, Alejandro. 1978. Immigrant aspirations. *Sociology of Education* 51: 241–60.

———. 1999. Immigration theory for a new century: Some problems and opportunities. In *The handbook of international migration,* edited by Charles Hirschman, Philip Kasinitz, and Josh De Wind, 21–33. New York: Russell Sage Foundation.

Portes, Alejandro, and Robert L. Bach. 1985. *Latin Journey: Cuban and Mexican immigrants in the United States.* Berkeley: University of California Press.

Portes, Alejandro, and Jozsef Borocz. 1989. Contemporary immigration: Theoretical perspectives on its determinants and modes of incorporation. *International Migration Review* 23: 606–30.

Portes, Alejandro, and Ramon Grosfoguel. 1994. Caribbean diasporas: Migration and ethnic communities. *Annals of the American Academy of Political and Social Science* 533 (May): 48–69.

Portes, Alejandro, and Rubén Rumbaut. 1990. *Immigrant America.* Berkeley: University of California Press.

Prashad, Vijay. 2000. *The karma of brown folk.* Minneapolis: University of Minnesota Press.

Puerto Rico Department of Labor. 1969. Proyecto piloto de la caña, 1967–1968. San Juan, Puerto Rico: Department of Labor.

Puerto Rico Junta de Planificación. 1948. Mapa de municipios y barrios: San Sebastián, nu. 8. Santurce, Puerto Rico: Junta de Planificación, Urbanización y Zonificación.

Puerto Rico Policy Commission. 1934. *Report of the Puerto Rico Policy Commission* (Chardón Plan). San Juan, Puerto Rico: Puerto Rico Policy Commission.

Quintero Rivera, Angel. 1978. *Conflictos de clase y politica en Puerto Rico.* Río Piedras, Puerto Rico: Ediciones Huracán.

———. 1988. *Patricios y plebeyos: Burgueses, hacendados, artesanos y obreros.* Río Piedras, Puerto Rico: Ediciones Huracán.

Ramírez de Arellano, Annette, and Conrad Seipp. 1983. *Colonialism, catholicism and contraception: A history of birth control in Puerto Rico.* Chapel Hill: University of North Carolina Press.

Ramos-Zayas, Ana Yolanda. 2003. *National performances: The politics of class, race and place in Puerto Rican Chicago.* Chicago: University of Chicago Press.

Ranney, David C., and William Cecil. 1993. *Transnational investment and job loss in Chicago: Impacts on women, African-Americans and Latinos.* Chicago: Center for Urban Economic Development, University of Illinois at Chicago.

Reed, Adolph. 1992. The underclass as myth and symbol: The poverty of discourse about poverty. *Radical America* 24 (winter): 21–40.

———, ed. 1999. *Without justice for all: The new liberalism and our retreat from racial equality.* Boulder, Colo.: Westview Press.

Reyes, Belinda Imar. 1994. New, repeat and return migration: The Puerto Rican experience and poverty. Ph.D diss., Department of Economics. University of California Berkeley.

Richardson, Bonham. 1989. Caribbean migrants, 1838–1985. In *The modern*

Caribbean, edited by Franklin W. Knight and Colin A. Palmer. Chapel Hill: University of North Carolina Press.

Ríos, Palmira. 1992. Comments on rethinking migration: A transnational perspective. In *Towards a transnational perspective on migration: Race, class, ethnicity, and nationalism reconsidered,* edited by Nina Glick Schiller, Linda Basch and Cristina Blanc-Szanton. New York: Academy of Sciences.

———. 1993. Export-oriented industrialization and the demand for female labor: Puerto Rican women in the manufacturing sector, 1952–1980. In *Colonial dilemma: Critical perspectives on contemporary Puerto Rico,* edited by Edwin Meléndez and Edgardo Meléndez, 89–102. Boston: South End Press.

Rivera-Batiz, Francisco L., and Carlos E. Santiago. 1996. *Island paradox: Puerto Rico in the 1990s.* New York: Russell Sage Foundation.

Rivera, Raquel Z. 1997. Rapping two versions of the same requiem. In *Puerto Rican jam: Essays on culture and politics,* edited by Frances Negrón-Muntaner and Ramón Grosfoguel, 243–56. Minneapolis: University of Minnesota Press.

———. 2003. *New York Ricans from the Hip Hop Zone.* New York: Palgrave Macmillan.

Rivera Montalvo, Rey F. 1993. *Los colonos Pepinianos y las cuotas azucareras: 1953–1956.* M.A. thesis, Department of History, Universidad de Puerto Rico, Rio Piedras.

Roberts, Dorothy. 1997. *Killing the black body: Race, reproduction, and the meaning of liberty.* New York: Vintage Books.

Rodríguez, Clara. 1991. *Puerto Ricans: Born in the U.S.A.* Boulder, Colo.: Westview Press.

———. 1993. Puerto Rican circular migration. *Latino Studies Journal* 4 (2): 93–113.

———. 1997. *Latin Looks: Images of Latinas and Latinos in the U.S. media.* Boulder, Colo.: Westview Press.

Rodríguez, Néstor P., and Jaqueline Hagan. 1992. Apartment restructuring and Latino immigrant tenant struggles: A case study of human agency. In *After modernism: Global restructuring and the changing boundaries of city life,* edited by Peter Smith, 164–80. New Brunswick, N.J.: Transaction Publishers.

Romero, Mary. 1992. *Maid in U.S.A.* New York: Routledge.

Rosario Natal, Carmelo. *Éxodo Puertorriqueño: Las emigraciones al Caribe y a Hawaii, 1900–1915.* Río Piedras, Puerto Rico: Editorial Edil.

Roseberry, William. 1989. *Anthropologies and histories: Essays in culture, history and political economy.* New Brunswick, N.J.: Rutgers University Press.

Roseberry, William, and Jay O'Brien. 1991. *Golden ages, dark ages: Imagining the past in anthropology and history.* Berkeley: University of California Press.

Rothenberg, Robert, and Gary McDonough. 1993. *The cultural meaning of urban space.* London: Bergin and Garvey.

Rouse, Roger. 1991. Mexican migration and the social space of postmodernism. *Diaspora* 1: 8–23.

———. 1992. Making sense of settlement: Class transformation, cultural struggle, and transnationalism among Mexican migrants in the United States. In *Towards a transnational perspective on migration: Race, class, ethnicity, and nationalism reconsidered*, edited by Nina Glick Schiller, Linda Basch and Cristina Blanc-Szanton, 25–52. New York: Academy of Sciences.

Royko, Mike. 1971. *Boss: Richard J. Daley of Chicago*. New York: Signet Books.

Rúa, Merida. 2001. Colao subjectivities: PortoMex and MexiRican perspectives on language and identity. *CENTRO: Journal of the Center for Puerto Rican Studies* 13 (2): 117–33.

Ruiz, Viki L. 1993. "Star struck": Acculturation, adolescence, and the Mexican American woman. In *Building with our own hands: New directions in chicana studies*, edited by Adela de la Torre and Beatríz Pesquera, 109–29. Berkeley: University of California Press.

Safa, Helen I. 1981. Runaway shops and female employment: The search for cheap labor. *Signs* 7 (2): 418–33.

———. 1990. Women and industrialization in the Caribbean. In *Women, employment and the family and the international division of labor*, edited by Sharon Stichter and Jane L. Parpart. London: Macmillan.

———. 1995. *The myth of the male breadwinner: Women and industrialization in the Caribbean*. Boulder, Colo.: Westview Press.

Sánchez, George J. 1994. "Go after the women": Americanization and the Mexican immigrant woman, 1915–1929. In *Unequal sisters: A multicultural reader in U.S. women's history*, edited by Vicki L. Ruiz and Ellen Carol DuBois. New York: Routledge.

———. 1997. Face the nation: Race, immigration, and the rise of nativism in late twentieth century America. *International Migration Review* 31 (4): 1009–30.

Sánchez, Luis Rafael. 1994. *La guagua aérea*. San Juan: Editorial Cultura.

Sánchez-Korrol, Virginia. 1994. *From colonia to community: The history of Puerto Ricans in New York City*. 2d ed. Berkeley: University of California Press.

Sandoval Sánchez, Alberto. 1997. Puerto Rican identity up in the air: Air migration, its cultural representations, and "cruzando el charco." In *Puerto Rican jam: Essays on culture and politics*, edited by Frances Negrón-Muntaner and Ramón Grosfoguel, 189–208. Minnesota: University of Minnesota Press.

Sanjek, Roger. 1990. *Fieldnotes: The makings of anthropology*. Ithaca, N.Y.: Cornell University Press.

Santiago, Carlos E. 1993. The migratory impact of minimum wage legislation: Puerto Rico, 1970–1987 *International Migration Review* 27 (4): 772–95.

Santiago Méndez, Helen. 1988. *La elite cafetalera de San Sebastian a finales del siglo XIX: Su ascenso y decadencia*. M.A. thesis, Department of History, Universidad de Puerto Rico, Río Piedras.

Santiago-Valles, Kelvin A. 1994. *"Subject people" and colonial discourses: Economic transformation and social disorder in Puerto Rico, 1898–1947*. Albany: State University of New York Press.

Scarano, Francisco. 1984. *Sugar and slavery in Puerto Rico: The plantation economy of Ponce, 1800–1850*. Madison: University of Wisconsin Press.

Schein, Louisa. 1998. Forged transnationality and oppositional cosmopolitanism.

In *Transnationalism from below,* edited by Michael Peter Smith and Luis Eduardo Guarnizo, 291–313. New Brunswick, N.J.: Transaction Publishers.

Sciorra, Joseph. 1996. Return to the future: Puerto Rican vernacular architecture in New York City. In *Re-presenting the city: Ethnicity, capital and culture in the twenty-first-century metropolis,* edited by Anthony D. King. New York: New York University Press.

Scott, Rebecca J. 1985. *Slave emancipation in Cuba: The transition to free labor, 1860–1899.* Princeton, N.J.: Princeton University Press.

Segal, Aaron. 1987. The Caribbean exodus in a global context: Comparative migration experiences. In *The Caribbean exodus,* edited by Barry B. Levine. New York: Praeger.

Sen, Amartya. 1997. Population: Delusion and reality. In *The gender/sexuality reader: Culture, history and political economy,* edited by Roger N. Lancaster and Micaela di Leonardo, 89–106. New York: Routledge.

Senior, Clarence. 1961. *Strangers, then neighbors: From pilgrims to Puerto Ricans.* New York: Freedom Books.

Sennett, Richard, and Jonathan Cobb. 1972. *The hidden injuries of class.* New York: Vintage.

Sevcenko, Liz. 2001. Making Loisaida: Placing Puertorriqueñidad in Lower Manhattan. In *Mambo Montage: The Latinization of New York,* edited by Agustín Laó-Montes and Arlene Dávila, 292–317. New York: Columbia University Press.

Silvestrini, Blanca. 1986. Women as workers: The experience of Puerto Rican women in the 1930s. In *The Puerto Rican woman: Perspectives on culture, history and society,* edited by Edna Acosta-Belen. New York: Praeger Publishers.

Slayton, Robert A. 1987. The Reagan approach to housing: An examination of local impact. Chicago: Chicago Urban League.

Smith, Michael Peter. 2001. *Transnational urbanism: Locating globalization.* Malden, Mass.: Blackwell Publishers.

Smith, Michael Peter, and Luis Eduardo Guarnizo. 1998. *Transnationalism from below.* New Brunswick, N.J.: Transaction Publishers.

Smith, Neil. 1996. *The new urban frontier: Gentrification and the revanchist city.* New York: Routledge Press.

Smith, Neil, and Peter Williams. 1986. *Gentrification of the city.* Boston: Allen and Unwin.

Smith, Raymond T. 1997. *The matrifocal family: Power, pluralism, and politics.* New York: Routledge.

Smith, Robert C. 1998. Transnational localities: Community, technology and the politics of membership within the context of Mexico and U.S. migration. In *Transnationalism from below,* edited by Michael Peter Smith and Luis Eduardo Guarnizo, 196–239. New Brunswick, N.J.: Transaction Publishers.

Souza, Caridad. 2000. Welfare debates and Puerto Rican teenage mothers in New York City. *Economic and Political Weekly* 35 (20–21): 24–32.

———. 2002. Sexual identities of young Puerto Rican mothers. *Diálogo* 6: 33–39.

Squires, Gregory. 1987. *Chicago: Race, class and the response to urban decline.* Philadelphia: Temple University Press.

Squires, Gregory, ed. 1991. *Unequal partnerships: The political economy of urban redevelopment in postwar America*. New Brunswick, N.J.: Rutgers University Press.

Stack, Carol B. 1974. *All our kin: Strategies for survival in a black community*. New York: Harper & Row.

Stansell, Christine. 1986. *City of women: Sex and class in New York, 1789–1860*. Chicago: University of Illinois Press.

Starn, Orin. 1986. Engineering internment: Anthropologists and the War Relocation Authority. *American Ethnologist* 13: 704–20.

Steinberg, Stephen. 1995. *Turning back: The retreat from racial justice in American thought and policy*. Boston: Beacon Press.

———. 1997. Science and politics in the work of William Julius Wilson. *New Politics* 6 (2): 108–20.

Stepan, Nancy Leys. 1991. *"The hour of eugenics": Race, gender and nation in Latin America*. Ithaca, N.Y.: Cornell University Press.

Steward, Julian, et al. 1956. *The people of Puerto Rico*. Urbana: University of Illinois Press.

Stinson Fernández, John H. 1994. Conceptualizing culture and ethnicity: Toward an anthropology of Puerto Rican Philadelphia. Ph.D. diss., Department of Anthropology, Temple University.

———. 1996. Hacia una antropolgía de la emigración planificada: El Negociado de Empleo y Migración y el caso de Filadelfia. *Revista de Ciencias Sociales* 1 (June): 112–54.

Stycos, Mayone J. 1955. *Family and fertility in Puerto Rico: A study of the lower income group*. New York: Columbia University Press.

Sullivan, Mercer. 1993. Puerto Ricans in Sunset Park, Brooklyn: Poverty amidst ethnic and economic diversity. In *In the barrios: Latinos and the underclass debate*, edited by Joan Moore and Raquel Pinderhuges, 1–26. New York: Russell Sage Foundation.

Suro, Roberto. 1998. *Strangers among us: Latino lives in a changing America*. New York: Vintage Books.

Suttles, Gerald. 1968. *The social order of the slum: Ethnicity and territory in the inner city*. Chicago: University of Chicago Press.

Taylor, D. Garth. 1988. Minority housing markets in Chicago. Chicago: Chicago Urban League.

Thomas, William Issac, and Florian Znaniecki. 1927. *The Polish peasant in Europe and America*. New York: Knopf.

Thorne, Barrie, with Marilyn Yalom, eds. 1992. *Rethinking the family: Some feminist questions*. Boston: Northeastern University Press.

Tienda, Marta. 1989. Puerto Ricans and the underclass debate. *The American Academy of Political and Social Science* 501 (January): 105–19.

Tienda, Marta, and William Díaz. 1987. Puerto Ricans' special problems. *New York Times*, August 28.

Tienda, Marta, and L. Jensen. 1988. Poverty and minorities: A quarter century profile of color and socioeconomic disadvantage. In *Divided opportunities: Minorities, poverty, and social policy*, edited by G. D. Sandefur and M. Tienda. New York: Plenum Press.

Toro-Morn, Maura. 1995. Gender, class, family and migration: Puerto Rican women in Chicago. *Gender & Society* 9: 712–26.

———. 1999. Género, trabajo y migración: Las empleadas domésticas puertorriqueñas en Chicago. *Revista de Ciencias Sociales* 7: 102–25.

Torre, Carlos, Hugo Rodríguez Vecchini, and William Burgos, eds. 1994. *The commuter nation: Perspectives on Puerto Rican migration*. Río Piedras: Editorial de la Universidad de Puerto Rico.

Torres, Andrés. 1995. *Between melting pot and mosaic: African Americans and Puerto Ricans in the New York political economy*. Philadelphia: Temple University Press.

Torres, Andrés, and José E. Velázquez, eds. 1998. *The Puerto Rican movement: Voices from the diaspora*. Philadelphia: Temple University Press.

Torruellas, Luz M., and Jose L. Vazquez. 1982. *Los puertorriqueños que regresaron: Un análisis de su participación laboral: El movimiento migratorio de retorno en el período 1965–1970 y su impacto en el mercado laboral*. San Juan, Puerto Rico: Centro de Investigaciones Sociales.

Torruellas, Rosa, Rina Benmayor, and Ana Juarbe. 1996. Negotiating gender, work and welfare: *Familia* as productive labor among Puerto Rican women in New York City. In *Puerto Rican women and work: Bridges in transnational labor*, edited by Altagracia Ortiz, 184–208. Philadelphia: Temple University Press.

Tuan, Mia. 1998. *Forever foreigners or honorary whites?: The Asian ethnic experience today*. New Brunswick, N.J.: Rutgers University Press.

U.S. Census Bureau. 1990. *Census of Population and Housing, 1990*. Washington, D.C.: Government Printing Office.

U.S. Census Bureau. 1940.*Characteristics of the Population, No. 2*. Washington, D.C.: Government Printing Office.

Urciuoli, Bonnie. 1991. The political topography of Spanish and English: The view from a New York Puerto Rican neighborhood. *American Ethnologist* 18: 295–310.

———. 1996. *Exposing prejudice: Puerto Rican experiences of language, race and class*. Oxford: Westview Press.

Valle, Victor M., and Rodolfo D. Torres. 2000. *Latino metropolis*. Minneapolis: University of Minnesota Press.

Vargas Ramos, Carlos. 2000. The effects of return migration on political participation in Puerto Rico. Ph.D. diss., Department of Political Science, Columbia University.

———. 2001. "Los de afuera que regresan": Demographic characteristics of Puerto Rican return migrants. Paper presented at the Center for Puerto Rican Studies Colloquium Series, May 15.

Vélez-Ibáñez, Carlos G. 1993. U.S. Mexicans in the borderlands: Being poor without the underclass. In *In the barrio: Latinos and the underclass debate,* edited by Joan Moore and Raquel Pinderhuges, 195–210. New York: Russell Sage Foundation,

———. 1996. *Border visions: Mexican cultures of the Southwest United States*. Tucson: University of Arizona Press.

Venkatesh, Sudhir Alladi. 2000. *American Project: The rise and fall of a modern ghetto*. Cambridge, Mass.: Harvard University Press.

Villa, Raúl H. 2000. *Barrio logos: Space and place in urban Chicano literature and culture*. Austin: University of Texas Press.

Wagenheim, Kal, and Olga Jiménez de Wagenheim. 1994. *The Puerto Ricans: A documentary history*. Princeton, N.J.: Markus Wiener Publishers.

Wagenheim, Olga Jiménez de. 1993. *Puerto Rico's revolt for independence: El Grito de Lares*. Princeton, N.J.: Markus Weiner Publishing.

Warren, Kay B., and Susan C. Bourque. 1991. Women, technology, and international development ideologies: Analyzing feminist voices. In *Gender at the crossroads of knowledge: Feminist anthropology in the postmodern era*, edited by Micaela di Leonardo, 278–311. Berkeley: University of California Press.

Waters, Mary C. 1996. The intersection of gender, race, and ethnicity in identity development of Caribbean American teens. In *Urban girls: Resisting stereotypes, creating identities*, edited by Bonnie J. Ross Leadbeater and Niobe Way, 65–81. New York: New York University Press.

Weismantel, Mary J. 1996. Children and soup, men and bulls: Meals and time for Zumbagua women. *Food and Foodways* 6 (3–4): 307–27.

West, Cornel. 1993. *Race matters*. Boston: Beacon Press.

Whalen, Carmen T. 1998a. Labor migrants or submissive wives: Competing narratives of Puerto Rican women in post-WWII era. In *Puerto Rican women's history: New perspectives*, edited by Felix V. Matos-Rodriguez and Linda Delgado, 206–26. Armonk, N.Y.: M.E. Sharpe.

———. 1998b. Bridging homeland and barrio politics: The Young Lords in Philadelphia. *The Puerto Rican movement: Voices from the diaspora*, edited by Andrés Torres and José E. Velázquez, 107–23. Philadelphia: Temple University Press.

———. 2001. *From Puerto Rico to Philadelphia: Puerto Rican workers and postwar economics*. Philadelphia: Temple University Press.

Williams, Brett. 1988. *Upscaling downtown: Stalled gentrification in Washington, D.C.* Ithaca, N.Y.: Cornell University Press.

———. 1992. Poverty among African Americans in the urban United States. *Human Organization* 51: 164–74.

———. 1996. "There goes the neighborhood": Gentrification, displacement, and homelessness in Washington D.C. In *There's no place like home: Anthropological perspectives on housing and homelessness in the United States*, edited by Anna Lou Devahenon. Westport, Conn.: Bergin and Garvey.

———. 1999. The great family fraud of postwar America. In *Without justice for all: The new liberalism and our retreat from racial equality*, edited by Adolph Reed Jr. Boulder, Colo.: Westview Press.

———. 2001. What's debt got to do with it? In *The new poverty studies: The ethnography of power, politics, and impoverished people in the United States*, edited by Judith Goode and Jeff Maskovsky, 79–102. New York: New York University Press.

Williams, Raymond. 1973. *The country and the city*. New York: Oxford University Press.

———. 1977. *Marxism and literature*. New York: Oxford University Press.

Wilson, Elizabeth. 1991. *Sphinx in the city: Urban life, the control of disorder and women*. Berkeley: University of California Press.

Wilson, William Julius. 1987. *The truly disadvantaged: The inner city, the underclass, and public policy*. Chicago: Chicago University Press.

Wolf, Eric. 1974. American anthropologists and American society. *Reinventing anthropology*, edited by Dell Hymes, 152–63. New York: Vintage Books.

———. 1982. *Europe and the people without history*. Berkeley: University of California Press.

———. 1990. Distinguished lecture: Facing power — Old insights, new questions. *American Anthropologist* 92: 586–96.

Zavella, Patricia. 1987. *Women's work and Chicano families: Cannery workers of the Santa Clara Valley*. Ithaca, N.Y.: Cornell University Press.

———. 1991. *Mujeres* in factories: Race and class perspectives on women, work and family. In *Gender at the crossroads of knowledge: Feminist anthropology in the postmodern era*, edited by Micaela di Leonardo. Berkeley: University of California Press.

———. 1993. Feminist insider dilemmas: Constructing ethnic identity with Chicana informants. *Frontiers* 13 (3): 53–76.

———. 1997. "Playing with fire": The gendered construction of Chicana/Mexicana sexuality. In *The gender/sexuality reader: Culture, history, political economy*, edited by Roger N. Lancaster and Micaela di Leonardo, 392–408. New York: Routledge.

———. 2001. The tables are turned: Immigration, poverty, and social conflict in California communities. In *The new poverty studies: The ethnography of power, politics, and impoverished people in the United States*, edited by Judith Goode and Jeff Maskovsky, 103–31. New York: New York University Press.

Zell, Steven. 1973. *A comparative study of the labor market characteristics of return migrants and non-migrants in Puerto Rico*. San Juan: Junta de Pacification de Puerto Rico.

Zentella, Ana Celia. 1990. Returned migration, language and identity: Puerto Rican bilinguals in dos worlds/two mundos. *International Journal of Social Language* (84): 81–100.

———. 1997. *Growing up bilingual: Children in El Barrio*. New York: Basil Blackwell.

Zinn, Maxine Baca. 1979. Field research in minority communities: Ethical, methodological, and political observations by an insider. *Social Problems* 27 (2): 209–19.

Zinn, Maxine Baca, and Bonnie Thornton Dill. 1994. *Women of color in U.S. society*. Philadelphia: Temple University Press.

Zorbaugh, Harvey W. 1929. *The gold coast and the slum*. Chicago: University of Chicago Press.

Zukin, Sharon. 1991. *Landscapes of power: From Detroit to Disney World*. Berkeley: University of California Press.

———. 1995. *The culture of cities*. New York: Blackwell Publishers.

Index